DECISION-MAKING IN
BRITISH EDUCATION

The Open University

Faculty of Educational Studies

Decision-making in British Education Systems (E221)

COURSE TEAM

Tony Bates
Robert Bell
Gerald Fowler (*Chairman*)
Tony Gear
Robert Glaister
Donald Holms
Vincent Houghton
Christine King
Ken Little
Colin Luckhurst
John Miller
Colin Morgan
Vera Morris
Jennifer Ozga
William Prescott
Alberto da Silva e Melo
Adam Westoby

Decision-Making
in
British Education

Edited by

Gerald Fowler

Vera Morris

Jennifer Ozga

at The Open University

HEINEMANN, LONDON

in association with

THE OPEN UNIVERSITY PRESS

Heinemann Educational Books Ltd

LONDON   EDINBURGH   MELBOURNE   AUCKLAND   TORONTO
HONG KONG   SINGAPORE   KUALA LUMPUR
IBADAN   NAIROBI   LUSAKA
JOHANNESBURG   NEW DELHI

ISBN 0 435 80310 7 (cased)
ISBN 0 435 80311 5 (paperback)

Selection and editorial material
copyright © The Open University 1973
First published 1973

Published by
Heinemann Educational Books Ltd
48 Charles Street, London WIX 8 AH
Printed in Great Britain by
Northumberland Press Ltd, Gateshead

LB
2901
.F63
1973

Contents

Acknowledgements

The editors and publishers wish to thank the following for permission to reprint copyright material: Hamish Hamilton Ltd for extract (1) from *The Art of the Possible* copyright © 1971, by Lord Butler, K.G., C.H.; George Allen & Unwin Ltd for two extracts (3 and 10) from *Central Department and Local Authorities* by J. A. G. Griffith; Longman Group Ltd for extract (4) from *Born and Bred Unequal* by Taylor and Ayres; Penguin Books Ltd for extract (5) from *Local Government* (Harmondsworth, 1970) by R. J. Buxton, Chapter 8, 'Comprehensive Education', copyright © R. J. Buxton, 1970; The Clarendon Press for extract (6) from *Policy Making in Secondary Education* (Chapter 5) by R. Saran; IPC Science and Technology Press for article (7) by M. Kogan in 'Educational Planning in Perspective' ed. T. Green from *Futures*, 1971; Cambridge University Press for extract (8) from *The Teachers' Unions and Interest Group Politics* by R. Coates; The Controller of Her Majesty's Stationery Office for extract (10) 'Governmental Response to Plowden' by A. H. Halsey from *Educational Priority Vol. 1*; Tyrrell Burgess Associates Ltd for article (11) 'The Impact of Robbins' by Layard and King in *Higher Education Review* Autumn 1968; The Controller of Her Majesty's Stationery Office for extracts (13 and 16) from *Educational Planning Papers No. 1 and 2*; Tyrrell Burgess Associates Ltd for article (14) 'Manpower forecasting since Robbins' by K. G. Gannicott and M. Blaug in *Higher Education Review*, Autumn 1969; Elsevier Publishing Co. for article (17) 'The Economics of the Open University' by L. E. Wagner in *Higher Education*, Vol. I, No. 2, 1972; NFER Publishing Co. Ltd for the article (20) 'Office and Expertise in the Secondary School' by L. E. Watson in *Educational Research*, Vol. II, No. 2, 1969; Basil Blackwell Ltd for the article (21) 'The Head Teacher and his Authority' by R. King in *Headship in the 1970s*; The Headmasters' Association for the article (22) 'The Planning of the Curriculum' by A. Bates from *Headmasters' Association Review*, Vol. LXX, No. 24, 1972, the remaining articles are reprinted by permission of the Open University.

Acknowledgements

Preface

There is not one system of public education within the United Kingdom, but several. In England, the Secretary of State for Education and Science has responsibility for the promotion of the education of the people, and for securing the effective execution by local authorities of the national policy for providing a varied and comprehensive educational service in every area. (Education Act, 1944, Section 1). In Wales, the schools are now the responsibility of the Welsh Secretary, and the Secretary of State for Scotland oversees the whole of public education in that country, except the universities; they remain, throughout Great Britain, and via the mediation of the University Grants Committee, within the purview of the Secretary for Education and Science. The Government at Stormont was from 1922 responsible for the whole of the education system of Northern Ireland, but the six counties are now (August 1973) under direct rule from Westminster, and the future governmental system is unclear.

Common to all of these systems is a diffuse pattern of power and control. It is not upon the Secretaries of State, but upon the local education authorities, that the duty of making adequate educational provision for the child population of their areas in general devolves. Below them again, the managers or governors of schools have powers and duties (even if they be restricted), and in most schools some at least of the teachers, and especially the head teacher, enjoy a wide measure of freedom in the organization of the school, the determination of what is taught and how it is taught, and even in the deployment of available resources. This does not however mean that central government lacks any power save that of encouragement. It has formal powers which are formidable, if rarely exercised, such as the power conferred upon the Secretary of State for Education and Science by Section 99 of the 1944 Act to give directions to any local education authority, or to governors or managers, whom he holds to be in default in the performance of a duty statutorily laid upon them. The informal powers of central government, exercised largely through financial control, are however wider still.

Thus, as we hope will be apparent from some of the material we have selected for this volume, the public system of education in Britain does not manifest the degree of centralized governmental control which is found in France or Sweden, but equally is less reliant on local initiative, and more narrowly circumscribes local power, than the education system of the United States.

Outside the formal structure of control lie other bodies which may have great influence upon the administration of education at national or local level—whether formally established as advisory bodies, like the Central Advisory Councils for Education or the Schools Council for the Curriculum and Examinations, or acting simply as pressure-groups, like the Confederation for the Advancement of State Education and some parent-teacher associations, or with a professional interest in the development of education, like the teachers' unions. There are also the politicians and the parties at local and national level, who are of central importance, since it is they who may control the local education authorities (though not all authorities are controlled by the representatives of one party), and from whose parliamentary representatives the government of the day is formed; the determination of a new party policy can therefore presage radical change in the organization and administration of education, and may be as much a part of the educational decision-making process as any event within the formal control structure.

All of these groups and individuals interact in the administration of education not only with each other, but with the permanent officials of the service, the civil servants at national level and the chief education officer and his staff within the local authorities. These may be professional educators or they may not (at local level most are, at national they more frequently are not, save for Her Majesty's Inspectorate, the 'eyes and ears' of the Department). They have all become professional administrators. That does not however mean that they leave the determination of policy to others, contenting themselves with its implementation. The interaction of individuals is infinitely more subtle, and the decision-making process infinitely more complex, than that: we hope that some of these readings will help to elucidate it.

It might still seem as if educational decisions were in broad measure kept 'within the family'; most of those we have mentioned are or have become educationists in some sense. The politician who becomes Secretary of State, or the chairman of the local education committee, and indeed most of its members, may be expected to have a strong commitment to the development of public education. But the Secretary of State is part of a Cabinet which may rank education low in its list of priorities in the allocation of national resources. The education committee, whatever its delegated powers, is ultimately just one committee of a local authority responsible for many services. At official level, a Treasury civil servant or a local authority treasurer, may or may not have an interest in education (and if he does it may not always lead him to look with favour on a particular proposal!).

Beyond all of these categories lie the parents of schoolchildren, most of whom do not belong to parent-teacher associations, or local or national educational associations, or political parties, and the pupils and students themselves. They too may demand, and win, a voice in the decision-making process. Their demand may not be articulately expressed; it may be apparent only through non-compliance with a set of rules, or lack of interest in 'what the school has to offer', or failure to learn what others intended that they should learn. But when this results in change, they have contributed to that change.

To make confusion worse confounded, the structure of local authority administration in much of Britain is in the course of upheaval. In England and Wales, outside London, new and often larger authorities will replace the old counties and new counties and new metropolitan districts will be responsible for education (among other services), alongside the unchanged Inner London Education Authority and Outer London Boroughs. Scotland goes through a similar, and in some ways still more radical, change in 1975. Since these changes affect all local authority services, and not just education, there are no readings in this volume which discuss them; but the reader should remember that references in the text to local authorities are all to the pre-1974/5 pattern.

At the same time, changes are taking place in the internal

management of both central and local government. At local level, there have been several experiments in recent years with systems of corporate planning or management for the services for which an authority is responsible; one of these is output budgeting, called in the United States planning-programming-budgeting, in which an attempt is made to measure the effectiveness of a 'programme' by its output (crudely, what it achieves) rather than by the input (what goes in to it by way of resources or money). The 'programme' may itself entail the co-ordination of contributions from several services hitherto regarded as separate: thus, duplication of activities designed to secure the same objective, or failure to co-ordinate overlapping activities, or the total neglect of a problem because it fell neatly between the central concerns of several departments, might be eliminated or reduced on this system of management. It will be clear to the reader that inefficiency of this kind might have occurred in the past when, for example, the education, health and welfare services were all concerned to solve or ameliorate the same set of social problems—even if those working in each service saw different aspects of it.

The application of such management techniques to education always seems peculiarly difficult, not least because of the imprecision of many educationists when asked to state their objectives (what they hope to achieve) and the related problem of measuring the output of education (what has been achieved). Nevertheless, there has in recent years been much work at national level on the refinement of these techniques for application to education, and this volume contains some readings illustrative of this work. At the same time, broader changes have been made by central government in recent years in its system of managing overall expenditure, including that on education, and these too are discussed; one aim here has been to plan more effectively and coherently for some years ahead, so that fewer *ad hoc* decisions are taken in particular areas of governmental activity, such as education, with ill-foreseen economic consequences.

Within education itself the past ten years have seen the use of new economic aids to planning future development. The growth of higher education in particular has resulted in controversy not only about desirability of further expansion beyond any given point (the 'more means worse' dispute), but also about how many students should follow what type of course in what discipline, to what level, and in what kind of institution. The Report of the Robbins Committee (the Committee on Higher Education appointed by the Prime Minister under the chairmanship of Lord Robbins) in 1963 was broadly accepted, in terms of the numbers to be admitted to higher education. But its recommendations about the relative size of the university and the non-university sectors of higher education, the latter including the polytechnics as well as the colleges of education, have been by-passed by the official adoption in the mid-sixties of the 'binary' policy. Robbins' preferred method of calculating the desirable size of higher education as a whole, the demand from students with the required standard of educational qualification, has continued to be the basis of official policy. Even Robbins however accepted that the alternative technique of forecasting manpower needs in particular professions or areas of expertise should help to determine the balance of student admissions between disciplines and between types of course. This technique has been applied not only to meeting the requirement for teachers and doctors, where, granted agreement on broad principles (the number of pupils per teacher in primary schools, or the average number of patients who should be on the panel of a GP), it should have yielded useful results, but also to much more difficult questions, such as the overall requirement for scientists and engineers. Here it might seem impractible to achieve any broad agreement on the method of measuring the requirement, and dispute has in fact ensued.

Others again might favour the wider use in planning the distribution of students between courses of rate-of-return analysis, which measures the increase in production (either of the society or the individual)—and compares this with the cost of educational provision, treated as an investment. Put crudely, will the ex-student be better off, over his earning life-time, than if he had simply put the money his higher education cost him into a building society when he was eighteen? Will the community be better off as a result of investing in the higher education of its younger people rather than using the available resources in some alternative way? And will there be a marked difference in the answers if our student read Mechanical Engineering instead of Latin?

Manpower forecasting techniques and rate-of-return analysis have been applied in Britain chiefly to further and
higher education, and they are therefore of general interest
to educationists as are modelling techniques. Here an attempt
is made to reproduce, as an aid to planning, a statistical
model of the education system, or of some part of it. By
changing features of the model it may be possible, with varying degrees of sophistication, to measure the effect of
implementing possible policy options, which might be
impossible in the real world without operating on a long-term
'suck-it-and-see' basis. (And even then, since other changes
might occur in the meantime, it might be impossible to isolate
the effects of a particular new policy.) We include in this
volume examples, criticisms, or explanations of each of these
techniques.

Changes in the methodology of decision-making are occurring in the schools and colleges too, and there is increasing
interest in the training of head teachers and others with
administrative roles in appropriate techniques. Some of these
derive from research in the social sciences, and especially in
organizational analysis. Here an attempt is made to analyse
the structure of educational institutions, their behaviour as
organizations and interaction with their environment, and the
organizational role of individuals or of groups within them.
The lessons can then be applied to the administration of
schools or colleges, or to planning change within them. It
is also possible to ask what interests and attitudes in the
teacher will fit him best for what type of role in a school,
seen as a complex organization. When a teacher is given an
ill-defined role in the organization, when the school has
accepted incompatible objectives, when it is seeking to
achieve something other than what is expected of it by external bodies, or when the aims of one member or group of
members of the organization conflict with those of another,
conflict may arise. It must be understood before it can be
resolved by administrative change. Finally, certain complex
decisions must be made at regular times in similar types of
organization; in the school curriculum-planning and time-
tabling are good examples. Efforts have therefore been made
recently to develop techniques which will at least facilitate
this kind of decision-making in educational institutions.

It is not possible in a Reader of this size to illuminate all of the topics we have mentioned in this Preface; thus, none of the readings discuss the role of the Schools Council or the efficacy of the Confederation for the Advancement of State Education. Those wishing to learn more of the functioning of British education systems are referred to *Education in Great Britain and Ireland*.[1] Nor is it possible to give any detailed account of the law governing education; for the law in England and Wales, readers are referred to *The New Law of Education*.[2]

We have however set out to present a set of readings which illustrate the administrative processes at national and at local level, the interaction between the two, the educational effects of particular decision-making structures, the role and effect of advisory bodies at national level, and of pressure groups and political parties, the new planning techniques which have been applied to educational development in Britain, and new approaches to management in schools and colleges. Some of the readings have direct applicability to only one of the four countries which form the United Kingdom; nevertheless, we believe that their administrative systems have sufficient commonality to give to the nationally particular a more general interest. All alike share an increasingly complex structure of educational decision-making well worthy of study and analysis.

---

[1] Published by Routledge and Kegan Paul in association with the Open University Press, and a set book for the Open University courses E221 and E352.

[2] By G. Taylor and J. B. Saunders (7th Edition), published by Butterworths.

Introduction

The volume begins with an extract from Lord Butler's memoirs (1), in which he describes the political processes which led to the 1944 Education Act; Lord Butler was the President of the Board of Education, the then title of the Minister now known as Secretary of State for Education and Science, who was responsible for preparing the Bill and piloting it through Parliament. He discusses the consultations which he held with the religious bodies before the Bill was prepared. The relationship of the education provided by such voluntary bodies to the State system was of course a central educational question for many decades prior to the 1944 Act. The importance which Lord Butler attaches to his discussion with the then Prime Minister, Winston Churchill, may be noted: the relationship between Prime Ministers and members of their Government varies, as does the degree to which major matters turn upon the collective decision of the cabinet rather than upon the views of key individuals.

The first major section of the book then deals with aspects of the public control of education. P. Armitage (2) analyses the techniques now used by central Government to control the allocation of finance to education, through the local authorities and the University Grants Committee. He shows how the figures which may be deduced from central government planning documents are not always precisely compatible one with another, and suggests that further improvements to the system are desirable.

J. A. G. Griffith (3), scrutinizes the process whereby central government permits local education authorities to indulge in major capital expenditure on schools and colleges. Since Griffith's work was published (in 1966) the Department of Education and Science has adopted a rolling three-year programme for school building, and sections of the circular in which the new system was set out are appended to the extracts from the book. In essence however his comments upon the system remain valid.

That the level of educational provision made by local education authorities can vary widely has long been known. The work of G. Taylor and N. Ayres (4), published in 1969, demonstrated these inequalities conclusively. Taylor brought both practical experience and theoretical knowledge to his study. It should be noted that the local authorities to which Taylor and Ayres refer will in many cases cease to exist with local authority reorganization.

One aspect of the legal system governing the relations of central and local government in education is discussed by R. Buxton (5) in the extract we print from his book on local government. The Wilson Government in 1965 attempted to persuade local education authorities to reorganize secondary education on comprehensive lines by means of a circular; this of itself had no legal force, but when changes were introduced by local education authorities, it was necessary for them to comply with specific legal requirements. In consequence there were some *causes célèbres* in the areas which are discussed by Buxton.

The law also affects the provision that local education authorities can make for the education of children living within their area at direct grant and independent schools. R. Saran (6) analyses the interrelationships of central and local government, and the effect of pressure from parental and religious groups, in the determination of the number of places taken up at such schools by the former Middlesex LEA. Her article also illustrates the interplay of views between officers and elected members in the determination of LEA policy.

Some educational innovation comes from above, as a result of decisions by central government. Sources of innovation are however as likely to be found in LEAs or in the individual schools or among the Inspectorate. M. Kogan (7) shows how the use of 'learning by discovery' methods in primary education in England had its origins at local and institutional level, although the movement received some impetus from the approval given to it by national committees.

Of all the pressure groups in the field of education perhaps the most important are the teachers' unions. In the extract we have taken from his book about them, R. D. Coates (8) examines the effect upon educational policies of the level of educational expenditure of the campaign for educational advance organized by the unions during the 1960s.

Section 2 of the Reader deals with educational planning
in Britain. One traditional piece of machinery for planning
educational development is the national advisory committee
or commission. Kogan (9) takes the Plowden Committee as
an example of the function of the Central Advisory Council
in educational change. He shows how the committee crystall-
ized the thinking of professional educationists and others
about primary education. The extract we have taken from the
report of the research project sponsored by DES and the
Social Science Research Council into educational priority
areas, edited by A. H. Halsey (10), demonstrates that in the
years immediately following the report of the Plowden Committee central government, for a variety of reasons, failed to
implement or to implement fully many of its recommendations. The political debate following the publication of the
report, and the views of the professional bodies and the local
authority associations, both affected the translation of the
report into policy.

The Robbins Committee which reported in 1963 has often
been regarded as the most successful national committee in
the educational area, since the then Government announced
the acceptance of many of its recommendations on the day of
its publication. While not all of them were implemented the
Robbins Report certainly seemed to result in a very rapid
expansion of provision for higher education. Armitage (11)
shows that the statistical techniques used by the Committee
in planning the expansion of higher education, and subsequently used by DES itself, may mislead the unsophisticated
observer, while R. Layard and J. King (12) analyse the effect
which the report had. Once the process has been transferred
from an outside committee to the Department itself, it becomes clear that the projections may influence, but will not
of themselves determine, policy.

We print a brief extract from *Educational Planning Paper
No. 2* (13) describing three approaches to educational planning: two of these approaches, that of cost-benefit analysis
(or the rate of return approach) and manpower forecasting,
have been developed by economists working in education
during the past ten years. The third approach, that of planning on the basis of individual choice and demand is the one
originally adopted by Robbins in 1963 before the more recent
investigations by economists. K. Gannicott and M. Blaug in

'Manpower forecasting since Robbins' (14) describe the attempts made by various committees to forecast needs for scientists and engineers and explain that these have as yet met with little success because neither the training costs nor employers' demands have been taken into account. They argue that only an approach to planning which includes some measure of the costs and benefits will meet with greater success. The results and policy implications of such an analysis are discussed in the article by Vera Morris on educational investment (15), in which the costs of obtaining different qualifications and the economic benefits associated with these qualifications are shown. This article presents evidence which may lend some support to the Gannicott and Blaug argument, and also serves as a partial explanation (albeit accidental) for some government decisions on educational expenditures. All three articles in this section point to the fact that successful educational planning depends on the use of a variety of approaches to supplement each other.

The contribution of economic analysis to educational planning has also been closely related to such questions as the efficiency of educational expenditure, the consideration of alternative policy options, the contribution of education to economic growth, and the effectiveness of different input mixes in meeting the several social and economic objectives of education. It has been possible to only include two examples of all this work in this volume. The first outlines a systematic approach to budgetary control for educational expenditure and has been developed by DES economists in *Educational Planning Paper No. 1* (16). The excerpts from this document show expenditure allocated to separate programmes which correspond to certain broadly-defined educational objectives. The inputs to the separate programmes are costed, and may be related to a series of suggested outputs, measures such as, for example, numbers of qualified students. This approach inevitably requires more detailed supporting research on effectiveness, which may be undertaken within a particular sector, school or college. The second article by L. Wagner (17) investigates cost estimates for traditional and non-traditional university systems.

The last article in this section is by Armitage on model-building (18) and represents an essentially statistical approach to planning based on projected student numbers and contrasts with the economist's concern to evaluate alternative policy options in terms of both numbers and budgetary problems.

The third section of the reader deals with the administration of the school. Analysis of the decision-making process within the school has become an increasingly complex exercise as schools themselves become larger, partly through secondary reorganization, while the school population continues to increase.

As schools increase in size and complexity, so the number of positions of potential power and authority expand, for example that of the head of department, or the school counsellor, while the role of the deputy head—or of the head himself—may be radically revised. As this network of decision-making has developed, so also has interest in the school as an organization, and this section of the Reader begins with an article by S. Bennett and R. Wilkie (19) which outlines some of the problems which the school presents to the organization theorist, and examines five specific areas—the membership, goals, structures, technology and environment of the school. L. Watson's article, which follows (20), analyses the effect of the bureaucratization of the school in terms of its effect on the school personnel—where does the school secretary, subject teacher, head of department, school counsellor, etc., stand on the 'pyramid of power', and how has the large secondary school affected the role of the head?

The power and authority of the head are examined in greater detail by R. King (21), who analyses different types of headship and the attendant differences in the structure and organization of the school.

From a broad-ranging discussion of the authority of the headmaster the focus is narrowed to concentrate on a specific problem of school administration which falls on heads or deputy heads—that of planning the time-table. In his article, A. Bates (22) underlines the haphazard way in which this exercise is carried out, and in view of the increasing complexity of time-tabling for larger numbers in an increasing variety of subjects, puts forward a model of the curriculum-planning process. The concluding article (23) examines some areas of conflict which have arisen within the school as it expands both its size and its social function—here the problems centre round choice in the curriculum, pupil guidance and counselling versus subject teaching, and the introduction of new posts, often in response to a need for a more efficient administrative structure, which upset the traditional structure of the school.

R. A. BUTLER

The Politics of the
1944 Education Act* †

The Prime Minister sent for me. He saw me after his after-
noon nap and was purring like a tiger. He began, 'You have
been in the House fifteen years and it is time you were promoted.' I objected gently that I had been there only twelve
years but he waved this aside. 'You have been in the government for the best part of that time and I now want you to
go to the Board of Education. I think that you can leave
your mark there. You will be independent. Besides,' he continued, with rising fervour, 'you will be in the war. You will
move poor children from here to here', and he lifted up and
evacuated imaginary children from one side of his blotting
pad to the other; 'this will be very difficult'. He went on: 'I
am too old now to think you can improve people's natures.
Everyone has to learn to defend himself. I should not object
if you could introduce a note of patriotism into the schools.'
And then, with a grin, 'Tell the children that Wolfe won
Quebec.' I said that I would like to influence what was taught
in schools but that this was always frowned upon. Here he
looked very earnest and commented, 'Of course not by instruction or order but by suggestion.' I then said that I had always
looked forward to going to the Board of Education if I were
given the chance. He appeared ever so slightly surprised at
this, showing that he felt that in wartime a central job, such
as the one I was leaving, is the most important. But he
looked genuinely pleased that I had shown so much satisfaction and seemed to think the appointment entirely suit-

* [From R. A. Butler, *The Art of the Possible*, Hamish Hamilton, 1971.]
  † [It was in consequence of the 1944 Education Act—the Butler Act—
that the Board of Education became the Ministry of Education, to be
renamed the Department of Education and Science in 1964—Ed.]

able. He concluded the interview by saying, 'Come and see me to discuss things—not details, but the broad lines.'. . . .

The crisis of modern war is a crucial test of national values and way of life. Amid the suffering and the sacrifice the weaknesses of society are revealed and there begins a period of self-examination, self-criticism and movement for reform. It is remarkable how in England educational planning and advance have coincided with wars. In the earlier years of the twentieth century the Boer War and the First World War had both provided an impulse. Alas, many of the proposals of the Fisher Act of 1918 were killed by the economic blizzard which was to freeze the educational pattern for most of the inter-war years. Grammar schools, which had emerged as part of the public provision of education when the century was young and which were the acknowledged route to the professions, were restricted to a small minority of children. The vast majority spent the nine years of their education in elementary schools, which still suffered from the blight of poverty and inferiority associated with the traditions of the past. Thus, through sheer lack of opportunity, much human potential was wasted. Already in 1926 the Hadow Report on the Education of the Adolescent had recommended reorganization of schools with the provision of separate post-primary schools for the senior (eleven-plus) age groups. The Board of Education had encouraged reorganization—in practice the building of new senior elementary schools—but among local authorities progress had varied and in many areas the old all-age elementary school persisted, indeed was not finally obliterated for another forty years. The Hadow Report had also recommended that the school-leaving age should be raised to fifteen—an increase called for by the need to make post-primary education a course with sufficient length to be meaningful. The Education Act of 1936 gave partial effect to this by laying down that, *as from 1 September 1939*, all children were to remain at school until the age of fifteen unless they obtained work which the local education authority approved as beneficial. On that day, however, German troops invaded Poland, the evacuation of school-children began, and the raising of the leaving age was indefinitely postponed.

War brought the building of schools and education itself to a halt in many areas. The evacuation of school children threw the educational system into serious disorder, and thoughts of reform were put aside. There were considerable doubts whether the structure itself could be held together. In January 1940 some half a million children were getting no schooling at all. Energetic action by the Board of Education gradually restored the position. But the revelations of evacuation administered a severe shock to the national conscience; for they brought to light the conditions of those unfortunate children of the 'submerged tenth' who would also rank among the citizens of the future. It was realized with deepening awareness that the 'two nations' still existed in England a century after Disraeli had used the phrase. The challenge of the times provided a stimulus for rethinking the purposes of society and planning the reconstruction of the social system of which education formed an integral part. Realization of a full democracy—an order of society free from the injustices and anomalies of the pre-war period—was the ideal. Educational problems were thus seen as an essential part of the social problem and the urgent need for educational reform was increasingly realized. The first active move came before the end of 1940, and from the Churches. The Archbishops of Canterbury and York, the Roman Catholic Archbishop of Westminster and the Moderator of the Free Church Federal Council wrote a letter to *The Times* on 21 December. In this, under the heading 'Foundations of Peace', they urged that extreme inequality of wealth and possessions should be abolished; that every child, regardless of race or class, should have equal opportunities of education, suitable for development of his *particular* capacities; that the family unit should be safeguarded, and that a sense of divine vocation should be restored to man's daily work.

A scheme for putting some of the aspirations of the time into practice was drawn up by officials of the Board of Education and issued in June 1941. From the colour of its cover, this became known as the 'Green Book'. Its object was to serve as a basis of preliminary talks with all the bodies associated in the educational service. The document was therefore marked 'highly confidential'; but, in Lester Smith's splendid phrase, 'it was distributed in such a blaze of secrecy that it achieved an unusual degree of publicity'. In answer to one of the first parliamentary questions I received on arriving at the Board, I promised to make public a summary of its contents. Though many of the Green Book's proposals, notably those to do with the knotty problem of the Church schools, did not survive exposure, its production did stimulate thinking about educational reform and inspired a spate of booklets on the subject, each in its own distinctive colour. Thus the National Union of Teachers produced a book in a more sombre and less vernal shade of green, the Association of Directors and Secretaries an orange book. (But it was many years before a Black Book was to appear.) With the Parliamentary Secretary, Chuter Ede, I gave the fullest consideration to this response, interviewing deputations and touring the country. Chuter Ede was a Labour man and a Nonconformist, many years my senior in age and experience. I pleased him at our first meeting by offering for his perusal any document that passed through my Private Office, whether personal or public, political or otherwise. In the end a convention grew up between us that we did not bother about each other's purely party correspondence. I was very lucky to have this consistently loyal and wise friend as my chief lieutenant. I was no less fortunate to be served by a quite outstanding group of civil servants: the brilliant Sir Maurice Holmes, Permanent Secretary, derisive of many of the persons and fatuities that came our way, yet acute in ideals and practice; Sir Robert Wood, who did much of our drafting; S. H. Wood, who kept us on the progressive path; the traditionalist, G. G. Williams; William Cleary, with his great reservoir of experience; and the young Neville Heaton, who was the secretary of so many of our committees and who, in my opinion, was of the calibre to be Permanent Secretary himself. Sylvia Goodfellow was my private secretary and worked her way passionately through a mass of paper. Her contribution was important and deserves special mention.

With such a team, it was natural to find intense activity and infectious enthusiasm when I arrived at the Board. Shortly after assuming office I told the House of Commons that it was necessary to reform the law relating to education, and a few weeks later I sent the Prime Minister a letter stressing the need to adapt the educational system to present social requirements. I instanced the need for industrial and technical training and for a settlement with the Churches about their schools and about religious instruction in schools. This was on 12 September 1941. The next day the Prime Minister replied as follows:

It would be the greatest mistake to raise the 1902 controversy during the war, and I certainly cannot contemplate a new Education Bill. I think it would also be a great mistake to stir up the public schools question at the present time. No one can possibly tell what the financial and economic state of the country will be when the war is over. Your main task at present is to get the schools working as well as possible under all the difficulties of air attack, evacuation, etc. If you can add to this industrial and technical training, enabling men not required for the Army to take their places promptly in munitions industry or radio work, this would be most useful. We cannot have any party politics in wartime, and both your second and third points raise these in a most acute and dangerous form. Meanwhile you have a good scope as an administrator.[1]

Sir Maurice Holmes took the Prime Minister's Minute as a veto on education reform and wrote me a philosophic letter:

R. S. Wood and I have discussed the PM's Minute to you. I do not think we need be unduly cast down. It seems to me axiomatic that a major measure of educational reform will be demanded in quarters which will make the demand irresistible, and the question then is not whether but when such reform will be brought about.

And there are, I feel, some advantages in having more time than ever your revised programme contemplated for reaching the greatest common measure of agreement on the more contentious issues, so that from this point of view the PMs frigid reception of your proposals has its brighter side.

However, if educational legislation is to be shelved till the war is over, we shall then be able to think more clearly in terms of bricks and mortar than is possible while the war is in progress, and so form reasonably sound estimates of the dates when this and that measure of reform can become operative. The delay is of course disappointing, particularly to those of us who, like myself, cannot hope to accompany you into the Promised Land, but that you will lead the Children of Israel there, I do not doubt.

Churchill's Minute was quite definite and Holmes's letter disappointingly compliant. But, having viewed the milk and honey from the top of Pisgah, I was damned if I was going to die in the land of Moab. Basing myself on long experience with Churchill over the India Bill, I decided to disregard what he said and go straight ahead. I knew that if I spared him the religious controversies and party political struggles of 1902 and side-tracked the public schools issue, I could win him over. I intended to have an Education Bill, and three years after receiving his Minute I had placed such a Bill on the Statute Book. And, as will be seen, I received on its passing a warm telegram of congratulation from him. This was typical of the man.

My first step was to push forward into the light the proposals made in the Green Book. On 23 October 1941 I made public a summary of its main contents. These were of unequal merit and practicality. On its 'lay' side, the Green Book stressed the need for a system of free secondary education for all as outlined in the Spens Report of 1938. This was imperative. On the other hand, the religious solution proposed in the Green Book, had I ever considered accepting it, would have led to a head-on collision with the Free Churches. This was because the Green Book proposed the abrogation in the secondary schools of the ban on denominational religious instruction imposed by the Cowper-Temple clause of the Act of 1870. This would have meant that such instruction could have been given in secondary schools provided by local education authorities ('provided schools') as well as in Church secondary schools ('non-provided schools'). During the winter of 1941-2 I worked on my own plans for educational reform and presented the lay aspects of these to the Conference of the National Union of Teachers on 9 April 1942, with the warm support of Chuter Ede who had been himself a teacher. The Union's President described the proposals as 'the most progressive ever outlined by a President of the Board of Education'. I said that the aim should be elementary education up to eleven and secondary education for all over that age. Educationally after the war Britain had to be one nation, not two. So there must be an education system providing a 'training suited to talents' of every individual. This would have to be combined with more expert training for industry, with a revivified system of apprenticeship, and with a practical form of continued education, later to be called County Colleges. I did not, however, go any further on the religious side than to call for a final settlement of the 'Dual System' of provided and non-provided schools. Since this issue was a particularly thorny one, I was to spend more time in trying to reach the settlement than on anything else.

For most of the nineteenth century, schools had been provided not by local authorities, but by voluntary bodies who raised money by public subscription and financed the building and running of schools. From 1833 the State had assisted these bodies with grants of money which increased in amount as time went on. The most important of the voluntary bodies was the Church of England's National Society. At the end of the nineteenth century it had nearly 12,000 schools in England and Wales and was responsible for educating nearly two million of the country's children. Of the other voluntary bodies that of the Roman Catholic Church was the most important. Altogether the voluntary or Church schools educated two and a half million children. At the same time, however, far fewer schools, provided by the local education authorities, were educating two and a quarter million children. Many of the Church schools were small, with a wide age-range of pupils, a limited number of teachers (sometimes, in villages, only one) and, very often, antiquated and ill-equipped buildings. Yet any attempt to increase central government help meant greater expenditure, which was resisted by the Treasury, and any proposal to assist Church schools from the rates aroused a furious and bitter opposition. A main reason for this was that Church schools gave the religious instruction of the Church to which they belonged, while local authority schools gave religious instruction unconnected with the formulary or beliefs of any particular Church. There were relatively few Nonconformist schools and in many areas, particularly in the villages, the Church of England school was the only school. These were known as 'single-school' areas. Nonconformists naturally resented sending their children to a school which taught the catechism of the Church of England, especially when the local parson took part both in the control of the school and in the religious instruction. There were political implications too—the Tory alliance of squire and parson in the village drew the village school and its master within their orbit as lesser satellites.

In preparing myself to deal with the religious question, I looked back to the precedents of the 1902 Education Act and read what historians had had to say. Elie Halévy's immortal

History of England and Jacques Bainville's smaller history were both illuminating.

Halévy described the school situation of 1902 as: 'State schools favoured by the Free Churches and free schools favoured by the State Church.' The 1902 Act, by making local education authorities responsible for paying for elementary education in Church schools as well as in their own, aroused a fierce religious dispute. The cry went up of 'Rome on the rates', and some Welsh authorities refused to pay for the education in Church schools in their area. Halévy comments, 'To read the Liberal newspapers of the day you would imagine that the Cecils were preparing to revive the policy of Laud if not of Strafford and that in every village a Nonconformist Hampden was about to rise against their persecution.' Winston Churchill remembered very vividly the battles over the Education Act of 1902 and the serious damage it did the Conservative party. When the Liberals took over in 1905 their efforts to settle this question met with no success; three Bills put forward by successive Presidents of the Board of Education failed. The first of these, Birrell's Bill of 1906, was not unlike my final settlement. I was anxious not only to achieve a solution to this problem, but in doing so not to do damage to the interests I represented.

Though religious tensions had lessened since the 1900s, the problem of the Church schools was becoming more serious. The Church of England had built hardly any schools since the 1914-18 war and had been giving them up at the average rate of 76 a year. Far too many were appallingly old and out of date. The Hadow reorganization, which involved the introduction of separate schools for the primary and post-primary pupils, meant new buildings. The Church of England particularly had great difficulty in responding to this new need, and its voluntary schools were largely unreorganized by the time war broke out. Many of them, particularly those in rural areas, were too small to be efficient. Educational progress would not be possible unless the problem of the Church schools could be solved. The radical solution of abolishing the Church schools and of putting all schools equally under local authorities was urged by such bodies as the TUC, the National Union of Teachers and the Free Churches. The NUT were concerned that the rights of school managers to appoint their own teachers meant that thousands of posts were open only to teachers of a particular denomination. The NUT stated in 1942 that 'the only fully satisfactory solution would be the achievement of a national unified system of education by means of the transfer of all non-provided schools, whether included at present in the elementary or secondary system, to the control of the local education authority'. The Nonconformists also wanted the Dual System to go, since they particularly resented the Anglican monopoly of schools in over 4,000 rural areas—schools which, to quote Halévy once more, were 'built with the squire's money and taught the parson's catechism'. The Free Churches, while strongly in favour of Christian teaching in the schools by qualified teachers, regarded undenominational religious instruction as essential and the Cowper-Temple clause of the 1870 Act as a Charter of their rights.

An important development which met the wishes of the Nonconformists and of many Anglicans was the 'agreed syllabus'. In Cambridgeshire in 1924 a committee of Anglicans, Free Churchmen and teachers had met and had drawn up a syllabus of religious instruction for use in the county's schools. By 1942 the Cambridgeshire syllabus was in use by over 100 local education authorities. Because of this, many Anglican managers were willing to hand over their schools to the local authorities in return for Christian teaching on these lines. The Prime Minister, I soon discovered, was fascinated by the idea of the agreed syllabus. He called it the 'County Council Creed' and on one occasion 'Zoroastrianism'. He asked me whether I intended to start a new State religion. I replied that the Roman legionaries in North Africa may have fallen for Zoroaster but that I was more orthodox.

There was a division of opinion in the Church of England between those who felt a truly Christian atmosphere and teaching could come about only in Church schools, and those who thought the 'agreed' syllabus was sufficient. On the question of the Dual System, many Anglicans wanted denominational schools put on the same financial basis as provided schools. Behind these Anglicans were many members of the Conservative party. The Roman Catholics, though not co-operating with the other Churches, disliked the agreed syllabus (Cardinal Hinsley called it 'disembodied Christianity' and the *Tablet* 'a synthetic article') and wanted to retain their own schools. When it came to negotiation they were not prepared to compromise. They argued that they had to pay rates and taxes for the upkeep of the local authority schools which their consciences would not let them use. Since 1870 they had spent millions of pounds in preserving their schools and they were determined that they would not be lost now. Thus Dr Downey, Archbishop of Liverpool, said on 31 May 1942, 'We shall continue to struggle for denominational schools even though we have to fight alone' and Cardinal Hinsley wrote in a letter to *The Times* on 31 November 1942: 'No equal opportunity will exist for a minority who are saddled with extra and crushing financial burdens because of their definite religious convictions and because they cannot accept a syllabus of religious instruction agreeable to many.' Churchill cut this out, and sent it to me with a curt covering note saying, 'There, you are fixed.'

In spite of all the difficulties it seemed a suitable moment, during a National government and with a loyal collaborator from the Labour party working with me, to attempt a solution of these political problems. Not long after I reached the Board, I had had to receive a massive deputation of Church leaders; but the absence of the Roman Catholics made it essential for me to say as little as possible at this stage, though I provided some innocent diversion and surprise by asking Cosmo Gordon Lang, the Archbishop of Canterbury, to conclude the interview with prayer. To begin with, discussions about the future of the Church schools centred on the plan outlined in the Green Book—very exquisitely drawn and much in favour of the Anglicans. In the spring of 1942 an alternative plan, largely the work of Chuter Ede, and known as the 'white memorandum', was privately circulated by the Board. Both plans broke down: that in the Green Book on the issue of denominational religious teaching in the future secondary modern schools; that in the white memorandum because Anglicans opposed compulsory transfer of their schools to the local education authorities in single-school areas. Wolmer, later Lord Selborne, in particular was most anxious that I should not stand by the white memorandum plan, saying that it had no chance of acceptance by the Anglicans. We accordingly set about drafting another plan, which would attempt to satisfy the Free Churches in that their children could feel, in most places, that they were entering a school which was not conducted in the atmosphere of the

Church of England alone, but which would attempt to satisfy the Anglicans by a continuation of some doctrinal teaching and would not involve any change in the ownership of the premises.

The solution I reached after much patience and experimentation was to make an offer of two alternatives. Thus a Church school could choose either to be 'controlled' or 'aided'. If 'controlled', the local education authority became responsible for all the expenses of the school, and for the appointment of all but a limited number of teachers; the religious instruction was, for the most part, to be in accordance with an agreed syllabus; and a majority of the managers or governors were appointed by public bodies. If 'aided', the local education authority was responsible for the teachers' salaries and the running expenses of the school; but the managers were responsible for any alterations and improvements needed to bring the school up to standard (for which they would receive a 50 per cent grant from the Exchequer), and they retained the right to appoint and dismiss teachers and to control the religious instruction; the Church had a majority on the managing body. 'Controlled' status met the needs of the Free Churches and the Low Church Anglicans. Sir Maurice Holmes was always adamant that to extend State help to one community without extending it to all denominations was impossible. The Roman Catholics felt that the 50 per cent grant was not enough. But we knew that if it were raised, and if many Anglican schools were involved, this would only continue the Dual System of Church-local authority schools under slightly different terms. For the plan to succeed Anglican schools would have to opt for controlled status in large numbers. This insistence was a key to the whole success of the plan. I thought that the aided status was perfectly fair to both Anglicans and Roman Catholics since they were going to get so much additional help from public funds, while retaining their rights with regard to teachers and religious instruction.

This was the solution of the problem which I hoped the various parties concerned would accept. But difficult negotiations lay ahead, with the Church of England and with the Roman Catholics. As I have indicated, the Roman Catholics still wanted to act independently. There was no question of an alliance between them and the Church of England. I had to deal with each body separately yet achieve a solution which would satisfy all parties concerned. In these negotiations the leading personalities were clearly of the greatest importance. [....]

There is little hope of agreement with prominent religious leaders, particularly of a minority, and what hope there is lies in getting hold of them personally and assuring them of the sincerity and sympathy of one's approach. The Free Churches knew quite well that my uncle, George Adam Smith, was one of them, having been himself Moderator of the Free Church of Scotland. As for the Anglicans, I was fortunate in having to deal with Archbishop Temple (who succeeded Lang in April 1942) and with the then Bishop of London, Fisher, who played an important part in helping me set up the Fleming Committee to deal with the public schools question and proved a most effective ally in getting my Bill through the Lords. [....]

The occasion when the Archbishop was tipped over to support a plan on my lines was one hot morning in the Conference Room at Kingsway, its windows blitzed out and covered with cardboard, no air in the room, in the summer of 1942. On that occasion I described to him and those few with him—including the Dean of St Albans and the Bishop of Oxford, two zealots indeed, and Mr Hussey, secretary of the National Society—the condition of the Church schools, the number of them on the Black List, and the small extent of reorganization. He was moved by the figures and said he had not realized what a bad state the Church schools were in. Of the 10,553 voluntary schools, 9,683 were over 40 years old. On the Black List were 543 voluntary schools out of a total of 731. I noted at the time that 'these statistics visibly impressed his Grace, who said he would have to do his best to wean his flock from their distaste at the challenged threat to their schools'. Ever after that date he adhered to his part of the understanding. He told me he had decided that the majority of the Church schools would opt for the controlled status and therefore depend on the agreed religious syllabus. He would rather compound for 'stoical ethicism', which is how he described the religious syllabus teaching, than attempt the impossible, namely for all the Church schools to undertake denominational teaching. How important Temple thought the religious syllabus to be, it is hard to say. In Dean

Iremonger's Life, he is quoted as saying that the raising of
the school age was the most essential element of the Bill:
'I am putting this very crudely, but I believe that our Lord
is much more interested in raising the school leaving age to
sixteen than in acquiring an agreed religious syllabus.' This
at any rate shows that Temple was so keen on the provisions
of the Act itself that he was determined not to allow a religious
quarrel to hold up educational advance.

Another very important figure in the whole negotiation
was Sir Robert Martin, the prominent layman in the Church
Assembly and the National Society. Taking advantage of a
visit to Leicester, I had gone to stay a night with Martin in
the early part of the year and had sat with him at 'The
Brand' until a late hour. He had told me that he thought if I
could grant the Church up to 75 per cent of their expenses,
they would be very satisfied. I was obliged to point out to
him that I would not be able to go as high as this and, having
heard what I had to say about the plan, he very gallantly
gave it the National Society's backing in speeches at the
Church Assembly, where he said: 'The Society had come to
the conclusion that where the amenities of non-provided
schools could not fulfil their legal obligations in regard to
repairs, alterations and improvements, there must clearly be
a wide measure of public control. This could be met by an
arrangement whereby its obligations as well as the appointment of teachers could pass to the local education authority,
subject to the appointment of reserve teachers to such an
extent as might be necessary for providing denominational
teaching as set out in the agreed syllabus.'

This revolution in policy aroused the wrath of the non-
compromisers, but they were reminded by Dr Temple of the
figures of black-list schools which I had given him. To bring
these schools up to a reasonable standard would take another
ten or fifteen years. The Assembly decided to approve and
support the policy outlined in the National Society's report.
This decision set up a landmark in the history of English
education and cleared the way for the resultant compromise
in the 1944 Act. [. . . .]

I now revert to the fact that with the Roman Catholics one
of the chief problems was that there was no special leader;
those at the summit were very old and it was difficult to establish any personal contact. I have already indicated that they

were not co-operating with the other Churches, and from the public pronouncements of leaders like Dr Downey and Cardinal Hinsley, it was evident that it would not be easy to come to a settlement. Their absence from the deputation of 1941 had made an impression on my mind which was subsequently confirmed. There was difficulty in negotiating with an individual bishop without that bishop repudiating responsibility for the others. After I had started talking to Cardinal Hinsley and had driven out to his home in the country to do so, I became aware that his powers showed clear signs of decline. He seemed unable fully to understand the benefits of the plan—in particular, the revival of the provisions of the 1936 Act, which enabled capital grants of up to 75 per cent to be paid by local authorities for new Church secondary schools needed for reorganization. This did not mean that one was not impressed by his sincerity. His influence was carried on by Bishop Myers, the Vicar-Capitular of Westminster, and it is wrong to say that had Cardinal Hinsley lived he would have obtained a more easy settlement, though the dignity of those with whom one had to deal could never equal his. I was advised that Dr Downey was a man ambitious not only for celestial, but also terrestrial renown. He spoke quite fairly in private but appeared, as an Irishman, to enjoy a public fight. Unfortunately he chose the period in which I was involved in negotiations to reduce his weight by some nine stones! This rendered his health precarious, with the result that, for the critical period of the summer of 1943, he retired from Liverpool to Ireland, where he was no doubt encouraged in his militancy by his non-co-operation.

I also negotiated with Archbishop Amigo of Southwark and the apostolic delegate Monsignor Godfrey. I visited the former on 24 November 1942, and my records state that 'after much sounding of the bell, a sad looking, rather blue-faced Chaplain let me in and we climbed a massive palace stair to the first floor where the Archbishop was sitting, fully robed, in a small room overlooking the ruins of Southwark Cathedral. His window was wide open on his left hand so that he could at once take in the tragic picture of the ruins and inhale the chilly morning air.' The Archbishop asked immediately we had sat down what I had come to see him for. I obliged by informing him; but it was not an auspicious beginning. He said that a 50 per cent grant was not sufficient and that he saw no chance of agreement with politicians. He said that if I had belonged to his community he would have suggested that we should pray. I said that I would be very ready to do so since I was also a churchman.

This interview indicated the nature of the head-on collision with the Roman Catholic Church. When the White Paper on Educational Reconstruction—the blue-print for the Education Bills—was published, the Roman Catholics attacked the proposals and Cardinal Hinsley said that in negotiating with the President of the Board of Education they had 'at no stage agreed to the financial conditions now made public'. Thereafter, in December 1943, I was invited, together with Chuter Ede and Maurice Holmes, to meet the Northern Roman Catholic Bishops. Near Durham we came to the imposing parterres of Ushaw College. We were greeted by the Bishop of Hexham, in full robes, and taken almost at once into the evening meal, which, in the tradition of the younger Pitt, was served at about 6 o'clock. There was a large *gigot* and tolerable quantities of a red wine. Immediately this feast was over we were taken to see the Chapel, and a magnificent ivory figure was taken down from the High Altar for our benefit. We were all filled with a certain awe, which was no doubt intentionally administered. Chuter Ede told me he thought he was going to faint. So we came to our conference with the Bishops, at the start of which I tried to explain that against the background of difficulties in 1902, the important thing was to handle this problem so as to remove bitterness and deal with the great majority of the Church schools, amounting to some 10,000. I sketched the growth of aid to voluntary schools by a process of geometrical progression from the settlement of 1870 to the present day. I said that, if the Catholics were patient and accepted this settlement, they could in my view (which has been proved correct by events) hope for more within another generation. If, on the other hand, they placed themselves athwart the stream of national progress, they would be doing their cause so much harm, especially in some districts, that it might never recover.

I was perhaps misled by the great understanding apparently shown of this speech by all the bishops present, and by the personal conversation of many of them. The Bishop of Salford, for example, said that he desired his followers to suffer and pay as part of their faith. Bishop Flynn of Lancaster told Maurice Holmes that he could work the scheme. Archbishop Downey told Chuter Ede and myself that it would enable him to get over all his troubles in Liverpool. But, in the event, none of them attempted to control their own supporters, believing that their anxieties justified them in encouraging a fuss. Still, it must have been quite a good speech; for Maurice Holmes passed me a note which said, 'Your utterance was at once so human and so statesmanlike that it nearly brought tears into the eyes of a very hardened administrator.' [. . . .]

The only reference to educational reform I was able to persuade Churchill to include in the King's Speech was to the factual effect that discussions were proceeding. Even this was secured after considerable initial hesitation—and quite deliberately no specific mention was made of a Bill. This was how matters stood publicly in March 1943 when I was invited to spend the night at Chequers. I drove down with 'the Prof', as everyone called Lord Cherwell, that sharp-witted, sharp-tongued, pertinacious, and more than slightly conspiratorial character who had long been Churchill's closest friend and confidant. He told me that the Prime Minister would be wanting to talk about education, especially in the context of a speech on 'the home front' which he contemplated making. The Prof hoped that I would encourage him to make the speech, though some of the wording needed attention. [. . . . .]

We spent much of the journey from Whitehall to Princes Risborough discussing what now seems the extremely academic thesis that a continuing fall in the school population (which did not, as it happens, take place) would still involve the country in additional expenses, since the slack (which did not, in the event, appear) would be taken up by reducing classes to the proper level (which, a quarter of a century later, we still had not done). Neither of us was prophetic enough to see the future 'bulge' in the birth rate, even less its duration. However, the Prof was understanding about my efforts in the religious sphere, saying that I made a good bargain with the Anglicans [. . . . .] When dinner was over everyone was sent away except the Prof and me, and the Prime Minister produced his draft speech from which he proceeded to recite at great length and with exaggerated gusto [. . . . .] He read four pages on education, which were in a flowing style and derived from Disraeli's view that a nation rules either by force or by tradition. His theme was that we must adhere to our traditions, but that we must move from the class basis of our politics, economics and education to a national standard. There were some sharp words about idle people whether at the top or the bottom, some very pungent remarks about the old school tie (the time for which, he said, was past), and a definite assertion that the school-leaving age must be raised to sixteen. He remarked that his daughter Mary had told him he must say sixteen, 'because it had been promised', and that he agreed with her as this would keep people off the labour market where 'blind-alley occupations' started so fair and often ended so foul. I said that I agreed with Mary too, but that perhaps I had better have a good look at the wording later on. [.....] I sat up for a considerable period rewriting. In particular, I added a piece on religion and its place in the schools, modified the reference to the school-leaving age by saying that it must be progressively prolonged, inserted a few lines on further education and part-time release from industry (using the Prime Minister's own words about blind-alley occupations), and substituted for the rather rude remarks about the old school tie a statement about the need for every type of school and every type of tie.

I was up and about well before nine next morning, and was rather shaken to be told that it wasn't certain whether the PM would actually want to see me. However, at a quarter to eleven my presence was demanded and I found him in bed, smoking a Corona, with a black cat curled up on his feet. He began aggressively by claiming that the cat did more for the war effort than I did, since it provided him with a hot-water bottle and saved fuel and power. Didn't I agree? I said not really, but that it was a very beautiful cat. This seemed to please him. He then asked me if I had done anything overnight or whether I had been lulled to sleep. So I produced my handiwork which was critically surveyed. He did not agree at all with my wording about religion, but allowed that there were people in the country who would have noticed its omission. I observed mildly that there were quite a lot. The PM said he would rather express the idea in his own way, if I would allow him to; whereupon he began to expatiate on the subject of freedom of conscience, toleration, consideration of the other man's point of view, and the kindly character of our country—into which pattern the schools must fit themselves. [.....]

We came to what for me was the crucial part of our conversation. 'I advise you,' he declared, 'not to come out too much on education immediately, because they will only drag you down in the present political atmosphere. I admired what you said about not bringing out snippets of policy. You will have to make a great statement when the time comes— a State Paper or a speech, a great speech.' So I said I was drafting a Bill, with the aid of my colleagues. To this he paid no attention at all. I repeated, in a louder voice, 'I am drafting an Education Bill.' Without raising his head from the papers before him on the counterpane, he said simply that I must show him my plans when they were ready and that he was sure they would be very interesting. I gladly left it at that, and we turned to the other and detailed amendments I had made to his speech, all of which he accepted quite calmly, saying he thought they were improvements. [.....]

The sequel to my visit to Chequers was that in April I sent a memorandum on educational reconstruction to the Cabinet, in July I published the White Paper, decorated by a quotation from Disraeli ('Upon the education of the people of this country the fate of this country depends'), and in January 1944 I moved the Second Reading of the Education Bill in the House of Commons. The original idea was that the Bill and the White Paper should come out together. But the Bill proved so complicated to draft that it was decided to issue the White Paper separately and references in it to what the Bill 'provides' were changed to what it 'would provide'. This was accepted as a thoroughly democratic way of proceeding. It also proved extremely advantageous from a tactical point of view. For the reception of the White Paper made it plain to my Ministerial colleagues that, whilst there might well be controversy over certain sections of the Bill, and particularly over the religious settlement, it would have the minimum of disruptive effect upon the Coalition character of the government. The *Times Educational Supplement* said of the White Paper, 'The ingenious and intricate compromise—product of many months of patient and unwearying negotiations on the part of the President of the Board of Education—which is proposed as a solution for the inveterate problem of dual control, though it commands the agreement and one would imagine the respect of all the moderates may yet not satisfy the intransigents or the extremists on either side. Yet he will be a rash and irresponsible man who is prepared to attack the settlement now proposed without offering to put in its place another which will command an equal degree of consent and will be equally well conceived to promote the success of the plan as a whole.' There were indeed strong attacks on the arrangements outlined for the voluntary schools, notably from the Roman Catholic community. But despite the anxiety raised by this opposition, indeed largely because of it, there was a desire on the part both of government and back-benchers to get this matter well out of the way before an election.

Another decisive argument in favour of an early Bill was that no other Minister on the home front had been able to bring his plans to fruition. Sir Granville Ram, the Parliamentary Counsel, who with Sam (now Mr Justice) Cooke was responsible for the drafting of the Bill, told me only ten days before it was issued that he had nothing else whatever on the stocks—not even a keel laid down. Thus, for example, the whole problem of how to implement the Beveridge Report on social security and allied services was still at the stage of drawings, and not under construction. This was due to the fact that most of the issues of post-war reconstruction impinged directly and immediately on the pocket, and appeared in one way or another to touch the sensitive political area of economic planning and control. It may seem strange that the enormous capital and current commitments which the full implementation of the Education Bill would entail were not considered an insuperable barrier to progress. But I was very careful at all stages to say, what was indeed the case, that their full implementation would take at least a generation. This was naturally a great comfort to Sir Kingsley Wood and Sir John Anderson, the two Chancellors with whom I had successively to deal, and they and their Treasury officials were therefore reasonable and helpful over finance. I was also encouraged by the Whips' Office, then under the direction of James Stuart, for whom the beauty of the Bill was that it would keep the parliamentary troops thoroughly occupied; providing endless opportunity for debate, without any fear of breaking up the government. Its provisions were broadly acceptable to moderate and progressive Conservative opinion and consistently supported by Labour men, both those inside the government (notably Ernest Bevin) and those 'in opposition' (notably our former colleague Arthur Greenwood). *The Times* noted that, in a two days' debate on the White Paper, 'not a single voice was raised in favour of holding up or whittling down any one of the proposals for educational advance'. For all these reasons I was able to carry on with my hands strengthened.

I began my Second Reading speech by observing that a schoolmaster friend had explained to me how, if it were too academic, it would be set by schools as a subject for prize essays. This was my excuse for getting down to the practical details of the Bill without too much philosophizing. For it was a long Bill—122 clauses and eight schedules—and to make a précis of it would take at least as long as to play a football match. I proposed, with this image in mind, to divide the speech into two halves—playing the first half 'with the wind', that is to say dealing with proposals about which everyone was pretty happy, and the second half 'against the wind', that is to say dealing with issues that might prove, or had already proved, contentious. In the first half I described the revised powers and influence of the central authority (soon to be renamed the Ministry of Education), the setting up of advisory councils for England and Wales with a wider scope than the old Consultative Committee, and most important of all, the replacement of the elementary code, with its emphasis on the three R's, by a continuous process of education conducted in successive stages and suited to the three A's, 'the age, ability, and aptitude', of each child. For children below the age of five the aim was a sufficient supply of nursery schools. The period of compulsory school attendance, and hence of free schooling, would be extended from fourteen to fifteen without exemptions and with provision for its subsequent extension to sixteen as soon as circumstances permitted. And this period would be divided into two stages—primary education up to about eleven, and secondary education for all, 'of diversified types but of equal standing', thereafter. When the period of full-time schooling ended, it was proposed that young people should continue under educational influences up to eighteen years of age, either by staying on at secondary school or by attending county colleges. Throughout all these stages the benefits of full medical and dental inspection and treatment would be available, and special schools would be provided for children suffering from physical or mental disability. Opportunities for technical and adult education would also be increased.

I had just got to the second part of my speech, in which I anticipated playing against the wind, when Mgr Griffin, the newly appointed Archbishop of Westminster who had been enthroned the day before, was ushered into the Distinguished Strangers' Gallery. There, with the sun illuminating his bright red hair and his pectoral cross, he sat looking directly down on me as I outlined the provisions of the religious settlement and replied to those who had criticized its compromises. 'I would ask those who feel deeply,' I said, 'to dismiss from their minds the wholly unwarrantable views that the Government desire either to tear away Church schools from unwilling managers or to force them inhumanely out of business. The best way I can reassure them is by quoting a verse from the hymn:

> Ye fearful saints, fresh courage take,
> The clouds ye so much dread
> Are big with mercy, and shall break
> In blessings on your head.'

The unexpected, gratifying and witty sequel was the delivery to me next morning of a large parcel, containing not a bomb but a set of Abbot Butler's *Lives of the Saints*, the classic Roman Catholic work on hagiography. Indeed, I must in fairness say that, though the Roman Catholic interest never accepted the financial basis laid down for voluntary school building, the religious clauses aroused far less acrimony and a much greater sense of responsibility in the House of Commons than past experience had suggested was likely.

The other two issues on which controversy was expected were the future of independent educational provision, and most particularly the public schools, and the proposed abolition of what the Act of 1902 had called 'Part III authorities', those responsible for the oversight of elementary education only. A system had been written into the Bill for improving sub-standard independent schools and for closing those that were inefficient or inadequately equipped. But the central political issue—whether, and if so how, public schools might be more closely associated with or integrated into the general

educational system—had been remitted for study by a committee under the chairmanship of Lord Fleming. I had been
advised that Fleming was a distinguished Scottish judge who
could be relied upon to provide impartiality; I had not been
prepared for the limitations of his views or for the humourless-
ness with which he gave them rein. The sensationally ingenu-
ous report produced in 1944, in common with its successor a
quarter of a century later,* tended only to confirm the view
of my old Corpus mentor, Sir Will Spens, that there was no
practical solution to the problem of public schools, since they
were *sui generis*. Certainly it had little influence on the
course of events. But, though Labour members breathed a
certain amount of ritual fire and fury about social exclusive-
ness and privilege, the appointment of the Fleming Committee had temporarily removed the fuse. Or, in a railway
metaphor, the first-class carriage had been shunted on to an
immense siding.

The abolition of the Part III authorities was, mercifully,
provided for in a schedule to the Bill. What would have happened if this issue had been fought out at an earlier stage is
anybody's guess. The proceedings in committee were very
slow to begin with—it took eight days to get through the
first 27 clauses—though later a voluntary time-table was
evolved and things went more rapidly until the fateful night
when the government were defeated on clause 82 on the question of equal pay for women teachers. Many sensational
accounts have been given of this incident. It arose because
of a clear resolve of the Tory Reform group, led by Quintin
Hogg to whom I had quite fruitlessly appealed for a modicum
of uncharacteristic restraint, to vote with the Labour rebels
against the government. Owing to their jubilant and over-
weening attitude, I did not feel it right to adopt an appeasing
line, particularly as they had for some time been creating
difficulties for my other colleagues in the government. We
should have escaped defeat if only one of the less sprightly
Ministers, like Sir John Anderson, who had been working in
their offices in Whitehall, had proved more fleet of foot. But
they arrived in the Chamber out of breath and too late to
prevent our being beaten by the margin of a single vote.

* [Butler here refers to the first report of the Public Schools Commission appointed by the 1964–70 Labour Government, H.M.S.O. 1960—Ed.]

After the event I was sorry to have shown a measure of irri-
tation; but I did take it rather hard that major political issues
with which I had been dealing for so many months should
have led to no trouble, whereas a matter (implicitly affecting
the entire Civil Service) which could not conceivably have
been settled within the context of an Education Bill should
have resulted in a government defeat due to the irresponsibi-
lity of a small minority in my own party.

However, the current gossip about my telling the Prime
Minister I was in an impossible position and appealing to him
for support, had no basis in fact. Having returned home to
dinner with my PPS, I was asked to go along with the Chief
Whip to see the Prime Minister at about a quarter to ten.
We found Churchill in a very resolute and jovial mood. He
said that he warmly supported my language, which he had
heard on the 9 o'clock news; he was sorry that the issue
should have been that of equal pay, but it was not the issue
that mattered so much as the opportunity to rub the rebels'
noses in their own mess. He had long been waiting for this
opportunity; the by-elections had been going against him, and
the House seemed to be utterly unaware that there was a
war on and that we had severe struggles ahead. Now the
Lord had delivered the enemy into his hands, and he reminded me of the strategy of the Battle of Dunbar ('Both sides
confidently appealed to Jehovah; and the Most High, finding
so little to choose between them in faith and zeal, allowed
purely military factors to prevail'). Happily, he had the big
battalions, and it would be valuable to secure a vote of confidence before the Second Front opened. So clause 82 as
amended must be expunged from the Bill and the original,
unamended, clause put back as a matter of confidence. He
dictated on the spot the statement to this effect which he
made in the House next day. It had the cordial backing of all
the other members of government who had been badgered
by the Tory Reformers from time to time. Anthony Eden,
then Leader of the House, was particularly firm in his support, while Ernest Bevin went so far as to say that, if my position were to be in any way prejudiced, he would leave the
government. These were indeed cheering reactions. It is
when one gets into a scrape that it is easiest to count one's
friends.

On the night before the confidence debate Churchill prepared a splendid piece of oratory which he invited me to read. It high-lighted the magnificence of the British Constitution, compared it in somewhat doubtful terms with the written Constitutions of Russia and the United States, and depicted Prime Ministers riding upon the sea of Parliament as our battleships do upon the waves. Polite and even gracious noises followed about my handling of the Bill; almost everyone was in agreement with it and with the manner in which it had been piloted through Parliament. But, he went on to say, to insert the massive and far-reaching issue of equal pay into its provisions was like placing an elephant in a perambulator. (In the original text, he had referred to my Bill as a milk cart, but, seeing that I was not overpleased by this description, changed it to what he called 'a less clattering vehicle'.) Unfortunately, the Chair's ruling prevented this speech from being delivered; so the House was sadly deprived and the PM sulked visibly on the Treasury bench. In the vote that followed the government had an overwhelming majority, and we continued, without further distractions of a similar magnitude, to pass the Bill through the Commons. Indeed the equal-pay fracas paid a handsome dividend. For thereafter no member proved so bold as to press an amendment which was unacceptable to the government if there was any prospect of its being carried. This made it very much easier to deal with the potentially controversial abolition of the Part III authorities which, as I have already mentioned, had been relegated by the unwitting prescience of Sir Granville Ram to the tail end of the Bill.

In the House of Lords the Bill was in the capable charge of Lord Selborne (whom Churchill incurably persisted in addressing by his previous title of Wolmer). 'Their Lordships', he wrote to me at a time when, having carelessly fallen from a tree in my father's Cambridge garden, I was incapacitated with a broken rib, 'are a very formidable assembly comprising four ex-presidents of the Board of Education and three ex-Lord Chancellors, and a million Bishops, to say nothing of ardent spirits of varying eloquence and wisdom.' Their ardour was somewhat quenched when they had to call off a vote because they simply did not know how to divide in the temporary quarters they were then occupying in Church House. But in any case the proceedings proved less exciting, certainly less troublesome, in the Lords than in the Commons. By August the Bill was law, and I received the following telegram:

Pray accept my congratulations. You have added a notable Act to the Statute Book and won a lasting place in the history of British education. Winston S. Churchill.

I cabled him back:

Very many thanks for your generous telegram which much encourages me on the inauguration of the reformed system of education. R. A. Butler.

The Act of 1944, in common with its predecessors of 1870, 1902 and 1918, affords a classic example of what Dicey called 'our inveterate prejudice for fragmentary and gradual legislation'. It did not, as some would have wished, sweep the board clean of existing institutions in order to start afresh. On the contrary, it established a financial framework within which schools provided by the local education authorities and schools provided by the Churches could continue to live side by side. The more generous assistance which it made available to the voluntary bodies enabled the physical reorganization of schools into primary and secondary to proceed, albeit slowly. It was therefore possible for the Act to cut right out of the educational vocabulary the word 'elementary', to which the stigma of an inferior kind of schooling for children of the poorer classes had continued to cling. Henceforth every child would have a right to free secondary education and in order that these secondary courses should become a full reality, they were to last for at least four and eventually five years. It was, however, equally important to ensure that a stigma of inferiority did not attach itself to those secondary institutions—and they were bound now to be the preponderant majority—which lacked the facilities and academic prestige of the grammar schools. Conditions in each of the different types of school, grammar, modern and technical, would therefore have to be made broadly equivalent: indeed, as my 1943 White Paper stated, 'It would be wrong to suppose that they will necessarily remain separate and apart. Different types may be combined in one building or on one site.' This forecast the comprehensive idea. Even so, equality of opportunity would remain something of an empty phrase if children entered the period of compulsory schooling from conditions of family deprivation, or left it to pursue what Churchill called blind-alley occupations. Accordingly, the Act made provision, on the one hand, for a major expansion of maintained and grant-aided nursery schools and, on the other hand, for compulsory part-time education up to the age of eighteen.

I

Public Control of Education

2

P. ARMITAGE

Central Government and the Allocation of Finance to Education

Educational planning has this in common with an iceberg: that it is only the tip which is immediately visible. This note is concerned with the submerged part, the mechanisms within the administration and especially the system of allocating finance to the universities on the one hand, and to the local education authorities on the other. It draws mainly on memoranda and replies by public officials to the House of Commons Select Committee on Expenditure.[1, 2] Our main purpose is to show the complexity of the administrative system and the difficulties encountered in educational planning; frequently the agents of the policy-making process are not even themselves fully aware of either the constraints of the real potentials which exist for change within this administrative structure.

First we must indicate who is responsible for what. Figure 2.1 shows the key agencies down to the individual institutions, showing especially those mechanisms which make financial allocations. The Government of the day is shown at the apex, with the Treasury and the Department of Education and Science immediately below. This section of the diagram represents the connection between the central administration of education and the rest of central government. Decisions on the overall allocation of funds to education are made at

[1] Second Report from the Expenditure Committee together with the minutes of evidence taken before the Education and Arts Sub-committee and Appendices. Session 1970-71. HMSO, 1971 (hereafter referred to as A).
[2] Session 1972-73: Further and Higher Education. HMSO, 1972 (hereafter referred to as B).

30   Public Control of Education

this level partly through the public expenditure surveys. Beneath the Department of Education and Science, the left fork refers to the regulation of funds for the universities by the University Grants Committee. The UGC was set up in 1919, and until 1963 dealt directly with the Treasury. Since then, the UGC has retained its role as a 'buffer' between the State and the universities. The regulatory mechanism here is the quinquennial settlement. Down the right fork beneath the Department of Education and Science lie the local education authorities, which have direct responsibility for the schools, colleges and further education institutions. Central government is involved here through the finance provided by the Rate Support Grant. In addition to the funds received from

Fig. 2.1

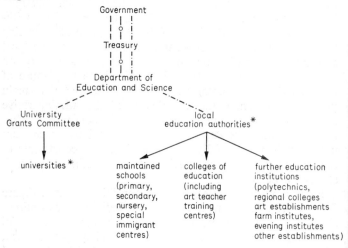

Notes: —o—o—o—o— Public Expenditure Survey
        — — — — — — — quinquennial settlement
        —·—·—·—·— Rate Support Grant

* [These agencies have the right to borrow on the open market, though in the case of universities 'sources other than income from the UGC are minor'.]

† [Pooling arrangements exist whereby local education authorities share the costs of running colleges of education and advanced further education.]

the Treasury, the local authorities themselves raise money on the rates and spend some of this on education. They may also borrow money on the open market. (Universities, too, can borrow money but are more inhibited in doing so.)

To understand the education decision process, we must grasp the mechanisms of the public expenditure surveys, the quinquennial settlements and the rate support grant. We start, therefore, with a straightforward description of this machinery.

The Public Expenditure Survey system has grown up since 1961, when the Plowden Committee on Expenditure reported that 'regular surveys should be made of public expenditure as a whole, over a period of years ahead, and in relation to prospective resources'.[3] The surveys are carried out annually and are now well-established, with the following rough time-table:

December:	Instructions on the conduct of the coming year's Survey are issued by the Treasury.
End-February:	Spending Departments submit preliminary expenditure returns to the Treasury.
March/April:	Discussions take place between the Treasury and the individual spending Departments to reach agreement on the figures and on the underlying policy and statistical assumptions —agreement here meaning no more than an identity of view on what present policies are and on the probable cost of continuing them.
May:	A draft report on public expenditure is drawn up by the Treasury and considered by the Public Expenditure Survey Committee.
June:	The report is submitted to Ministers.
July/October:	Decisions are taken on the aggregate of public expenditure and its broad allocation to the major functional heads.[4]

As a result of this process a Government White Paper is

[3] Report of the Committee on the Control of Public Expenditure under the chairmanship of Lord Plowden. HMSO, 1961, para. 12A.

[4] A. p. 4, para. 15. Memorandum by the Treasury on the Public Expenditure Survey System.

published towards the end of each calendar year presenting 'the Government's consideration of the prospect for public expenditure'[5] for the next five years.

These exercises are major surveys and the Public Expenditure Survey Committee is a large and important internal body of the Civil Service. It involves the main finance officers of all the principal spending ministries and is chaired by a Deputy Secretary of the Treasury. The Committee's task is not to decide or propose action but provide a factual report which will enable Ministers to recast policies 'in accordance with their own views of economic, social and political priorities'.[6] The proceedings of the Public Expenditure Committee are not published, but it is clear that the individual ministries make assessments of their needs as the basis of their bids for public funds. How far the bargaining process is begun in committee and completed in the Cabinet is not clear, though Ministers are, of course, responsible for final decisions.

The Public Expenditure Survey system is one means of relating education to all the other activities for which the Government is responsible with money provided from public funds. The quinquennial settlement is a mechanism internal to the educational system and the way in which it dovetails into the Public Expenditure System is not clearly defined though the consequences of decisions upon either will be assimilated into the next round of deliberations about the other.

It is through the quinquennial settlement that the Government's grant to the recurrent expenditure of universities is settled in advance for a five-year period. Capital grants are distributed on the basis of an annual programme similar to the annual 'starts' of the school building programme.

The quinquennial settlement does not adhere to a standard pattern, but a number of stages can be distinguished. Initially each university sends the estimates of its proposed income in the final year of the current quinquennium, and of the increases in spending in the next quinquennium which would be needed for the developments the university would want to make if finances were available. These estimates of future

[5] Public Expenditure: A New Presentation. Green Paper, HMSO, 1969. Cmnd. 4017. p. 4, para. 5.
[6] A. p. 4, para. 18. Memorandum by the Treasury on Public Expenditure Survey System.

spending are not unconditional but are circumscribed in a general way by 'guidance', though there may be specific indications of the desired ratio between arts-based and science-based students or between undergraduates and postgraduates to be reached by the end of the quinquennium, and of the building priorities in the intervening years needed for these proportions. For the present quinquennium (1972-77) the UGC's initial guidance indicated 320,000 university students by 1976-7, 55 per cent science-based and 45 per cent arts-based.[7] However the UGC pointed out that 'the Government are aware of the planning hypothesis on which the Committee are working but are not in any way committed by it',[8] and that, at the same time, the Public Expenditure White Paper was based upon different estimates which suggested 341,000 university students in 1976-7. (The settlement, as finally determined, provided grants on the basis of provision for 306,000 university students of whom 53 per cent should be science-based and 47 per cent arts-based and 83 per cent undergraduate and 17 per cent postgraduate.)

At the next stage discussions take place between individual universities and the UGC until provisional agreement is reached. The information on existing commitments and costs is assessed and a number of UGC sub-committees, dealing with different disciplines (e.g. physical sciences, biology, arts, etc.) look at development in their area in all universities. Their conclusions are then built into the UGC's final proposals for the university sector as a whole for each year of the quinquennium, and submitted to the Government. These proposals are in global terms; they are not concerned with the position of individual universities. When the Government has decided on the overall funds available and the associated student numbers, the UGC then make allocations to particular universities. These allocations are unlikely to be in exact agreement with the agreed submissions of the individual universities reflecting the differences between the Government's decision and the UGC's advice. In notifying the universities

with such guidance as is necessary about the student

[7] A. p. 194, para. 3. Paper No. 1 by the Secretary of the University Grants Committee.
[8] A. p. 194, para. 3.

numbers and mixes finally proposed for that university, and about the developments, academic or otherwise, for which provision has or has not been made ... the Committee will not earmark sums for particular purposes, nor indicate to universities how much has been allowed in their recurrent grant for various different purposes, unless there is an exceptionally strong case for doing so in a particular situation. The Committee have always taken the view, and successive Governments have agreed, that the universities should be allowed as much freedom as possible to fix their own priorities for the use of resources allocated to them, subject to the broad guidance described above and to the financial constraints which the procedure necessarily imposes.[9]

The Rate Support Grant system is the means whereby the liability of the Exchequer in helping to finance local authority services is determined in advance for a two-year period. The Grant covers all services except housing subsidies. The system began with the Local Government Act of 1966, and there have been variations in each application of the process so far. The Act requires the Secretary of State to consult the local authority associations and to take into account:

(a) the current level of prices, costs and remunerations; any future variation in that level which can be foreseen; and the latest information available to him as to the rate of relevant expenditure;

(b) any probable fluctuation in the demand for services giving rise to relevant expenditure, so far as the fluctuation is attributable to circumstances prevailing in England and Wales as a whole which are not under the control of the local authorities; and

(c) the need for developing these services, and the extent to which, having regard to general economic conditions, it is reasonable to develop them.[10]

The local authority associations negotiate with the central government Departments to decide the total relevant expenditure. In earlier periods, negotiations were based upon sum-

[9] A. p. 195, para. 8. Paper No. 1 by the Secretary of the University Grants Committee.
[10] A. p. 136, para. 11. Memorandum of Evidence by the County Council Association.

maries of forecasts produced by *individual* authorities, but for the 1971-2 and 1972-3 period, five small service groups were set up, one of which consisted of local authority and Department of Education and Science representatives. The basic approach of these groups was:

> to assume present policies would continue unchanged, but any new policies already announced were to be reflected in the expenditure forecasts. In addition, improvements in the standards of certain services were also costed so as to provide an agreed basis for policy decisions to be taken at the negotiations.[11]

These forecasts provide an agreed basis for discussion at the main negotiations. The extent of aggregate Exchequer aid is finally calculated as a percentage of the relevant expenditure, and in recent years has been approaching 60 per cent. From this result various grants for specific purposes (mainly police services) are subtracted; the residue is the total of the Rate Support Grant. This is then divided into three elements to determine the distribution:

(i) the needs element (the largest, about 80 per cent of the total). It is distributed on the basis of objective factors such as population, numbers of pupils and students and mileage of roads;
(ii) the resources element, to help authorities with below average rateable resources; and
(iii) the domestic element; this is not distributed to the (spending) local authorities but to the rating authorities to reduce the rates payable by householders.

Further arrangements are made for annual increase orders, to allow for changes in pay and prices.

It is important to note that:

> Although forecasts for individual services play an important part in determining the total amount of grant to be distributed, the Rate Support Grant which each authority receives (needs element and resources element) is not earmarked to particular services but is a grant in aid of expenditure as a whole.[12]

[11] A. p. 137, para. 14. As above.
[12] A. p. 137, para. 14. As above.

Consequently, as 'local authorities are responsible bodies, competent to discharge their own functions, and they exercise these responsibilities in their own right',[13] authorities are at liberty to decide expenditure on any particular service, even though more than half the finance comes from central funds. Technically, about 80 per cent[14] of total public expenditure on education is directly financed by the local education authorities, though their actual freedom is very limited since much of this spending is mandatory.[15] Their obligations take many forms such as providing compulsory schooling, awards to students on advanced courses, paying teachers on nationally determined scales, and running the colleges of education on a scale intended to fulfil the judgement of the Secretary of State for Education on the supply of teachers. It has been estimated that 'something like 80 per cent of the expenditure on education is completely outside the discretion of local government'.[16]

The various parties involved in these three main regulatory mechanisms have expressed many qualifications and criticisms about its effectiveness. Asked whether or not the Secretary of State is the head of a single managerial system with authority running through it, Lord Boyle (Conservative Minister of State for Education 1962-64) replied that 'there can't be a straight, single control here for the very simple reason that the Ministry directly controls so very little money'. Anthony Crosland (Labour Secretary of State for Education from 1965 to 1967) replied to the same question: 'No, you couldn't conceivably describe it in these terms—there is in no sense a single organization with a managerial chain of command. On the other hand, I was very struck by how much influence, control, power, or whatever the right word is, the Department has.'[17] Most of the controls available to the central administrator are negative in the sense that he gives guidance and has powers of approval, but may initiate proposals less easily.

[13] A. p. 107, para. 3. Memorandum by the Association of Municipal Corporations.

[14] A. p. 6, para. 29 et seq. Memorandum by the Treasury on the Public Expenditure Survey System. See also Appendix A. pp. 30-32.

[15] A. p. 155, question 649, evidence of Mr J. C. Alexander.

[16] Edward Boyle, p. 124 of *The Politics of Education*, Boyle and Crosland in conversation with Maurice Kogan. Penguin, 1971.

[17] Anthony Crosland, p. 169 of *The Politics of Education*, Boyle and Crosland in conversation with Maurice Kogan. Penguin, 1971.

The UGC and the Committee of Vice-Chancellors and Principals have both praised the financial security given them by the fixed quinquennial system, and though the universities' capital programme has been cut back in times of financial stringency, there has never been an occasion when the recurrent grant, once announced, has been reduced. There have been some complaints that the supplements allowed for increased academic salaries and other costs measured by the Tress-Brown index have been delayed and subject to negotiation between the UGC and the Government. This objection was partly removed when, in 1972, the Government guaranteed that henceforth 50 per cent of the compensation would be obligatory and the remainder negotiable. Vice-Chancellors have also been perturbed by the delay in reaching the latest quinquennial settlement, which left them operating in the dark and inhibited implementation of the initial stages of plans. The Association of University Teachers even described the universities as 'working from hand to mouth for at least two years, the last year of the quinquennium and the first year of the next'[18] and in subsequent evidence to the House of Commons Sub-Committee, they extended the uncertainty to three years. The quinquennial grant system has also been criticized because it encourages universities to spend the whole of their predetermined allocation, rather than to attempt to reduce their total financial commitments, and because there is no reward for efficiency or penalty for inefficiency apparent in subsequent UGC allocations. It is possible that universities which choose not to observe the letter of guidance given to them, or otherwise express their autonomy in unsanctioned ways, will be penalized, but since any 'correction' can only come at five-yearly intervals, the system cannot be described as highly responsive.

The Education and Arts Sub-committee of the House of Commons Expenditure Committee commented critically on the quinquennial settlement arrangements:

> We recognize that many people in the university sector are strongly attached to the present arrangements for a fixed quinquennium, though even here there is by no means unanimity. However, most of the arguments in its favour seem to us weak and even specious. One is that present

[18] B. Volume III, p. 587, question 1592, evidence of Professor H. J. Perkin. See also question 1600.

arrangements lessen uncertainty in university planning. It is hard to see how such an argument can be seriously upheld at a time when universities have been handicapped in their planning for a period of a year or more while awaiting the outcome of the next quinquennial settlement which, when it is announced, will have not much more than four years to run. Another argument was that it encourages universities to undertake a major planning exercise every five years. We feel that planning and self study should be undertaken continuously and not need the stimulus of periodic bargaining for public funds. Finally it was suggested that abandonment of the fixed quinquennium would undermine the sanctity of the quinquennial settlement during periods of economic stringency when the Government is seeking financial savings. An Expenditure Committee of the House of Commons can hardly be expected to endorse such a view. Furthermore we do not find the argument valid. If the universities should need to be subjected to a stringent settlement this year because of economic conditions, they will surely want to re-open the issue before five years have elapsed.[19]

The greatest concern with present planning arrangements arises from the financial relationships between central and local government. Representatives of the local authorities have complained that the government often had too little awareness of the needs and priorities of local authorities who they felt had a contribution to make 'at the formative stage of policy-making'.[20] Despite experiments to give them more general loan sanction, the local authority associations maintain that they have very little room for the true exercise of their legal discretion. They also complain that 'there have been occasions when the same Departments have spoken with two voices, one encouraging the development of services while the other urges restraint',[21] and that they have been faced with the full burden of the cost of providing additional services, and with such problems as the inability to cut back expenditure on the scale expected when the Government have imposed economy measures as a result of devaluation. Moreover:

[19] B. pp. xvi and xvii, para. 52.
[20] A. p. 134, para. 3. Memorandum of Evidence by the County Councils Association.
[21] A. p. 139, para. 24. Memorandum of Evidence by the County Councils Association.

The LEAs are very conscious of the lack of any central planning body which could ensure the proper allocation of resources within their sector of higher education. 'There is no single permanently-established machinery which at national level represents the local authority sector of higher education in such a way that all those concerned with higher education can effectively consider its needs, requirements and relative priorities within the total available resources. The determination of such questions, in so far as they are determined is left to the DES, individual LEAs, direct contact between the DES and individual colleges and ad hoc negotiations with the local authority associations.'[22]

Asked about the local authorities' reactions to the Public Expenditure White Paper, the House of Commons Sub-committee noted that their representatives:

find it a frustrating document. White Papers ... in their present form, are of limited use to individual authorities in planning the development of their services because the content is too generalized and does not take into account the differing needs and rates of development of local authorities. The Public Expenditure Survey is produced in Whitehall without any direct reference to the local authority associations; the associations and through them the individual authorities, are unaware of the basic assumptions which have been made in arriving at the figures.

The associations were also anxious about the effect of the PESC predictions on the biennial Rate Support Grant settlements. They complained that the PESC figures and the Rate Support Grant figures were on a different price basis and could not therefore be related to one another in their present form. The association wished ideally to see Rate Support Grant and PESC as parts of a single inter-related exercise rather than as two separate and, as they suspected, conflicting operations. Their underlying fear was that the White Paper forecasts might in some way prejudice the estimates which they had taken pains to agree with departments for the purposes of Rate Support Grant.[23]

As a result of long consideration of the financing and administration of further and higher education, the Education and

[22] A. p. xiii, para. 31, and also p. 115, para. 8.
[23] A. p. vi, para. 6-7.

Arts Sub-committee of the House of Commons Expenditure Committee were dissatisfied with the varying arrangements in the different sectors, particularly the variable time spans and the lack of cohesion. They made some drastic recommendations:

> We recommend that the basic financial and planning mechanism for higher education institutions should be a rolling five-year plan co-ordinated with and on the lines of the Public Expenditure Surveys ... We recommend therefore that the rolling quinquennial arrangements embrace both recurrent expenditure and capital projects ...
> We consider that an overall plan is necessary for the efficient distribution of the resources available for higher education, and that this will prove possible under a unified system of financial provision. We therefore follow the Select Committee on Education and Science in recommending the creation of a Higher Education Commission to have overall responsibility for advising the Minister on the administration and financing of the whole higher education sector, and for its planning and co-ordination.[24]

Whether or not the Government adopts these recommendations it is clear that there are grounds for dissatisfaction with the present structure of planning. It should, of course, be stressed that the whole process is changing. Some application of output budgeting and the system of Programme Analysis and Review has been made in the Department of Education and Science. But little information has yet been given, and a proper appraisal of this method is therefore not possible. These techniques have similarities in that they place the emphasis on considering objectives in particular areas of policy, on measuring resource—inputs and outputs, on identifying relationships between expenditure incurred and returns obtained, and on investigating alternative ways of achieving objectives. At this stage 'programme review' is cautiously described as a complement and reinforcement of the Public Expenditure Survey System and

> Nothing in the Programme Review scheme supersedes the Public Expenditure Survey arrangements, or the application of the Plowden principle that individual expenditure

[24] B. p. xvii, para. 54 and p. xxi, paras, 67-68.

decisions are taken against the background of expenditure as a whole.[25]

Finally, we should make some general observations about the mechanisms we have described. The system is characterized by several hierarchies which are 'imperfect', in the sense that the ranking of the parties involved is not rigid and dominance of each by another is not total. Each round of the decision-making process begins at the bottom, proposals being filtered by agencies on their way upwards and finally presented for Government decision. When decisions have been made in overall terms at the top, they are again filtered by the agencies on the way down, and interpreted and applied in detail.

The two processes we have described have much in common. In the first case, individual universities are asked to formulate plans of what they would do if the money were forthcoming (though the free play of their imagination may be heavily curtailed by the guidance given by the UGC).

The initial stages of the Rate Support Grant process are more obscure (and less well established) but at present they appear to involve a general review of the current patterns of local authority expenditure, taking into account how the pattern is changing, and the desire to improve services subject to general economic conditions. In one system, the guidance given by the UGC may be at variance with presumptions about the same issues in other government exercises (e.g. the Public Expenditure Survey); in the other system, the local authorities and their representatives are not fully aware of the Government's assumptions, and have difficulty in relating their planning to that of the central government. In both systems, as proposals pass upwards they are sifted and reviewed as part of the bargaining process by the co-ordinating agencies before being presented to Government—in global terms in the case of the quinquennial settlement and in such general terms in the case of the Rate Support Grant that the allowance for educational needs is never specifically identified. When government decisions have been made they are normally in the form of the total budget allowed, and though they may be accompanied by some guiding observations in

---

[25] A. p. 5, para. 26. Memorandum by the Treasury on the Public Expenditure Survey System.

principle, they do little more than define the over-riding budgetary limit within which resources must now be reallocated. In the downwards reinterpretation of how the funds should be used, the autonomy of the local authorities and the universities is zealously respected. The allocations of the Rate Support Grant are not earmarked and the local authorities are free to determine their own expenditure, once they have fulfilled the mandatory requirements placed upon them and met the need for approval to go ahead with capital projects and advanced courses of further education. The UGC 'hold strongly that ... each individual university should be left to manage its affairs with the minimum of detailed directions' and they 'believe that the combination of block grants and Memoranda of Guidance is the best means so far of meeting these objectives. They have, therefore, kept to a minimum earmarked grants which can only be spent on specific purposes.'[26] The desire to avoid the danger of over-influencing the universities is carried to such lengths that the allowances that have been made within a block grant may be concealed. Despite the wish to maintain as much university freedom as possible the extent of the guidance at each quinquennial settlement seems to be increasing.

One important aspect of this process is the way in which proposals are formulated on the way up and guidance is given on the way down. Although it would appear that the fullest discussion is possible between all the participants, the scope of actual proposals may be greatly inhibited. The universities frame their proposals in the light of UGC guidance, which does not commit the Government (though it may be aware of it). There is a natural tendency for this advice to be conservative; and this is justified with the argument that it is comparatively easy to add when the Government is generous, but much more difficult to have to subtract when the Government is ungenerous.

Similarly, from the initial stages the local authorities assume the continuation of present policies, but try to reflect new policies already announced and to cost some possible improvements in services. Just as the DES makes projections which extrapolate existing trends and do not prejudge policy,

[26] Universities Grants Committee, Development Plan for the Quinquennial settlement to 1976-77, sent to universities. See *Times Higher Education Supplement*, 19 January 1973, pp. 1-3.

so the Public Expenditure Survey Committee tries to provide a factual report which does not make decisions or recommendations. Consummating the upwards process, it is the supreme authority of Ministers to make decisions on major policy directions which is being respected and safeguarded. Consequently submissions are dominated by the view of no change in policy, with cautious proposals for new developments left to compete for any funds left over after all existing commitments have been fully met. Such a system lacks motivation for major change and it is difficult to see how the real decision options open to Ministers can be more than rudimentary if the factual reports which they are given do not prejudge policies and do not provide a wider exploration of possible alternatives. It is a system in which new developments will be the first to be abandoned or postponed when resources are tight and, not being given any effective guidance on how best to cut existing commitments when they exceed the total available budget, Ministers will tend to order a percentage decrease 'right across the board'.

Although the present system can be strongly criticized, it possesses durable features which we would expect to find repeated at different levels. The problems of allocating resources between the faculties within an individual university or between the institutions within an authority or between the departments within an institution are of much the same kind. In all cases we would expect to find some form of hierarchy in which periodic planning discussions took place. We would expect these negotiations to be most detailed at the lowest level and to be in broad, possibly vague, terms at the top. We would expect both the submission of proposals upwards and the reallocation of resources downwards to constrain the autonomy at each level. There is a natural tendency for any such system of recurrently reviewing and allocating central financial resources to partly autonomous spending authorities, to acquire such features, and they are not peculiar to education.

Oversimplified descriptions of central planning paint the picture of the Secretary of State periodically collecting together free submissions of the needs and aims of all those involved in different parts of the system before making a judgement on the disposition of resources which is supposed to be the best overall compromise. All involved parties are then regarded as bound to execute to the letter the Secretary's decisions and the system is presumed to pursue this direction until the whole procedure is repeated afresh.

In practice the planning process is not so clear cut and coherent. Developments are taking place all the time and decisions must be taken sequentially. What actually happens is not the direct result of the Secretary's supreme authority but is shaped by the various people and bodies whose actions are affected by central decisions but otherwise express their own objectives as modified by their appreciation of central intentions. There is plenty of scope for actions leading to consequences far removed from those hoped for by the Secretary of State and by the participants, who may not be entirely clear about their own aims, and are likely to be even less well-informed on the objectives and outlook of everybody else.

Consequently planning has evolved as the precarious and sometimes vague interplay of different agencies and forces putting out tentative feelers and making limited responses to each other against a bargaining background of highly imperfect mutual knowledge. The outstanding question is— how can this system be improved so that it is more reliable and robust and so that planning becomes more efficient and successful?

3

J. A. G. GRIFFITH

The School Building Programme - The Roles of Central and Local Government[*]

The Department[†] negotiate future programmes with the Treasury over a period of years.

The function of the Treasury is to ensure that the claims which the Department put forward for future school building programmes are well substantiated and, thereafter, to provide the material (and to make recommendations on that material) on which the Government's decisions of investment in school building, in education generally, and in all the other services, can be based. This function was put in these words by an Under-Secretary serving the relevant Supply Division of the Treasury when he was giving evidence to the Select Committee on Estimates in 1961: 'It means taking a view about the amount of investment the country can stand at a time and within that figure, for public investment. Within that, the figure provided for educational building is well up, year in and year out. It is a fairly steady figure. There is no particular animus between the Ministry and the Treasury about educational building. They know very well that they have had a fair share of the cake for quite a long time but I am not saying that they have had all the cake they reasonably desire.'[1] The speed and the extent of the school building programme are matters of government policy which is reflected in the investment figures.

Although the Treasury require to be shown how the Depart-

---

* [From J. A. G. Griffith, *Central Governments and Local Authorities*, Allen & Unwin, 1966.]

† [The Department of Education and Science: this article is about precedents in England and Wales, but the Scottish system is similar in many respects—Ed.]

[1] H.C. 284 of 1960-61, Q. 408.

ment have arrived at their estimates of expenditure—and in school building this means particularly the facts and figures relating to population growth and population movements— no control is exercised over the Department on where the money is sent. Not only is there no Treasury control over individual projects, but there is no Treasury control over the allocation to regions and thence to local education authorities. The Department might well resent being told by the Treasury or by any other body that it ought to cause schools to be built in some areas rather than in others. Nevertheless, it is not possible to regard school building as an isolated operation. If the Government wish to foster regional development and growth then the schools programme is important. As the Government report on the North East said: 'The quality and range of schools available will clearly make a big difference both to the efficiency of the region and to its attractiveness for the kind of people needed for economic vitality.'[2] The report went on to outline the educational defects in the North East and added: 'But a number of major secondary-school replacements have been included in annual school building programmes, and a considerable measure of priority was given to the North East when projects were being selected in this category for 1964-65.' This seems to say that the North East was given 'a considerable measure of priority', because it was the North East. But no special amount was allocated by the Department to that region for the major school building programme because of the Government's concern for the improvement of the North East.

The section of the report concluded cautiously: 'The complete replacement of all old schools will be of necessity a long-term matter, as not all can be rebuilt or remodelled at once and the needs for schools in equally inferior buildings in other parts of the country must not be overlooked. But the normal capital allocation will in any event serve to provide a considerable number of new schools in pace with new housing development, and these will in themselves make an important contribution to the better development of the region.'[3]

The provision of technical colleges and other further education facilities is even more obviously an important part of the development of a region. The report said that it was hoped

[2] Cmnd, 2206, 1963, para. 100-101.
[3] Ibid., para. 101.

gradually to increase the investment in this kind of work and that in any event new buildings would be provided from year to year to keep pace with population growth and increased economic activity.[4] These are not fighting words [.....]

The Architects and Building Branch of the Department is the branch primarily concerned with investment problems. The Department's proposals are submitted to the Treasury under the heads of the various programmes: major school building, minor works, special schools, further education, teachers' training, youth service, colleges of advanced technology.* The negotiations centre on each of these programmes. The major works programme is considered under two heads: basic needs; and improvement. Basic needs are the provision of school places, by the building of schools or additional classrooms, for new population. Improvement in this context means building for all other purposes, and includes replacement. The Department is required to justify its claims for meeting basic needs and the figures for this purpose are based on the estimated increase in school population and on movements of population. They are not based on the proposals of local education authorities which are not necessarily known at this stage. The Treasury is concerned to ensure that the methods of assessment used by the Department in its estimations are sound and that the figures are therefore justifiable. But it is accepted on both sides that the basic needs must be met. There is no similar assumption for improvements. The amount of money to be made available for this purpose is more arguable.[5] Improvement work will provide more primary than secondary school places for the same amount of money. But the decision of how the money for improvement is to be spent is regarded as an educational matter and so the final responsibility rests with the Department. The major works allocation which is eventually received by the Department does not distinguish between basic needs

[4] Ibid., para. 103.

[5] The serious inadequacies in secondary modern schools were emphasized in the report of the Central Advisory Council for Education (England) *Half our Future*, 1963, (the Newsom report), and in *The School Building Survey* 1962, published in 1965.

* [The colleges of advanced technology have now become universities, and there is hence no separate programme for them. Major school building at the time when Griffith was writing consisted of projects costing more than £20,000; minor works were those costing less than this. The division now comes at £55,000—Ed.]

and improvement and if the Department find they have under-estimated or over-estimated basic needs, the amount for improvement varies accordingly. If the estimate on basic needs proved to be consistently or considerably inaccurate, this would throw doubt on the Department's method of assessment.

Preparation of Major Capital Works Programme by Local Education Authorities

A primary function of each local education authority is to consider the needs of its area and to put forward proposals to the Department for the building of new schools to meet these needs.

Today the pressure which ultimately results in the inclusion of the proposal for a new school in the list of projects forwarded to the Department develops from one or more of a number of reasons. Most importantly, it is the function of local education officers concerned with future development, and of divisional education officers, to make plans to meet anticipated growth of population in particular areas. A new housing estate, whether provided by a local authority or by private developers, is the most obvious indication that the future position of existing schools serving that neighbour-hood must be looked at. Sometimes, for less clear reasons, a school, which has for some time managed to meet the local demand for places, becomes overcrowded. More general changes, such as the great (and perhaps quite sudden) popu-larity of a suburban or exurban district, may flood the schools.

If this description suggests a certain lack of planned de-velopment and rather a series of emergency moves by the local education authority to meet unforeseen overcrowding, it is not inaccurate. This is not the fault of the education officers. Far too little is known in advance. The difficulty of forecasting the need for school building is considerable. It flows, as we have seen, from the growth of population and the movement of population. New housing developments must, of course, be approved by local planning authorities or the Ministry of Housing and Local Government. But while this gives some indication, it relates to permission only and not to execution and the time which elapses between the granting of planning permission and the occupation of houses varies greatly. If the building is by a private developer, his starting date and the rate of his progress will depend on his own financial resources, on the progress of work on other sites, on the readiness of purchasers to buy at his price. Whether the building is by a housing authority or by a private developer, it may be delayed by the weather, by shortage of labour and materials. All these considerations, moreover, affect short-term planning. And a local education authority would prefer to plan for periods of four or five years ahead, so that sites can be obtained well in advance.

Long-term planning is additionally inhibited by the difficulties of forecasting the birthrate and the ways in which the trend towards remaining at school after compulsory school-leaving age are likely to affect particular areas. National and regional statistics are available[6] but they cannot greatly help the making of decisions on whether a particular school in a particular locality should be built in 1966 or in 1967 or whether it should be a three-form or four-form entry school. A few of the larger local education authorities do employ, in their education department, an officer whose job it is to give as accurate a forecast as possible. And it is the nightmare of every education officer that a newly opened school will remain half-empty—or, what is regarded as not quite so alarming, over-full. But unless more accuracy can be obtained, the unpredictability of population demands will continue to limit the period over which school building programmes can be projected.

Planning control under the Town and Country Planning Acts is too imprecise an instrument for this purpose.[7] In particular, although conditions can be attached to a grant of planning permission to seek to ensure that the development begins within a prescribed period, this period will be one of years and can relate only to the starting of projects, not to their completion. The private developer who acquires land and obtains permission to build may in effect be banking his money in an asset almost certain to appreciate in value and there may therefore be no great incentive for him to begin his operations either immediately or ever. He may prefer to re-sell and the prospective buyer will be likely to obtain, on

[6] See, for example, *Statistics of Education* 1964, Pt. 1.
[7] There is dispute about how precise it could be made. But one view is that it could be made much more so if proper predictors were used.

a new application, an extension of any period limited by the first permission.

In the absence of any radical reform of planning legislation, one can urge only the importance of greater co-ordination and collaboration between the local authority's planning department, housing department (which in a county will be that of the county district council), and education department for the area. There is evidence that these departments frequently do not combine and pool information as much as they could.

It naturally falls, as we have said, to education officers to make recommendations for new schools, or for the enlargement of existing schools, to meet the movement and the growth of population. Further, existing school buildings may be below the standards required by the Department, either in the size of their classrooms or in the ancillary accommodation (including playgrounds). In rural areas in particular the major problem was for many years not one of a shortage of places alone but of the reorganization of schools (including additional buildings) so that both primary and secondary education could, in accordance with the Act of 1944, be provided in place of 'all-age' schools normally housed in old 'elementary' school buildings.

Others, besides education officers, are likely to make their views known about future development. Her Majesty's Inspectors, concerned primarily with what is taught and how it is taught, are inevitably interested in the physical environment in which teachers and pupils seek to work. The teachers themselves, both individually and through their organizations, exert their own pressures. And if the pupils do not yet, in this country, complain collectively about their conditions of work, they may not be silent in their homes. And so parents, again either individually or through parent-teacher associations, may complain. So also, in the case of existing schools, governors or managers will make their representations about overcrowding and substandard conditions to the appropriate authorities.

Members of local education authorities stand at the crossings of many of these complaints. Teachers, parents, governors and managers (who are themselves often councillors), may all turn to these members who are expected to substantiate and emphasize the representations.

At this point it is again necessary to be wary of generalization, for practice differs from authority to authority. But by one means or another, either a divisional executive or the appropriate sub-committee of the education committee must decide, in principle, on the merits of the argument for the new school or other major development. This decision in principle does not normally give any indication of the date when the proposal will be put into an annual programme by the authority. But it does enable the next important step to be taken, that of finding a site for the school. A sites sub-committee of the executive or the authority will consider, by inspection, the various possibilities and a conclusion will be reached by the appropriate committee or sub-committee of the executive or the authority. If land has to be purchased this will either be done at once or the land earmarked and the purchase deferred.[8] In certain circumstances the owner can require the land to be purchased forthwith.

Since 1945, local education authorities have normally wished to build more schools in each financial year than the Department, under the procedure to be described, have been able to allow. This limitation on projects makes for competition within the authority for the inclusion of particular proposals in the list to be submitted to the Department. Apart from the attitude of the Department, there are certain built-in limitations within the authority itself such as the number of architectural and other professional staff it employs, its estimate of the availability of building labour and materials in the area, and the capital expense which it is prepared to incur for school building. This last consideration needs a little more explanation.

Individual local education authorities differ in their attitude to school building and to expenditure on education generally. Much depends on the personal attitude of the chief education officers and of the chairmen of the education and finance committees. Education officers are professionals and not only have their own standards but also their own laudable desire to be well thought of amongst their fellow professionals. The job of a chief education officer is to provide as good a service as he can for the area for which he is responsible. He does not wish his tenure of office as chief (for which he has been

---

[8] Local education authorities vary considerably in the extent to which they anticipate their needs for land.

preparing and working during the earlier years of his career) to be remembered as a period when little progress was made, when problems remained unsolved, and when the standard of education failed to improve. He has therefore had a very great incentive, in the post-war period when the demands for better education have been so strong, to embark on extensive schemes.

The chairman of an education committee is also, in a somewhat different sense, a professional. Running an education service is not, indeed, his career. But he is likely, if he retains any enthusiasm for local government, not to wish to see 'his' committee suffer in comparison with other committees. It may be, of course, that his is not a strong personality and it is more common to find a weak chairman than a weak chief officer. But he will be driven, if he is weak, by his chief officer to get what share he can of the capital outlay of the council for his committee. It is only if both chief officer and chairman are weak or if the chairman is strongly against considerable expenditure on public education, that the work of the committee will greatly suffer.

The education committee, having regard to these limitations on its activities and to its view, based on past experience and announced government policy, of what the Department are likely to approve in total for its area, determines its requirements for school building for a one or two or three year period prescribed by the Department. Only a few of the individual projects which have been approved in principle can be included in a particular programme. There will, in effect, be a queue of projects, standing in order of priority outside the door of the committee room. At the head of the queue will be those which were put forward by the authority to the Department on the previous occasion but which failed to get approval. Behind them will be others which narrowly failed to be included in the previous list of those forwarded. With them may be a very few projects which now appear for the first time in the queue and which are there because of some emergency unforeseen before. Further down the queue will be some hardy annuals the case for which has been urged each year, the merits of which are accepted, but which seem always to be overtaken by other projects having an air of immediacy which they lack. This hard core of very slow moving projects will include, for example, those for the replacement of existing buildings which are below standard.

From this contemplation of the queue, it will be obvious that, save exceptionally, a particular proposal has been long thought necessary and desirable before it is finally submitted by the authority to the Department. Much of the local agitation about school conditions—angry letters to the local Press, outbursts by councillors—is in this sense beating on an unlocked door. While the Government adheres to a national sum for capital investment in school building and while, inevitably, it allocates some share of this to individual local authorities, and while the authorities accept these and other limitations, then any one particular project is merely in the competition with other projects. This does not mean that each decision, each place in the queue, is invariably determined by its objective merits. It is possible for a councillor by continuous campaigning and personal persuasiveness at the vital times to promote a project to a place higher in the queue than its bare merits would indicate. So also the Anglican and Roman Catholic authorities will bring their own pressure to bear on councillors and officers. But it is the job of the appropriate chairman of committee or sub-committee and even more of the chief or other education officer concerned to see that not too much of this happens. Each member of the committee will have his own projects. And if it is too much to expect that all members will seek objectively to weigh the claims of these against the claims of others and to vote according to the result even if that is against their own local interest, yet something like justice is generally done, both because of the views of these officers who alone perhaps know the merits of all the proposals, and because much advocacy tends to cancel itself. Everyone has a hard luck story about school accommodation in his area. So no-one is particularly impressed. Finally, there will be many parts of the area of the authority for which no councillor speaks because the member for that ward or division is not a member of the appropriate committee. Here again, it is the function of the education officer and the chairmen of committees to ensure that those parts are not overlooked.

The determination of the final list of projects to be submitted to the Department will normally (and this is common for most major decisions in local government) pass through two or three levels within the council, committee and sub-committee structure of the authority. The first, lowest, sub-committee level is the arena for free argument (within the limits of any prior political party determinations) of the merits of various projects competing for inclusion. We have already noted the important role of objectivity, which is the function of the education officers and, sometimes to a less extent, of the chairman, that is, of putting the comparative need of these projects. Much of the argument may be concerned with those which are said to be emergency cases and thus to justify the jumping of places in the queue. In the result, unless the party controls are very strong and the position of the officers, as a consequence, relatively weak, it is the view of the officers and chairman which is likely to prevail. The second level is the consideration by the education committee of the recommendations put forward by the sub-committee. At this stage, those who feel they have been unfairly treated may seek to have inserted their own projects. This is also the opportunity for councillors who were not members of the sub-committee similarly to make the case for projects, in their own divisions or wards, which have not been included. Neither of these groups is likely to succeed in changing the recommendations.

In most authorities the decision of the education committee will be final as it will be acting as the delegate of the council. It is possible that the finance committee and thence the council may at this stage consider the financial implications of the list to be submitted to the Department. But often it will not concern itself with the programme to be submitted to the Department [. . . .]

The pattern is of local education authorities clamouring for approval of far more projects than the Department can possibly allow within their own capital allocation from the Treasury. The Department seem to be convinced that the programmes submitted by local education authorities are inflated not only far beyond their reasonable expectations but also beyond their capacities. The '1963 Campaign for Education' conducted a national survey in that year by asking all local education authorities, *inter alia*, what was the total value of projects submitted to the Department for 1964-65, what was the total value of approved projects and how far the programme submitted was inflated. According to their figures, the total value of projects submitted was £187,880,000 and the total value of approved projects was £47,138,000. And they reported: 'The information supplied makes it abundantly clear that there is no evidence for any suggestion that local education authorities deliberately inflate their submissions to the Ministry in order to secure a bigger building allocation than they might otherwise obtain.'[9] In support they quoted the views of many chief education officers to the effect that they could embark on much larger programmes than were permitted by the Department.

In this dispute, two questions must be distinguished. The first is whether some local education authorities put forward programmes which are larger than they expect the Department to approve. It is certain that they do. Chief officers and chairmen of education committees know fairly accurately what is likely to be the permitted level of investment for their authorities. And their proposals habitually exceed their expectations. The second question is whether local education authorities could handle all the projects they apply for. This is more arguable. Many local authorities, particularly the larger, could certainly manage more projects than are approved and some could probably double their production. The limitations are those of their own staff, especially of architects, of the availability of sites, and of the capacity of the local building industry. Certainly most authorities would find a sudden large increase in their school building programmes to be beyond their immediate resources. While, therefore, most authorities could do more than they are permitted, very few could do all they ask for.

Local education authorities submit building programmes which they can justify in the sense that the need for each project in the programme can be properly made out. They select the projects from a longer list. They re-submit projects year after year to impress the Department with their view of the importance of those projects. Very few authorities can believe that the greater their demands the greater will be their allocation. Chief education officers and chairmen of committees are under considerable pressure to include particular projects and if they are convinced of the genuineness of the need it is both simpler and fairer to add projects, and let the Department decide, than to omit them. But though it is simpler and fairer

[9] *School Building—A survey of the Present Programme and its Limitations.*

—and makes for more peace—to include projects which will certainly not be approved by the Department for inclusion in the programme, yet it is an abdication of responsibility. Marginal cases, which the Department might approve, will inevitably and naturally be submitted. But the submission of the more remote cases shifts the burden of refusal firmly on to the Department and while this may be politically conveni-ent to the local authority it is an act of weakness. As the Parliamentary Secretary said in the House of Commons on 26 March 1963, the Minister did not object to local authorities submitting lists which they knew to be larger and more expensive than could be authorized because it gave him a broader picture of their needs and might facilitate the right selection.[10] If local education authorities wish to have a greater part in this decision-making, then clearly they would be better advised to submit programmes more realistic in terms of the total allocation they can expect to receive and so limit the Minister's area for manoeuvre.

A few local education authorities abdicate responsibility more completely. The Department require projects to be sub-mitted in order of priority.[11] Some authorities refuse to follow this requirement on the ground that all their proposals are equally urgent. The Department is then forced to decide which projects to approve without this vital and local evaluation. In these cases the local authority can truthfully and conveni-ently rebut local criticism by saying that a rejected project went forward to the Department as high on the list as every other and that the whole blame rests with the Department. But the ostrich is not the most intelligent of animals in its attempts at self-preservation [.....]

The district HMI is the local liaison officer between the Department and the education authority. As we shall see, his view may carry weight with the Department when the pro-posals are considered. It is therefore surprising to find a con-siderable divergence of practice amongst local education authorities on the extent to which the views and support of HMI are sought when the programme is being drafted. Some authorities take him very largely into their confidence and try to be sure that he accepts not only the need for the pro-posals they submit but also the degree of their urgency and

[10] Vol. 674 of House of Commons debates, 5th series, column 1162.
[11] See circular letter from the Department dated 18 October 1963, para. 3.

their relative priority. Others actively resent the part he plays in departmental decision-making and, not altogether logically, disregard him in the drafting of their proposals. By some, the district HMI is regarded as their advocate with the Department; by others, as an intruder.[12] Perhaps the most common relationship is one where HMI is not directly drawn into the preparation of the draft proposals but where his views are known, because of his ordinary contacts with the education officers, and are taken into account.

The reasons for the relatively small part played by the district HMI in the drafting of proposals are, first, the responsibility which the chief education officer naturally feels for the programmes submitted by his authority, and, secondly, the opportunity which the education officer has of direct contact with those who make the decisions in the Department. The programme is the programme of the local authority; it is their function to assess the needs; it is their duty to ensure that their claims are properly put and heard. HMI, however independent he may be both in theory and in practice, is regarded by local authorities as more of a departmental man than a local authority man.[13] Local education authorities do not willingly yield any part of their statutory duties or share any part of their statutory responsibilities with other persons. Moreover, chief education officers and others in the local authority know they have direct access, if they wish it, to the civil servants at the headquarters of the Department. The district HMI acts indeed as a liaison but he is in no sense an intermediary through which local officers must pass. It is not intended that he should be. And he does not act as such. If a chief education officer wishes to express certain views to the Department, he does so directly and would not necessarily feel under any obligation whatever to inform HMI.[14]

From all this it can be seen that the programme is drafted by the officers concerned whose recommendations are normally accepted by the committee. Perhaps surprisingly, neither individual members nor party caucuses play a significant part in the preparation and submission of school building projects.

[12] All this relates to the functions of the district HMI in programming, not to the functions of HMIs generally as advisers on educational matters.

[13] The Department, on the other hand, sometimes regard HMI as biased in favour of the local authority.

[14] It is common for copies of all formal correspondence between the local education authority and the Department to be sent to HMI by the authority.

The interest of members of education committees is considerable but for the reasons we have given the judgement of chief
officers is normally accepted. At the same time the programme
may be consequential on other decisions which have been
made very largely by the elected representatives themselves.
Most obviously, a majority party group may decide to change
the organization of secondary schools—perhaps introducing
more comprehensive schools or sixth-form colleges. This is
the sort of decision which may be made independently of
the chief education officer and possibly against his advice.
Then his proposals for the school building programme must
reflect this change of policy. Similarly, on a smaller scale, a
choice may have to be made between building a co-educa-
tional school or two single-sex schools and this is a subject
capable of arousing considerable controversy. When, however, as is usual, what is being determined is the relative need
of various projects, the chief officer is the person who is best
able to judge. The willingness of councillors to accept his
view is not therefore to be necessarily regarded as weakness
but rather as a recognition of his expertise and knowledge.

Again, a warning must be given. This description, with its
emphasis on the central role played by the chief education
officer, is not of universal application. In some local authorities, the chief education officer is instructed by the committee (which often means the party caucus behind the
committee) in considerable detail. And the result may be the
promotion of projects not easily justifiable, in terms of the
need for school places, when compared with other projects
either not proposed or given a low priority. And, as with the
road programme, it is not unknown for a chief education
officer to inform the Ministry of proposals which, in his
view, are not to be encouraged. H. C. Dent puts it in these
words: 'There have even been occasions when the Ministry
has been advised by a Chief Education Officer over the telephone not to approve something which his authority has
formally proposed; and *vice versa* when an officer of the
Ministry has suggested to a local authority ways of circum-
venting some Ministerial pronouncement which appeared to
bar a favoured project.'[15]

[15] *The Educational System of England and Wales*, 2nd ed., 1963, p. 83.

Departmental Treatment of LEA Proposals

The share of investment in the public sector authorized for the Department for the school building programme is first divided and allocated to five regions for England and to Wales.

This allocation is made by an Assistant Secretary in the Department to each territorial Principal in charge of a region. Initially, this allocation is made on the basis of the school population of the region which for the programmes 1965-68 is that estimated for 1970. Any special considerations affecting a region or a large part of a region[16]—such as unemployment, bad housing conditions, secondary schools known to be substandard—will come into the account at this point so as to vary the allocation between regions. Thus for 1966-67, out of a programme of £80m, a reserve of £4·5m was retained mainly to cover future urgent requirements in areas of substantial housing developments and population growth in the South and South East. This initial allocation may absorb up to as much as seven-eighths of the total authorized investment programme. The remainder (less a reserve sum which the Assistant Secretary withholds) is allocated after a comparison of marginal cases. For this purpose the Assistant Secretary collects information from territorial Principals about the projects which, in each region, would be marginally included and marginally excluded by the initial allocation. It may also happen that promises have been given, but not honoured, to include particular projects in the previous programme—a minor change in economic policy can produce a situation in which the Department has been led by the Treasury to expect, or has been unduly optimistic in hoping for, a larger programme than was eventually authorized. The honouring of these promises will affect the allocation of the remaining part of the programme.

The responsibility for the allocation to regions is therefore that of the Assistant Secretary who will use whatever technique seems appropriate. It will reflect the first priority urged by the Department on local education authorities[17] of satis-

[16] Thus, the London County Council received a large allocation even though its basic needs (because of depopulation) were small. Here the special consideration was the political strength of the local authority. [The L.C.C. area is now covered by the Inner London Education Authority.—Ed.]

[17] Circular 12/63.

fying basic needs for new accommodation arising from increases in the school population and new housing. The
decisions are made, after the initial allocation, in consultation with the territorial Principals and after the examination
of marginal cases which indicate the extent to which the
initial allocation has satisfied the basic needs.[18] And in the
further allocation, the satisfaction of basic needs again has
priority. This method is therefore a combination of assessing
basic needs on estimated population figures and of examining
the actual proposals put forward by local education authorities and vetted by the territorial Principals.

The next step in the process is for each territorial Principal
to select individual projects from amongst all those put to
him by local education authorities to the total of his allocation. He therefore examines in detail the projects in the programmes of those authorities. He has first to satisfy himself
that the case for meeting basic needs by the construction of
new schools or the enlargement of existing schools is clearly
made out. For this he does not rely solely on the written justification he receives but also, in addition to any personal knowledge he may have from his visits to the region and from his
meetings with chief education officers from time to time, on
two other sources. The first of these is the district HMI, whose
job it is to be familiar with the conditions in his area and
with the projects put forward by the local education authority.

As has already been said, HMI may or may not have been
consulted by the local education authority on the details of
the programmes the authority intend to submit to the Department. But even if he has not been consulted, he will be well
aware of the local educational needs and so in a position to
give his views on the merits of the arguments put forward by
the authority. His knowledge will be supplemented by that
of other HMIs in the district. His function is therefore three-
fold: to advise the local education authority; to advise the
territorial Principal; and to act as a liaison between the local
authority and the Principal. This advice to the Principal will
be an evaluation of the case put by the local authority on
facts which are usually not then in dispute. And no one else

---

[18] It has been recent practice for the Assistant Secretary to decide personally the allocation to territorial Principals. Particular instructions of a
'political' nature may, of course, descend from above from time to time.
And, of course, as is emphasized, the stated departmental policy on priorities is the context within which the Assistant Secretary decides.

attached to the Department is in this position. Normally the district HMI is responsible for one local education authority only.

The meeting between the territorial Principal and the district HMI to examine the proposals of a local education authority can be of the greatest importance in the process of deciding what projects are to be approved. The extent to which the Principal relies on the judgement of HMI will obviously vary considerably according to the personalities, the view which the Principal takes of HMI's ability, and the view which each of them takes of the local education authority and its officers. The position of the district HMI is not altogether easy. HMIs are proud of their independence, and do not regard themselves as 'ordinary' civil servants in the Department. Their status helps them to remain distinct both from the Department and from the local education authorities. Yet they naturally tend to become involved in the educational affairs of their district and to become prejudiced in favour of the local authorities who themselves often regard HMIs as someone who *ought* to be their advocate with the Department even when he is more of 'them' than of 'us'. But once HMIs become partisan they begin to lose their independence and so some of their influence in the Department. To attempt any generalization would be of little value. But the opinion of HMI is one of the factors—and may be one of the most influential factors—which the Principal takes into account.[19]

The other major source of information available to the Principal is the local education authority itself. The written justifications are not necessarily their last contact with the Department before decisions are taken. The Principal may seek elucidation, by telephone or by letter, from the local authority on any doubtful questions of fact or argument in their justifications. Most importantly, the chief education officer or his deputy will often meet the Principal, either in the Department or in the locality, to discuss the proposals submitted. This meeting is frequently attended also by the district HMI. One of the peculiarities of this whole process is the fact, not that this

[19] Some chief education officers resent the fact that HMI has the private ear of the Principal—especially when they suspect that HMI may be opposing their arguments. Where the three persons concerned are wholly frank with each other, the resentment will not exist.

meeting takes place, but that it takes place for some local authorities but not for others. Any chief education officer could request such a meeting and obtain it. Yet by no means all do so. It may be, of course, that because of contact at other times, the chief education officer is satisfied that the proposals of his authority are well known and understood by the Department so that a meeting is unnecessary. There are other reasons why this meeting is not held. A chief education officer may feel that he has nothing more to say and does not wish merely to repeat what the written submissions contain. Or he may not have enough freedom of manoeuvre to make discussions fruitful. At one extreme, an education committee may simply approve a programme, leave to its officers the arrangement of the priority of projects within the programme and give them the power therefore to change the priorities in discussion with the Department if this will result in the approval of a larger programme. At the other extreme the education committee may refuse to allow its chief officers to bargain with the Department and, in this case, a meeting is of little value. Finally, some local education authorities are reluctant to 'wrangle' or 'horsetrade' with the Department. They have decided what they need on the best evidence they can get; and they have put forward a genuine and realistic programme. If the Department wishes to reduce it or change its priorities, that is the Department's concern.

If the meeting is held, it is the crucial stage in the making of the decision. The local officers will put the case for their programme and for individual projects within it, with more or less vigour and persuasive power. The Principal will raise the doubts he has about some of the projects and in particular will seek the views of the local officers on those projects which are on the margin of inclusion and exclusion. HMI will express his own views and may therefore sometimes agree with the local authority and sometimes with the Principal. The ultimate decision will be that of the Principal.

This decision will be dictated first by the overriding necessity of meeting basic needs—of ensuring that there are places in schools to meet the increase in school population. So the territorial Principal must be certain that the population increases in the figures submitted by the local education authorities justify new or enlarged buildings. This entails the examination of the movements of age groups through the years, which reveals immigration. For each project, he must consider the numbers on the rolls of the existing schools, the sizes of the actual classrooms, and the possible alternatives of extension or alteration of existing schools, and all the other information submitted in the justification statement. What is required to meet basic needs must be kept to a minimum if any money is to be left for other demands and so it may be necessary to omit classrooms from a project and to reduce the size of entry or to build a school in two phases.

Like all decisions of this kind where the evaluation of cases must be made, where written statements vary in quality, where face-to-face discussions take place, and where the demand far exceeds the supply, subjective judgement cannot be excluded. Many of the projects applied for must clearly be approved; their case is so strong that they write themselves into the programme. So also another group of projects is clearly unacceptable. There remains the difficult middle group where discretion must be exercised and where finally the distinction between what is included and what is excluded can only be arbitrary or a matter of chance. The need for a new school cannot easily be assessed with mathematical precision. The principal difficulty is that the criteria—for example the anticipated rate of housebuilding—are so often very variable in the short term. Again, some geographical spread of approved projects is politically inevitable. If comparative need were the only basic factor, some part of the rural countryside and some of the smaller county boroughs would never see a new school.

What is left after the basic needs have been met is available for distribution for purposes of improvements—which themselves may help the meeting of basic needs. As the territorial Principal seeks to evaluate the proposals for new schools submitted by the local education authorities in his area, so he seeks to evaluate the relative worth of the proposals for improvement. But here also he may spread the allocation to ensure that each local authority receives approval for at least one improvement project.

The territorial Principal does exercise a real control and does not merely draw a line below one project and above another on each local authority list. It is of course arguable that he should do so—that he should accept the order of priority put to him by the local education authority and decide only how many projects should be approved. But in practice he considers each project in detail and may engage in lengthy consultation with the local education authority on its merits or demerits.

The results of the handling by the Department of local priorities are inconsistent—there is no reason why they should be other since they are an evaluation by the Department of an evaluation by the local education authority, or, more precisely, an evaluation by the territorial Principal (with advice from the district HMI) of the wisdom, objectivity and conformity to departmental policy of the chief education officer and the local education committee. Some chief officers are well-known personally in the Department, others far less so. The reputation of chief education officers and their committees varies in the eyes of the Department, their past record producing an image favourable or unfavourable. (So also territorial Principals are variously regarded by chief education officers and committees.[20]) Some local authorities find their priorities often changed, others hardly ever. Some of those whose priorities are changed feel themselves ill-treated while others of these accept the alterations with equanimity.

The sort of considerations which, in the Department's eyes, justify their overriding of the priorities of local education authorities include: wilful disregard of departmental policy; the submission of priorities determined by divisional executives and not assessed and ordered at the county level; undue emphasis on the need to spread projects over the whole area of the local authority (usually, a county); local pressures deriving either from political groups or individual councillors or aldermen not based on proper educational needs; and bias against Church schools. Because of the financial straitjacket, it may happen that a less expensive project is promoted out of order when to prefer the higher priority would result in an unduly large programme for a particular authority.

To say that territorial Principals pay as much regard as possible to local priorities is to say very little. The priorities form a base which in some cases will be found to accord, year in and year out, with the views of the Principal. But the personalities, both in the locality and in the Department, change—the Principal, HMI, the chief education officer and

[20] Some chief education officers complain of the quick turnover of territorial Principals and of their consequent failure to know them.

his assistants, the chairman of the education committee, the members of local committees—and so the kaleidoscope of relationships is shifted. So also policy changes in the Department, as does the political complexion of local authorities. While the Principal's powers and duties continue to be so vital a part of this decision-making process—and only a radical change in practice can alter this—the priorities fixed by local education authorities can be considered as proposals only and so always liable to be overriden.

Territorial Principals do, to a large extent, personally make the decisions on allocations to local authorities. As with the Assistant Secretary, they may be under 'political' instructions from above in particular cases, and they are consciously seeking to achieve departmental policy. In one sense the contact between Principals, Assistant Secretary and those above is close and continuous. But each is left to make the decisions appropriate to his or her level.

When a local education authority is informed by the Department of the projects included in a building programme, an appeal against that decision is often contemplated and sometimes instituted. In its simplest form this appeal is a letter of protest to the Department and a special plea for the reconsideration of one or more specific projects which have not found a place. Alternatively the Department may be asked to receive a deputation. The help of Members of Parliament may be called on. And occasionally a full-scale onslaught may be made whereby all possible pressures including, where appropriate, the Anglican and Roman Catholic Churches, are brought to bear.

The level at which these appeals are dealt with in the Department depends on two main factors: the size of the local authority and the extent to which the issue has become 'political'. This slippery word does not here mean, necessarily, party political. It reflects the volume as well as the source of the pressure. Responsible government is also responsive government and if we regard the possibility of embarrassing politicians as a desirable safeguard we must not be surprised if they seek to avoid embarrassment. There can be no doubt that a properly mounted campaign can sometimes produce a change of decision. Whether that change results in a more equitable decision will be a matter of opinion in each case. Ministers and civil servants are largely hardened to resisting pressures which seek to change decisions made after full investigation of the facts, especially where rival pressures are exerted or where to yield to pressure from one interest will mean that another interest which is not vocal will suffer. Civil servants are not greatly impressed by special pleading in these circumstances and like all human beings resent attempts to influence them if they feel that they have already performed a difficult task to the best of their ability. But politicians, although also human (or perhaps because even more human), are willing to make 'exceptions' if this will placate a particularly vociferous or a particularly powerful interest. Appeals can, however, be met only within the limits of available money. And this money must be taken from the reserves held back by the Assistant Secretary or the territorial Principals when they make their allocations to regions or to local education authorities, respectively.

Where the appeal is made by letter or at office level, the territorial Principal deals with it alone. A deputation from the most powerful local authorities will normally insist on being seen by the Secretary of State or other Ministers. The civil servants in the Department may encourage this if they feel the Secretary of State needs to be made aware of the pressure for larger school building programmes. The presence of Members of Parliament in the deputation seems to add little to its strength. Representations of the Anglican and Roman Catholic Churches may be included if the project is a voluntary school but they have their own lobby with the Department which is probably more effective than their membership of a deputation.

Chief education officers do not normally show much faith in deputations—perhaps because they are too familiar with the administrative process to believe in the efficiency of this form of pressure, the main defect of which is its openness. The Department, forced to adjudicate between so many rival claims for a share of limited money, cannot afford to have the reputation of yielding to deputations. The reputation for fairness which the Department have acquired in their school building allocation could be most easily and quickly lost if it were felt that they were weak when faced with a deputation. And the interest of the Secretary of State in supporting the decisions of his civil servants is obvious.

If an appeal is successful, it may be so in one of two ways.

A local education authority may succeed either in substituting their own more expensive project for one already approved or in having another project added to their programme.

The process for the local education authority of obtaining final approval for a project begins, after the inclusion of the project in a programme, with the preparation of the schedule of accommodation which is then passed to the architect's department (or to the private architect if one is employed) for the preparation of sketch plans. Drafts of these plans are examined by the education officers, their advisers or specialists, by HMI, sometimes by teachers' representatives, sometimes by divisional executives, sometimes by managers or governors when already in existence. Amendments will result and the final draft will generally (though not universally) go to the appropriate sub-committee where it will be observed but rarely altered.

It is usual for these plans to be submitted [to the Department] in every case and the submission is often followed by meetings in the Department with the territorial architects of the Architects and Building Branch.[21] In the result, the local education officers and architects know, when sketch plans (as amended after discussion in the Department) are approved, that the final drawings based on the sketch plans will also probably be approved.

There may be discussion on building regulations and more commonly on cost limits which the local authority may find they are obliged to exceed. Where tenders exceed these limits the approval of the Department will have to be obtained to proceed and this may call for a second meeting in the Department.

It is the Department's policy to give final approval if the project, first, provides accommodation adequate both in amount and in standard for the purposes to be served and, secondly, can be carried out within the cost limits laid down by the Department.

The first of these requirements is governed by the Standards for School Premises Regulations[22] prepared by the

[21] Not all local education authorities submit sketch plans to the Ministry. Some of the largest authorities act more independently and seek less advice and help. For aided and special agreement schools, the Church authorities are required to submit sketch plans and final plans to the Ministry through the local education authority.

[22] S.I. 1959, No. 890. [As amended by S.I. 1969, No. 433.—Ed.]

Architects and Building Branch and supported by the guidance provided by the Ministry's Building Bulletins. The Regulations prescribe minimum standards.

The second of the Department's requirements for the giving of a final approval to a project is that it falls within the
cost limits. The Department determine the limits of net cost
per place.

These limits are determined by Architects and Building
Branch in consultation with the Ministry of Public Building
and Works and agreed with the Treasury. They are based on
actual and expected increases in building costs derived chiefly
from various indices. Cost limits are not reviewed at regular
intervals but only when pressure from local educational
authorities for their amendment has become intense and when
the evidence for the increase in costs is strong. Costs vary in
different parts of the country but the Department have always
rejected proposals for regional limits. They are, however,
always willing to consider supplementary allowances in those
areas where building costs are shown to be high.

The Department claimed before the Estimates Committee
that the introduction of cost limits in 1949 had in ten years
saved well over £200m or in real money terms about 50 per
cent and, with the other two key controls or annual building
programmes and the Building Regulations, enabled the
central departments to set the designs of schools free from
the sterile, time-wasting business of having to justify their
decisions, often when it was already too late to make changes,
to the departmental watchdogs. Phrases like 'a substantial
increase' in quantity, 'equally dramatic increase in quality'
are used.

There is something to be said on the other side. In 1953 the
Department raised the existing limits by 4 per cent and announced that in future periodic adjustments would be made
in relation to the Department's calculated index of building
costs. In 1955 limits were accordingly increased. But in 1956,
despite substantial rises in building costs, no further increase
was made and local authorities were asked to use 'their
imagination, skill and energy' to absorb these rises. The
Department was of the opinion that it was 'still possible in
the majority of cases to build schools of good quality within
the cost limits'. The Association of Chief Education Officers
has observed that this meant it was 'clearly understood at the

Ministry that in a minority of cases (and how large that minority was is not stated) it was not possible to build schools of good quality within the cost limits.[23] This, as the Department agreed, was a deliberate choice by the Government at a time when an attack was being made on cost inflation.

This use of cost limits as part of a deliberate general policy would seem to bear very hardly on local authorities and to enable the Government to avoid criticism. If the Government decide that, because of the nation's economic position, local authorities should spend no more on schools, then it is not proper to trap local authorities between the upper stone of cost limits and the nether stone of Building Regulations. If the authorities keep within the cost limits, standards must fall save in those authorities where some 'slack' can be taken up. It is true that Building Regulations set minimum standards and cost limits set maximum cost. But when the Department agree, as it did in 1956, that, on its own bases, cost limits should have been increased, it is unfair to pose local authorities with problems which for many of them are clearly insoluble. And to cheer them on with reference to imagination, skill and energy adds insult to injury. As the Sheffield Education Committee observed 'a point is ultimately reached at which imagination is left to carry on the struggle alone'. Moreover experiments tend to be initially expensive and so a rigid cost limits system may stifle experimentation.

That Committee added other criticisms: adjustments in cost limits were found to lag behind rising costs in building; national cost per place formula cannot take account of differences in tendering conditions in different places or at different times: local authorities building schools in areas where the topography makes construction of buildings and playing fields particularly difficult are not properly compensated by the normal 10 per cent for additional cost items.[24]

Criticisms have been made of the introduction of undesirable expedients necessitated by the level of cost limits: the use of poor materials especially for roofs and floors resulting in increased maintenance costs; inadequate sound-proofing; the reduction of circulation and storage space below desirable limits; the severe restriction of cloak and washing spaces and dual use of accommodation; the serious inhibition of normal

[23] House of Commons Paper No. 284 of 1960-61, Question 513.
[24] The percentage is now 12½. It is not inflexible.

educational advance and experiment because the minima of Building Regulations have become maxima; the insufficient regard of the limits to the appreciable change-over from arts to science.[25]

Perhaps the fairest conclusion was that reached by the Association of Chief Education Officers when asked by the Select Committee in 1961 if they agreed there was 'enormously more value for money today' than in 1949. The President of the Association and Chief Education Officer for Shropshire replied: 'We would not go quite so far as the Ministry. While we think that the Ministry have done very well in this field we feel that some of their phrases about a dramatic increase in quality are stretching things a little.'[26]

CONCLUSIONS

The three principal methods by which the Departments control local education authorities in their school building activities are the approval of projects in building programmes, the imposition of minimum standards of accommodation and the limitation of costs.

Are the decisions made by the Department those which are appropriate for central, national decisions? Or do any of them impinge on the scope of discretion which a local authority might properly expect to be its responsibility?

Building programmes derive from investment programmes. This is not necessarily so and indeed there were building programmes in the last twenty years before the control of investment in the public sector was at all comprehensive. But today the figures for school building are a reflection not only of other educational spending but of all other public spending also. For present purposes we may accept that decisions of capital expenditure on school building will be taken as part of a larger exercise. £80m is the figure we can start from, being the annual allocation to the Department for school building on major projects at present agreed.* If local education authorities are to continue to build schools then that £80m must be divided amongst them. Short of inventing some new 'independent' authority, the Department is the only candidate for this act of division.

---

[25] Evidence of Association of Chief Education Officers.
[26] Ibid., Q. 1058.
* [£80m was the figure for 1965. The figure is now much higher.—Ed.]

As it is, then, inevitably, the function of the Department to allocate to each local education authority their share of the £80m, we are left with the selection of individual projects within that share. At present, this selection is done by territorial Principals, with the help of district HMIs, from amongst the projects proposed by local education authorities. Is the Department the proper body to make this selection or should it be entrusted to local education authorities, within an allocation of money?

The basic need for new school places is a local need, however much the meeting of the need is a national necessity. It can, of course, be expressed in national terms: more school places are needed because the birth rate is high, because the population moves, because more children are staying on at school after compulsory school age. But the effect of these changes varies vastly from area to area. The natural increase of population is higher in some areas than in others. The migration within England and Wales populates some regions and depopulates others. And in 1952, the proportion of sixteen-year-olds (as a percentage of thirteen-year-olds) remaining at school in the metropolitan region was 15·6 per cent rising to 28·1 per cent in 1961 while in the northern region the figures were 9·2 per cent rising to 15·3 per cent.[27]

These variations are, however, in broad terms, and over regions composed of many local education authorities. The need for new schools arises more locally still. In county boroughs, the emergence of new populations is comparatively predictable but in the counties, as we have seen, sudden demands can arise because of development which could not have been or was not foreseen. To be told, for example, that the population of the South East is expected to increase by at least $3\frac{1}{2}$ million by 1981 does not give any useful hard information to local education authorities because there is no indication where these people will live. 'Most of the population growth in the South East,' said the Government's Study,[28] 'can be looked after by normal planning processes; but local planning authorities will have to allocate much more land. Their development plans will have to provide land to accom

[27] *Statistics of Education* 1963 *Part I*, Table 3; and 1964 *Part I*, Table 3. [The percentage of pupils staying on beyond statutory school age has continued to increase, but regional disparities remain.—Ed.]
[28] *The South East Study, 1961-1981*, 1964, p. 99.

modate well over 2 million more people by 1981.' In the past, normal planning processes and development plans have not helped local education authorities to forecast where the need for school building is likely to arise. There is no reason to assume that the future will be different.

It is noteworthy that the arguments on capital investment in school building become more generalized the higher the level of decision-making. Those which result in the annual allocation to the Department of £80m* are the most imprecise, and can be supported only by evidence of the most general kind. The figures put forward by the Department are not derived from the detailed arguments put forward by local education authorities in support of their needs. The Department make the best projection they can on national and regional trends. Similarly the Treasury think in general terms of a percentage growth rate in educational expenditure. As a result of these imprecise negotiations, a figure is arrived at.

The division of the £80m amongst the territorial Principals is a little, but not much, more based on precise calculations. Regional considerations will be taken into some account— but not areas smaller than regions. Figures of school population for the area of each Principal are the basis for seven-eighths or so of the allocation with an examination of marginal cases determining the allocation of the remainder.

The next stage, when territorial Principals decide what schools shall be built where, is a wholly different operation— being a detailed examination of detailed submissions. Although the allocation is to local education authorities, it is not their needs as authorities which are considered but those of the catchment area for each specific proposal. In no real sense is one local education authority in competition with other local education authorities nor is evidence adduced to show the general educational situation in separate authorities. While attempts will be made in small part to ensure that even the authorities with the fewest problems receive some allocation from time to time, the competition is principally between projects not authorities. Only at this level, therefore, are the actual needs regarded. But at this level they are regarded most minutely.

The provision of school building is therefore to meet the most local of needs. The amounts made available are arrived

* [See note on page 70.]

at by having regard to the most general of considerations. And the selection of projects is a decision of the Department, from amongst proposals received from local education authorities, after they have been assessed in relation to other projects of the same and other local authorities.

[Arrangements for the determination of school building programme change from time to time. Since Griffith wrote, there have been two changes of major significance:
1. In Circular 13/68, of 8 July 1968, the Department set out a new system based on a three-year 'rolling programme'. The relevant sections of the Circular read:

The Need for Change

The system of annual programmes introduced in the early post-war years succeeded well in focusing attention on educational priorities, concentrating resources on limited and realistic policy objectives and in giving authorities the assurance they needed in planning to meet local needs. The increasing scale and complexity of educational building and the necessary co-ordination with other aspects of urban development including housing programmes have, however, made it more and more difficult to operate the system in its present form. Moreover, the carrying over of unstarted projects from year to year has seriously weakened the credibility of the annual programme as a forecast of work to be started in the year in question. A more flexible system is required which will offer adequate notice of work to be done and adaptability to meet changing requirements.

In other sectors of public investment there has been a movement towards arrangements under which lists of projects are agreed in general terms covering a period of several years ahead (the length of time depending mainly on the size and complexity of the projects) and these lists are extended from time to time as earlier projects are started. Such arrangements are often referred to as a 'rolling programme'. In a typical system of this kind the degree of commitment to a particular project increases in step with the progress of the preparatory work and the earmarking of the necessary investment. At the final stage the project, on which planning is nearing completion, is included in a firm programme of projects to be started in the ensuing year. Basic to this system is the early and realistic assessment of needs to be met within the given period, having regard to the resources likely to be available. This should be followed by the identification of individual projects to meet these needs and their probable timing. Once agreement is reached on these points, planning can start on the basis of reasonably firm assumptions while leaving open for a later stage final decisions on timing which, as experience has shown, can be affected by a variety of unforeseen factors.

The New System

Within the framework outlined above, the new system will have three phases corresponding with the normal sequence of events which lead up to the commencement of building operations:

- (a) the 'preliminary list' of projects for the completion of which a need is reasonably foreseeable within the next five years, but which can at this stage only be arranged in a provisional date order;
- (b) the 'design list' of projects, drawn from the preliminary list, on which detailed planning and design work is taking place and which can be expected to start in a specified year;
- (c) the 'Starts programme' of fully-planned and costed projects to be started in the specified year.

Transfer from one phase to another will depend mainly on the progress which has been made on the preparatory and planning operations and on the resources available. Although most projects of similar types will progress at a similar rate, the system is intended to be flexible enough to accommodate without the strains involved in the present system both the complicated and slower-moving projects and those which can (and sometimes must) be planned and executed very quickly to meet urgent needs.

THE PRELIMINARY LIST

Under the new procedure the preliminary list, and not the annual building programme, will be the first formal stage at which new building projects are identified by the Department. When projects have been included in this list, the authority and the managers, governors or promoters of voluntary schools will be able to carry out preliminary work such as securing sites (if they have not already done so) obtaining outline planning permission, putting forward proposals under section 13 of the Education Act 1944 if necessary and preparing the brief for architects, so that there will be no foreseeable delays to the progress of planning and building. In the long term the Secretary of State envisages that authorities will consult the Department about additions to this preliminary list from time to time as they identify their future needs. In the initial stages, however, it will be made up on the basis of replies to formal requests by the Department.

The length of time that a project will need to be on the preliminary list before starting will depend on its size, complexity, and any delays which may be foreseen in such matters as acquiring a site. Inclusion in the list will not therefore imply a start in any particular year, but projects should not normally be included in the list unless the accommodation will be needed within five years. It will be the Department's responsibility to ensure that the aggregate value of the preliminary list is kept at a realistic level, having regard to capital investment prospects for the future.

THE DESIGN LIST
Projects will be eligible for transfer to a 'design list' when the preparatory stages referred to above have been completed, or are sufficiently well in hand to give an assurance of smooth progress. Normally this will imply, *inter alia*, that the site has been acquired and that, in the case of schools, any action required under Section 13 of the Education Act 1944 has been completed. This list will be designated by the year during which most of the design work will take place and will consist of projects intended to start in the following year (e.g. the 1970-71 design list will consist of projects on which building work is intended to start during 1971/72 and will be related in size to the prospective starts programme for 1971/72). It will therefore need to be drawn up on the basis of a firmer commitment and estimate of cost than the preliminary list and at this stage authorities will be asked to confirm or modify the information submitted earlier in support of the proposal. The Secretary of State intends to draw up the design lists about a year and half before the beginning of the financial year in which projects are intended to start, in order to allow sufficient time for them to pass through the necessary stages of detailed design and approval. Since the approvals and contractual arrangements for projects which are to start early in the financial year must be substantially completed

in the previous year, it follows that the preparation of working drawings for these projects will be one of the most important activities to be carried out at the design list stage. The general procedure does not, however, preclude the commencement of design work on projects still in the preliminary list; indeed, it is hoped that, as experience is gained, authorities will be able to plan the work in their offices as a steady flow without any serious interruption by the administrative stages.

Once a project has been included in the design list, the normal assumption will be that it will form part of the starts programme for the following year, provided that the following conditions are satisfied:

(i) the authority (or the promoters, in the case of voluntary schools) still wish to start it in that year;
(ii) progress on the detailed planning suggests that it will be ready to start in time;
(iii) the estimated cost is within the agreed expenditure limit.

The procedure for compiling a starts programme will be directed mainly to seeking confirmation on these points during the summer preceding the programme year.

THE STARTS PROGRAMME

The starts programme will be drawn up some six months before the beginning of the programme year in accordance with the capital investment programme for that year, and will take account of all the information available about individual projects. As explained in the previous paragraph drawing up the starts programme will in the main consist of the promotion from the design list of projects on which satisfactory progress has been made. On the other hand projects which have fallen behind their time-table will have to be retained in the design list (or, if their urgency has diminished, revert to the preliminary list). It must be emphasized that the starts programme will be established on the basis that projects are capable of starting within the year in question. While it may in some cases be possible to include exceptionally urgent projects in the starts programme without the normal preparatory periods in the preliminary and design list stages, this will be done only if the authority can give an assurance that it will start within the programme year, and capital investment can be made available for it, if necessary by the deferment of another project or projects. If a project included in the starts programme for a given year fails to start in that year, it will be able to start in a subsequent year only on the basis that it will be transferred to the starts programme of the authority concerned for the later year. This will normally imply the deferment of another project or projects which might otherwise have held a place in the authority's starts programme.

No comment on this change seems necessary, save that it must facilitate sensible forward planning by both central and local government.

2. An experiment has been initiated by the Department whereby five local education authorities—Canterbury, Cornwall, Croydon, Kent and Liverpool—receive a block allocation for their major building programme, and are allowed to determine their own priorities within it. Were this experiment to be judged successful, and the system to be extended more widely after the reorganization of local government, the procedures analysed by Griffith might undergo radical change.—Ed.]

4

G. TAYLOR and N. AYRES

Levels of Educational Provision in Local Authorities in England*

School buildings

School buildings, unlike factories, are not subject to stringent regulations rigorously enforced in respect of hygiene, amenities, lighting and heating. Post-war schools conform to the standards laid down by the Department of Education and Science at the time when the plans were approved; inter-war schools were built in accordance with the not very exacting regulations then in operation. There are, however, schools still in use built as early as the 1830s which, apart from the installation of electric lighting, remain substantially unmodified.

According to the Department of Education and Science Survey made in 1962 of the stock of school buildings, there were two-thirds of a million primary school children attending pre-1875 schools and nearly a million attending schools dating from the period 1875-1902. The proportion of primary school children within a region attending schools built before 1902 is shown in Fig. 4·1.

The distribution of older schools is similar to that for sub-standard and overcrowded dwellings but, as in the case of housing, percentage figures do not reveal the full extent of the problem. For example, in the North West there were 120,000 children in pre-1875 schools and 160,000 in schools belonging to the period 1875-1902; included in these figures were the 8,000 children who were attending all-age schools

* [From G. Taylor and N. Ayres, *Born and Bred Unequal*, Longman, 1969.]

(i.e. former elementary schools retaining children up to the age of fifteen). The Northern region, with a smaller proportion of old schools had a larger number of children (10,000) in attendance at all-age schools. Although reorganization into separate primary and secondary schools has proceeded rapidly since the date of the survey, the fact remains that, as late as 1962, children continued to remain in primary schools until the age of fifteen.

There is a similar correlation between the incidence of substandard housing and old schools in the West Yorkshire and West Midlands conurbations. In the Eastern and South Western regions the problem is one of remote rural schools in villages whose school population has declined sharply during the last fifty to a hundred years. The two Southern regions have only a comparatively small proportion of pre-1902 schools.

Despite the regional pattern of old schools, the main impact of the school building programme is not in areas where the need for replacements of obsolete buildings is urgent. Direct evidence to substantiate this statement does not exist so that indirect methods of corroboration must be used.

To cover their expenditure on new schools, local authorities raise loans which are repaid with interest over a period of sixty years; repayments made each year appear in a local authority's budget under the heading 'debt charges'. Since, as a result of this method of repayment, loans for pre-1914 schools are largely repaid, current debt charges relate mainly to inter-war and post-war schools. Relatively high charges are indicative of a considerable volume of post-war building, low charges of few or possibly no new schools built in the post-war period.

Chart 4·1(a) shows the total debt charges (for every 100 primary school-children) incurred for the building of new primary schools on a regional basis, and 4·1(b) the extent to which individual authorities differ from the county or county borough average. From these charts it can be inferred that the volume of new primary school building in the North West is below average and that few of the many old schools in this region are being replaced. Particularly noteworthy are the following authorities, all declining in population, in which primary school debt charges are among the lowest in the country:

Fig. 4.1 *Age of primary school buildings (1962)—old regions. Primary School population for each region inserted*

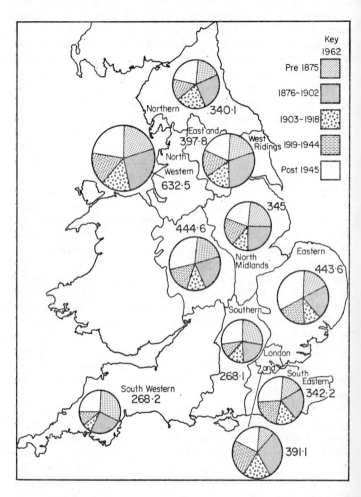

Source: Department of Education and Science 1965, School Building Survey 1962

Blackburn	£335	Liverpool	£267
Burnley	£173	Oldham	£361
Salford	£313	Wigan	£326

The North West Study* suggested that one house in two in Burnley required replacement; the lack of new school building in the town suggests also that the primary schools are in need of replacement on the same scale as the houses. Deficiencies in the environment in Salford, Liverpool and other Lancashire towns have already been noted; the comparative lack of new school building suggests that the school environment is similarly deficient. For the region as a whole, it is evident from the chart that expenditure on primary school building is well below the national average.

By contrast, most authorities in the West Midlands, East Anglia, South Eastern and South Western regions are building on a massive scale. Analysis of the distribution in the South East calls for comment: seventeen of the twenty-three authorities have above average charges, and in those with below average charges the deficiency is very much less than that of the authorities in the North West.

Chart 4.1 (a)

Debt charges per 100 primary school children 1966-67 (new regions)

* [HMSO 1965.]

(b-j) Debt charges per 100 primary school children by authorities. Deviations from the appropriate (i.e. county or county borough) average are shown. County average £697. County borough £607

Chart 4.1 (b)

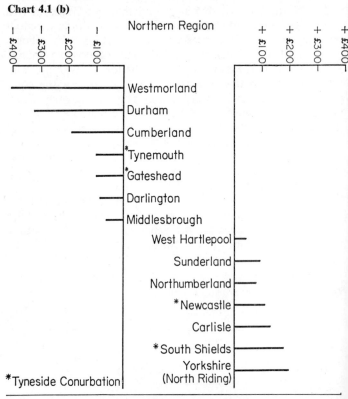

Northern Region

Westmorland
Durham
Cumberland
*Tynemouth
*Gateshead
Darlington
Middlesbrough
West Hartlepool
Sunderland
Northumberland
*Newcastle
Carlisle
*South Shields
Yorkshire (North Riding)

*Tyneside Conurbation

In other regions the incidence of new buildings is uneven. Durham, Gateshead and West Hartlepool, all areas of declining population and of unfavourable environment, have debt charges well below the national average, as also do authorities in the West Yorkshire conurbation (Bradford, Dewsbury, Halifax, Leeds and Sheffield). Although the West Midlands region has a high rate of debt charges, it is clear that new building is unevenly distributed, being largely confined to the newer and expanding towns such as Coventry and Solihull; the older parts of the conurbation (Warley, Walsall and Birmingham) are replacing their old schools only slowly. These three authorities have been described as areas with unfavour-

Chart 4.1 (c)

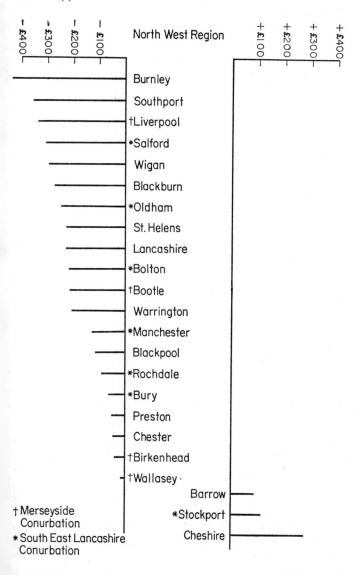

North West Region

Left axis (reading towards centre): −£400, −£300, −£200, −£100
Right axis: +£100, +£200, +£300, +£400

Burnley
Southport
†Liverpool
*Salford
Wigan
Blackburn
*Oldham
St. Helens
Lancashire
*Bolton
†Bootle
Warrington
*Manchester
Blackpool
*Rochdale
*Bury
Preston
Chester
†Birkenhead
†Wallasey·
Barrow
*Stockport
Cheshire

† Merseyside
  Conurbation
* South East Lancashire
  Conurbation

Chart 4.1 (d)

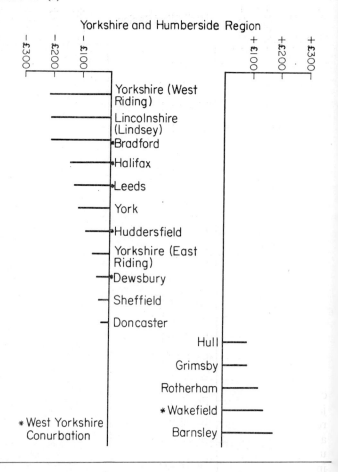

Yorkshire and Humberside Region

able environment—on to which the complication of a considerable immigrant population has been added.

The unevenness of new school building over the country as a whole stems from national policy and population dynamics. Capital expenditure on schools, closely controlled by the Government, is devoted to providing new schools for

Chart 4.1 (e)

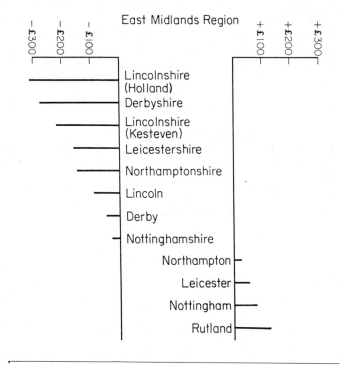

East Midlands Region

| | −£300 | −£200 | −£100 | | +£100 | +£200 | +£300 |

Lincolnshire (Holland)
Derbyshire
Lincolnshire (Kesteven)
Leicestershire
Northamptonshire
Lincoln
Derby
Nottinghamshire
Northampton
Leicester
Nottingham
Rutland

children in expanding areas, 'roofs over heads' in the current jargon. Though this may be the only feasible policy, its regional implications are far reaching. As long as a child has a roof over his head, however old and unsuitable the structure under the roof may be, he stands little chance of being taught in a school conforming to modern standards. Just as the reasonably well housed citizen is unable to visualize life in an 'unfit' house, so do teachers, parents and administrators who are familiar only with schools in the newer suburbs find it difficult to imagine education in 'unfit' schools.

Lavatories for staff and pupils, at the far side of the school yard, are uncovered and freeze for weeks or months in a severe winter; heating of lofty classrooms is dependent on the skill of the caretaker in stoking an old-fashioned and often temperamental boiler; daylight enters from windows too high to look through; there is no provision for a sick child; there may be a makeshift room for the head teacher— though a staffroom is less likely; improvised arrangements for dining are a disturbance to work and a nightmare on wet days. Classrooms, which may also be corridors, vary in size, with the consequence that organization is based on the peculiarities of the building instead of the needs of the cur-

Chart 4.1 (f)

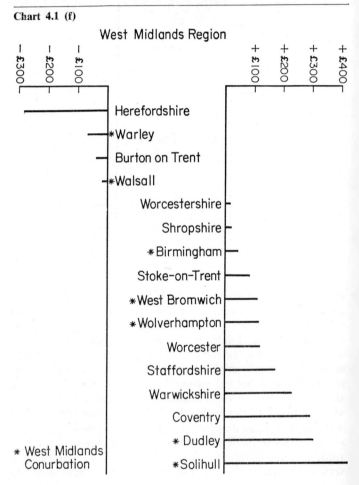

West Midlands Region

Chart 4.1 (g)

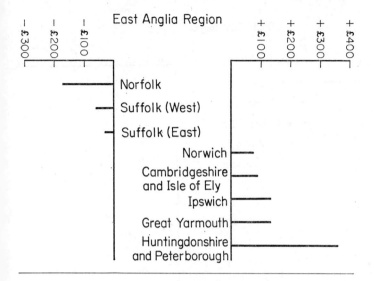

riculum. Designed for the traditional pedagogic methods of the last century, schools of this type are ill adapted to current practice or to the introduction of modern aids. They are certainly in no condition to attract and retain teachers.

In the second half of the twentieth century, two nations are growing up. One is of children living in new or expanding areas with Favourable environments, attending well-equipped and well staffed schools. The other nation consists of generations of children conditioned by obsolete and inefficient schools; they are children who come from homes whose standards and environment are as deplorable as those of their schools. That the two nations can and do co-exist within a short distance of one another is certain. What is significant and alarming for the future of our society is the concentration in large areas, principally located in the three northern regions, of children so handicapped in comparison with more fortunate children elsewhere that the majority will fail to achieve their potential intellectual and aesthetic development. It cannot be doubted that the marked regional differentiation in the provision of new schools is increasing the gap between the two nations.

Chart 4.1 (h)

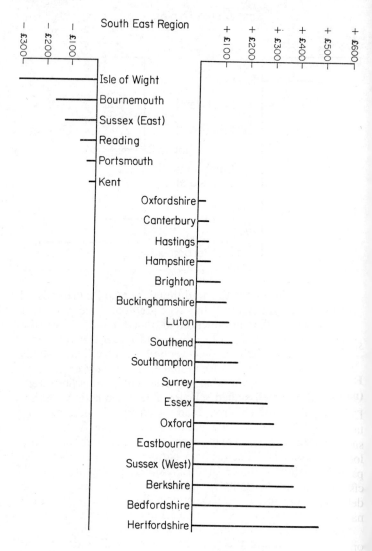

South East Region

Chart 4.1 (j)

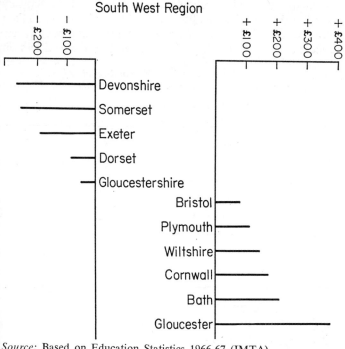

South West Region

Source: Based on Education Statistics 1966-67 (IMTA)

Expenditure on Schools
(maintenance and provision of materials)

Local authorities not only build new schools but also maintain existing schools. Over expenditure on repairs, decoration, small improvements, furniture and educational materials, a local authority has complete control. It is, in fact, the only part of an authority's budget where generosity can be exercised or economies made; all other parts (teachers' salaries, debt charges, university awards) are largely regulated by national policy.

An overall picture of the level of expenditure in the regions on the maintenance of primary schools may be obtained from Chart 4·2; under this heading are included repairs to buildings and playgrounds, decoration and small improvements, new furniture and fittings. The size of the budget for these items is decisive in ameliorating or depressing the working conditions in older schools, but in assessing the adequacy of regional or local expenditure three factors have to be taken into account. First, authorities with a large number of new schools (i.e. those with high debt charges) need spend less on

Chart 4.2   *Expenditure on maintenance and repair of buildings, furniture and fittings per 100 primary pupils 1966–67*

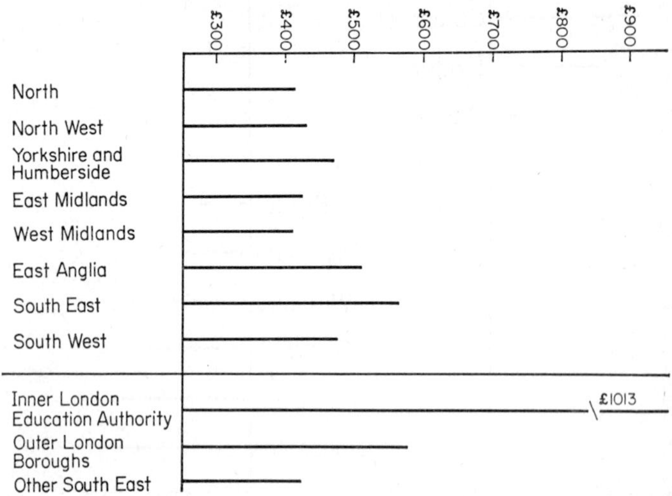

Source: Based on Education Statistics 1966-67 (IMTA)

repairs or replacement of furniture; second, older schools (particularly those in older industrial areas) require frequent decoration both in the interests of cleanliness and of making them more attractive places; third, authorities with a significant number of aided schools (Church of England and Roman Catholic) have smaller charges for exterior decoration since this is the responsibility of the managers who receive assistance from the central government for this purpose.

Despite these variables, it is possible to form some impression of the extent to which authorities are discharging their responsibilities as landlords. But to do so, Chart 4·1(a) must be compared with Chart 4·2.

The Inner London Education Authority, with a small building programme for new primary schools, is compensating by a large expenditure on existing schools while the area described as 'other South East', building schools on a massive scale, can maintain their smaller number of older schools without an excessive outlay. East Anglia and the South West, both with sizeable building programmes and little atmospheric pollution, probably spend enough to keep their schools in good repair. If this is the case, it is quite clear that the three northern regions spend too little to counteract the effects upon a large number of old schools (for which there is little prospect of early replacement), of atmospheric pollution and of dereliction and poor housing in the immediate environment of these schools. Although the general picture of the standard of maintenance in these regions is gloomy, a number of authorities are, by increased expenditure, making considerable efforts to overcome the depressing effects of older schools (see Table 4·1). Liverpool, in particular, is extremely generous (expenditure £726) and so, to a lesser extent are Lancashire, Barrow, Manchester and St Helens in the North West. Durham in the North spends an above average amount on maintenance and so also do the West Riding, Hull and Sheffield in the Yorkshire and Humberside region.

Why some authorities are better landlords than others is far from clear; 'keeping down the rates' is a major factor when the level of expenditure is discussed but, unexpectedly, it is not always authorities with the least resources that are the most parsimonious. A lack of sensitivity on the part of some elected representatives enables them to be satisfied with a policy of infrequent decoration and one suspects that the theory of 'where there's muck, there's brass' is not yet dead.

Another aspect of working conditions that is vital for educational standards concerns the supply of books, materials and apparatus, supply which is more important now than it has ever been because curricular reform in primary schools —the Nuffield projects in mathematics, science and French— involves considerable expenditure. New schools are normally well equipped on opening, not only with new books and equipment which will need no replacement for several years, but also with modern aids such as tape recorders, strip projectors and television. Apart from consumable materials new schools are inexpensive to run; old schools are, or should be, much more expensive. Books and apparatus require constant replacement: in areas of social deprivation, they receive harder wear and should be supplied on a more generous

Table 4.1

Expenditure per 100 primary pupils on maintenance, repairs and furniture

County borough average, £417; County average, £447; London borough average, £579

Region	Above average		Below average		
	20% or more	*Between 10 & 20%*	*Between 10 & 20%*	*20% or more*	
North	Northumberland	Durham	Darlington West Hartlepool	Cumberland Westmorland Yorkshire (North Riding)	Middlesbrough Newcastle upon Tyne Sunderland Tynemouth
North West	Liverpool	Barrow St Helens	Blackpool Bootle	Cheshire Birkenhead Blackburn Bolton Bury Chester	Burnley Preston Southport Stockport Wallasey Warrington Wigan
Yorkshire and Humberside	Huddersfield Hull Sheffield	Yorkshire (West Riding) Halifax	Yorkshire (East Riding) Wakefield	Barnsley Leeds	Rotherham
East Midlands	Derbyshire		Northamptonshire Derby Leicester Nottingham Northampton	Lincolnshire Lincolnshire, Rutland Lincoln	Holland Kesteven
West Midlands		Staffordshire Coventry Solihull Stoke-on-Trent	Walsall Wolverhampton	Shropshire Worcestershire West Bromwich Worcester	
East Anglia	Norfolk Suffolk, East	Cambridgeshire and Isle of Ely Suffolk, West Ipswich		Great Yarmouth	
South East	Sussex, East	Bedfordshire	Surrey Isle of Wight	Sussex, West Canterbury Hastings	Luton Portsmouth
London Boroughs	Ealing Enfield Newham Waltham Forest	Hillingdon Hounslow	Barking Merton Sutton	Bexley Brent Harrow	Kingston upon Thames Richmond
South West	Somerset Bristol Plymouth		Wiltshire	Cornwall	

Source: IMTA Education Statistics 1966-67

scale to compensate for the lack of materials at home. In the interests of equality, more correctly termed uniformity in this context, authorities often base their expenditure on the number on roll in each school and not on the school's needs. The Plowden Committee drew attention to the desirability of positive discrimination in favour of deprived schools and areas, but how far this idea has proved generally acceptable it is not possible to judge.

Table 4.2 suggests where there may be considerable deficiencies in the supplies, materials and equipment available to teachers and children. That a considerable number of authorities in the three Northern regions economize on educational material is a matter for concern, particularly when other authorities in the same regions, with no greater financial resources, have appreciated the need for generosity in the matter of equipment. The small number of entries in the left-hand column for other regions is an indication that the majority of authorities budget for a reasonable, if not generous, standard of supply of educational material.

Supply and Distribution of Teachers

One of the major factors influencing the quality of education in an area is the supply of teachers. To be efficient a school

Table 4.2

School supplies (text and library books, stationery, materials and equipment) expenditure per child

Region	10% below appropriate average		10% above appropriate average	
North	Westmorland Yorkshire (North Riding)	Gateshead Newcastle upon Tyne Sunderland	Carlisle Darlington South Shields	Tynemouth West Hartlepool
North West	Lancashire Barrow Bury	Chester St Helens Salford Southport Wigan	Blackburn Bootle Manchester Rochdale	Wallasey
Yorkshire and Humberside	Yorkshire (West Riding) Barnsley Dewsbury	Leeds Rotherham	Doncaster Halifax	Hull York
East Midlands	Great Yarmouth Northampton		Derby Lincoln	
West Midlands	Coventry		Dudley Stoke Walsall	Warley Wolverhampton Worcester
East Anglia			Cambridgeshire and Isle of Ely Norfolk Suffolk, West	
South East (excluding Outer London Boroughs)	Kent Oxfordshire Sussex, West	Isle of Wight Luton	Bedfordshire Buckinghamshire Surrey	Bournemouth Oxford Reading Southend
South West	Cornwall Bath		Somerset Gloucestershire	

Source: Based on IMTA Education Statistics, 1966-67

requires a staff which is stable, experienced and sufficient in number; for schools serving districts of social deprivation these staffing requirements are basic. While this is generally appreciated, there is little information available that indicates how far teachers are deployed where they are most needed. Pupil/teacher ratio over a whole region is meaningless; rural areas with a large number of one, two and three teacher schools need many more teachers than an urban area; an urban area may have well staffed schools in the suburbs although the 'down-town' schools are acutely short of staff.

One method of gauging the supply of staff in individual authorities is to consider the cost of their salaries; this information is set out for primary schools in Table 4·3. Although conclusions drawn from these figures must be treated with some caution, it is generally true that low costs arise from one or all of the following circumstances:

1. An authority's inability to recruit teachers up to the quota permitted by the Department of Education and Science.
2. An authority's inability to recruit part-time teachers owing to their non-availability in the area. In discussion of the level of parental education, it emerged that women who had undertaken education to the age of twenty or beyond were less numerous in some parts of the country, particularly in the Midlands, than in other parts. It is mainly from this group of women that trained part-time teachers are drawn.
3. A low salary bill owing to a larger than average proportion of teachers recruited direct from college or with little experience. When an authority is heavily dependent on recruiting young teachers, instability of staff is an inevitable consequence since young women do not remain long in their posts.

On the reasonable assumption that low staffing costs indicate staffing difficulties, analysis of Table 4·3 suggests some interesting regional differences. In a considerable number of North Western authorities the supply of teachers is better than might be expected. Judged by expenditure, the Northern and Yorkshire regions are also not seriously short of teachers. Only Darlington, Barrow, Bury, Rochdale, Salford, Southport, Stockport and Barnsley in the three northern regions incur an expenditure on primary-school teachers' salaries of 5 per cent or more below the county borough average. In other authorities with 0-5 per cent expenditure below average, teacher shortage may exist because there are few teachers living in the area who are available for part-time work.

Reasonable staffing standards in the three northern regions do not, however, imply that all the schools are adequately staffed. Still less do they imply that schools most in need of a stable and experienced staff are appropriately served. It is not without significance that five of the eight boroughs mentioned above have major environmental deficiencies.

That the northern regions do not experience serious shortages may be accounted for in several ways. They produce a large number of teachers and are, on the whole, self-supporting; the quota system designed to distribute teachers evenly over the country has been highly successful, preventing excessive migration to the south; obsolete schools have been staffed because no alternative posts are available. But it is the experience of most authorities that as the number of their new schools increases, it becomes progressively more difficult to persuade teachers to work in the remaining old schools in deprived areas.

The position in the Midlands, particularly in the conurbation, is less favourable. In Birmingham, Solihull, Walsall and West Bromwich the cost of teachers' salaries is well below the national average. Generally within the conurbation and in Nottingham and Northampton, there is a continuing shortage of teachers, due largely to the fact that, unlike the Northern regions, the Midlands does not produce sufficient teachers for its needs. There is a shortage exacerbated by the absence of a reservoir of married women teachers. The West Midlands Study* commented on the situation in the following terms: 'Taking the region as a whole, the proportion of teachers to pupils is well up to the average for England and Wales and slightly better ...; the difficulty in recruiting teachers in some parts of the region is very marked. These are usually areas with a poor environment, and it is such places that have had fairly substantial flows of Commonwealth immigrants with consequent educational problems.'

* [HMSO 1965.]

The eastern and southern regions have few difficulties in attracting staff; only one county borough (Luton) spends less than average on salaries. Apart from Essex, all the counties incur costs above, or very little below, the county average. Whether these regions recruit the most competent teachers can only be a matter for conjecture, but it is suggestive that advertisements for headships and other posts of responsibility produce many more applications than they do in other regions. Northern and Midland authorities do not expect or receive applications from other regions. Migration of teachers is predominantly in a southerly direction.

Table 4.3

Salaries of teachers in primary schools: cost per unit of 40 pupils 1966–67 1967–68

| Average for county boroughs £1882 } 1966–67 | | | £1996 } 1967–68 | |
| Average for counties   £2010 } | | | £2120 } | |

	£	£			
North Region			Liverpool	1884	2024
Cumberland	2318	2442	Manchester	1962	2049
Durham	2085	2218	Oldham	1924	2019
Northumberland	2064	2160	Preston	1931	2017
Westmorland	2547	2665	Rochdale†	1753	1880
Yorkshire			St Helens	1996	2110
(North Riding)*	1926	2055	Salford†	1781	1899
Carlisle	1922	2053	Southport†	1765	1859
Darlington†	1780	1890	Stockport	1788	1927
Gateshead	1898	1939	Wallasey	1872	2005
Middlesbrough*	1819	2008	Warrington*	1843	1936
Newcastle upon			Wigan*	1879	1914
Tyne*	1825	1940			
South Shields*	1834	1968	*Yorkshire (E. and W.*		
Sunderland*	1860	1958	*Ridings) Region*		
Tynemouth	1954	2083	Yorkshire		
West Hartlepool*	1875	1990	(East Riding)	2315	2382
			Yorkshire		
North West Region			(West Riding)*	1976	2065
Cheshire*	1823	1933	Barnsley†	1687	1819
Lancashire*	1889	1982	Bradford*	1794	1917
Barrow-in-Furness†	1723	1858	Dewsbury	1895	1999
Birkenhead*	1878	1956	Doncaster	1977	2108
Blackburn	1970	2047	Halifax	1951	2154
Blackpool	1920	2027	Huddersfield*	1821	2062
Bolton*	1780	1881	Hull	1918	2059
Bootle*	1847	1999	Leeds*	1806	1932
Burnley*	1873	1973	Rotherham*	1799	1880
Bury†	1655	1780	Sheffield*	1822	1930
Chester	1968	2055	Wakefield	1946	1998

	£	£		£	£
York	2032	2189	Huntingdonshire and		
			Peterborough	1963	2169
North Midland Region			Norfolk	2433	2523
Derbyshire	2015	2135	Suffolk, East	2346	2452
Leicestershire*	1920	2020	Suffolk, West	2277	2431
Lincolnshire,			Great Yarmouth	2016	2111
Holland	2344	2423	Ipswich	2017	2113
Lincolnshire,			Luton†	1764	1789
Kesteven	2153	2238	Norwich	1903	2066
Lincolnshire,			Southend	1967	2066
Lindsey	2032	2103			
Northamptonshire*	1943	2036	*South East Region*		
Nottinghamshire*	1875	1964	Kent*	1910	2032
Rutland	2032	2169	Surrey	2079	2212
Derby	1963	2040	Sussex, East	2156	2268
Grimsby*	1813	1941	Sussex, West	2010	2104
Leicester*	1829	1960	Brighton	2034	2125
Lincoln	1929	2035	Canterbury	2012	2113
Nottingham†	1756	1805	Eastbourne	1971	1984
Northampton†	1748	1922	Hastings	2018	2061
Midland Region			*South Region*		
Herefordshire	2401	2563	Berkshire*	1986	2095
Shropshire	2089	2211	Buckinghamshire*	1980	2136
Staffordshire	1955	2074	Dorset	2194	2289
Warwickshire	2020	2134	Hampshire	1938	2058
Worcestershire	2007	2109	Isle of Wight	2251	2340
Birmingham†	1778	1910	Oxfordshire	2030	2156
Burton-on-Trent	2096	2143	Bournemouth	2005	2146
Coventry*	1836	1961	Oxford	2034	2137
Dudley	1909	1986	Portsmouth	2006	2077
Solihull†	1744	1856	Reading	1972	2073
Stoke-on-Trent	2022	2180	Southampton	1951	2109
Walsall†	1780	1838			
Warley*	1808	1890	*South West Region*		
West Bromwich†	1726	1878	Cornwall	2078	2185
Wolverhampton*	1880	1977	Devonshire	2146	2329
Worcester	2032	2078	Gloucestershire	2069	2199
			Somerset	2123	2232
East Region			Wiltshire	2084	2192
Bedfordshire	2022	2105	Bath	1981	2132
Cambridgeshire and			Bristol	2010	2150
Isle of Ely	2156	2230	Exeter	1983	2124
Essex*	1863	2001	Gloucester	2058	2119
Hertfordshire	2051	2001	Plymouth	1940	1992

Greater London Region

Owing to London weighting of salaries, these figures cannot be compared with those for other regions.

Average for London Boroughs £2014 (1966–67), £2118 (1967–68)

	£	£		£	£
Barking*	1853	1924	Croydon*	1961	2086
Barnet	2113	2190	Ealing	2050	2109
Bexley*	1990	2090	Enfield	2084	2210
Brent*	1949	2039	Haringey	2012	2132
Bromley	2032	2108	Harrow	2066	2157

	£	£		£	£
Havering*	1883	1990	Redbridge	2010	2145
Hillingdon	2104	2239	Richmond upon		
Hounslow	2074	2231	Thames	2130	2256
Kingston upon			Sutton*	1963	2049
Thames	2093	2197	Waltham Forest	2020	2130
Merton	2070	2137	*Inner London Education*		
Newham*	1926	2039	*Authority*	2098	2235

Source: based on IMTA Education Statistics 1966–67; 1967–68

  * Authorities below appropriate average.   } in 1966–67

  † Authorities 5 per cent or more below appropriate average. }

5

R. BUXTON

Comprehensive Education: Central Government, Local Authorities and the Law[*]

We have chosen this topic because the strains caused by the implementation of the Labour Government's policy of comprehensive education have revealed much about the relations of local government both with the national government and with the law. We cannot, of course, discuss here all the points of governmental and educational principle involved, but will rather concentrate on two aspects of the subject, the relationship between local and national government, and the opportunities which exist for the individual citizen to interfere with the process of educational administration. In this latter connection we will consider the protracted litigation over the Enfield comprehensive scheme, as an example of the intervention of the law in local government affairs.

Central and Local Government

BACKGROUND[†]
It shall be lawful for His Majesty to appoint a Minister (hereinafter referred to as 'the Minister'), whose duty it shall be to promote the education of the people of England and Wales and the progressive development of institutions directed to that purpose, and to secure the effective execution by local authorities, under his control and direction, of the national policy for providing a varied and comprehensive[1] educational service in every area.[2]

[*] [From R. Buxton, *Local Government*, Penguin, 1970.]
[†] [See Griffith, Chapter 3 of this reader—Ed.]
[1] 'Comprehensive' is used here with its ordinary meaning of 'all-embracing', and not in any technical sense.
[2] Education Act 1944, s. 1 (1).

It shall be the duty of every local education authority to secure that there shall be available for their area sufficient schools:

> (a) for providing primary education, that is to say, full-time education suitable to the requirements of junior pupils; and
> (b) for providing secondary education, that is to say, full-time education suitable to the requirements of senior pupils.[3]

These two sections of the ruling statute,* the Education Act 1944 (hereafter called the 1944 Act), well illustrate the confused coexistence between national and local government which characterizes the education service. In introducing the Act in the House of Commons Mr R. A. Butler attempted to clarify matters by saying that, whilst the Minister remained responsible to Parliament for 'policy', 'the central authority must continue to rely on the local education authorities for the administration of all national policy and the variety and scope of the provision must depend on local initiative';[4] but this left unclear what the distinction between national policy and local administration in fact was. The 1944 Act does not provide any effective means of coercing the local authority to do what the government requires, the crucial controlling factor, here as elsewhere, being financial rather than legal. [.....]

Not only is the education service a principal beneficiary of the government grant system, but also even the introduction of the block grant in 1958, giving local authorities more discretion over the way in which governmental bounty was used, did nothing to free capital expenditure, necessarily the main instrument of policy-change, from the rigours of loan sanction. In any case, any lack of definition of the relative roles of central and local government was not likely to cause difficulties whilst there was general agreement between administrators at local and national level about the organization of secondary education and, although there were

---

[3] ibid., s. 8.
[4] *Hansard* (House of Commons Debates), 19 January 1944, vol. 396, col. 209.
* [In England and Wales—Ed.]

occasional squalls during the 1950s,* for nearly twenty years after the 1944 Act local councils and their officers showed no greater wish to challenge the accepted principles of selection at eleven-plus than did successive Ministers of Education, both Labour and Conservative.

The adoption by the Labour Party of comprehensive education as a major, and distinctive, feature of its party policy, and the Labour victory in the 1964 General Election, disrupted this concord. The argument over comprehensive schools was now identified as a clear party issue, and one which could cause a division on party lines between the Labour Government and a Conservative-controlled local authority. In most local government questions the tension between local and national administrations of differing political views does not take this stark form, because disagreement will usually be over the speed and precise form if advance towards goals of social reform which both parties claim to support, and positive policy differences tend to be limited to issues with small practical impact, such as the sale of council houses. The organization of secondary education, however, not only affects the whole community, but also involves great financial expenditure and the infringement of heavily vested interests. In this situation, the lack of clear definition of the central government's powers threatened to be very troublesome, particularly since the Labour administration decided to press on with its programme for comprehensive education without seeking any greater legal powers than those given it in the 1944 Act.

It was, therefore, fortunate that a number of features of the educational situation muffled the clash between national and local government. In the first place, various authorities had already succeeded in going comprehensive, with lukewarm support from the Ministry, and the new schools were usually 'purpose-built' and thus showed the new system working in the way most attractive to other authorities. Secondly, it had already become clear that hard economics and practical efficiency,† rather than any abstract theory, required the setting-up of some form of comprehensive system in scattered rural areas. if children were to be able to attend a school

* [An account of one or two cases is given in Pedley, The Comprehensive School, Penguin Books, pp. 44–45—Ed.]
† [Pedley, *The Comprehensive School*, Penguin, 1966, p. 47.]

large enough to offer the whole range of modern educational resources. In the town the case was not so obvious; but this division had the advantage, from the political point of view, that urban councils tended to be Labour and rural councils Conservative. If the latter were in any case being forced to go comprehensive by the exigencies of the educational situation the possibility of political discord was immediately reduced. Thirdly, it may not be unduly partisan to suggest that as a general rule enthusiasm for comprehensive education tends to increase as one becomes more knowledgeable about educational issues. To put it at its lowest, education officers would be aware, as their members often were not, of the positive arguments in favour of comprehensive education, and in some cases one does not doubt that the dominant position of the council officials enabled them to press the results of current informed thinking upon the members.

GOVERNMENT BY CIRCULAR

Whether emboldened by reflections such as those above, or inspired by simple faith, the new government went into action with Department of Education Circular 10/65, which reviewed progress up to that date towards the introduction of comprehensive education, and 'requested' all local education authorities to submit to the Ministry, within one year of the publication of the circular, plans for the reorganization of secondary education in their areas along comprehensive lines.[5] There might be some doubt about the constitutional propriety of proceeding thus by ministerial fiat, without altering the, to say the least, ambiguous terms of the 1944 Act; the status of circular 10/65 was, however, made the more puzzling by the confused background of local–national relations against which it had to be set.

The circular expressed the hope that the growth towards comprehensive education would be encouraged by the 'clear statement of national policy' which it thought itself to contain,[6] but, as a commentator has pointed out, the circular seems to be a statement of national policy without the means to enforce it.*

[5] Circular 10/65, para. 43.
[6] ibid., para. 46.
* [J. A. G. Griffith, *Central Departments and Local Authorities*, Allen and Unwin, 1966, p. 511.]

If a local authority refused to submit plans in the form requested, or to submit plans at all, there does not seem any way for the Ministry to coerce them. Even the submission of plans and their approval by the Ministry has in itself no legal effect, though this preliminary administrative move would, of course, put the Ministry under some pressure when building programmes were submitted by local authorities to implement the approved plans.

The Ministry does, however, have some sanctions in reserve, though these are of an *ad hoc* and arbitrary nature, and were certainly not developed with the intention of giving Whitehall power to impose nation-wide reorganization of the sort envisaged in circular 10/65. If a local authority were to submit plans for building which contravened the comprehensive policy, no doubt loan sanction would be refused, and the authority told that it would only be allowed to spend on schools which complied with the terms of the circular. This lever, however, could be available for use only if the authority took the initiative and planned capital expansion, and even then the Ministry might hesitate to hold up one badly-needed project as a means of forcing the authority into line over general policy. The civil servants may however have reflected that, although this seems to give the local authorities the whip hand, they would in fact be likely to be forced into school building, not only by pressure from their own ratepayers, but also by changes in the scale of educational provision required of local authorities by the national government. For instance, a decision to raise the school-leaving age forces local authorities into finding places for the extra children that they are obliged to educate; but the decision is taken by the national government, and the threat of this impending expansion strikes an ominous note when it is referred to in paragraph 44 of the circular.

NATIONAL POLICY IN ACTION

Erratic though these relationships are, they did succeed in securing the government's first objective, in that by the autumn of 1967 159 out of 194 local education authorities had submitted schemes in response to the circular.[7] Nevertheless, various features of the intended reorganization were less than satisfactory, and whilst not all of these can be blamed on the

[7] *Times Educational Supplement*, 6 October 1967, p. 710.

relationship between central and local government, some can.

In the first place, the *ad hoc* growth of comprehensive schemes before 1965 meant that schools varied greatly in size and age-range in different parts of the country,[8] and this mixture of schemes was allowed to continue under the Ministry's arrangements for nation-wide comprehension. This was of course partly due to the need to use makeshift arrangements of existing premises on grounds of economy, but some of the Ministry's reluctance to challenge local arrangements on educational grounds must be attributed to the in any case delicate state of relations between Whitehall and the Town Hall, and the feeling that, under the terms of the 1944 Act, the local authorities were supposed to have some say about what was 'education suitable to the requirements of secondary pupils'.[9] The Ministry even showed reluctance to turn down local plans which incorporated features which authorities had been warned against on policy grounds. For instance, the circular stated that approval would not be likely to be forthcoming for 'middle schools', straddling the age-range between primary and secondary education,[10] but this did not prevent thirty-four authorities from submitting such schemes, of which at least eleven were approved in the two years after the publication of the circular.[11]

This division of responsibility between local and national government also enables Whitehall to be evasive about aspects of its policy that it does not want clearly to reveal, or has not clearly thought out. There can be no doubt that the existence of direct grant schools is inconsistent with the ideal of comprehensive education as the Labour Party conceived it; but, since local opposition was likely to focus most strongly around this point, and the Ministry did not appear in any case to have calculated the effect of the abolition of direct grant provision on the educational system as a whole, the circular confined itself to some delphic and, apparently, hostile references to the direct grant schools,* which seemed to

---

[8] The various systems are summarized in circular 10/65, para. 18.

[9] Above, n. 2.

[10] Circular 10/65, para. 22.

[11] *Times Educational Supplement*, above, n. 6.

* Circular 10/65, paragraph 44. A direct grant school is one which is independent of the state system, but which receives a grant from the Ministry of Education on condition that 25 per cent of its pupils are paid for by the local authority.

suggest that the local authorities were expected to make up their own minds on the subject, and take on their own heads the unpopularity of doing what the government apparently really wanted. The direct grant schools would have been a difficult problem in any case. None the less, the formal insistence of the present scheme of government on local autonomy enables Whitehall the more easily to procrastinate and confuse the public as to who has responsibility for policy-making, even if in the process the policy-makers become confused themselves.

THE VIRTUES OF LOCAL OPTION

As Dr Pedley says, the policy of the Labour government is open to criticism because 'while it countenances half a dozen possible schemes we are in danger of having, not a national system, but the kind of chaotic variation in different areas which the 1944 Act was intended to prevent'.* Some of this variation was forced on the government by the need to re-organize on the cheap; some of it, however, has been produced by a reluctance to take steps which might lead to the spelling out in too precise terms of the actual state of relations between Whitehall and the local education authorities. [. . . . .] The possibility of tension between Ministry and council over questions of general policy was not thought to need resolution in the 1944 Act because of the general atmosphere of agreement existing at that time about the shape of things to come. The use by the Ministry of government by circular and loan sanction, and the uneven pattern of progress that this has produced, does, however, raise the issue of whether educational questions of this sort are suitable for decision at local level.

The question of whether to go comprehensive or not, and of what sort of comprehensive system to adopt, is a matter of general principle which needs to be discussed in the light of informed opinion about size of schools, variety of provision, and children's aptitudes. It will not, therefore, come as a surprise to those who have followed the argument thus far to learn that, in our opinion, such issues are uniquely unsuited for decision by local government as it at present operates. The impossibility of submitting any issue of principle

* [Pedley, *The Comprehensive School*, Penguin, 1966, p. 46.]

to the local electorate in a meaningful way prevents any serious involvement in the question except on the part of those who have a special interest in the subject, which is often limited to the preservation of a particular institution. Moreover, when it comes to deciding the best form of re-organization, there seems little reason to think that councillors and their officers, with the experience of only one local area to draw on, are better qualified to make decisions than administrators at national level. The Labour Government thought it necessary to keep the activities of local education officers under close surveillance,[12] but if this control is necessary, it would seem only to make for confusion to encourage local initiatives in the first place.

It might of course be argued that there is some abstract merit in allowing each area to decide its own educational arrangements, however illogical an outcome this may produce. But what reasons can there be for Devon to be comprehensive and Plymouth not, or Glamorgan to have a single-tier system of comprehensive schools and Cardiff a two-tier system? Certainly, the needs of the children in adjoining areas, and the uses to which they will have to put their education, are not likely to be so radically different. If local government elections gave the opportunity to the people of an area to make a genuine informed decision for or against comprehensive schools, there would be something to be said for the present set-up on grounds of democratic principle, even if not on grounds of reason or efficiency. But local government elections do not give the electors the chance to make this choice and are not likely to do so under any of the schemes of local government reorganization currently under discussion.

These considerations make it the more alarming that 'democracy' was one of the main grounds advanced by the Conservative government in justification of its decision of June 1970 to withdraw circular 10/65 and rely instead for secondary reorganization on local enterprise, or lack thereof. National government may, of course, have many good reasons for not taking the lead in educational policy; it is hard to believe that the superiority, as an exercise in democracy, of local over national elections ought to be one of them.

[12] Circular 10/65, para. 44 (b).

The Citizen, the Council and the Courts

With the perhaps surprising degree of accord which has existed between national and local government about the introduction of comprehensive education, it has been necessary for the small but articulate groups who have been strongly opposed to the disappearance of the grammar schools to take action outside the political arena. Litigation on local government questions has usually been restricted to those fields where the citizens' financial and property interests are involved: principally, planning and compulsory purchase. Because educational issues are more abstract, and do not threaten anyone's pocket, they have not been thought worth the financial expenditure and trouble of going to law, especially since, as we shall see, the law's control here, as in many other areas of local government, is over procedure rather than policy. Nevertheless, the passions set loose by the amalgamation of grammar with secondary modern schools, added to the indecent speed and somewhat makeshift arrangements of many local authorities, put educational issues firmly in the foreground of controversy, and in the London Borough of Enfield led to litigation wherein the courts, whilst disclaiming any interest in the question of substance of whether the scheme proposed was educationally sound,[13] exercised their right to ensure that the procedure adopted by the council and by the Minister was that laid down by statute.[14]

THE EDUCATION ACT 1944
The legal framework within which educational organization

---

[13] 'We are not concerned in this court with the policy of the Minister or of the education authority. Nor have we to consider whether it is a good thing to change from a selective system of education to a comprehensive system. We have only to consider whether the requirements of the law have been fulfilled.' Lord Denning M.R. in *Bradbury* v. *Enfield London Borough Council* [1967] 1 W.L.R. 1311 at 1320C. 'At no time have the courts been concerned with the merits of this educational controversy ... the court is not concerned with the merits of what is proposed but solely with its legality.': Donaldson J. in *Lee* v. *Department of Education and Science* [1967] 66 L.G.R. 211 at 215.

[14] 'In cases of this kind, it is imperative that the procedure laid down in the relevant statutes should be properly observed. The provisions of the statutes in this respect are supposed to provide safeguards for Her Majesty's subjects. Public bodies and Ministers must be compelled to observe the law; and it is essential that bureaucracy should be kept in its place.': Danckwerts L. J. in *Bradbury* v. *Enfield L.B.C.* at p. 1325E.

has to work is that of the Education Act 1944. As we have already suggested, this Act was passed at a time when official and, indeed, any other, thought on educational matters was dominated by the belief that children could be segregated on grounds of ability at an early age, and that intelligence could be tested independently of any consideration of the children's class or home background.* These assumptions pointed clearly to the extension of the selective system of education from the age of eleven onwards, with egalitarianism demanding, not a change in this system, but only a guarantee that any working-class child who did succeed in passing the tests for grammar-school education should not be prevented from taking up the opportunity on financial grounds.

However, most importantly, although these views about the proper organization of secondary education inspired the 1944 Act, they were not written into it, in the sense that the Act does not in specific terms require the presence of selection or of any particular type of secondary school.[15] Had the ideal of selective education been incorporated into the Act, it would of course have proved impossible to extend comprehensive education without legislation on the subject and, although opinion progressed a good deal in this area in the twenty years after 1944, it is very doubtful whether either party would have wanted the public discussion and the need to adopt definitive positions that the legislative process demands. The extension of comprehensive education was thus able to proceed by the more covert methods of action by local authorities and informal pressure by the Ministry, and citizens who wished to go to law to oppose this policy were forced back on to the far from all-embracing rules for educational organization that the 1944 Act did provide.

PARENTAL CHOICE

At first sight, an opportunity for direct popular intervention might be thought to be provided by section 76 of the 1944 Act, which says that 'In the exercise and performance of all powers and duties conferred and imposed on them by this

---

[15] 'The Act nowhere provides for grammar school education, or secondary modern education as distinct from grammar.': Goff J. in *Wood* v. *Ealing London Borough Council* [1967] 1 Ch. 364 at 384.

* [For a brief summary see Pedley, *The Comprehensive School*, Penguin, 1966, pp. 37–44.]

Act, the Minister and the local education authorities shall have regard to the general principle that, so far as is compatible with the provision of efficient instruction and training and the avoidance of unreasonable public expenditure, pupils are to be educated in accordance with the wishes of their parents.' However, on analysis, this section proves to be yet another example of an Act of Parliament stating an ideal of administration in general, and vague, terms, without providing any means of ensuring that its principles are in fact put into practice. As Denning L. J. put it in *Watt* v. *Kesteven County Council*,[16] 'section 76 does not say that pupils must in all cases be educated in accordance with the wishes of their parents. It only lays down a general principle to which the county council must have regard. This leaves it open to the county council to have regard to other things as well, and also to make exceptions to the general principle if it thinks fit to do so.'

Not only the form of words adopted by Parliament but also considerations of administrative convenience have encouraged the courts to adopt this attitude, since it would clearly make for chaos if every parent could in fact insist on his child being educated in accordance with his wishes. Furthermore, the courts concluded that Parliament could hardly have intended parents as a whole to be consulted on the details of educational provision, since there is no reliable method of canvassing their opinion, which might in any case change erratically from year to year. This latter consideration weighed heavily with Goff J. in *Wood* v. *Ealing L.B.C.*,[17] where the plaintiffs claimed that the local authority had broken section 76 of the 1944 Act by introducing comprehensive education without sufficiently discovering parental opinion upon it. In answer to this contention, his Lordship said[18] that 'it would be wholly impractical if section 76 meant the wishes of parents in general, since they would almost certainly not agree in most, if not all, cases and would be, moreover, a constantly fluctuating body'. Nor could an individual parent appeal to section 76, as individual parents attempted to do in *Wood* v. *Ealing L.B.C.*, since 'in my judgement, education in section 76 must refer to the curriculum, and whether it includes any,

[16] [1955] 1 Q.B. 408 at 424.
[17] [1967] 1 Ch. 364.
[18] At p. 383G.

and if so what, religious instruction, and whether co-educa-
tional or single-sex, and matters of that sort, and not to the
size of the school or the conditions of entry'.[19]

Whether parental rights even in respect of these questions
would effectively survive the severe limitations placed on them
in *Watt* v. *Kesteven C.C.*[20] is perhaps open to doubt, even
though it is not in fact at all clear that the bare words of
section 76 justify the distinction which Goff J. here draws
between organization and curriculum. Nevertheless, the clear
implication of the *Wood* case was that the courts were not
going to take the political risks involved in intervening in a
controversial matter on the basis of a section drafted in the
non-committal terms of section 76.

CONSULTING THE PUBLIC

The restraint shown by the courts in the *Wood* case was not,
however, the end of the matter as far as judicial intervention
was concerned, since it was still possible for a local authority
to fall foul of the more detailed rules about public consultation laid down in the 1944 Act. In particular, section 13 of
that Act provides that 'Where a local education authority
intend to establish a new county school or to cease to maintain any county school or voluntary school they shall submit
proposals for that purpose to the Minister', and then give
public notice of the proposals in order to allow local government electors in the areas affected an opportunity to object
to the Minister.

It will be noted that the Act is phrased as if the initiative
for reorganization of schools comes exclusively from the local
authority, the Minister acting only as some sort of independent referee who becomes involved only when the local
authority makes a formal submission of proposals. However,
with the sort of overall reorganization that the introduction
of comprehensive education requires, and which the drafters
of section 13 doubtless did not envisage, as we have discussed above, things do not work like this in practice. In the
case which we are about to consider, not only were the
Enfield Council working under the impetus of circular
10/65,[21] but also correspondence took place between the

[19] At p. 384G.
[20] Above, n. 15.
[21] Above, n. 4.

local authority and the Ministry before the formal submission of Enfield's own comprehensive scheme, the Minister indicating that earlier plans were not acceptable, and suggesting various desirable revisions. These revisions having been duly made, the Minister was able to say, within a week of receiving the proposals, that 'they would, in principle, form an acceptable element in the authority's general scheme of reorganization'.[22] and although he was careful in the same letter to refer to his duty to consider objections made to the proposals under section 13 of the 1944 Act, potential objectors might have been forgiven for thinking, in view of the previous transactions between Ministry and local authority, that such consideration was likely to be of a formal nature only.

In this case, however, the Ministry went further, and advised the council that, in its opinion, no public notice was required under section 13 in the case of eight of the schools involved in the reorganization. Amongst these schools were Enfield Grammar School and Chace Secondary Modern School, which it was proposed to combine into one comprehensive school, using the Grammar School premises for boys from fourteen to eighteen and the Secondary Modern premises for boys from eleven to fourteen. Similar proposals were made for other groups of schools, with the additional change that in one case a previously all-girl school should be used for the accommodation of part of a mixed comprehensive.

Contrary to the view of the Ministry's lawyers, however, the Court of Appeal held,[23] when various ratepayers of Enfield sought an injunction to prohibit the local authority from implementing the scheme, that changes in the age and sex of pupils attending a school, as opposed to changes in its curriculum or method of entry, were sufficiently fundamental to constitute 'ceasing to maintain' the old school, and thus needed to be publicly advertised, and an opportunity given for complaint to the Minister under section 13. Since the authority had failed to carry out the procedure there laid down, its acts were *ultra vires* and would therefore be forbidden by the court.

However inconvenient for the authority in its immediate consequences, the defect seized on by the courts, being merely

[22] See [1967] 1 W.L.R. at p. 1319H.
[23] *Bradbury* v. *Enfield London Borough Council* [1967] 1 W.L.R. 1311.

procedural in nature, could be rectified by submitting the proposals with regard to the eight schools to the same process of advertisement as had already been adopted in the case of the remainder of the schools in the scheme. In the *Bradbury* case, however, the ratepayers attempted to go further than this, and to involve the courts in questions affecting the substance of the reorganization scheme, as well as the methods adopted to put it into action. Sub-sections (6) and (7) of section 13 of the 1944 Act, after dealing with the question discussed above, went on to say that

> After proposals for the establishment of a new school have been approved by the Minister ... the authority ... shall submit to him in such form and in such manner as he may direct specifications and plans of the school premises, and the Minister, on being satisfied that the school premises will conform to the prescribed standards, may approve the specifications and plans.... When the proposals, specifications and plans for a new school have been approved by the Minister ... it shall be the duty of the authority ... to give effect to the proposals in accordance with the specifications and plans so approved.

In the Enfield case all the schools had been established without the submission of specifications and plans to the Minister, and it was further alleged that in many respects the new establishments fell short of the prescribed standards. The Court of Appeal, however, thought that, although the intention of the 1944 Act had been that the local authority should not establish a new school in advance of submitting plans to the Ministry, there was no legal remedy available if such plans were not submitted.

The judges advanced various reasons for this conclusion: (a) that section 13 (6) and (7) of the 1944 Act spoke only of the local authority having a *duty* to give effect to the specifications, once those specifications had been approved, but did not in terms say that the authority had no *power* to establish a new school before the submission to specifications;[24] (b) that section 13 (5) of the 1944 Act, by forbidding the local education authority to do anything for which proposals were required to be submitted to the Minister until such proposals had been approved by him, by implication excluded the

[24] Per Diplock L.J. at p. 1334D.

courts from adjudicating once that approval had been given, as it had in the case of Enfield,[25] and (c) that the proper remedy was not to go to law, but to complain to the Minister under section 99[26] of the 1944 Act.[27]

None of these reasons for the court's refusal to intervene seem on analysis, to make the plaintiff's case on the 'specification' point any different from the failure to give notice on which they had succeeded in the first half of the action. If the court had been as anxious in the case of the specifications as they were in the case of the notices, or lack thereof, to find the local authority's actions illegal, it would have been easy to hold that section 13 (6) and (7), in addition to imposing a duty on the authority to maintain the school once the proposals had been approved (ground a, above), also laid down a procedural code which, similarly to section 13 (3),[28] was a necessary preliminary to any valid action by that authority. It must likewise be an open question whether the specific prohibition of one course of action makes any other course of action not so mentioned *ipso facto* valid (ground b, above), and the argument based on section 99 of the 1944 Act (ground c, above) applies equally to the notice or to the specifications.

The suspicion must remain, therefore, that despite the aggressive posture adopted by the court[29] their Lordships were reluctant to become involved in questions which touched, however indirectly, upon the merits of a difficult matter of political policy, even though there might arguably seem to be statutory justification for them to intervene. Safer by far to confine oneself to matters of pure procedure, which could be used to give pause to administrators, whilst at the same time enabling them to correct the actions complained of without undue inconvenience.

BREAKING THE SCHOOL RULES
Nevertheless, the requirements imposed by the Court of

[25] Per Lord Denning M.R. at p. 1324D, and Diplock L. J. at p. 1335C.
[26] 'If the Minister is satisfied ... that any local education authority ... have failed to discharge any duty imposed on them ... the Minister may make an order ... giving such directions for the purpose of enforcing the execution thereof as appear to the Minister to be expedient.'
[27] Per Diplock L. J. at p. 1335H, and (*semble*) Lord Denning M.R. at p. 1324C.
[28] Above, p. 202.
[29] Above, n. 13.

Appeal presented an immediate practical problem. The court delivered judgement in *Bradbury* v. *Enfield L.B.C.* on 23 August 1967; the term had been due to start at the new comprehensive schools on 7 September 1967. It was clear that the original scheme could not be carried out as planned, since the statutory consent of the Minister, following the issue of the public notices required by the Act, could not be expected to be forthcoming until late in the term. It will be recalled that under the reorganization scheme Enfield Grammar School was to become a school for fourteen- to eighteen-year-olds, with Chace Secondary Modern School as a school with an unselective entry for eleven- to fourteen-year-olds. As an interim measure, therefore, until the full scheme could be implemented, the Council decided that the fourth-year pupils should stay at the Chace school, rather than transfer to the Grammar School as the original scheme required, and that admission of first-year pupils should take place at both the Grammar School and at the Chace School, instead of only at the latter. The first year at each school would, therefore, consist of a three-form entry, not on any 'selective' basis, but drawn from children who would have formed the first year of the new comprehensive school, the curriculum at both the Chace School and Enfield Grammar to be as far as possible that which would have been followed in the first year of the intended comprehensive school, pending the establishment of the latter institution.

Enfield Grammar School was thus still in existence, and still governed by the Instrument of Government made for it by the Minister under section 17 (2) of the 1944 Act. By section 11 of this Instrument, 'the arrangements for the admission of pupils to the school shall be such as may be agreed between the governors of the school and the local education authority and shall take into account the wishes of parents and any school records and other information that may be available ... provided that the local education authority shall determine which candidates are qualified for admission by reason of their having attained a sufficient educational standard'. In an attempt to comply with the requirements of this article, the governors of the Grammar School were prevailed upon to agree to the council's interim measures, and the council for its part resolved that any pupil who had completed a course of primary-school education had *ipso facto* attained a sufficient standard for admission to the Grammar School. One of the governors, however, sought an injunction to prevent the council from implementing the interim scheme, on the grounds that the articles of government, apart from these points, required admission to Enfield Grammar School to be on a selective basis, which it would clearly not be if the new first year were taken arbitrarily from a 'pool' of candidates for the first year of a comprehensive school.

Donaldson J. had little difficulty in granting the injunction,[30] since the requirement in the articles that admission should be on the basis of the pupils' school records and other information only made sense on the assumption that admission was selective and, until this requirement was deleted from the articles, 'it is quite impossible for the local education authority and the governing body to agree upon a non-selective scheme of entry'.[31] In making the school non-selective the governors would be acting contrary to their own constitution, and this the courts would forbid them to do.

His Lordship also made observations on two other, more general, matters. Firstly, he held that the authority were in breach of section 76 of the 1944 Act (see above) in not asking parents to express a preference between Enfield Grammar School and the Chace School before allocating their children between the two. How far this point could have been relied on in the absence of other grounds for holding the authority's acts illegal is unclear. Certainly, Donaldson J. seemed to think, and this view would be in accordance with the remarks of Denning L. J. in *Watt* v. *Kesteven C.C.*,[32] that the authority's obligations under section 76 would be discharged by asking the parents which school they wanted their children to attend, without necessarily acting on the preferences so expressed. Secondly, it was held that, in this case, section 99 of the 1944 Act[33] did not exclude the jurisdiction of the courts, since this was a case of positive wrongdoing by the authority, as opposed to a failure to perform a duty.[34] This latter point is in fact somewhat tenuous, since most administrative actions could, if needs be, be analysed as either the

---

[30] *Lee* v. *Enfield London Borough Council* [1967] 66 L.G.R. 195.
[31] ibid., at p. 207.
[32] Above, n. 15.
[33] Above, n. 25.
[34] [1967] 66 L.G.R. at p. 210.

doing of one thing or a failure to do another thing; in the
Bradbury case, for instance, the failure to submit the specifications was analysed as just that, but it could as easily have
been said to be the wrongful establishment of a new school.
Psychologically, however, the difference is an important one.
In *Lee* v. *Enfield L.B.C.* the local authority had broken a
clear and positive rule, and this the court would not allow.

REASONABLE ADMINISTRATION

The administrators' only answer to this decision was to change
the rules, and the Minister of Education was accordingly
asked on 14 September 1967 (the day after judgement was
delivered in *Lee* v. *Enfield L.B.C.*) to exercise his powers
under section 17 of the 1944 Act of varying the instrument
of government by cutting out the provisions about a selective
intake. Acting with unusual dispatch, the Minister announced
on the same day his intention of complying with this request.
Unfortunately, however, for the speed with which both council and Ministry now wished to move, section 17 (5) of the
1944 Act required the Minister, before altering the instrument of government of a school, to 'afford to the local education authority and to any other persons appearing to him to
be concerned with the management or government of the
school an opportunity of making representations to him'. The
Minister sought to discharge this obligation by asking the
governors of the Grammar School, in a letter written on
14 September 1967, to make representations to him by twelve
noon on 18 September, the intervening period between these
dates including a weekend when, as the Minister helpfully
pointed out, his office was shut.

The objectors, on receipt of this missive, again sought the
help of the law, to give them more time to organize their representations, and they were again successful.[35] The issue facing
Donaldson J. in this case was less clear-cut than in *Lee* v.
Enfield L.B.C., since the Ministry had gone through the
motions of doing what the section required, and intervention
by the courts might have been looked on as a claim to a right
to criticize the administrative arrangements made by civil
servants, as opposed to simply keeping them within the
boundaries of their legal powers. His Lordship was, however,

[35] *Lee* v. *Department of Education and Science* [1967] 66 L.G.R. 211.

saved from difficulties of this sort by the concession made by counsel for the Ministry that, although not specifically so stated, the duty imposed on the Minister by section 17 (5) of the 1944 Act required him 'to give a real and not an illusory opportunity to make representations'.[36] On the basis of this formula the judge held that 'the time so far allowed by the Secretary of State is wholly unreasonable, in the circumstances of this case, and amounts to a denial to the persons named in section 17 (5) of the rights conferred upon them by that sub-section'.[37] The judge accordingly extended the time allowed by four weeks.

If this concession had not been made, the judge would no doubt have still been able to find that Parliament must have intended in section 17 (5) that at least a period of time greater than that allowed in the Enfield case should be given for representations to be made. The courts have been extremely reluctant to scrutinize administrative action on grounds of reasonableness alone,[38] but where, as here, a specific duty is laid on administrators, the courts will not be slow to make sure that, in terms of procedure at least, those administrators act in the way that Parliament is assumed to have wished.

Comprehensive education thus had to be introduced in Enfield according to the procedure laid down in the 1944 Act, and had to wait until the public notice required in the *Bradbury* case had been given, and objections considered by the Minister. The council was required, if the children were to go to school at all during the winter term, 1967, to admit them to grammar and secondary modern schools according to the old selective methods, rather than adopt the stop-gap expedients, pending a full reorganization, which had been declared unlawful in the *Lee* cases.

THE LESSONS OF ENFIELD

The Enfield litigation was welcomed in some quarters as a great victory for the citizen against the bureaucrat and, indeed, against the politician as well, but in fact little of substance was achieved by it. The statutory framework of the education service nowhere gives any real right of control to

[36] 66 L.G.R. at p. 219.
[37] ibid., at p. 221.
[38] *A.P. Provincial Picture Houses* v. *Wednesbury Corporation* [1948] 1 K.B. 223; see ch. 5, section on delegation.

the parents, or to the ordinary citizen, and the courts have reinforced the wide discretion which this confers on the administrators by their refusal, even where the normal principles of statutory construction might arguably seem to allow it, to become involved in any question of policy or the merits of what is being proposed (see the section on consulting the public, above). Even the apparent safeguard of an independent adjudication by the Minister on detailed proposals initiated by the local authority, which the 1944 Act seems to envisage,[39] loses its meaning in a world where the Minister requires a detailed statement of the local authority's programme to be discussed with his officials before being formally submitted to him,[40] and where widespread change is taking place under Ministerial guidance and, in some cases, pressure.

We have already discussed the merits of the division of responsibility between local and national government that the 1944 Act embodies, and the suitability of this system for carrying through the national government's educational plans. This division of function was, however, only one part of the ethos of the 1944 Act, which pre-supposes that the *general* pattern of school provision would not undergo radical change in the future, and that therefore rules about consulting the public over alterations in the number and nature of schools could safely be limited to situations where individual schools were closed and others opened, rather than allowing for public discussion of the whole pattern of secondary education. It was indeed the difference between the world envisaged by the 1944 Act and the facts of educational controversy in 1967 that gave the Enfield litigation much of its air of unreality. The parents and others who opposed the council's plans must have known that they had no chance of ultimate success when local authority and Ministry had agreed on a policy, the 1944 Act giving them no right to interfere with policy-making as such. Therefore, in opposing the overall policy of the Ministry, they had to have recourse to methods designed to give some public voice to those interested in the fate of one particular school.

The Enfield victories therefore lacked any permanent effect, not only because of the courts' concentration on procedural

[39] Above, n. 3.
[40] Circular 10/65, para. 45.

questions, but also because of the failure of the 1944 Act to give the citizen any control, apart from a procedural one, over educational policy-making in general. It so happened, in the case of Enfield, that statutory provisions designed for another purpose were (quite properly) construed as impeding the local authority's pursuit of its policy; but the fact that the courts' intervention had to be of this fortuitous and short-term nature reveals the lack of force of legal sanctions, once it has been decided that questions of policy must be left to the policy-makers.

This is not to say, however, that the Enfield battle was fought entirely in vain. Quite apart from the fact that it is always admirable for citizens to stand up for their legal rights, the light which was thrown, however obliquely, on the process of administration revealed some interesting facts. In the first place, there is little doubt that the Enfield scheme, like some others, was put through with undue haste, and without pre-paring the citizens for the very fundamental change in edu-cational provision that it entailed. The Ministry were at least warned against maladministration of this sort, exposed as it was to the publicity that litigation brings in its train. Secondly, it became clear during the hearings that the interim scheme fixed up after the Court of Appeal, by its judgement in *Bradbury* v. *Enfield L.B.C.*, had postponed the full com-prehensivization of the schools had been adopted by the Council despite the fact that their chief education officer considered it to be open to grave objection as anything but a very temporary measure.[41] This was clearly something that the public had a right to know, and of which they would have remained in ignorance had the normal local government machinery operated untouched by outside scrutiny.

It may also be counted for merit on the part of the Ministry that its response to the Enfield cases was to promote the Education Act 1968, which provides that the requirements for public notice under section 13 of the 1944 Act should apply to 'any significant change in the character' of a school,[42] such changes to include not only alterations in the age- and sex-range of the school, but also 'the making or alteration of

[41] *Lee* v. *Department of Education and Science* [1967] 66 L.G.R. 211 at pp. 220-21.
[42] Education Act 1968, s. 1 (2) (a).

arrangements for the admission of pupils by reference to ability or aptitude.[43] True it is that any question of whether a particular change is 'significant' is to be determined by the Minister and not by the courts;[44] but the important point is that the Government has now added positive statutory instructions to local authorities to its previous informal exhortations[45] about good administration requiring that the public should be kept informed.

Statutory consultation in the education field was carried further even than this in the 1970 Education Bill, which required local authorities to consult teachers, and inform parents of their plans, at an early stage of any comprehensive scheme. The Bill also required authorities to submit plans for comprehensive education where they had not already done so, thus appearing to give the confirmation of legality to the previous informal urgings to co-operate in national policy. No additional sanctions are, however, provided for use against recalcitrant authorities, and it is therefore difficult to see how differences of policy between local and national government were in fact going to be resolved. Both the importance of public participation, and the status of local government in educational planning, are therefore left unclear, pending what may or may not prove to be a rational re-organization of the whole method of educational policy-making and administration.

For the moment, however, the imposition of statutory requirements about consultation, however dubious their exact status may be, does suggest a certain reserve, here as with planning questions, about the degree to which normal local government processes are apt to produce the sort of public knowledge of important proposals that both parties now wish to encourage. We have already ventured to doubt whether policy-making at the local level is an ideal method of re-organizing the educational service; the obscure way in which much local government business is conducted creates similar doubts about whether public participation is best achieved by placing responsibility for the formulation and execution of detailed proposals in the hands of local education authorities.

[43] ibid., s. 1 (2).
[44] ibid., sch. 1, para. 3.
[45] Circular 10/65, para. 41.

6

R. SARAN

Decision-Making by a Local Education Authority*†

The majority of secondary school day pupils attend maintained schools, but a small minority are sent as LEA-financed
pupils to fee-paying schools. Townley LEA exercised its statutory powers to buy grammar school places in the private
sector[1] for approximately 2 per cent of its eleven-year-olds.
LEA dependence on the private sector was much more important than this small proportion of pupils might suggest.
For the individual schools, the LEA's small proportion often
represented quite a large one. Furthermore, broad issues of
secondary schools policy in the maintained sector were affected by the existence of the non-maintained schools and their
use by the local education authority. [. . . .]

* [From *Policy Making in Secondary Education: A Case Study*, Oxford
University Press, 1973.]

† [There are few accounts of how decisions are made by local education authorities. This study by Dr Rene Saran forms a part of chapter
5 of her recent book on *Policy Making in Secondary Education: A Case
Study*. The extract covers one decision taken in 1963 by a large LEA to
reduce the number of secondary school places purchased by them in direct
grant and independent schools. As much of the source material used by
Dr Saran was confidential, the area she studied was given the fictitious name
'Townley'. Townley is a large urbanized county in the south of England,
with a two-tier local government structure. The LEA had the usual education committee and sub-committees and there were also divisional executives, and all these bodies were involved in the decision-making process.
As education authority, Townley Council was responsible under the 1944
Education Act to provide school places—Ed.]

[1] The direct grant schools are here treated as part of the private
—and fee-paying—sector, despite the fact that three quarters of their
current income comes from public funds. These schools are sometimes considered an integral part of the state sector, but the evidence here clearly
shows that LEA placements in direct grant are in many respects similar
to those made in independent schools. The Public Schools Commission (in
its second report published in 1970) also held that it would be 'inconsistent to treat the two categories of school differently'.

This detailed study covers the period 1960–63, and traces the decision taken by Townley Council in 1963 to reduce the number of secondary places purchased by the LEA in direct grant and independent schools. During the 1950s the authority increased its provision of places in maintained grammar schools in order to meet the increased demands arising from the population bulge, and towards the end of the period found that it had sufficient grammar schools places in the maintained sector. Accordingly it sought to reduce the number of places taken up in the private sector.

Over the years some 500 to 560 fee-paying places had been taken up for eleven-year-olds annually. Since it can be safely assumed that such pupils would normally remain at their new school for at least five years, Townley purchased a total of $2\frac{1}{2}$ to 3 thousand places at fee-paying grammar schools. In the early 1960s, the total annual cost of these places was in the region of a quarter of a million pounds. In 1963, after nearly three years of discussion and consultation, the number of children placed in fee-paying schools was cut from 556 (1962 quota) to 496 (1964 quota). On the face of it this was a minor matter, affecting a mere sixty potential applicants for fee-paying school places per year. But it raised important issues and provides a good opportunity for examining the manner in which such decisions are made. The interaction between the LEA, the Ministry and the affected interests is important, and there were significant differences of approach within the LEA between officers and elected representatives over the application of the complex legal provisions[2] governing the authority's policy.

Under the 1944 Education Act, an LEA has the duty to secure that there shall be sufficient schools in its area. The schools available are not deemed to be sufficient

> unless they are sufficient in number, character and equipment to afford for all pupils opportunities for education offering such variety of instruction and training as may be desirable in view of their different ages, abilities, and aptitudes, and of different periods for which they may be expected to remain at school, including practical instruction and training appropriate to their respective needs.[3]

[2] See *Policy Making in Secondary Education: A Case Study*, Chapter 2(b) sections (ii) and (iii) for a summary of the most important legal provisions.

[3] Education Act, 1944, Section 8(1)(b).

An LEA with sufficient schools of its own seems to have no need to buy fee-paying places in either direct grant or independent schools. Since the cost of doing this is invariably higher per child—certainly if independent schools are used—than a place in a maintained school, it is of interest to know why LEAs spend public money in this way. One reason is shortage of school places in the maintained sector; the authority's desire to extend parental choice of school is another. The fact that fee-paying places formed part of the *grammar* school provision of the LEA is crucial in examining these two criteria.

To take parental choice first, only children eligible for grammar school had the chance of securing a fee-paying place. Almost a third of the parents whose children passed the LEA's eleven-plus gave a fee-paying school as their first preference, followed by two maintained grammar schools. This illustrates the prestige many parents attached to a school place outside the state sector and their appreciation of such an extension of parental choice. Actual admissions to fee-paying schools were decided not by the LEA, but by the heads of particular schools, who received from the authority —before maintained grammar school placements were made —the names of all children who had passed the eleven-plus and whose parents had listed the school as their first preference. The fee-paying school heads thus had the first pick of the brightest children over a wide catchment area.

As regards the second criterion, a definition of 'shortage' in relation to grammar school places was not arrived at until the early 1950s. Pre-war, part of Townley's provision for grammar school children had been in direct grant and independent schools, so the authority could ill-afford to lose these places immediately after the war. Indeed, in 1945 the Education Committee empowered its Chairman and Vice-Chairman to negotiate with the governors of certain direct grant schools the maximum quota of places under the new direct grant schools regulations.[4] For these places, as explained earlier, the LEA paid full fees.

[4] Under these regulations, 25 per cent of the previous year's intake must be given *free* places—full remission of fees to be financed by the LEA, by an endowed foundation or by the governors. Pupils qualify for *free* places only if they have attended a grant-aided primary school for at least two years. As preparatory departments of direct grant schools are not eligible for grant-aid, pupils in them cannot be considered for *free*

Until 1952 the Education Committee also paid full fees for all its pupils placed in independent schools. In that year, however, due to clarification of the statutory position in a Ministry of Education manual of guidance,[5] a distinction was drawn between *free* and *assisted* places at independent schools, parents contributing to fees on an income scale for the latter. The manual defined more closely the powers of LEAs to pay fees for pupils at independent schools. It pointed out that parental choice under Section 76[6] of the 1944 Act was limited by the requirement to avoid unreasonable public expenditure, and stressed that, by and large, school places in the maintained sector and in accessible direct grant schools should suffice to give effect to parents' wishes. Only when there were 'deficiencies of an *educational* character'[7] were LEA *free* places at independent schools justified. Later, this clarification was embodied in the 1953 Education Act, which contained the word 'shortage'. An LEA could pay full fees at independent schools only when '... the authority are satisfied that by reason of shortage of places in schools maintained by them and ... by another LEA'[8] was it necessary to educate the pupil at an independent school.

The manual also dealt with *assisted* places at independent schools. These could be made available to widen parental choice of school[9] by the exercise of powers under Section 81 of the 1944 Education Act, even when the provision of free places was precluded. But under this Section, which covered cases of hardship, the authority could do no more than assist

places unless they have received at least two years of their primary education in a maintained school.

If the LEA desires places beyond the quota of free places, the governors of the school have to offer a maximum of another 25 per cent as *reserved* places, or more, if the authority and governors agree. *Reserved* places are open to pupils irrespective of the school previously attended. The remaining *residuary* places in a direct grant school are filled by the governors from among applicants whose parents are prepared to pay fees. Parents may apply for remission of fees on an income scale. The Department of Education and Science reimburses the school with the difference between the approved fees and the amount actually paid by parents.

[5] Manual of guidance, Schools No. 1. *Choice of Schools*, HMSO 1950. Reprinted, with minor amendments in 1960, this manual still represents DES policy.

[6] Section 76 is quoted on pp. 108–9.

[7] Manual of guidance, para. 16.

[8] 1953 Education (Miscellaneous Provisions) Act, Section 6, (2)(a)(ii).

[9] Manual of guidance, para. 18.

parents to meet fees at an independent school.

Without a definition of 'shortage', it was now impossible for the LEA to determine how many free and assisted places at independent schools should be offered. How, then, was 'shortage' of grammar school places in the maintained sector to be defined? This question received attention after the manual of guidance had appeared.[10] The CEO advised the Education Committee on future policy. If the Committee held that too high a proportion of Townley children were placed in grammar schools, it would have to conclude that no 'shortage' of places existed. A cut of a mere one per cent in the proportion was enough to eliminate all the LEA-financed independent school places.

Clearly it was no easy matter to judge what was the right proportion of children to receive a grammar school education. Opinion among officers and councillors in Townley had always been that the general intellectual quality of their children was high by national standards and that it was therefore reasonable that the provision of grammar school places should be above the national average. Thus 25 per cent, as compared with a national average of 20 per cent, was accepted as approximately the right proportion, despite the fact that some children at grammar schools failed to complete the course or to pass the school certificate examination.

Within this broad framework of 25 per cent, the Education Committee accepted in 1951 that 'shortage' for any particular area in Townley be assessed on the basis of the number of children who reached the qualifying mark in the eleven-plus examination, plus one-third for marginal candidates. This number was set against the number of grammar school places —including LEA-supported places at fee-paying schools— actually at the disposal of any of the five sub-areas into which Townley was divided. On this basis, as from 1952, children in two sub-areas were debarred from securing *free* places at independent schools because there was in those zones a 'surplus' of grammar school places. A divisional executive in one of the sub-areas immediately protested. Parents were, however, able to apply for the *assisted* places, awarded for the first time that year. The total number of places offered was left unchanged, but only one-third were now free, two-

---

[10] See *Policy Making in Secondary Education*, chapter 3(c)(i).

thirds assisted. Introduction of an income scale for the assisted places resulted in a decline of parental demand. A graph on page 127 shows the sharp reduction in places actually taken up.

During the policy review of 1950–51 which led to this drop, neither the schools nor parents were consulted by the Education Committee. The affected independent schools soon made their view felt. Year after year approaches were made to the CEO, offering the Committee additional places, preferably free ones. By 1958 total LEA recruitment to independent schools had risen to the former level, and over two-thirds of the places were free, under one-third assisted. Within six years the Committee had virtually reversed the decision governing the 1952 LEA entry to independent schools. The fact that the post-war population bulge was moving into the secondary schools during these years gave support to the argument that 'shortage' of grammar school places in the maintained sector existed and that therefore more places (particularly free ones) were justified.

Ten years later, between 1960–63, both direct grant and independent school places financed by the LEA came under scrutiny. It is the decision made at this time which will now be examined. The actual number of fee-paying schools concerned in the early 1960s was twenty-five. Six were direct grant, nineteen were independent schools. But fifteen schools between them took 90 per cent of LEA-placed pupils: these fifteen were the schools where the cuts would in the main be felt. The remaining ten schools each had very small numbers of Townley LEA admissions.

By the late 1950s, the LEA's school building programme had increased the number of grammar school places in the maintained sector at the very time when, after the year of peak entry in 1958, numbers transferred from primary to secondary schools were declining. Maintained grammar school places were being filled by less able pupils than hitherto. The expense of buying LEA places in fee-paying schools thus became an important consideration.

In this new situation Townley's LEA officers first tried to curtail fee-paying placements by administrative measures. The difficulties they encountered increased when specific proposals were placed before the Education Committee. The officers suggested that LEA places at direct grant schools and

Fig. 6.1

SECONDARY SCHOOL TRANSFERS TOWNLEY LEA
1950–1964

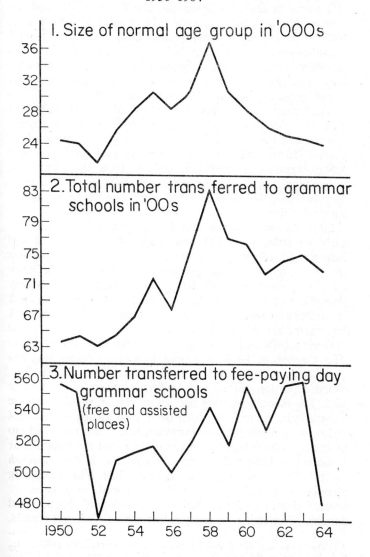

at non-denominational independent schools should be cut by 50 per cent. The total at Roman Catholic independent schools was to remain the same as there was a shortage of RC places in maintained schools. But for both RC and the remaining independent schools there was also to be a shift back from *free* to *assisted* places. During discussions and consultations, pressures were brought to bear to minimize the proposed cuts, and eventually places were cut by 15 per cent only. The shift from free to assisted places was also minimized, especially for the RC independent schools.

The results of the decision is shown in the graph on page 127 in relation to total numbers transferred to grammar schools and the side of the normal age group, covering the years 1950–64. Whereas the age group and total grammar school transfers reached their peak in 1958, the number of pupils placed in fee-paying schools reached its all-time peak only in 1963, the 1958–63 trend continuing to be in an upward direction.

So much for the actual decision. How was it reached? As early as 1958, the CEO had drawn the attention of the Schools sub-committee to the need to re-examine supplementation of maintained grammar school places: the peak entry of secondary pupils had passed into the schools that year. He suggested that the list of additional places should be drastically revised and that all additional places should be *assisted* rather than *free*.

During 1960 and 1961 the issue remained at officer level. The number of LEA-sponsored fee-paying places was reviewed at officers' meetings held regularly for all the divisional education officers and leading members of the CEO's staff. The officer's meeting had set up certain small panels or sub-committees, one of which dealt with all aspects of secondary school transfers. In the summer of 1960, the panel on secondary school transfers made it clear that the question of reduction in independent school places should be discussed by the officers' meeting as soon as possible. The panel had already decided that, if possible, the form[11] completed by parents should in future include a warning of the possible dangers of selecting an independent school. It is not certain

---

[11] This form was distributed by the LEA to parents with children in their last year at the primary school. On this form parents stated their preference for three modern and three grammar schools.

what 'dangers' were meant—possibly the fact that if parents were offered an assisted place at an independent school, they would be liable to contribute to fees, and to pay travelling expenses. The existing form actually gave ample warning about this. At a subsequent panel meeting it was explained by a senior officer that the inclusion or deletion of individual schools from the form was an administrative matter. Presumably the officer had in mind that the names of certain schools might simply be omitted from the form, thus reducing parental options for them. Reductions might initially be made in independent rather than direct grant schools, since costs per place were higher than in the LEA's own maintained schools.[12] After much discussion the panel agreed that when the lay-out of the form was reviewed in the following year, availability of independent and direct grant school places should be played down. Evidently the whole topic was a delicate one even among officers; only 'guarded reference' was to be made to the panel's discussion in any report to the full officers' meeting.

In April 1961 a much more detailed case was argued before all the education officers by one of their number. Discussion among officers in one of the five sub-areas had preceded this. Extra grammar school places had become available through the building programme, and through two previously independent RC grammar schools becoming maintained voluntary aided schools. Classes in the sub-area could now be reduced from thirty-three or thirty-four to the prescribed thirty. The time had come to dispense with places in direct grant and independent grammar schools. If these or similar measures were not adopted, undesirable consequences would ensue. First, pupils unlikely to benefit from a grammar school course as at present envisaged would be admitted to such schools, resulting in lower standards. Secondly, the growth of varied and extended courses in secondary modern schools would be checked. These had been developed to meet the needs of pupils of good but not outstanding ability,

---

[12] Comparison of costs per place in direct grant and maintained grammar schools is discussed in the second report of the Public Schools Commission, Vol. II, Appendix 7, pp. 241–242. It is there argued that on average LEAs are probably slightly worse off per pupil if they use direct grant places rather than educate the child in a maintained grammar school. At any rate LEAs do not gain in financial terms by sending pupils to direct grant schools, as is sometimes suggested.

or with more diverse aptitudes, and such pupils would no longer be in the secondary modern schools. Indeed, the development of seven-year courses in modern schools might be endangered.

In December 1961, the CEO informed his education officers of the decline in numbers of eleven-year-old children, the number of pupils placed in 'external'[13] grammar schools, how many were taken by individual schools and in which area of Townley the children resided. The authority's obligations under Section 6 of the 1953 Act and under Section 81 of the 1944 Act were also outlined. The CEO concluded that:

(i) Townley ratepayers valued opportunities afforded by free and assisted places for able pupils at a wide range of schools;
(ii) Cancellation or drastic cuts might have serious or even catastrophic effects on many fee-paying schools whose recruitment was based on a large Townley contingent;
(iii) The schools would have to accustom themselves to variations in admission as 1958 conditions (the year of the bulge) were likely to recur, necessitating supplementation of maintained places.

The officers agreed that—despite the difficulties—some restriction of present quotas of places should be accepted. They were asked to submit to the GEO their individual views.

At least seven did so early in 1962. One strongly favoured a large cut in places because there were vacancies at maintained grammar schools; another wanted the authority to take only free, but not reserved places at direct grant schools and to cut assisted ones at independent schools; officers from two other areas pointed to their continued need for additional places because the size of classes exceeded the prescribed number, or because it was still not possible to place all qualified children in maintained grammar schools. One officer thought opposition in his own area would be considerable if places eagerly sought by parents were severely curtailed. It became apparent later than 17 per cent of his area's grammar school children were placed in fee-paying and out-county schools, at a time when the maintained grammar schools in

[13] All schools not maintained by Townley, i.e. fee-paying schools and 'out-county' places at schools maintained by other LEAs.

the area had acute pupil recruitment difficulties.

So far only the officers had taken part in the discussions. Elected members became involved between February 1962 and March 1963. There were five meetings of the Schools sub-committee, one of a three-member *ad hoc* sub-committee, two of the Education Committee and one of Townley Council, at which reduction of LEA fee-paying places was on the agenda. In between there were consultations between the CEO on the one hand and the Council's Treasurer, the Chairman of the Education Committee, the schools, the RC authorities and the Ministry of Education on the other. It is not possible to describe in full the views expressed at every stage, and

Table 6.1 QUOTA OF LEA PLACES IN DIRECT GRANT AND INDEPENDENT SCHOOLS

(*Cuts Proposed in April* 1962 *and Cuts finally accepted in* 1963)

	Existing Quota	CEO's Suggested Cuts as put before Sub-Committee of three April 1962		Modified Cuts accepted by Council February 1963
	1962	1963	1964	1964
Free Places				
Direct Grant	265	188	122	225
Independent:				
Non-Denominational	85	44	23	55
Roman Catholic	79	47	21	63
Total Free	429	279	166	343
Assisted Places				
Independent:				
Non-Denominational	48	53	47	58
Roman Catholic	79	111	137	95
Total Assisted	127	164	184	153
Grand Total	556	443	350	496
Per cent Cut on 1962 *Quota*		%	%	%
Direct Grant		29·9	54·0	15·1
Independent:				
Non-Denominational		27·1	47·4	15·1
Roman Catholic*		—	—	—
All Fee-Paying Schools		20·3	37·0	10·8

* For RC schools only a shift from free to assisted places was proposed throughout the discussion, never a cut in the total of number of places. Ultimately only sixteen of the seventy-nine free places were made assisted.

how these gradually modified the proposed cuts. The original proposals and how these were ultimately amended can best be made clear in a table: 6.1.

Whenever the Schools sub-committee considered the matter, the CEO's guidance on the statutory position was given. His reports pointed out that Townley now had 6,600 maintained grammar school places, whereas 5,750 places were sufficient to admit 25 per cent of the age group to such schools. The consequences of this situation for the authority's own grammar and modern schools were shown.

The majority of officers accepted the necessity for substantial cuts after a further round of consultations at sub-area meetings. Proposals were then prepared by the CEO's staff, amended by the CEO, submitted for approval to the Chairman of the Education Committee, and presented to the sub-committee of three which accepted them. Cuts to be made in 1963 and 1964, amounting to a total of 50 per cent, are shown in the table setting out quota of LEA places. Special consideration was to be given to the RC schools because of the demand for such places.

The fee-paying schools were consulted next. Most expressed regret and concern about the proposed cuts. Some non-denominational independent schools stressed their long association with Townley and asked for less severe cuts. RC independent schools all pleaded for reconsideration of the proposals—parents, they added, did not readily apply for assisted places. The individual schools' distress was taken up by the RC diocesan authorities, who based their opposition on Section 76 of the 1944 Act. In the end the Chairman of the Education Committee received an RC deputation and amended proposals agreed between them were endorsed by the Schools sub-committee in October.

The direct grant schools also pressed their case. It was hoped the LEA would at least continue taking the 25 per cent free places. This plea was reinforced by the Ministry of Education in an exchange of views between the CEO's and the Ministry's representatives in May. The Ministry stated that no objections could in principle be raised, as the decision about direct grant school places lay with the LEA. It was also appreciated that the proposals arose on account of the financial advantages gained by keeping the maintained grammar school entry at normal level. Nevertheless, the Ministry

spokesman pleaded for as much latitude as possible in implementing the proposed cuts at direct grant schools, both
with a view to easing the problems of the schools concerned
and to reducing parental discontent, much of which found
its way to the Ministry. The first plea, that as much notice as
possible be given of the reductions, was met by the authority's
proposal to spread the cuts equally over 1963 and 1964. If
they could be delayed a little longer, so much the better. The
difficulty for the schools was that a reduction which left them
with less than 25 per cent of their entry taken up by the LEAs
in the form of free places—that was, pupils with a primary
school qualification—meant that the school governors had to
make up the free places to 25 per cent. That in turn meant
the admission of additional suitably qualified pupils without
payment of fees, entailing an annual loss of income which
had to be made good in some way. Generally the only way
to do this was to raise the tuition fees, a thing nobody liked
to do. It would therefore be most helpful to the schools if
the axe fell primarily on the reserved rather than on the free
places.

Following these representations, the CEO reassured the
Ministry spokesman that the LEA looked upon the direct
grant schools as part of the state provision of schools. It
would remain the authority's policy to offer parents freedom
of choice over as wide a field as possible, and to avoid harm-
ing the direct grant schools. These same views were incorporated into the CEO's next report to the Schools sub-committee,
although he made no reference to the fact that exchanges with
the Ministry had taken place. The CEO still concluded that
it would be improper to allow an undue proportion of
empty places in the maintained schools.

The CEO had to pay attention to the comments of the
schools and was certainly impressed by his consultations with
the Ministry. In the light of these he proposed less severe cuts
for direct grant and non-denominational independent schools,
to be implemented over three instead of two years. By 1965
places would have been cut by a total of 34 per cent instead
of by 50 per cent. For RC independent schools the proposed
shift from free to assisted places was left almost as before, but
its impact would have been less sudden. Without explanation,
these amended proposals were withdrawn by the Chairman of
the Schools sub-committee in June. The available evidence

allows no conclusion as to whether the withdrawal occurred primarily because of the aggrieved reactions of the RC schools and authorities. What is known is that subsequently—in October—the Chairman of the Education Committee received an RC deputation, and that the CEO on the day following withdrawal of the report consulted Council's Treasurer about the financial implications in law of *taking additional free places* at independent schools. This suggests that the Chairman and/or some councillors, who were concerned about the effect on either the RC or all independent schools, proposed an increase in independent school places, although *cuts* were then under discussion because of vacancies in state schools.

The treasurer drew attention (as had the CEO) to the proviso that free places at independent schools were justified only when 'shortage' of maintained school places existed, and to Section 76 which referred to 'the avoidance of unreasonable public expenditure'. He produced detailed estimates from which it was apparent that on the modified cuts at that stage proposed for 1963-5, the authority would save, after five years, between £60,000-£70,000 per annum. He also showed that assisted places at independent schools cost the authority, on average, 75 per cent, parents 25 per cent, of the fees. The offsetting cost of educating pupils in maintained schools instead would not be great since pupils would be spread over many schools in various areas. These views and figures were made known to the Education Committee Chairman during the summer.

Withdrawal of the modified proposals delayed matters for a few months. In October the Schools sub-committee accepted them, except that two further amendments of substance were suggested by the Chairman of the Education Committee and agreed. Firstly, concessions were made to the RC schools as a result of their deputation to the Chairman. Their quota of free places stood at seventy-nine. Instead of fifty-eight of these being converted into assisted places, only sixteen were so converted. This left the RC schools with sixty-three free places instead of a mere twenty-one. Secondly, only the first stage of the proposed reductions was to be implemented, and that not until 1964, so as to allow adequate time for notice to schools and parents. This meant that direct grant and non-denominational independent schools would be subject to a one-time cut of 15 per cent instead of an ultimate one of 34 per cent.

When these new sub-committee recommendations were put before the full Education Committee, a further delay occurred. The Education Committee refused to follow its sub-committee and decided to ask the sub-committee to reconsider the proposals. This reference back was moved by a Labour councillor and carried by twenty-five to twelve votes. Clearly the controlling party (Conservative at this time) did not carry the day. Some evidence suggests a degree of cross-party voting at this stage. On the full Education Committee political pressures could be brought to bear more effectively. Both party groups on the Council contained some RC members, and it is likely that Conservative RC councillors voted for the Labour motion.

The reference back was argued on 'means test' grounds (which would appeal generally to Labour councillors). It was the shift in the proportion of free to assisted places at independent schools to which exception was taken. Parents were liable to contribute not merely to fees, but also to pay travelling expenses and school meals, if their child secured an assisted place. A child's transfer to secondary school should not be governed by its parents' financial circumstances, argued Labour opponents.

When the Schools sub-committee reconsidered its own recommendations, the party whips were probably put on. In any case, the same recommendations were re-submitted to the Education Committee, and this time accepted. It then only remained for the Council, in February 1963, to endorse the revised policy for LEA fee-paying placements.

Discussion and conclusion

After nearly three years of consultation and discussion, a decision was reached which affected only sixty instead of 206 children out of 30,000. Behind this apparently trivial outcome far more was at stake. What were the issues?

There were two basic, inter-related issues, namely the extent to which the public sector can or should make use of the private sector, and the extent to which parental wishes are to be respected. The first turns on the interpretation of shortage, and raises the question of the impact on the maintained schools of creaming-off to the benefit of the private schools. The second raises difficult problems of legal interpretation and makes it necessary to examine whose parental preferences are expressed and how.

There was a clear division of opinion between officers and councillors in this case. The fact that vacancies existed in maintained grammar schools was not challenged by either side; what was in dispute was the consequences which should follow therefrom. Officers argued that in this situation under Section 6 of the 1953 Education Act cuts ought to be made in LEA fee-paying school places, especially free ones at independent schools. Councillors held that continuance of, or even an increase in, such places was nevertheless justified, quoting Section 76 of the 1944 Education Act, which safeguards parental choice. Officers in reply pointed to the financial limitations which Section 76 places upon parental choice. However, this merely prevented councillors from pursuing the attempt to *increase* free places at independent schools.

'Shortage' under the 1953 Act and concern for public expenditure were not all that mattered to the officers. It was important to assess how use of the private sector affected the public sector. It had been made very clear during officer discussions that creaming by the fee-paying schools was reducing standards in maintained grammar schools and endangering extended courses in the modern schools. The logical consequence of accepting this might have been to sever the link between the two sectors at a time when there was no longer any need to depend on private school places. However, the majority of officers, whilst accepting cuts, did not ask for the elimination of fee-paying places. Only one argued explicitly against taking *any* places in the private sector. The remainder were content with a review of *the number of* places taken. They regarded these places as an integral part of the provision of selective secondary education. The arguments for creaming of the ablest children first by fee-paying, and then by maintained grammar schools were never in question.

To return to the position of the councillors, it is often suggested that they are in the hands of their officers. This may be true for much of the time, but this case study shows that it need not be so. In fact councillors whittled away the cuts in fee-paying school places proposed by their officers. The principal reason must be sought in the influence of vocal or potentially vocal parents. Whilst in this case there was no evidence of organized political pressure being brought to bear by parents—except for the representations on behalf of RC parents—councillors were aware of the keen parental interest in access to grammar schools in general, and to fee-paying schools in particular. They might have had in mind the fact that when parents were notified of the secondary school to which their child was to be transferred, a considerable number used to telephone or visit their education offices. Complaints concerned failure to obtain a place in an independent or direct grant school or to secure the maintained grammar school next on their list. Moreover, some councillors were themselves parents, or may have been ex-pupils of fee-paying schools.

In certain circumstances, councillors are able to withstand pressures of this kind, in particular if the issue is one of clear party policy. None of the evidence suggests that on the issue of LEA placements in fee-paying schools either party group on Townley Council had a clear-cut policy. This probably made both party groups much more accessible to pressures exercised by interested groups inside and outside the Council. There was evidence of cross-party voting on at least one occasion.

On this occasion, the Conservative Chairman of the Education Committee, who initially had supported the proposals of his officers, had to take note of the influence RC councillors exercised in his own party. This may have prepared the ground for concessions made to RC independent schools, subsequent to the Chairman receiving an RC deputation.

On the Labour side, it was an RC councillor who, on the Education Committee, moved the reference back of the sub-committee's report, using 'means test' rather than denominational arguments to gain support from other party colleagues. At the same time Conservative RC councillors supported him probably on denominational grounds. Once concessions had been made to the RC schools, the Chairman may well have considered it unfair that these schools alone should benefit. It was actually his suggestion that only the first stage of the proposed cuts be implemented, and by this the non-denominational independent and the direct grant schools were to benefit as well.

As far as the direct grant schools were concerned, the part

played by the Ministry was decisive. When consulted by the CEO, it jumped to their defence, following which the CEO proposed less severe cuts. The Ministry feared the effect of cuts in LEA places on school fees. The burden of higher fees would fall not merely on LEAs buying places, but also on fee-paying parents opting out of the maintained sector of education.

How can the attitude of the Ministry be explained? Undoubtedly the Ministry, like the councillors, had discontented parents in mind. For such discontent makes itself felt at the Ministry, in Parliament and on local councils. Furthermore, both the Ministry and the CEO treated the direct grant schools as part of the state sector. Even after Circular 10/65 had been issued, the Secretary of State for Education and Science argued that the direct grant schools 'should negotiate direct with their local authorities' on secondary reorganization. The fact that in 1967, the direct grant schools were referred to the Public Schools Commission indicated a change of outlook—clearly placing them alongside the independent schools in the private sector.

It is now clear that the officers were rebuffed when they proposed drastic cuts in fee-paying places because they put themselves in conflict with Ministry, councillor and parental opinion. The LEA's dependence on the private sector, therefore, could not be explained in terms of 'shortage' of maintained provision alone. It existed also because of parental pressures on policy makers.

If it is accepted that parents exert an influence over policy the further question arises: how representative are these parents? This chapter shows that parental choice was effectively exercised mainly in connection with access to selective schools. Lord Boyle has said that people had to 'search their consciences about how much choice there was for those who were not selected for grammar schools'.[14] It is now generally known that middle-class children have a far better chance to go to grammar school than working-class ones. It is mainly middle-class parental pressure which exerts a subtle influence over policy makers in the education service. In the case examined some parents expected to opt out of the state sector of secondary education by sending their children to private

[14] Addressing the Northern Education Conference. See *The Times*, January 1966.

schools—but at public expense—and this expectation was respected.

It may be concluded that in this case parental wishes were respected at the expense of the ratepayer on the one hand and of the standard of work in maintained schools on the other. This raises the general question of how much weight is to be given to parents' wishes—even irrespective of whether they form a minority as in this case, or a more representative group of parents—when these wishes conflict with other legitimate claims.

This is a question of fundamental importance. The Act itself gives some guidance by placing certain limitations on parents' wishes. These wishes shall be respected in so far as they are compatible with the 'avoidance of unreasonable public expenditure' and 'the provision of efficient instruction and training'.[15] These stipulations have been on the statute book for nearly thirty years. Yet this study has shown that the problems arising in their application are not easy to solve.

[15] 1944 Education Act, Section 76.

7

M. KOGAN

English Primary Schools - the Interrelationship of Government Structure and Educational Innovation*

Social reform, and the reform of institutions which mediate social policies, might involve the creation of beneficient myths or even of white lies. There is something of this in current American assumptions that the British have produced open schooling for the mass of their children, that their primary schools are everywhere free and inventive. . . .

The origins of the movement are described at the beginning of the Plowden Report on primary education, published by the Department of Education and Science's Central Advisory Council for Education.[1] This began by referring—as its base line—to the reports of official committees on primary schools under Sir Henry Hadow published in 1931 and 1933.[2] The Plowden Report said that the reports 'virtually laid the foundations of what exists today'. The purposes to be achieved and the tests by which its success can be recognized, the 1931 Hadow report defined in these words: 'What a wise and good parent will desire for his own children, a nation must desire for all children'. This aspiration was written, of course, well before the objectives industry got under way. It is a simple and eloquent statement of values rather than a prag

* [From M. Kogan, English Primary Schools, a model of institutional innovation? in 'Educational Planning in Perspective', Ed. T. Green Futures, I.P.C. Scientific and Technical Publications, 1971.]
[1] Children and their Primary Schools, Report of the Central Advisory Council for Education, HMSO, 1967.
[2] Board of Education Reports of the Consultative Committees on the Primary School; and on the Infant at Nursery Schools, HMSO, 1931 and 1933.

matic utterance. Its authorship, incidentally, is beyond doubt. Precisely the same words appear in R. H. Tawney's *Equality*. Tawney was a member of the Committee.

In brief, the Plowden Report in its chapter of recommendations and conclusions (Chapter 32), came to the following conclusions:

Children are unequal in their endowment and in their rates of development and their achievements are the result of the interaction of nature and of nurture. 'The Hadow emphasis on the individual was right though we would wish to take it further. Whatever form of organization is adopted, *teachers will have to adapt their methods to individuals within a class or school.*'

On curriculum, the insights of the Hadow Report, thirty-five years previously, 'have been justified and refined by experience. *"Finding out" has proved to be better for children than "being told".* Children's capacity to create words, pictorially and through many other forms of expression, is astonishing. The third of the three R's is no longer mere mechanical arithmetic, French has made its way into the primary school, nature study is becoming science. There has been dramatic and continuing advance in standards of reading. The gloomy forebodings of the decline of knowledge which would follow progressive methods have been discredited. Our review is a report of progress and a spur to more'.

'... Research ... (some commissioned by the Committee) .. has suggested that the *most vital factor in a child's home is the attitude to school*—and all that goes on there—*of his mother and father.*' ...

Yet another official report about primary education—in Wales—implicitly assumed that the progressive English primary school should be the model for other parts of the system to emulate. The Gittins Report on Welsh primary education[3] stated that: 'Curricula have tended to remain too narrow and teaching methods traditional and formal, rather than forward looking and experimental.' It refers to the best known dictum of the Hadow Reports that 'the curriculum is to be thought of in terms of activity and experience rather than knowledge to be acquired and facts to be stored'. It says it found a theoretical rather than a practical acceptance, 'though

[3] *Primary Education in Wales*, A Report of the Central Advisory Council for Education (Wales), HMSO, 1968. Also published in Welsh.

there are some striking exceptions to this, particularly in our most forward looking schools'. The Gittins Report felt that a somewhat narrowly utilitarian view of education, associated with the strong emphasis in Wales on education as the ladder of socal mobility predominated, rather than the more purely educational and developmental value placed on it in English schools. [. . .]

What is the extent of English 'open schooling' (an expression used by Americans but hardly ever by British educationalists) in England? Again, we can quote the Plowden Report (Chapter 8). An assessment of primary education was made by Her Majesty's Inspector of Schools. 20,664 primary schools were included—all English primary publicly maintained schools—apart from a few which could not be assessed for technical reasons. They found 10 per cent of schools to be in two categories—'of outstanding qualities' or 'a good school with some outstanding features'.

28 per cent of the children attended 'decent' schools, 5 per cent of the schools were distinctly out of touch and 44 per cent of the children were in schools that were decent enough but without real merit, although some of them were on the move. Over 1,300 schools containing 5 per cent of the children were 'remarkably out of touch with current practice and knowledge and with few compensating features'. 28 school with 0·1 per cent of the children were bad schools 'where children suffered from laziness, indifference, gross incompetence or unkindness on the part of the staff'.

The survey's categories are a bit smudged at the edges but it describes a public education system covering a wide range of social and geographical conditions, and of school populations yet able to produce a really strong minority—a leading cohort —of schools where beneficent movement has taken place...

The outstanding characteristics of the 'good' English primary school are as follows:

1. Curriculum, internal organization, relationships between children and teachers and relationships between the school and home rest on the assumptions that children are 'agents of their own learning', and that since the educational process depends strongly upon children motivation, the school environment should allow flexible interaction between the child and the school in terms of time and space allocation.

2. The school should be free to find its own level, style and content of educational performance.

The progressive movement is different from two movements in American educational history. First, the American progressive education movement of the 1930s hardly ever got under way and when it did it often centred on middle class and professional neighbourhoods In England, this is not so. The 'best' areas for primary education are: a quite squire-archical county area; a county area in which mining villages predominate; a large city with many downtown schools; and so on. Traditional schools, on the other hand, are often found in the middle class suburbs of large cities where middle class parents are anxious about measurable performance. Secondly, the movement is different from the sort of attempt to *structure* elementary or primary education that can be found in, for example, Operation Headstart, which attempts to bring about experiments in operant conditioning, programmed instruction, and so on.

The better schools thus represent not so much a movement in educational technology as a change in social values and humane convictions which seem about to help build up human relationships and a society quite different from the Britain of the 1930s and 1940s. But, by the same token, its characteristics are difficult to define, let alone measure.

The curriculum and internal organization of the schools are thus far different from those of schools elsewhere. In the USA, in Sweden and in France, for example, curriculum is laid down prescriptively in state or school district regulations and the assumptions are of a managerial and strongly instrumental kind. In England, a marked characteristic of the schools is their freedom to go their own way. They are allowed to be traditional or progressive and the sanctions applied by educational administration are relatively non-prescriptive and subtle in their effect.

Most head teachers would say that they are 'autonomous' of a public management structure.[4] The management structure is that the central government department—the Department of Education and Science—has strong control over the

[4] A. Cook and H. Mack, *The Role of the Head Teacher*, a pamphlet of the Anglo-American Primary Education Project. A contrary view is given in M. Kogan, *The government of education*, in the same series.

overall rate of educational development—through finance, school building programmes, the determination—with local education authorities—of teachers' salary scales, the amount of teacher training permitted, and so on. But the Department explicitly falls short of controlling curriculum. Interventions —but this is too strong a word—are made through the existence of something like 500 Her Majesty's Inspectors of Schools who 'advise' the schools, the local education authorities and the Department.

A central body, the Schools Council for the Curriculum and Examinations, provides advice and encourages and mounts research and development projects for the schools to either take or leave.

The real management of schools in England and Wales begins with the 169 local education authorities. They are— with the exception of the London area, which has a special arrangement—effectively committees of counties and county boroughs, and they comprise at present the largest form of local government.*

There is always a chief education officer, or director of education, who is the chief executive to the education committee. There have been few adequate statements of his role but it seems that he is the manager of his schools in as much as he can, in the last resort, apply organizational sanctions and he has authority to make recommendations on overall policy to his committee. But even this extremely strong role —one in which rewards and penalties can be employed—is rarely used to dictate to the schools what type of curriculum or organization they ought to have. A strong chief education officer can, however, determine the style of education in his area through the voice he has in the appointment of head teachers.

Within a school, a head teacher occupies a role which they themselves state ambivalently. They might call themselves 'advisers' or 'trainers' of their teachers. It would seem that they are managers of their teachers. While they may not be able to appoint whom they want, they have authority in that they allocate tasks to them, can reward them financially through the award of special responsibility allowances, and

* [This was of course written before the reform of local government in England and Wales outside London which becomes operational in April 1974, and which reduces the number of LEAs to 101.]

can help or hinder their chances of promotion elsewhere. A head teacher almost certainly sets the style of his school, although, of course, in some schools variations in style are obvious.

What is evident here is that there are, in effect, 23,000 sources of educational innovation in England because of the strong discretion, though not autonomy, allowed to the heads of primary schools. This is where change began. A few quite small schools, mainly rural, began to let the children follow their own bent.

Such developments were encouraged and strengthened by writings of such as Froebel, Montessori and Susan Isaacs. But a somewhat mysterious movement took place in that it was humble and evangelical in style rather than anything that could be graced by the name of a Change Model. The progressivism of a few teachers in their schools was taken up by a few leading administrators and then reinforced by the encouragement given by an increasingly progressive body of HMIs (Her Majesty's Inspectors of Schools). HMIs them- selves had changed their role. Until 1944, there was a statu- tory Elementary Code but in 1918 an official Handbook of Suggestions for the Consideration of Teachers said: 'The only uniformative practice that the Board of Education ... desired to see in the teaching of the public elementary schools is that each teacher shall think for himself, and work out by himself such methods of teaching as may use his powers to the best advantage and best suited to the particular needs and conditions of the school.'

This statement was not only made but meant. When change has been positively mounted it has occurred through advisory teachers rather than inspectors, in-service training rather than managerially dominated systems.

The model that we now have, therefore, is one in which change has certainly taken place over a large number of institutions. We can describe the main characteristics of the primary school. We cannot be certain of the results other than by statements of informed impression. And those results are hardly definable as outputs. We more certainly have a model of educational government which has allowed teachers, or at least head teachers, to employ discretion in such a way that they have been able to do their own thing, and it has been a thing which has attracted admiration.

8

R. D. COATES

Teacher Organizations and Educational Policy: the Alliance for Educational Advance*

The goals of the teachers' associations invariably involve the spending of public money, on such items as schools, equipment, training, salaries and pensions; and the ability of the Department of Education and Science to respond to those demands is ultimately limited by the availability of resources for educational provision. Indeed, in an economic situation such as Britain's in the 1960s, where the rate of economic growth did not keep pace with the growth rate of the school population, even the maintenance of prevailing educational standards, not to mention educational advance, required that the DES capture a growing proportion of available resources.

There were only three general ways in which the Department could do this: either by capturing an even greater share of total public expenditure; or by retaining a fixed share of public expenditure as total government activity itself absorbed (by taxation and by borrowing) an ever greater share of the Gross National Product; or by a mixture of the two. The first involved the Department of Education and Science in competition with the political heads of other spending departments; the second in a running battle with the Treasury—traditional guardian of the level of total public expenditure. In each case, the resulting level of educational expenditure was both the product and the manifestation of a political decision, on the degree of priority to be attached to education as an area of government activity.

* [From R. D. Coates, *The Teachers' Unions and Interest Group Politics*, Cambridge University Press, 1972.]

Traditionally, the teachers' associations have relied on a strong Secretary of State to compete for resources both with other government departments and with the Treasury. As Sir Ronald Gould told Anthony Crosland as recently as 1966, the associations judge the success of a Minister by 'how much money he wrings from the Treasury'.[1] But in the 1960s they attempted to achieve a more direct influence on the level of educational expenditure. [...] In this chapter we will concentrate on attempts by organized teachers to strengthen the hand of the Secretary of State in bargaining with his Cabinet colleagues on the share of public expenditure going to education. They did this by forming an alliance of educationally-minded interest groups, in order to create such a level of demand for education in the electorate as a whole that Government expenditure would move in favour of education in response to democratic electoral pressures.[2]

A number of Ministers have appealed to the teachers' associations for this sort of assistance in negotiations with Cabinet colleagues. Sir David Eccles told the NUT in 1961 that

We do our cause no good if we appear to assume that we have a prescriptive right to more and more public money. We have no such right ... We must justify the demands we make upon the Exchequer and the rates ... I hope therefore you will constantly seek to convince the public that we want more money to enable us to give their children the best possible start in life.[3]

A similar call for a campaign to mould public opinion in favour of educational advance came from a later Secretary

---

[1] *The Teacher*, 15 April 1966. (This drew from Crosland the reply quoted later that on the contrary what mattered was how much he won in competition with his Cabinet colleagues.)

[2] The associations' traditional reliance on MPs was not sufficient to this task. As a recent observer of Parliament has recorded, the Commons, 'cannot easily find the occasion to debate the relative priorities of expenditure within a given total, the total itself, or the long-term implications for the economy of preferring expenditure in one sector of public activity to expenditure in another', R. Butt, *The Power of Parliament* (London, Constable, 2nd ed. 1969), p. 392. Indeed, Butt makes a strong plea for 'fuller Parliamentary debate of Government spending plans' (p. 396). The Labour Government drew up a paper, around which such a debate was held, in 1969.

[3] *The Schoolmaster*, 29 April 1960, p. 1138.

of State, Anthony Crosland. Replying to Sir Ronald Gould's assertion, quoted earlier,[4] he told the NUT,

> With respect, this is not the point: it is how much money he wrings from the Cabinet as compared with his colleagues, the Ministers of Housing, Pensions, Health, etc. And when the Cabinet comes to decide these priorities, they try to do so first of all on merit; but they also, since we live in a democracy, take account of popular desires. And here I must be frank with you ... what have you done to create an irresistible public demand for more educational spending? ... If you ask me for more money you for your part must give me a stronger hand to play with.[5]

Anthony Crosland's accusation of NUT inactivity here was unwarranted. All the teachers' associations, and especially the Union, maintain a persistent pressure on the electorate through the mass media. In 1942, the NUT had allied with the TUC and the WEA in a Council for Educational Advance; and (more damning still of Crosland's accusation) all the associations had participated in 1963 in a major, year-long publicity drive for educational expansion, the 1963 Campaign For Education.[6]

---

[4] Supra, p. 147.

[5] *The Teacher*, 15 April 1966, p. 1.

[6] An alternative route through which to move government spending priorities in favour of education would be by direct affiliation to a political party, or at least by pressure to reduce government expenditure elsewhere by, say, policy statements on defence expenditure. The associations have traditionally avoided both. In line with the personal preferences of normally the majority of their executives, the associations have found strong organizational reasons for retaining their position of political neutrality. Their need to maintain cordial relationships with all governments regardless of party, the fear that political alignment would cause large membership defections, and their lack of sanctions (and therefore, to large measure, possible influence) over government departments other than the DES have repeatedly led the associations to oppose moves to align with political parties or to publicly commit themselves on politically controversial issues arising from government activity in other (non-educational) sectors.

The executives have normally strictly limited the area of debate and policy to issues determined within the education sector alone, or to others with clear and immediate educational implications. The boundary line has never been automatic (it is in essence arbitrary) but by and large the associations have accepted as constraints on the range of their dialogue the dictates of the Government's own division of functions between its departments. This had been challenged systematically only by the organized

The 1963 Campaign for Education

There were a number of reasons for the formation of this Campaign in 1963. NUT conferences in 1961 and 1962 had demanded a greater percentage of public expenditure for educational provision, and had urged the Union to campaign for educational advance. The time was propitious. A General Election was looming, which the Government was unsure of winning; and a number of major educational reports were pending (both the Newsom and the Robbins reports were expected in 1963)[7] on which leading educationalists wished to see more Government action than on such reports in the past. There was also leadership. The initiative for the Campaign came from one man, Fred Jarvis, then Secretary of the Publicity and Public Relations Department of the NUT. The Campaign was his idea, which he organized and inspired with his drive and enthusiasm throughout.

In July 1962, the NUT invited more than fifty educational bodies, and organizations interested in education, to discuss a possible educational campaign. At this first meeting in July, and at later meetings in 1962, the Union found a large degree of support for an educational campaign from the associations of teachers, industrial workers, education and welfare workers, church bodies and women's organizations that attended. From these meetings emerged the detailed aims and structure of what became the 1963 Campaign For Education.

The prime aim of this year-long publicity drive was 'to win public support and secure public action for a general advance in education'; and through its local activity to bring local parents into closer contact with the work and problems of the schools. The Campaign took three specific targets as the key to the general educational advance that it sought:

Left within the NUT (over Suez and the bomb in the 1950s) and with little success until the late 1960s when both the NUT and ATTI conferences passed resolutions critical of the level of defence expenditure. Otherwise, 'politics' have started where the education sector ends, and have been ignored by the teachers' associations. For the very different attitude to politics of French teachers, see J. M. Clark, *Teachers and Politics in France* (New York, Syracuse University Press, 1967), *passim*. See also M. Harrison, *Trade Unions and the Labour Party since 1945* (London, Allen and Unwin, 1960), Chapter 8: 'The Non-Political Unions'.

[7] The Newsom Report, 'Half our Future', on the education of the child of average or less than average ability; and the Robbins Report on 'Higher Education'.

the spending of more money, an increased supply of teachers, and the expansion of higher education without which that supply could not be provided. The winning of a larger share of public sector expenditure for education (to make education the first expenditure priority of Government) was the Campaign's primary target, 'since no advance [could] be expected without it'.[8]

The Campaign was initially supported by 54 bodies and eventually by 86, with nine others giving sympathetic support as 'observers'. The 86 included all the major teachers' associations, with a number of Church organizations, educational bodies, trade unions and civic groups. More than half the associations supporting the Campaign were educational bodies; and the rest, almost entirely trade unions or civic (predominantly women's) organizations. In addition, more than 100 distinguished people in the academic, business and public worlds accepted invitations to be its patrons.

The Campaign opened with a January manifesto and a large rally in the Central Hall, Westminster, attended by 3,000 people. This was followed by a series of public meetings in nine provincial centres between January and March. Attendance at these varied, with 1,150 at Bristol but only 500 at Cambridge. Press and television coverage was consistently high. Through the year, the national committee issued booklets, speakers' notes, films, a survey of the school building programme, and a mobile exhibition; and in June held a series of much publicized public meetings attended by many leading public figures, and addressed by the leaders of the three major political parties, supported by their educational spokesmen. And in the aftermath of the publication of the reports of both the Robbins and the Newsom committees, leading members of each committee addressed public meetings organized by the Campaign For Education.

It had always been the intention of the organizers that the bulk of the Campaign should be carried out at local level, though when this local activity began in earnest in March, only 80 local co-ordinating committees were in existence. Over the year local activity was nationwide, but its incidence was uneven and its range varied. Even so, throughout the country between March and November, local co-ordinating

[8] *The Schoolmaster*, 2 November 1962, p. 12.

committees held nearly 300 public meetings, and organized brains trusts, film meetings, study conferences, exhibitions, displays, and school open days.

This local activity came to its peak in the country's first 'National Education Week' in November; and the Campaign ended with a mass rally of 5,000 people in the Albert Hall in November, amid an accolade of support from leading politicians—with leaders of all three parties competing to give the greatest praise to the Campaign and to promise the greatest priority to educational advance.

The Council for Educational Advance

Amongst the intentions of the sponsors of the 1963 Campaign was a desire for their activity to coincide with the publication of the long-awaited Robbins Report on Higher Education, and with the General Election expected all through 1963. But the Robbins Report was delayed, and there was no General Election until October 1964. For both these reasons, and because of a reluctance to abandon so wide an alliance, the 1963 Campaign For Education continued in 1964 as the Council for Educational Advance. By early 1965, this new council was supported by 71 organizations from a field as wide as that represented by the bodies that had supported the 1963 Campaign.

The new body had a wider function than the Campaign For Education. Like the Campaign, it pressed for educational advance, and intended to promote National Education Weeks. But it was also (and indeed, these were listed first in its official functions)[9] to coordinate national-level activity by its member associations, to provide a forum for the discussion of educational issues, and to act as a clearing house for the exchange of information. It was also to 'police' the promises made by the political parties on the total and detail of educational advance.

The level of activity adopted by the Council was lower than that of the Campaign. Local activity was minimal, and so there were no more National Education Weeks. The finance available to the Council was less than in 1963; the local associations proved unwilling to give as much effort (often

[9] CEA: Aims and Organization, p. 2.

none at all) to the Council as they had to the Campaign. Activity increasingly differed in kind too. The Council began, as the Campaign had ended, preoccupied with the impending General Election; but with the election over, such publicity activity aimed specifically at the political parties gave way in importance to two other forms of activity that reflected the absence of mass local support: deputations and conferences.

The Council regularly sent deputations, letters and memoranda to the Secretary of State and his Ministers. It also organized conferences on specific educational issues. In addition, the Council wrote on occasion to MPs, commissioned research on teacher shortage, issued newsletters, and in 1964 published a school building survey. It was symptomatic of the differences between the Council and the 1963 Campaign that, largely for financial reasons, the Council decided against a mass rally of the 1963 kind as a means of commemorating the centenary of state education in 1970. It commissioned a booklet instead.

Unlike the 1963 Campaign, the Council by 1970 was indistinguishable from the large number of other educational bodies surrounding the DES, and it had resorted to an almost total reliance on the traditional forms of teacher pressure— the deputation, the memoranda, and the occasional use of MPs—which were subject to all the limitations discussed earlier.[10] In particular, they were singularly inappropriate as a means of influencing decision-making outside the education sector (on, for example, the percentage of public expenditure going to education) or of defending educational expenditure at a time of retrenchment in national economic policy. These limitations were clearest at the time of the education 'cuts' of 1968, and it is worth considering the role of the Council here in detail.

When the Labour Government devalued sterling in November 1967, they deflated initially by cutting public expenditure, and only later (in the 1968 Budget) by restricting private consumption. The cuts in public expenditure came in January 1968, and fell most heavily on education. £100m was taken off the education bill for the following two-year period; and in addition, and still more ominous for the rate of growth of educational provision, the Prime Minister announced restric-

[10] [Omitted here—Ed.]

tions on the rate of increase of local authority expenditure that would inevitably restrain spending on education.

The Secretary of State for Education and Science made clear the implications of this for educational expenditure. Education would no longer receive a growing share of the Gross National Product. All that Patrick Gordon-Walker could anticipate was that 'education [would] at least keep in step with the expected growth in Gross National Product'.[11] It appeared that the unprecedented growth of education since 1955, that had brought a greater share of available resources to education each year, was finally over.

Against this, the Council for Educational Advance could do little. In December 1967, it joined the other teachers' associations and educational bodies in publicly insisting that education should escape the cuts; and when this did not come about, it denounced the resulting postponement of the raising of the school-leaving age as 'a bitter disappointment', and, at its later Annual General Meeting, passed a motion highly critical of government policy. But all that the Council could do in addition, beyond exchanging and publicizing a series of letters with the Secretary of State on the exact meaning of the 3 per cent limit on local authority expenditure, was to 'appeal to all affiliated organizations to maintain the utmost vigilance on this matter'.[12] But 'this matter' was nothing less than the availability of money for educational advance, which the 1963 Campaign and the Council itself had been created to win. To leave pressure on this central issue to its affiliated associations in 1968 was an indication of how far the Council had come from the days of the 'educational crusade' of 1963.

The Impact of the Campaign and the Council

Even so, it is not easy to assess the impact of either the Campaign or the Council. Even in situations of apparent failure, as in 1968, it is always possible that the education cuts would have been greater but for the public outcry of the educational bodies of which the Council was one. Certainly it seems likely that the raising of the school-leaving age might have been postponed for longer but for this pressure.

It seems fair to conclude that the Campaign For Education

[11] *The Teacher*, 19 January 1968, p. 1.
[12] *CEA: Annual Report for 1968–69*, p. 5.

had a major impact on the political *dialogue* of the period. Education was a major issue in the 1964 Election, and though the Conservatives' long-standing commitment to further and higher education, and the Labour Party's controversial proposals on secondary reorganization, would probably have made education an election issue anyway, the Campaign and the early Council maintained pressure on the politicians in the long run-up to a closely fought election.

Yet as the Campaign itself recognized, 'what eventually counts most in assessing [its] impact is the extent to which those who have to take the decisions on the allocation of the nation's resources come to accept its point of view'.[13] On this criterion, neither the Campaign nor the Council had a major influence. For both were created in the middle of a period of unprecedented growth in educational expenditure that began in the mid-1950s, and which continued at least until 1968. In each year after 1955, an ever increasing percentage of GNP was spent on educational provision. But this trend did not markedly increase for the presence of either the Campaign or the Council, though conceivably it might have fallen for their absence.

1963 marked the *end* of the period in which government social expenditure had been moving in favour of education to the detriment of health and public housing. The effect of the Campaign and Council here should have been to accentuate that trend, but in fact the distribution of social expenditure stabilized in 1964, and even moved slightly against education between 1963 and 1966. Before the Campaign, the NEDC's *The Growth of the United Kingdom Economy to 1966* gave educational expenditure exactly the same growth rate as did *The National Plan* which came two years after the Campaign; and between these two documents, government social priorities moved slightly against education in spite of the Campaign and the Council. The NEDC, for example, gave education a growth rate of 5·7 per cent, whilst allowing house building to rise 'at less than the rise in the gross national product of 4 per cent'.[14] Not so *The National Plan*: it had public housing expanding by 33 per cent in the five-year period, half a per

---

[13] *The 1963 Campaign For Education: a report on its origins, work and achievements*, p. 4.

[14] NEDC *The Growth of the United Kingdom Economy to 1966* (London, HMSO 1963), p. 45.

cent *more* than education. Expenditure on roads and social security payments was equally to rise more rapidly than that on education under *The National Plan*.

At best, all that can be said is that the Campaign and the Council helped to prevent an even greater move away from education to health and public housing. This seems a fair assessment of the impact of the 1963 Campaign For Education. As its report said, 'the Government of the day has declared that it aims to make education its first priority ... [and] this was not the state of affairs ... when we decided ... that a Campaign For Education was required'.[15] But it is hard to see that the Council for Educational Advance had any impact at all on the political standing of education as an area of government expenditure. It is worth considering why the impact of the two should possibly have been different.

The Campaign and the Council Compared

The Vice-President of the 1963 Campaign For Education talked of the need for an 'educational crusade', a clear statement of a 'systematic, orderly, balanced programme of realistic objectives' and the creation of 'popular enthusiasm' for such a programme.[16] The 1963 Campaign, and not the later Council, came nearest to providing education with a crusade of this kind. The support for the Campaign was wider, its local activity more sustained, and its strategy different from that of the Council that followed it; and on all of these dimensions it was better able to meet the initial purpose of its creation—'to win public support and secure public action for general advance in education.'

As the Campaign organizers recognized, 'the most significant thing about [it was] that it unite[d] a large number of different organizations in pursuit of common aims'.[17] Because of this, the Campaign could do what the teachers' associations alone could not, namely appeal to the political parties as the spokesman for a movement that united the educational world, and included many pressure groups be-

[15] *The 1963 Campaign For Education: a report*, op. cit. p. 4.
[16] Dr L. White quoted in *Education*, 8 November 1963, pp. 885–6.
[17] *1963 Campaign For Education: A Guide to Campaign Activity*, p. 11.

yond it. Yet the width of support for the alliance dwindled
after 1963, and the Council lost a large part of its non-
educational support, as Table 8.1 shows.

More important, the degree of involvement by the remaining associations was far less in the Council than in the Campaign. Officials of the smaller associations interviewed were
unanimous in stressing both their involvement in the Campaign and their lack of interest in the Council, which had
become, one said, far more a 'talking shop' than an educational crusade. The Council's organizers recognized from the
outset that activity would be at a lower level than in 1963,
but even they did not anticipate the paucity of local activity.
Many of the already hard-pressed officials of the local associations involved in 1963 undertook activity then on the understanding that it was a once-and-for-all involvement; and
successive Annual Reports of the Council for Educational
Advance repeatedly note and regret the dearth of local
activity.

Table 8.1: THE SUPPORT FOR THE CAMPAIGN AND THE COUNCIL

	Campaign For Education	CEA (Feb. 1965)	CEA (mid-1969)
Educational bodies			
Teachers' associations	20	19	16
Local auth. assocs	1(3)‡	1(2)	1
Church bodies	7(2)	5(1)	6
Others*	23(1)	20(5)	17(1)
Total	51(6)	45(8)	40(1)
Trade unions†	29	19	14
Civic groups	5	5(1)	2
Industry	0(2)	0(2)	0
Others	1(1)	2	1§
Total	86(9)	71(11)	57(1)

* Including unions of educational workers.
† And professional bodies not in the education sector.
‡ The bracket indicates those associations with 'observer' status.
§ The Communist Party.

Yet it was primarily at local level that the 1963 Campaign
aimed to create and to tap a 'groundswell of public opinion'
in favour of educational advance, by the force of its publicity

and by the involvement of parents locally in the work and problems of the schools. Denied this local support, the Council for Educational Advance had nothing to deliver to Governments but the co-ordinated views of its member associations at national level, who were anyway normally quite capable of taking their views to Government unaided by the Council. The Council could less validly say, as the Campaign had said, that substantial groups within the electorate at large supported its demands for educational advance. They may have, but the Council, denied local support, was in no position to know. Yet it was this popular support that appears to have given the Campaign whatever impact it had in the run-up to the 1964 General Election.

Reflecting and underpinning this difference in popular support for the Campaign and the Council was a difference in strategy that explains much of the difference in their respective impacts. The prime focus of the Campaign For Education was the political parties; that of the Council for Educational Advance became increasingly the DES itself. Yet the DES needed no convincing of the need for educational advance. The need was rather to persuade the Cabinet, of which the Department's political hand was only a middle-ranking member.[18] To achieve this, the 1963 Campaign tried to create a 'public opinion for educational advance' which it could then deliver to the Government through its impact on the electoral promises of the political parties. This was why its broad base of support and its many active local outlets were crucial, as a mechanism for generating a public opinion of this kind.[19]

Yet the Council for Educational Advance abandoned a strategy of preoccupation with the political parties after the 1964 General Election; and only revived the practice for that of 1966. Locally it lacked the organization to even pressure election candidates in a sustained way; and in 1966, of 1,400

[18] As the CEA's Annual Report for 1965–6 recognized, the Council's deputations 'ought probably to have gone to see the Treasury, since the obstacles to what the Council was seeking appeared to reside there rather than at the DES' (*CEA Annual Report*, 1965–6, p. 5).

[19] Obviously this strategy is particularly relevant before General Elections, but only a *sustained* 'public opinion for educational advance' could hope to protect education expenditure from 'cuts' between elections too. And the run-up to a General Election is often quite long, so the strategy need not be used only once every five years.

candidates approached, only 264 replied.[20] Instead, the Council took on two extra functions: of co-ordinating the policy of its member associations; and of 'policing' electoral promises. Then, submerged in the technical debates with the DES that these two functions produced, it lost sight of the initial goal of the 1963 Campaign, namely the creation of public opinion as an electoral pressure for educational advance.

For it was only for this latter task that the wide base of support for the Council was appropriate. Only if it could, like the Campaign before it, deliver a 'public opinion for educational advance' to the Government through the political parties, could it also safely spend time on 'policing' promises made. (In any case, its separate member associations could do this just as well.) But as co-ordination and policing become all, the Council could not mobilize the width of its alliance in support of its activity; and the alliance became moribund.

The impotence of this strategy of the CEA—its preoccupation with co-ordination and policing without first generating a public opinion for educational advance—was clearest in 1968. By then, the Council controlled no coherent public opinion to stop the Labour Government placing the heaviest of its expenditure cuts on education. All that it could do was mobilize the bureaucracies of the teachers' associations and of the national educational bodies. It emerged as what it had become: a source of national press releases and conference resolutions that spoke for no one but the representatives of the national associations affiliated to it, and co-ordinated the opinions of no one but themselves.

The 1968 cuts might well have inspired the teachers' associations to revive a body to 'crusade' for education; and indeed the 1970 NUT conference called upon the executive 'to campaign more intensively for a much larger share of the national resources for education'.[21] But by then, the larger associations had turned to an alternative kind of alliance to influence the distribution of public sector expenditure and the formation of national economic policy. They had turned to an alliance with organized labour.

[20] CEA: Annual Report 1966–7, p. 1.
[21] The Teacher, 10 April 1970, p. 3.

II

New Developments in Educational Planning

9

M. KOGAN

The Function of the Central Advisory Council in Educational Change[*]

The Formal Position of the Central Advisory Councils for Education

The Secretary of State for Education and Science is required by Section 4 of the Education Act, 1944, to appoint Central Advisory Councils for Education for both England and Wales. These are meant to be continuing advisory bodies and this immediately differentiates them from the Commissions and Committees described elsewhere. The Councils, in effect, replaced the Consultative Committees on Education which before the Second World War produced several famous reports—for example, the Hadow Reports on the Education of the Adolescent (1926), on Primary Education (1931 and 1933), and the Spens Report on Secondary Education (1938).[1]

The Act lays down that the CAC will 'advise the Secretary of State upon such matters connected with educational theory and practice as they think fit, and upon any questions referred to them by him' (Section 4 (1)).

---

[*] [From M. Kogan, *Central Development and Local Authorities*, Allen and Unwin, 1966.]

[1] Report of the Consultative Committee on the Education of the Adolescent, 1926.

Report of the Consultative Committee on the Primary School, 1931,

Report of the Consultative Committee on Infant and Nursery Schools, 1933.

Report on Secondary Education, 1938.

So while, in law, the CACs can make their own terms of reference, or equally well have them remitted to them by the Secretary of State, in practice almost all of the famous series of CAC Reports—Early Leaving (1954), Crowther (1959), Newsom (1963), and Plowden (1967),[2] were based on terms of reference handed to the Councils by the Minister. Some of the earlier discussions and reports of the Council were based on terms of reference created by them themselves, but it was soon thought preferable by everybody concerned that the Department should take the initiative.

The same ministerial initiative is preserved by the fact that by regulations made under Section 4[3] appointments are for a period of three years and that while they are renewable— and one or two members were reappointed so as to preserve some continuity between different Councils—most members have given way to newcomers with expertise more directly related to the new terms of reference to be followed.

The membership and the secretariat are entirely appointed by the Secretary of State. This contrasts with many bodies ostensibly appointed by him, such as the now defunct Secondary School Examinations Council and National Advisory Council for the Training and Supply of Teachers, who were formally appointed by the Secretary of State but the majority of whom were actually appointed by nomination, by the educational 'stage army' of local authority, teacher and other relevant associations. Only a few independents were appointed solely on the motion of the Minister. By contrast, the CACs, although certainly containing their share of figures well known in the education service, have been appointed from, as it were, first principles. The statutory provision is that 'Each Council shall include persons who have had experience of the statutory system of public education as well as persons

[2] Reports of the Central Advisory Council for Education (England), HMSO.
  'Early Leaving', 1954.
  '15 to 18', 1959 (Crowther), 2 Vols.
  'Half Our Future', 1963 (Newsom).
  'Children and Their Primary Schools', 1967 (Plowden), 2 vols.
[3] S.R. and O. 1945. No. 152 (Central Advisory Councils for Education Regulations, 1945) allowed for members to be appointed for six years and Chairmen for three years. This was amended to allow for three-year appointments in S.I., 1951, No. 1742.

who have had experience of educational institutions not forming part of that system.'[4, 5]

There is no easy explanation of the decision to appoint the
Plowden Committee. The official announcement was made by
Sir Edward Boyle in an answer to an obviously inspired
Parliamentary Question from Dr Horace King on 18 June
1963. The terms of reference were 'to consider primary education in all its aspects and the transition to secondary education'. It followed a long period of discussion within the
Ministry and consultation with the Treasury about its scope.
The then Prime Minister, Mr Harold Macmillan, was also
consulted about the chairmanship. But it resulted from no
dramatic initiative from government or anyone else. The
Secretary of State is bound to have Central Advisory Councils
even though this fact has been ignored by successive ministers
since the Plowden Committee reported and was disbanded in
1967. This being so, until Crosland decided not to reappoint
it (see below), officials had to find new terms of reference
if only to give the Council work to do. It emerged, first of
all, because something had to, but, secondly, because the
CACs had studied the main components and many of the
main problems of secondary and further education. Primary
education was obviously overdue for study. The last official
inquiry had been that of the Consultative Committee published in 1933.

'The years following the passing of the 1944 Education Act
have been a period of advance in both the resources and
content of primary education. The time appears opportune
for a major study of the primary schools and thought about
their future development.' This was how the first of the
Ministry's Reports on Education (July 1963) put it.

So Lady Plowden and Professor C. E. Gittins were appointed as Chairmen of the English and Welsh Councils respectively. Professor Gittins and another member of the Welsh
Council (Miss Ena Grey) were members of both councils
This greatly helped the two councils to keep themselves
informed of each other's thinking. The Secretary to the Welsh
Council, Dr G. A. V. Morgan, HMI, attended many council

---

[4] The intention of this subsection is quite clear—to ensure that Councils
are not packed with gifted amateurs. But whom does it exclude? Only the
ineducable, it seems.

[5] Education Act, 1944. Section 4 (3).

and working party meetings and received all papers. He also contributed to the work of the council from the point of view of his own expertise which is in educational psychology. The Gittins Report was able to take many of the Plowden recommendations and accept or modify them. The resulting Welsh Report substantially supported the main conclusions of the Plowden Report and thus was able to concentrate on the distinctively Welsh aspects of its remit—the question of bi-lingual education, of the special problems of Welsh rural schools and so on. The two secretariats worked closely together although one was based in London and the other in Cardiff. Any student of British primary education will do well to study both reports and, indeed, students of comparative education will also find much to reward them in the comparisons between two related systems which can be drawn from the two reports.[6]

The Developing Role of the Central Advisory Councils

That the Plowden Committee was appointed as part of a regular and ongoing official process rather than as the result of strong public or professional pressure is neither surprising nor reprehensible. The CACs were evidently devised to provide a continuing, ruminative and contemplative service to the Department of Education and Science and to the education service and no dramatic results have ever been expected from the Reports. None has been given terms of reference resulting from sharp political or public pressure. Within the education service, they may be contrasted with the Robbins Committee, a Committee set up by the Prime Minister— and appointed in response to sophisticated public demand for an enquiry into the future of higher education. Robbins produced recommendations that changed—within a decade— the whole landscape of higher education. The appointment of the Robbins' Committee by Macmillan evidently resulted from a government intention to permit, if not indeed to encourage, radical thinking about the size, functions and

[6] The Gittins Report is contained in a single volume of 646 pages. It was also translated into Welsh by four professors of Welsh.

The two councils were given identical terms of reference but this essay will concern itself only with the English Council—the Plowden Committee.

organization of such sacred institutions as universities.

The CACs have never had that type of role. Nor have they had the almost quasi-judicial type of role of, say, the Wolfenden Committee on Homosexual Offences and Prostitution, or the Fulton Committee on the Civil Service (if we dare mention both in the same sentence). One of these tested the equity and usefulness of a piece of social control while the other held up for review a part of the system of public administration. Both of these were under quite specific political and other challenges at the time that the committees were established.

The CACs have had instead the function of summing up practices in education and the present state of progress as seen at the time that the Reports were written, for the government, for educational practitioners, for the education service, and for the community in general, and of identifying problems and needs. The Reports have thus had a mixture of objectives and of outcomes that account for what some would regard as the inordinate length of some of the Reports. The Councils could hardly meet the demands made on them in less space.

An examination of the four Reports that preceded Plowden will show how these quite mixed purposes were met. The Reports have, first, an evangelical role: they provide teachers and teacher trainers with examples of the best practices in the area of education being studied. Look, for example, at the roseate picture of the English sixth form in Crowther,[7] or of practical work in secondary modern schools in Newsom[8] or of the freedom and flexibility of 'open schooling' in primary schools in Plowden.[9] The Reports all contain exhortatory writing which has relied on the best to be found in the schools by Her Majesty's Inspectors of Schools and others who have advised the Councils. There is, it is not unfair to say, a decided tendency not to describe *the worst* that can be found. These are not reports that attack abuse. They encourage the best by describing it.

Secondly, the Reports have all mounted arguments for

---

[7] '15 to 18'. Report of the CAC (England), HMSO. Vol. 1 Report, Chapter 21, 1959. To be fair, the chapter says it 'deliberately attempts to sketch the Sixth Form at its best'. But all CAC Reports have described the best.

[8] See Note 2.

[9] See Note 2, particularly Chs. 15 and 16, Plowden Report.

changes in policy which were already being mooted within
the education and wider social service world. 'Early Leaving'[10] made a judicious review of how and why some of our
best talent seeps away because too many people leave school
at fifteen years, and made specific recommendations. The
Report recommended that there should be an end to the
practice of requiring grammar school pupils' parents to sign
agreements that they would not leave school before the age
of sixteen and instead to do something about giving them
adequate allowances which would make it easier for poorer
parents to keep their children at school. The Crowther Report, among many important recommendations, provided
powerful arguments for raising the age of compulsory schooling to sixteen—all the more powerful because the Report
rehearsed the arguments for and against and also brought
in the full weight of educational economics.[11]

The Plowden Report contained 197 recommendations.
They included the provision of universal nursery education,
the changing of the compulsory ages of entry to full-time
education and of transfer to junior (or middle) and secondary
education, the creation of educational priority areas and
many other important recommendations. Many of these recommendations were already being evolved within the education service. But the Plowden Report picked them up, studied
them, added the weight of evidence from the education service
and from research, and codified them into a plan for a better,
if not a revolutionized, primary education service. Some proposals were new. Others had been the stock in trade of education conferences for twenty years.

Finally, these reports between them came at precisely the
right time to legitimate new thinking about the relation between education and society and, particularly, to reinforce
current changes in official thinking about selectivity in all
stages of education. The Reports of the Consultative Committees and of such other Committees as the Secondary
School Examinations Council which produced the Norwood
Report (1943) had performed much the same function before
the war. These Reports advanced the case for systems by
which pupils were selected according to ability and also were

[10] See Note 2.
[11] The Crowther Report '15–18', 2 vols, HMSO 1959.

concerned with the techniques of selecting them. The authors of the Report were implicitly concerned with ensuring that the able poor got a fair chance in life. By the mid-1950s educational sociologists had renounced what Anthony Crosland[12] called the 'weak concept of equality'. In talking about the CACs later (1971), Crosland agreed that: 'The CAC did document the good and the bad of the system and, in particular, legitimized the radical sociology of the fifties and sixties. Better than any other group of documents.'[13] This role perhaps emerges as one of the most important. The Department of Education and Science or the Ministry of Education was, in the late 1940s, and throughout the fifties and much of the sixties, one of the few government departments that put resources into development work.[14] Its Architects and Building Branch and Teacher Supply Branch became fine examples of how a government department could put resources and effort into advancing its own knowledge and the knowledge of its service, and of how to improve the system that it administered. But government departments find it as difficult as any other organizations to take account of all the movements with which they have to interact, particularly when some of the external forces are necessarily in conflict with the policies being enunciated by government at the time. Thus in the 1950s and 1960s several educational and social developments were at work and the Department was slow to catch up with some of them. Some, indeed, were already part of the progressive policies enunciated by the Ministry and by Her Majesty's Inspectors of Schools. For example, the child-centred educational theories which were so eloquently stated in the Hadow reports in the 1930s were carried forward by the work of HM Inspectors in the schools, and in-service courses, and so on. They were worked out in more detail, with more evidence from the field, and over broader fronts in the Newsom, Crowther and Plowden Reports. A second theme was never fully taken up by the official committees largely because it was, and still is, a fighting point between the main political parties —the substitution of comprehensive education for selective systems of education. The third theme was that of education

[12] A. Crosland, *The Conservative Enemy*, 1962, Jonathan Cape.
[13] E. Boyle, A. Crosland and M. Kogan, *The Politics of Education*, Penguin, 1971, p. 174.
[14] The Defence and Supply Departments have always done this, of course.

as a 'distributor of life chances'[15]—the assumption being that education had a distributive function and that one of its roles was to redress social equality. This argument was carried out throughout the 1950s and 1960s in surprisingly muted tones, almost as a technical argument between the educational psychologists who in the 1920s and 1930s had done so much to substantiate the weak concept of equality—that all children should have a chance to be educated to the level of their discoverable ability—and the sociologists and psychologists who in the 1950s were showing that educational testing was inaccurate, that selective systems placed a premium on a child's social background, and that the waste of ability was enormous.

Such doctrines as these, of radical educational sociology, were not only written into the CAC Reports but were legitimized by them. And successive CACs enabled some of the important original work on these problems to be undertaken by such as Gilbert Peaker (an HMI) who provided most of the data for CACs on early leaving, on reading ability and on the ways in which social factors affected secondary modern school pupils' performance. This work was directly commissioned and encouraged by the CACs. It is doubtful whether the Ministry of Education, left to itself, would have undertaken it.

Indeed, the Councils not only brought in, or legitimized, thinking otherwise unlikely to arise from ordinary process of government—they were in a better position than the Ministry to absorb and make sense of the work of academics of the generations at work while they made their studies. They also reflected well, and to some extent anticipated, ideological conflicts and consensuses. Plowden was the first report to state the principle that public authorities should exercise 'positive discrimination'[16] in favour of the under-priviledged. This conclusion was reached at precisely the point in time when the controversy about universality and selectivity was being mounted by Richard Titmuss[17] and others. It was, curiously

[15] A. H. Halsey, J. Floud and C. Arnold Anderson, *Education, Economy and Society: a Reader in the Sociology of Education*, The Free Press 1961, Intro.

[16] Education Act, 1944, Ch. 5, para. 151.

[17] See particularly R. M. Titmuss, *Commitment to Welfare*, Allen & Unwin, 1967, Part III.

enough, a doctrine that could appeal to both the universalists and the selectivists on the council.

A careful reader of the CAC reports would thus find them important source materials for the political and ideological history of the periods in which they were written. In the main they were slightly in advance of official opinion; the tug boats of gradualist radicalism.

The Pressures For and Against Plowden

It will be seen, then, that the Plowden Committee was not established to evaluate a contentious issue, or to make specific recommendations on the reform of a system felt generally to need reform, but evolved from a statutory provision made with a quite general intention to ensure that ministers were informed of how the best opinion viewed the education service and its problems over time.

No parliamentary questions had been asked seeking an enquiry into primary education for at least some years before the Committee was appointed, although questions had been asked concerning some of the main issues which the Committee discussed—such as the lifting of restrictions on nursery education.

If there was no pressure for its establishment, there was a spontaneous, and as far as one can judge, genuine welcome for its establishment. A few newspapers niggled.

The *Daily Express* (19 June 1963) wrote that 'Too often educational ideas are accepted because their supporters are vocal and influential. Now these theories are to be put to the test. Be stern, Sir Edward! And judge purely by the results.' *The Guardian* pointed out that Boyle's announcement had been overshadowed by the Profumo affair but thought the appointment of the Committee a move of major importance. *The Times* sat on both sides of the fence in warning against a report that would not be too expository for teachers as had been the Crowther Report, but which would trim unattainable ideas. 'We need a firm appraisal of priorities.' In spite of these warnings, however, it thought the Report would be the primary schools' Robbins Report. The *Times Educational Supplement* (16 August) objected to the omission of members from the Incorporated Association of Preparatory Schools and secondary modern schools, a point that coincidentally had been urged repeatedly by the Deputy Chairman to the Council, John Newsom, to all who would listen to him.

There were some criticisms about the establishment of the Plowden Committee but they were few, idiosyncratic, and were really requests for more rather than for less. One critic, the militant National Association of School Masters, wanted a Royal Commission rather than a mere Central Advisory Council inquiry into primary education.[18] The same body objected to a study of the education service through piecemeal inquiries into different areas.

The general enthusiasm matched well the perking up of interest in primary education in the earlier 1960s. One contribution was personal and political—Edward Boyle who established the Committee had, particularly during his period as Parliamentary Secretary, brought his own charismatic force and interest in educational issues as such, which distinguished him from other ministers, to bear on the problems and achievements of primary education. He was unashamedly interested in promoting curriculum development, in such issues as the retention or rejection of streaming in primary schools[19] as was shown in one or two of his parliamentary speeches and in many of his speeches around the country as a junior minister. In the early 1960s, too, the Nuffield Foundation made the first of the philanthropic moves in this country towards creating development projects in primary education—in science, mathematics, and foreign language teaching. The short-lived Curriculum Study Group in the Ministry of Education[20] listed such areas as primary school science, mathematics, and modern language teaching in the first list of problems it intended to study. Educational psychology and sociology happened, at that time, to be paying particular interest to primary education—the work of J. W.

[18] The National Association of Schoolmasters, 'Primary Education', Memorandum submitted to the Central Advisory Board for Education, 1964, p. 5.

[19] Hansard, 24 July 1963, and Address to Annual Conference of the Association of Education Committees in *Education* 19 July 1963, pp. 98–106.

[20] Established a year before the Plowden Committee was appointed by David Eccles with the job of 'foreseeing changes before they happened'. It was killed by the suspicions of the teachers' associations but was intended to be a resource to the CAC.

B. Douglas[21] and of Basil Bernstein[22] was catching up on the studies made by Halsey and Floud[23] and others in secondary education.

The Committee was welcomed but was, in fact, taken more seriously by the educationists and by the public generally than by the Department which appointed and serviced it. Eight years later Anthony Crosland, the minister who received the report in 1967, stated that 'the Department didn't much like the CAC'.[24] Crosland's reception of it, in his Preface[25] to the Report and in his reply to a debate in Parliament on it, was somewhat tepid.[26] And members of the Council felt, although they were too polite to say so while the Council was sitting, that during its existence the Department did not give it the moral support or follow it with the interest they felt it deserved, although they would be the first to say that the DES supplied all the data they asked for without stint.

The reasons for this reluctant acceptance by the Department are complex and cannot be tactfully stated, let alone properly documented. One of them might have been a persistent reluctance by government and the DES to take seriously its own role as promoter of educational policy. For a long while after the 1944 Act, the Department considered itself not as an educational planning department, or as leaders on policy, but primarily as a mediator between the 'real' agents of educational government—the local education authorities, the teachers and the denomination and the government-wide network of control and economic policy lead by the Treasury.[27] Some of the changes in that attitude have already

[21] J. W. B. Douglas, *The Home and The School*, MacGibbon & Kee, 1964.

[22] B. Bernstein, particularly 'Social Class and Linguistic Development' in A. H. Halsey (ed.) *Education, Economy and Society*, The Free Press, 1961.

[23] For example, J. Floud, A. H. Halsey, F. M. Martin, *Social Class and Educational Opportunity*, Heinemann, 1956.

[24] Boyle et al., op. cit., p. 173.

[25] The Council were thanked for their 'thoroughness'. 'The many recommendations in the Report, some of far-reaching significance, will be studied with the greatest care by the Government and the work done by the Council, with so much diligence and public spirit, will enable decisions to be reached on a more informed basis by those who are charged with securing the best development of English education within the resources available.'

[26] Hansard, 16 March 1967.

[27] Boyle et al., op. cit., p. 25–34.

been mentioned. When Boyle ceased to be Minister in October, 1964, and while his successors, and particularly Crosland, in no sense renounced the leadership role—indeed, under Crosland it reached a new and different dimension—the Department's interest in curriculum and education as such receded and there was a perceptible decline in the developmental approach to them—partly it is true because of the establishment of the Schools' Council in 1964. This may have been because of the appointment from other departments of the two most senior officials—the Permanent and Deputy Secretary—responsible for schools' policy.

And other and more complex forces were at work. The Department had its own policy priorities and did not particularly welcome powerful and thrusting encouragement from one of its own advisory councils. Thus, the Department had already decided to loosen the legal restrictions on the creation of middle schools,[28] and, with it, the passing of the 1964 Education Act. Yet this proposal was central to the Council's studies. Equally, Anthony Crosland's Circular 10/65 which 'requested' local authorities to submit plans for comprehensive education again vitally affected the Plowden Committee's thinking about the age of transition from primary to secondary education—an explicit part of their terms of reference. The Committee later devoted a long, complex and sophisticated chapter to the different alternatives (Chapter 10). An active Minister like Crosland could well find an active Council under a vigorous Chairman such as Lady Plowden, something of a nuisance. In 1971, while conceding the value of the reports, Crosland said, '... but there's a danger of too many and too lengthy reports. And they can slow up action, as Plowden would have done on comprehensive reorganization if I hadn't been firm....'[29] In fact, Lady Plowden would almost certainly have made sure that the Council's thinking did not slow up action. But Crosland was not to know this.

Leaving aside the tensions caused by the relationship between this particular Council and the Department which, at that time, had immediate preoccupations placed on it by an

[28] The 1964 Education Act enabled schools to be established which cut across the legal definements that there should be separate schools for primary education (from three to eleven or twelve years), and for secondary education (from eleven or twelve to eighteen years).

[29] Ibid., p. 174.

active minister, there are structural issues—concerning the way in which a Department formulates its policies—which vitally affected the role of the Plowden Committee. This point will be discussed later.

Methods of Work

The Committee's methods of work were largely affected by its membership. It was appointed with twenty-three members but, at its own request, further members were appointed to bring in expertise from the secondary modern school and the primary school areas. The membership was unusual inasmuch as it contained, not only a lay Chairman, and a Deputy Chairman (Sir John Newsom) who was formerly a chief education officer, an educational publisher and Chairman of the previous CAC, but a wider range of interests than previous Committees. There were four practising primary head and assistant head teachers and two heads of secondary schools.[30] There were two chief inspectors. There was a local authority educational psychologist. There were two former Chairmen of education committees. The big change was in the introduction of a group of academics. These included A. J. Ayer, the Wykeham Professor of Logic at Oxford, David Donnison, Professor of Social Administration at the London School of Economics, and the sociologist, Michael Young, J. M. Tanner, Reader (later Professor) in Child Growth and Development at London University, and Ian Byatt, an economist from the London School of Economics. There was also a leading Principal from the teacher education world—Molly Brearley. Two other interesting additions were the Editor of *New Society*, Timothy Raison, and two representatives of parents—one from the Confederation for the Advancement of State Education.

In appointing this 'non-educational' group, both Edward Boyle and those who advised him were obviously concerned that the Report should not only contain the best opinions of the education service but also show how the primary schools might be viewed from the point of view of the social and biological sciences more generally, as well as from the somewhat more objective point of view that might be expected

[30] One of them, Eric Hawkins, is now a professor of modern language teaching.

from a leading exponent of logical positivism,[31] or the progressive conservatism of Tim Raison.

The Council was served by a full-time team consisting of a Secretary and an Assistant Secretary who were a Principal and Higher Executive Officer from the DES, an HMI as main educational adviser, an ILEA School Inspector and, for a shorter time, another HMI. There were two principal DES assessors—the Under Secretary in charge of Schools' Branch and the Chief Inspector for Primary Education—and a larger number of specialists from different parts of the Department —a medical officer, a statistician, many HMIs, architects and administrators from different branches were available to produce information and views on any point asked for. This large group advised the Council directly or through its working parties.

By any standards the Council was too large. This was because of its multiplicity of objectives—to ensure that educational opinion was fully represented and yet subject to effective criticism or support from non-educationists. There were also problems in organizing its work, in getting all members to participate fully. There was too much of a burden on the secretariat, and also general discomfort, particularly since the DES Headquarters in Curzon Street House has only two rooms which are capable of housing a council of twenty-five and its advisers. And, during much of the Council's period of life, at least one of those rooms reverberated to the sound of workmen demolishing the façade put up to protect Field Marshal Montgomery who used the building as part of his headquarters during the war.

In practice, the Council remitted much of its detailed work to working parties and study groups. There were separate study groups for visits to different parts of the country and to other countries. The working parties studied such detailed aspects of the terms of reference as the growth and development of children, the social factors affecting primary education, the overall organization of primary education and the transition to secondary education, the curriculum and internal organization of primary schools, the training of primary

[31] Sir Alfred Ayer will be the first to agree, however, that his professional pursuit of philosophy did not inhibit him from having strong opinions about many of the issues, educational and otherwise, discussed by the Committee.

school teachers, the economics, finance and research programmes of primary education. Other smaller teams looked
at problems of school building and design and the special
problems of handicapped children. Each of these working
parties met a large number of times and received and generated a large number of papers. They produced reports to the
Council which became incorporated in the main Report.

The Council visited twenty-three English local authorities,
289 schools,[32] universities and colleges, and also paid short
visits to Russia, Poland, Denmark, Sweden, France and the
USA. It had a total of some 116 days of meetings and visits
but even this figure is no true account of the committed time
because travel to and from a half-day meeting, and preparation for a meeting, also added to the burden of members.
One member has written that his duties kept him out of school
two days a week in term-time.[33] Some 465 papers were
written and the list of evidence, solicited or otherwise, which
was received, fills seventeen pages. No member was paid for
this work and travel and subsistence allowances were at the
usual thin government service level.[34]

Throughout this period enthusiasm was sustained and the
Council's meetings were extremely well attended. A strong
camaraderie developed among members and with the secretariat, and much of this must be attributed to the Chairman's driving and positive interest which held the Council
together. Yet as one looks at those criticisms of the Council's
work (see, for example, R. S. Peters, 1969),[35] some of which
accurately discern the Committee's unawareness of some aspects of the theories they discussed, one has to ask whether
so large a burden should have been placed on so hetero-
geneous and large a body. Throughout, the full-time officials
were seriously overworked and many of the issues unresolved
by the Report could have been better tackled were there more
leisure with which to study them and less pressure generated
by the need to service so large and varied a Council.

[32] Including a few in Scotland.
[33] F. M. White, 'Three Years' Hard Labour—or Life on the Plowden
Committee', *Preparatory Schools' Review*, June, 1967.
[34] They travelled first-class but taxis were not generally permitted. A 24-
hour absence entitled them to £3·15 subsistence allowance. (September
1965 figures.)
[35] R. S. Peters (ed.), *Perspectives on Plowden*, Routledge & Kegan Paul,
1969.

For the most part, the Council's working methods were those traditional to government commissions although there were a few significant differences from previous CACs. The secretariat prepared the main papers in which data were put together, conclusions suggested and new lines of exploration proposed. The Council or its working parties considered the papers and authorized draft reports to the Council and draft chapters of the whole Report. Almost all of the first drafts of chapters were written by one or other members of the secretariat (with one or two notable exceptions where the content was of a highly technical and scientific nature: these were written by a member of the Council). Some chapters were barely changed while others were substantially written and rewritten by members of the Council and, perhaps, by the secretariat again. The Chairman throughout the life of the Council made the main decisions on the shape of the Report and on its style of writing although she did not herself draft chapters. On such strategic issues as the age at which children should enter and leave the different stages of primary education, the Chairman herself put together the arguments, including some extremely detailed technical arguments, and DES officials and HMIs contributed to several decisions, while preserving their correct distance from the Council. At no time was pressure put on the CAC who were, in any case, anxious to produce a 'useful' report that the DES could hope to implement.

The making of the Report differed from previous CAC reports in several respects. First, the DES sought and received agreement from the Government for a large research programme which powerfully affected some at least of the Committee's conclusions. Researches were undertaken by members of the secretariat, HMIs, the Government Social Survey division of the COI working closely with two HMIs, Miss Stella Duncan and Gilbert Peaker, by Professor Stephen Wiseman (University of Manchester), the NFER, Dr G. Baron and Mr D. Howell of the London University Institute of Education Unit on School Management and Government of Education, Mr Bleddyn Davies, the Research Division of the Ministry of Housing and Local Government, the National Child Development Study, and three researchers from different universities, Mr (now Professor) A. T. Collis, Mrs Julia

Parker and Mr D. Miller on the social services affecting primary school children.[36]

In order to get this research programme off the ground and back again to the Council in time for decisions on the main recommendations, the secretariat had to work fast. They were appointed a few months before the Chairman or the Council and by the time the Council met in the autumn of 1963, proposals for at least one of the most important pieces of research—the 1964 National Survey of School, Parental Attitudes, and Circumstances Related to School and Pupil Characteristics—had been prepared so that the Council, and particularly its expert working party under David Donnison, could rapidly decide whether to ask the Social Survey, HMIs, and others to make the necessary starts. Almost all of the research findings were received in time for the main drafting of the report which began in the early months of 1966. Much of the initial design was undertaken by the remarkably able HMI who worked full-time with the Committee—Stella Duncan.

The use made of research by the Council was not always what would be acceptable to some researchers but it seems perfectly legitimate to this author. All research findings were written up fully in Vol. 2 and referred to appropriately in Vol. 1. But the Council did not scruple to follow the judgement of its own members, and of the weight of non-research evidence from its witnesses, rather than follow the results of such research findings as that which 'showed' that, for example, schools with large classes produce 'better' school performance than those with smaller classes or that 'formal' education produces 'better' results than informal education.[37] There are good reasons why these research results are valid but not decisive to the issues being argued.) In such cases the Council accepted the onus of arguing with the research evidence when it could not accept it.[38] In other parts of the Council's Report the research reinforced judgements of impression. For example, the place of parental attitudes in children's performances was clearly brought out by the regression and other analyses of the National Survey Data recorded

---

[36] These researches are reported in Vol. 2 of the Report.

[37] See Note 2, Vol. 1, Paras. 780 to 788.

[38] 'Although positive evidence from research in favour of small classes lacking, this does not outweigh professional advice, public opinion and the example of other countries.' (para. 86)

in Appendices 3 and 4. This research was early seen by the secretariat as a key area which needed further study on the basis of the somewhat intuitive findings of earlier researches such as those of Elizabeth Fraser,[39] and Floud, Halsey and Martin.[40]

This last example also demonstrates how research led to the important recommendations in Chapter 4 of the Report about the relationships between school and home and the way in which schools ought to build up a policy for parental participation.[41] These recommendations have had some effect (although not as much as might be desired) but they were among the earlier statements about the influence of client participation in social service institutions—an issue likely to be explosive and already beginning to tick in the early 1970s. Other research—on the way in which the primary schools relate to social services—led to the recommendations in Chapter 7 that later fed into the Seebohm Report which was being written at that time. Indeed, the careful reader will find in paragraphs 240 and 248 of Plowden the concept of the Area Team which has been a fundamental concept of both the Seebohm Report[42] and the 1970 Act[43] which followed it.

Other researches were also important. Chapters 4 to 7 of the Report about the social factors affecting primary education, the creation of the policy of positive discrimination through the creation of educational priority areas, were able to rest not only on the Council's research but also on the substantial findings of educational sociologists of the previous decade. The Council was able to get pre-publication copies of such works as J. W. B. Douglas's *Home and School*,[44] upon which it relied extensively. At the same time, the environmentalist findings of sociologists could be balanced against the somewhat more biologically determined views of the child development experts. Chapter 2 of the Plowden Report is a skilful mid-way statement between the two.

[39] E. Fraser, *Home Environment and the School*, University of London Press, 1959.

[40] Floud et al., op. cit.

[41] This research, so important to the Committee's proposals, has been held up to learned scrutiny. Jean Floud in *The Teacher*, 10 February 1967, found the design, and hence the conclusions, limited.

[42] Report of the Committee on Local Authority and Allied Personal Social Services, HMSO, 1968.

[43] Local Authorities Social Services Act, 1970.

[44] Douglas, op. cit.

So research findings had an important part to play in the writing of the Report. Where the Report did not depend well on research, it identified gaps in knowledge.[45] But there were, too, large areas of its remit that were not well researched, so that discussion of some of the more controversial issues was a bit blurred. Thus, the predominantly child-centred and Froebelian flavour of the Report, derived from thirty or so years of experience of the primary schools, was powerfully presented to the Committee through a large amount of evidence, much of it impressionistic, and gained from visits to schools as well as from the written statements from HMIs and other witnesses. This type of thinking could not easily be reconciled with some of the early findings of, say, Basil Bernstein[46] some of whose data appeared in the Council's offices on the day that the final text was being cleared with the printers. Bernstein emphasized the importance of verbal codes developed in the home. If one were to take his findings to their logical conclusion, as some of the American attempts to reverse deprivation by operant conditioning have done, children would be exposed to programmes of verbal and other reinforcement which would be in conflict with 'learning through discovery' under the informal guidance of teachers. Plowden was anxious that there should be maximum freedom for both teacher and pupil, this being a key feature of British primary education, and that educational procedures should only be structured so as to ensure that a rich environment was created in which children could find their own way. Such issues as this begin with discussions of a technical nature but can powerfully affect policy as any comparison of the role structure of a British with, say, French or Swedish primary school will show. The Committee did not, and could not, take all of these issues on board. Time, its own composition, and the state of research in these areas, were all against it.

There has been sophisticated criticism of the use made of research by the Plowden Committee.[47] But the critics would agree that the Council at least made a conscientious effort to commission what research could be performed in time and to use the findings as well as they could be used.

The second novel feature of the committee's work has

[45] These were listed in Ch. 30 of Vol. 1.
[46] Bernstein, op. cit.
[47] Peters, op. cit.

already been referred to. The mix of its membership undoubtedly affected the breadth of its studies. While somewhat over half of the Report is concerned with 'education' proper, large sections of the Report are concerned with the developmental and social aspects. Other chapters on the government of primary education, its status, on school building, and so on, demonstrate the range that was attempted.

A further new characteristic of the Council and of its Report can be found in Chapter 31. Here the Council attempted to show the financial and legal consequences of their findings, to put cost figures on them, and to express priorities. There is even a time-table for implementation. They also attempted to discuss more generally the cost and benefits of primary education. This proved to be an extraordinary intractable subject and the attempt demonstrates, perhaps, the hypnotic effect that economics was then beginning to exercise over educational thinking.

These differences in style and content of report-making and writing have not been widely followed. The Fulton Committee,* for example, did not cost its recommendations. And other social service departments still appoint large committees whose members are mainly drawn from the area of activity being examined. Indeed, in appointing the James Committee on teacher education the DES seem to have learnt the need for full-time work, but have gone almost wholly over to a membership of those directly or indirectly concerned with teacher education. They also assumed that further research was not needed. One of the lessons of the Plowden Report, and of the mixture of membership that Boyle brought into it, was that there are advantages in not having committees of cavalry officers assessing the advantages of the tank.

Before discussing the effects of the Report, it will be convenient to summarize its main recommendations. One group of recommendations confirm the role of parents in the school by proposing that schools create programmes for contact with children's homes. Parents and other adults were to be invited to participate in school activities, and the concept of 'community schools' was commended.

It commended the development of a national policy of 'positive discrimination' whereby schools in neighbourhoods where children were most severely handicapped by home con-

* On the Civil Service, which reported in 1968.

ditions should be declared educational priority areas. Special resources of staff, buildings and money were to be made available to them.

There were recommendations about the way in which schools should relate to health and social services through a grouping of existing organizations that would include social workers 'largely responsible for school social work' (Vol. I, para. 255 (ii)). This was an important precursor of the Seebohm recommendations for area teams but emphasized the need for specialist work on educational problems.

Several recommendations concerned the organization of primary education. There should be a large expansion of nursery education which was to be paid for by a relaxation of the law concerning the age at which children must attend school full-time. Children should begin school gradually and only become full-timers when they were ready, as individuals, to cope with a whole day of schooling. The schools should offer a three-year course in the first school and a four-year course in the middle school. But generally there should be flexibility for individuals in their entry to school and transfer between the different stages of education.

The Report commended the use of selection procedures other than 'externally imposed intelligence and attainment tests' in those areas where authorities continued to insist on selection procedures (para. 415).

The Report concerned itself with the optimum size of primary schools (a first school to be of 240 children and a middle school to be of 300 to 450 children). Special arrangements might apply to rural areas (para. 467).

The Report contained several chapters on curriculum and internal organization of schools. The Committee wanted recurring national surveys of attainment similar to those undertaken on reading by the Department of Education. There were strong divisions within the Committee on religious education but no attempt, by the majority, to seek a repeal of the law requiring children to attend religious education and acts of worship.

It was recommended that the infliction of physical pain as a method of punishment in primary schools should be forbidden and that independent schools which continued to inflict physical pain as a recognized method of punishment should not be registered.

Schools should be organized flexibly so as to provide a combination of individual groups and classwork and the trend towards individual learning should be encouraged. Flexibility in the length of the school day and the spacing of the school year should also be encouraged. The Report discouraged 'streaming' (division into groups according to the ability of children) in the infants school and hoped its abolition would continue to spread into the junior school. There were careful recommendations about the staffing of schools. Apart from a need for more generous staffing the Committee was concerned with the development of better conditions for part-time service, for help to teachers through assistants, secretaries and for trained teachers' aides. It was suggested that there need be a general review of advisory services (a need which becomes more obvious as time goes on). And the Committee recommended that there should be a full inquiry into the system of training teachers. This recommendation has been followed up by the appointment of a full-time committee, the James Committee, which is looking into the structure of the training system.

There were detailed recommendations about the training of nursery assistants and teachers' aides who would make it possible for there to be a major expansion in nursery education and a reduction in the workload of individual teachers.

The Committee asked for the application of more stringent criteria for the registration of independent schools.

There were recommendations about the improvement of primary school buildings—not all of which suggested the use of extra money. One of the recommendations read: 'The Department should undertake a careful study of present requirements for nursery education which may well be lavish in some respects.' (para. 113 (v).)

There was an important chapter on the status and government of primary education. The Committee stated that primary school teachers should be represented on local education committees and sub-committees. There was concern that the present somewhat muddled status and functions of school managers should be clarified. It was recommended that there should be representatives on the managing body of parents of children attending the school. (This recommendation has since been followed by the Inner London Education Authority.)

The last of the recommendations read 'All unnecessary and unjustified differences of treatment between primary and secondary education should be eliminated' (para. 1150 (xxi)).

There was, in fact, hardly a concern of the primary schools that was omitted. The Report contains chapters on the education of handicapped children and of gifted children. The heart of the Report is concerned with the educational content of the curriculum for normal children but this is paralleled by the major recommendations for the special arrangements to be made for deprived children. Much of the Report is concerned not simply with the merits of the proposals made but with their feasibility and their costs. While many of the recommendations were directed towards the Department, many more were directed towards the teaching profession, parents, and the community at large in the hope that attitudes as well as policies would change.

Effects of the Report

The Report was received on the day of publication and immediately afterwards with acclamation by the main associations and the press, although there were inevitably some reservations. *The School Government Chronicle*[48] complained of its length and of its price. It was also fearful of the cost of implementing the main recommendations. The *Daily Telegraph* wrote that 'the report displays some of the worst features of official expert enquiries into aspects of social policy. Far from applying the tests of objective science to the conclusions of current prejudice, it merely reproduces the prejudice.' It described the policy of positive discrimination as 'merely another expression of contemporary egalitarian dogma, the view that at every point the interests of those who have shown themselves capable of benefiting from education should be subordinated to those who show no wish to receive it'. The *Financial Times* described the proposals as 'sensible and necessary, if somewhat expensive'. 'New School Charter', 'Children's Charter', 'The Classroom Revolution' were headlines in the popular press. *The Times* and the *Guardian* were gingerly approving. Edward Boyle was reported as saying that the Report was all he had hoped for.

[48] *School Government Chronicle*, February, 1967. Leading article.

Forty thousand copies of Volume I were sold in one month and a total of 146,000 copies had been sold (excluding those issued for official purposes) by the end of October 1971. More surprisingly, nearly 22,000 copies of Volume 2—a hefty volume of research findings—have been sold.

The results have been of several kinds. The deepest disappointment has been the government's failure to undertake any *systematic* follow-up of its own Council's findings. Crosland[49] states that 'We set up a special working group inside the department to go through all the recommendations in minute detail, but their work wasn't finished by the time I left. As you know, I made a rather anodyne speech in the House of Commons welcoming the Report when it came out, and later a speech to the NUT ... accepting certain parts of the Report on the management of schools and things like that. I had a lot of work going on inside the Department and it was one of the things which I was coming back to in the autumn of 1967....'*

In fact, Crosland accepted the general conclusions on the establishment of educational priority areas while almost wholly ignoring the criteria and mechanisms proposed by the Council. And while he might have been a bit short of time in which to follow up the Report, he was not all that short. The draft Report had been seen by officials as it was written and a virtually final copy was in their hands in the summer of 1966. It was physically handed to Crosland, in return for a glass of sherry, by Lady Plowden at the end of October 1966—some ten months before he left the DES. With much the same processes, it had proved possible to accept the recommendations of the Robbins Report on the day of publication. Crosland's successors, Patrick Gordon Walker and Edward Short, had nearly three years of office in which to pursue the recommendations further. The official reception of the 197 recommendations is all the more baffling because of the Council's conscientious attempt to make their recommendations uncostly. Thus it proposed not additional resources for educational priority areas or for an expansion of nursery education, but a diversion of resources from what they felt to be the educationally unsound provision for full

[49] Boyle et al., p. 197.
* [Crosland left the Department to become President of the Board of Trade at the beginning of September 1967.—Ed.]

time education for all children from the age of five onwards. The policies for parent participation, for improving social service collaboration, for continuous surveys into reading and other forms of ability, for reform of school management, for lengthening the first school period, would have required considerable expenditure of forethought and energy by the Department but hardly more resources. Such key recommendations as an improvement in in-service training for teachers would have cost money but would have been extremely cheap in comparison with other government-sponsored proposals, of far less importance to the build-up of a public service.

So as an immediate planning and social engineering exercise, Plowden scored no great success. Its success lies in other and less easy to define fields. First, it undoubtedly reinforced and strengthened the liberating effects of progressive education in a large number of schools—this being the evidence of HMIs who have assessed the results of the Report over time. It has succeeded in its evangelical purpose.

The second and wholly unexpected result has been its impact abroad, and particularly in the USA. On the basis of Plowden, a large number of American visitors have sought to describe, explain, and emulate the 'British infants school' or the 'British open school'. One superb commentary written by Joseph Featherstone in the *New Republic*, 1968,[50] sold 100,000 off-prints. Some States have officially adopted the British primary school in the terms described in the Plowden Report and there has been a sudden rush of writing on the subject. The results of such adoptions are probably best not contemplated since the model is so inarticulately stated in Plowden and elsewhere that the American systems' installers might have difficulty in deciding what they are emulating.[51] Historians of cultural transfer will find something here to follow up.

Finally, there has been a quiet 'ripple' effect—not only have schools followed the examples given but surely many more teachers, parents and students have become aware of the existence of a remarkable phenomenon in the British social services as well as of what are now the commonplaces of

[50] Joseph Featherstone, 'The Primary School Revolution in Britain', *New Republic*, 1968.

[51] M. Kogan, 'The British Primary School: a Model of Institutional Innovation', Educational Planning in Perspective, *Futures*, IPC, 1971.

educational sociology and developmental theory.

Plowden and the Machinery of Government

In retrospect there are several lessons to be learned from the Plowden example. First, the CAC mechanism—of long-term assessment of parts of the educational service—is only likely to be directly useful to government (leaving aside its usefulness in the ways indicated above) if there is a prior decision by government that the service ought to be assessed and the results of the assessment taken seriously. Ministers in a hurry can advance on the most superficial or ignore the most careful findings of any inquiry. This being so, it seems likely that if it is to be resurrected the CAC ought to be tied up much more closely with the DES planning mechanisms.[52] Here the model is the Swedish Commission which considers problems put to it, in policy terms, by government and produces 'answers' which can be taken seriously.

Secondly, if this formula is followed, something will have to be done about membership. The uneasy compromise between expert membership and representatives of the various interests has to be broken down perhaps by allowing expert Commissions to get on with the work which is then submitted by government to review by the professional bodies, or by some other device. Twenty-five people and a small secretariat cannot cope with the multiplicity of objectives and pressures put on such a body as Plowden. Thirdly, however, any such device requires the DES to be clearer about its objectives in the areas where study is needed. Its programme assessment and review mechanisms should make this possible. Finally, the dependence of the secretariat upon the DES needs to be considered. If CACs are overtly part of government machinery, the secretariat can be dependent on the DES and the Civil Service for their careers. If, however, the secretariat is to take on a role of genuine independence, the duality created by loyalty to a CAC, which might be in conflict with the Department where promotion lies, ought to be avoided. This is not to say that the DES has been at all beastly to the administrators who served the CACs. On the

[52] These are described in several DES papers in the Second Report from the Expenditure Committee. (Education and Arts Sub-Committee), Session 1970–71.

contrary, two former secretaries to the CAC are now Deputy Secretaries in the DES. But it is a rough period of one's career to live through.

The CACs are now, illegally, in abeyance. Crosland never intended to reappoint them and Edward Short and Margaret Thatcher have not done so. Crosland said in 1971[53]: 'The Reports grew longer and longer, and more and more monumental and took up more and more of the time of already hard-worked officials.... I hadn't taken a final decision but I think I would have reappointed it once more for a fairly quick inquiry into teacher training, and then sought a change of law enabling it to be disbanded as a permanent body.... We've got to the point now where the general theme of educational and social background ... has been taken in and it doesn't need more inquiries to drive it home. We've got a large body now of active educationists who can carry this discussion on themselves. The point of having outside committees should now be to inquire into more precise and specific issues.' Edward Boyle,[54] speaking at the same time took a different view: 'I was personally sorry when it ceased to exist and nothing put in its place. The discipline of an *ad hoc* body sitting for some time is considerable.... It isn't only the report. If you read the evidence given to Robbins ... they are fascinating reading. Much of Plowden's is of the same order. The research on what makes a good school— parental attitudes and other variables—and the whole of the second volume is important stuff.'

Crosland's view was contrary to conventional wisdom and, as with everything from that source, it is worth considering carefully. To criticize it first: how would educational sociology have found its way into official acceptance if CACs had not applied it in four successive Reports? The Councils, including Plowden, turned the radical sociology of nearly ten years into conventional wisdom. Might not this be true of other facts and views of the education service? For example, might we not expect the recently created but terribly messy higher education system to produce problems and issues in the next decade that should be reviewed by those outside the government that itself creates the system? Would we be safe in assuming that the DES, left to itself, would undertake such

[53] Boyle et al., pp. 173 to 174.
[54] Ibid., pp. 132 to 133.

reviews? It did *not* do so with most of the issues tackled by the CACs. Crosland's scepticism about the methodology is well founded. There is, however, a danger in assuming that because the CAC formula was not particularly successful, one need not search vigorously for alternative formulas. No one is doing that now.

From this essay it will be plain that the origins or impressions on the Plowden Committee are not easily described by any political or scientific model. There was little pressure for its appointment, a lot of spontaneous enthusiasm for its findings—the subject is important to every citizen with young children—but no coherent pattern of action on or reaction to its conclusions. It most usefully throws up questions of how government departments, inevitably headed by Ministers of short political life span, can review fundamental policies in the light of developments of general, professional, and social scientific and other technical opinion and knowledge. The attitude of the Government on this issue has been cyclical. First, it kept clear of the external intelligentsia in formulating policy and preferred well-established members of the educational professions to gently assess themselves. Then, with Robbins and Plowden it went strongly the other way. Now it is seeking to strengthen its intelligence services through internal planning arrangements largely undertaken without external help. There needs to be some balance between these three different methods.

10

A. H. HALSEY

The Governmental Response to Plowden*

The idea of educational priority areas, as formulated in 1966 in the report by the Plowden Committee, was widely acclaimed both in Parliament and among the professional and administrative bodies concerned with education, though the welcome accorded it by the DES was tempered by extreme caution and refusal to commit the government to the increased spending recommended.

In introducing the concept of educational priority areas the committee was trying to formulate a scheme for helping those schools and neighbourhoods in which children were most severely handicapped. In distinguishing EPAs for special attention the committee recognized that the benefits of economic advance were not automatically and evenly spread throughout all social groups nor would they, given the present pattern of public services, secure for every child 'increasing opportunities for contributing to the nation's progress'. Thus the argument for special treatment for poor areas came in two parts; first to compensate for the poor living conditions which affected the children's progress in the schools and drastically reduced their chances of further education and, second, to enable children to develop their abilities in order to contribute to economic progress. '... From the earliest stages of education, the schools enlarge or restrict the contribution their pupils can make to the life of the nation. Money spent on education is an investment which helps to determine the scope for future economic and social development.'[1] The EPA proposal represented both a measure of social justice

* From A. H. Halsey (Ed.), *Educational Priority*, Vol. 1. HMSO.
[1] Plowden, p. 54.

and a way of improving the efficiency of the educational system as a means to economic advance.

The help to be concentrated on schools in poor areas was not designed only to bring them up to the level of those in better off areas in terms of buildings, equipment and teachers. The committee insisted on the compensatory principle. 'We ask for "positive discrimination" in favour of such schools and the children in them, going well beyond an attempt to equalize resources. Schools in deprived areas should be given priority in many respects. The first step must be to raise the schools of low standards to the national average; the second, quite deliberately to make them better. The justification is that the homes and neighbourhoods from which many of their children come provide little support and stimulus from learning. The schools must supply a compensating environment. The attempts so far made within the educational system to do this have not been sufficiently generous or sustained, because the handicaps imposed by the environment have not been explicitly and sufficiently allowed for. They should be.'[2] The aim was equal opportunity for all and this could only be achieved if some children had 'unequally generous' treatment.

The EPA scheme was to be translated into administrative terms by identifying schools needing special help in accordance with agreed criteria which it was hoped would provide a measure of educational and social need. The Plowden Committee suggested a tentative list of significant factors relating to occupation, family size, the receipt of state benefits, housing conditions, poor school attendance, the proportion of handicapped children in ordinary schools, incomplete families and children unable to speak English. On the basis of information supplied by local authorities the Minister would designate schools or groups of schools as priority schools or areas and they would then qualify for particularly favourable treatment. The form such treatment might take and the way in which it could be guaranteed was not precisely specified in the report, but a number of suggestions were made. More experienced and better qualified teachers should be recruited, there should be extra allowances for teachers serving in the difficult areas and teachers' aides should be

---

[2] Ibid., p. 57.

provided. Efforts should be made to develop links between teachers in training and the EPA schools. Money available for minor works should be concentrated on improving the most dilapidated schools. Nursery education should be provided to allow all children between four and five to attend part-time and 50 per cent of them full-time. Social work should be developed in association with the schools, and the schools themselves should be developed as community schools.

In making their proposals for implementing an EPA programme the committee envisaged two stages. The period up to 1972 was to be in some ways experimental. The special measures suggested were to be introduced in those areas and schools containing the 10 per cent of most deprived children (two per cent in the first year, rising to 10 per cent by 1972): and research was to be planned to evaluate the success of different innovations and so to provide some guide to the most appropriate future developments. The initial stage would add an extra £11 million to the current costs of maintained primary schools. The second stage, the more long-term programme, would depend to some extent on the discoveries of the experimental years. The committee envisaged that compensatory measures should continue for 10 per cent of the population, though left open the possibility of including a higher proportion. In any case the policy would call for additional resources over and above those then allocated to education. 'Positive discrimination ... calls both for some redistribution of the resources devoted to education and, just as much, for an increase in their total volume.... It would be unreasonable and self-defeating—economically, professionally and politically—to try to do justice by the most deprived children by using only resources that can be diverted from more fortunate areas.'[3]

Professional reactions to the EPA idea

The Plowden Report was debated in the Lords on 14 March 1967 and in the Commons two days later. It was received enthusiastically by all who spoke, though Mrs Shirley Williams noted that the attendance of members in the

[3] Plowden, p. 65.

Commons was very poor. The recommendation about EPAs to which the Plowden Committee had given first importance was singled out by speakers for special welcome, though many pointed out that there would be problems of definition. Only Lord Newton qualified his acceptance of the principle of positive discrimination: 'But I do not think ... (it) ... should be pushed too far ... I do not think that more generous staffing in priority areas ... should be allowed to result in levelling down over the whole field.'[4] He believed the Socialists had placed themselves in a dilemma in arguing against selection for clever children for a privileged education but in favour of selection for children from poor homes for such treatment. 'What I want to see is the widening of opportunity without loss of excellence.'[5] On the whole however the Conservatives in both houses were more inclined to welcome the idea of positive discrimination as consistent with and expressing their own convictions about the need for selectivity throughout the public services generally and for distributing benefits according to some kind of need or means test. Lady Plowden particularly emphasized the importance of the EPA idea, insisting that it should be put into practice if necessary by diverting resources from other parts of the educational budget. The Commons followed the Lords in endorsing the EPA principle though doubts were raised about the procedure for defining and designating the areas and about the proposal to give extra allowances to teachers in priority schools.

Here for the moment the matter rested, the government refusing to commit itself to any definite statement of what it intended to do about the Plowden recommendations until it had considered the views of the various professional and administrative bodies concerned with education policy. These were submitted to the Department over the next few months. The National Union of Teachers gave an enthusiastic welcome to the report and a resolution at the 1967 conference called on the government to make available the resources necessary to carry out the major proposals. The union agreed that EPAs should have highest priority, that education should attempt to compensate for social deprivation, and it welcomed the idea of positive discrimination. The definition of areas should

[4] *Parliamentary Debates, Commons*, 14 March 1967, cols. 177-8.
[5] Ibid.

proceed experimentally, however, and local education authorities and teachers should be responsible. If the DES were formally responsible for designation this should follow automatically on the recommendations of the local authorities. The National Association of Head Teachers were especially interested in the proposed extra payment for teachers in EPAs and sceptical as to whether this was the best way of attracting and retaining suitable staff. The actual teaching conditions were seen as more significant in encouraging teachers to work in the deprived areas. The Headmasters' Association had some reservations about the proposals for positive discrimination in EPAs, envisaging scarce resources for education and pointing to the claims of newly established comprehensive schools for specially favourable treatment. The Association of Head Mistresses on the other hand were insistent on the need to give special help to the deprived areas, welcomed the proposals for attracting teachers to them, but went on to urge that improving the schools was only one element in the reform of such districts, 'in which youth and community work and all the facets of the social services should also be involved'. The Assistant Mistresses were more cautious about the EPA strategy, agreeing that schools in poor districts should have special treatment but questioning the desirability of extra payments to teachers and placing more hope in positive efforts to make teachers more aware of the needs of such areas and the opportunities for service within them. In accepting the idea of EPAs the Assistant Masters' Association argued that the case for special treatment applied with equal force to secondary schools. The Association also insisted that extra help for deprived areas should not be to the detriment of other areas and should be financed by additional grants and by the recruitment and training of extra teachers. The Assistant Masters went on to stress that the problems of the poor areas could not be solved by the schools alone but would have to be tackled by all the social services.[6] Teachers in colleges and departments of education followed school teachers in generally welcoming

---

[6] Other professional bodies than the teachers submitted their views to the Department. The Council for Training in Social Work declared itself 'much interested' in the idea of EPAs though considered that it had raised important matters of principle which should be further discussed since it had implications for other services than education.

the report and the proposals for special treatment for priority areas. They also approved the suggestion relating particularly to themselves, for establishing close links between the colleges of education and the schools in the poor districts.

There were varied reactions from the administrative bodies. The Association of Education Committees was notably restrained, pointing out that implementing the report must be a long-term project which would involve determining relative priorities and that recent decisions of the Secretary of State had ruled out the possibility of carrying out all Lady Plowden's proposals. The Association did not think it practicable to define EPAs precisely or objectively and thought that the best way to help schools in difficulties would be by making extra money available to local authorities for building purposes. Given the problems of defining EPAs the Association of Education Committees opposed extra payments to teachers working within them. Nor did the Association think extra payments could be justified unless the schools were designated as schools for handicapped pupils and this they thought neither necessary nor desirable.[7] The official journal of the AEC, *Education*, argued that the EPA proposals presented a dilemma; they implied more resources for education than would be forthcoming.[8] In a later issue Sir William Alexander elaborated the argument. It was not realistic to think that more money would be available for education and the government must determine its priorities. Sir William's priorities were clear: '... It is hard to avoid the conclusion that those parts of the education service which impact most directly or increased productivity must take priority over any proposals however desirable, in the field of social welfare which do not have such direct impact on our economic problems'.[9] The real need, he said, was to increase the wealth of the nation so that it could carry the burden of increased spending or education. There had been suggestions, he went on, that extra charges for school milk and meals might help to pay for the Plowden proposals, but such charges were, he insisted essential to help to meet existing commitments.

The local authority associations were more favourably disposed. The County Councils Association welcomed the

[7] AEC Executive Committee minutes, March 1967.
[8] *Education*, 13 January 1967, editorial.
[9] Ibid., 20 January 1967.

proposal for positive discrimination for deprived areas as 'a generous one which must command everyone's sympathy and support'. Like the teachers, though, they pointed out that other services must be involved in the approach to the priority areas and emphasized that possibilities for discrimination within the limits of existing resources were very small. They also stressed the problems involved in defining EPAs.[10] The Association of Municipal Corporations agreed with the priority given to aid for deprived areas but, at the same time, raised queries about the criteria for identification, the period for which designation should last and the possibility of help for schools which were deprived though not officially designated.

The proposals for teachers' aides in the priority schools was seen as a threat to some of the interests of the professional bodies and, to a much lesser extent, the administrative authorities. The suspicions of the professional bodies were concentrated on the possibility that aides or ancillaries might be involved in actual teaching. The NUT thought the recommendations of the Plowden Committee about the conditions of employment and the period of training for aides implied that they would have some teaching functions and this the union opposed. The joint executive committee of the Association of Head Mistresses, the Association of Head Masters, the Association of Assistant Mistresses and the Association of Assistant Masters was more welcoming to the idea of ancillary helpers but also stressed that they should work in a non-teaching capacity and under the direction of teachers. The National Association of Head Teachers were more uncompromising. 'The NAHT can support the principle of teachers' aides only if they are used *in addition* to the school's proper establishment.'[11] Thus professional welcome for the idea of teachers' helpers was tempered by anxiety to regard professional status through insistence that terms of employment and training should distinguish very clearly between the aide and the qualified teacher.

The fears of the teachers were echoed to some extent by the administrative bodies. The AEC thought that the proposed two-year training for ancillaries was too long and likely to

---

[10] County Councils Association, *Observations on the Plowden Report*, July 1967.

[11] NAHT, Commentary on the Plowden Report, May 1967.

establish a new grade of teacher which would be unacceptable. The AMC however gave unqualified approval to the recruitment of aides, accepting the two-year training, and had doubts only about the possibility of attracting enough suitable trainees.

The Plowden Committee had also emphasized the importance of introducing parents into the work of the schools in priority areas and in fact of developing the community school. This notion, vague as it was, received widespread support, though the NUT was careful to point out that there was a limit to the time teachers could spend on community relations, given the variety of ways in which they contributed already to the life of the community in other respects. The Union also insisted that no activities be proposed without full consultation with the profession, and there was a general feeling among teachers that the profession itself was in the best position to judge what particular kinds of programme were most useful and appropriate in their areas.

The third major recommendation was an increase in nursery schooling—particularly in the deprived areas. Again this received general approval though the AEC pointed out that the establishment of nursery classes must be limited in order to restrict calls on teaching manpower.

The progress of the idea

Action over the Plowden Committee's proposals was a slow business. On 19 January 1967 the Secretary of State, Mr Anthony Crosland, was asked to make a statement on the report and in a written answer he welcomed it as 'a major contribution to educational thinking'. He also pointed out however that some of the proposals would involve substantial expenditure and even legislation and that, although the government had begun to study them, the formulation of policy would inevitably take time. On 4 April it was announced that £3 million out of £54 million to be devoted to school building in 1968–69 was to go to areas likely to emerge as EPAs. But later in the month Mr Crosland refused to make any statement about his intentions about nursery education.[12]

[12] *Parliamentary Debates, Commons,* 20 April 1967, col. 781.

In July the government announced a special allocation of £16 million for building in priority areas over the following two years.[13] The EPAs were not at this point formally designated by the Department. Mr Crosland believed that local authorities were well placed to judge special needs, though he told the local authorities that he would attach particular importance to evidence that children were suffering from a number of disadvantages and to the general quality of the physical environment. Action was to be concentrated in urban areas since, although the problems of rural areas were recognized, the Secretary of State believed deprivation to be greatly accentuated in densely populated districts. The kinds of projects envisaged were replacement of unsatisfactory schools, improvements to existing schools including better staff and amenities, additions related to planned educational development and measures designed to associate the schools directly with the life of the local community. Circular 11/67 (issued by the Department on 24 August) invited local authorities to submit argued proposals for action which would amount to claims on the £16 million. The government was rather hesitant about pressing the general EPA notion on local authorities. On 7 December 1967 the new Secretary of State, Mr Gordon Walker, reported that 92 local education authorities had applied for grants for priority areas. He was asked whether he would give 'strong and detailed' advice to the local authorities about discriminating in favour of EPAs in their current expenditure, over and above the capital allocations agreed by the Department, but Mr Gordon Walker avoided committing himself and asserted that local authorities must have discretion in spending their money. When pressed he rather reluctantly agreed to encourage local authorities to do all they could.

This unwillingness to try to influence or impinge upon the responsibilities of the local education authorities to implement the Plowden proposals was evident in other ways. Questioned about the steps he was taking to improve contact between home and school in EPAs, the Secretary of State replied that this was mainly a matter for the local authorities, though the Department did intend to publish a pamphlet on home/school relations.[14] And there was a similar response to an

[13] DES circular 11/67.
[14] *Parliamentary Debates, Commons*, 3 March 1968, cols. 1602-3.

enquiry about what was being done to increase the number of teachers' aides in priority areas. 'It is for the local education authority to decide on the employment of teachers' aides, in the light of the resources available and the needs of the area. . . .'[15]

Early in 1968 the Secretary of State was asked what the government was doing about the Plowden recommendations apart from the allocation of the £16 million for building. He replied that some £10 million of the normal major building programme had been allocated to EPA schools and also some of the additional £8 million a year recently announced for 1968 and 1969. Further, in the quota calculations a number of teachers were being held back for service in priority areas. Protests that the government was being too dilatory were rejected. 'Quite a lot of the proposals of the Report are being . . . carried out, but some . . . will be very expensive . . . restrictions on central and local government expenditure will hold up these and other desirable reforms.'[16]

The government had persistently refused to commit itself to expanding nursery education and at this point, in reply to a further question, Mr Gordon Walker argued that, apart from problems of cost, more nursery classes would simply take teachers from the primary schools. Later replies to questions in the House confirmed that the government had no intention of making extra funds available to develop nursery education in general, though they might sanction proposals for extra classes which were included in the schemes being submitted by the local authorities with priority areas.[17] The Secretary of State was also questioned about the possibility of changing the weighting of the rate support grant to help areas of high population density, a matter which, he replied, was being considered.

From 1 April 1968 teachers employed in schools of exceptional difficulty were to receive an extra £75 a year—such schools to be recognized by the Secretary of State on the recommendation of the local authority. Criteria for selection were to be the social and economic status of parents, the absence of amenities in children's homes, the proportion of

[15] *Parliamentary Debates, Commons,* 19 November 1970, col. 435.

[16] *Parliamentary Debates, Commons,* February 1968, cols. 1534-5.

[17] *Parliamentary Debates, Commons,* 8 February 1968, cols. 629-30 & 637-8.

children receiving free meals or whose families received supplementary benefits and the proportion of children in the schools with serious linguistic difficulties. Problems arose, however, over the matter of designation for purposes of the extra allowances for teachers. In 1967 the Burnham Committee had allotted £75 to teachers in schools of special difficulty on the understanding that local education authorities should apply to the Secretary of State for the schools to be so recognized. But in July 1968 the Secretary of State maintained that he could not select from the lists submitted by local authorities without creating 'serious anomalies' and asked the Burnham Committee to consider other ways of distributing the £400,000 set aside for the purpose. The Committee did not however wish to consider alternatives, and in November the Minister again agreed to be responsible for selection.

By April the allocation of the £16 million had been settled and distributed among over 150 school building programmes. Altogether 51 authorities in England and six in Wales shared in the programme. The English regions benefiting most were the North West, the North East, the Midlands and London, all being authorized to spend between £3 million and £4 million while Wales was allowed £1 million. In a comment on these arrangements the Secretary of State remarked that government action in going ahead with the programme despite the country's economic difficulties was a measure of the importance it attached to improving school conditions. 'The concept of EPAs is one of the most imaginative proposals of the Plowden Report. This building programme together with the special allowances for teachers ... is evidence of the government's determination to follow up the Plowden recommendation as fast as resources allow.[18]

In fact at the beginning of 1968 there were 424 schools containing 104,431 children in England, 143 with 40,144 children in London and five with 1,226 children in Wales which were recognized for purposes of special payments to teachers. This meant a total of 572 schools with 145,801 children. The schools so designated corresponded roughly though not exactly with those benefiting from the building programme. The schools distinguished as meriting special

[18] Press notice by the DES, 4 April 1968.

treatment thus accounted for 145,801 children out of a total of 3,694,975—very far short of the 10 per cent envisaged in the Plowden Report for designation by 1972.

The identification of schools needing priority treatment was rather an arbitrary procedure and in practice reflected not so much the circumstances of the schools as the amount of money the government chose to make available for improving them. This was made very clear by the Minister of State in reply to a question about what estimates the Department had made of the number of schools needing priority treatment. The answer was as follows: 'None. It is not practicable to try and list such schools centrally. The procedure adopted has been to decide centrally the resources available and the criteria of need, and then to seek bids from local education authorities and to select from among them those schools where the needs are judged to be most urgent.'[19]

Meanwhile, the question of expanding nursery education continually engaged the attention of MPs. In the summer of 1968 the Minister of State refused to withdraw the circular preventing local authorities setting up nursery classes, but added that she was considering the possibility of limited expansion.[20] It was also reported that 23 of the proposals approved under the £16 million building programme included plans for replacing existing nursery classes or building new ones.

Possibilities of further advance in nursery education were reopened by the Urban Programme, announced by the government at the end of July 1968, which embodied an attempt to tackle some of the problems of the most severely deprived areas through increased expenditure on education, housing, health and welfare. A new grant was to be introduced, payable retrospectively on expenditure incurred by local authorities on schemes approved under the Urban Programme. The government declared itself ready to sanction immediately expenditure up to £25 million over the succeeding four years. It planned to select a number of local authorities showing clear evidence of urgent need and to agree with them projects which could start without delay. The Home Secretary added that he expected that in the first

[19] *Parliamentary Debates, Commons*, 22 July 1968, col. 39.
[20] *Parliamentary Debates, Commons*, 27 June 1968, cols. 785-6.

year the projects would be mainly concerned with nursery education and child care.[21]

In October a joint circular from the Home Office, the DES and the Ministry of Health[22] explained the details of the Urban Programme to the 34 selected local authorities and invited them to submit their proposals—specifically limited for the initial phase (the remaining months of the financial year) to nursery classes and children's homes which might be approved up to a value of £3 million.

In February 1969 the second phase of the Urban Programme was introduced covering the period up to the end of 1970 and involving expenditure up to a further limit of about £2 million. At this point all local authorities were invited to submit proposals, the rate of government grant being fixed at 75 per cent of approved expenditure, and schemes were no longer limited to nursery schools and children's homes. The government indicated to the local authorities that it would give specially favourable consideration to plans for teacher centres, for in-service training courses, for language classes for immigrants, for family advice centres, for aid to voluntary societies and for expenditure on educational materials, equipment and transport.[23]

A year later, in June 1970, a third joint circular[24] set out the government's future plans for the Urban Programme and the arrangements for the third phase. The original four-year programme was to be extended for a further four years up to March 1976, it being anticipated that local authority expenditure between 1972 and 1976 would amount to between £35 and £40 million. During the third phase the government was prepared to approve plans for capital expenditure up to the value of £4 million for the period up to March 1973 and for new revenue items up to £400,000 for the year 1970–71. All local authorities were invited to submit proposals along the lines suggested in previous circulars and were informed that, although the Urban Programme had too small resources to be able to contribute to housing development, grants would be available for extra staff to deal with housing problems in areas of special need.

[21] *Parliamentary Debates, Commons*, 22 July 1968, cols. 40-1.

[22] Joint Circular, Home Office 225/68, DES 19/68, Ministry of Health 5/68.

[23] Joint Circular, Home Office 34/69, DES 2/69, DHSS 2/69.

[24] Home Office 117/70, DES 9/70, DHSS 9/70.

The joint circular also contained a review of progress to date under the earlier phases of the Urban Programme. Altogether expenditure amounting to £8·5 million had been approved which was to provide over 10,000 new places in nursery classes, over 2,000 new places in day nurseries and 20 more homes for children in care. A variety of other approved schemes, listed in an annexe to the circular, were concerned with the development of playgroups and community work, aid to voluntary bodies of different kinds, holiday projects for children, centres for different groups of handicapped children and adults, and the appointment of advisory staff.

Meanwhile, it became clear in reply to questions in the House that the government did not propose to make any further specific capital allocations for priority areas beyond the £16 million for 1968–70.[25] The Department did however propose to concentrate the resources available for building and improvements in the priority areas: 'The Secretary of State believes that the principle of EPAs is now widely accepted; and although he does not underestimate the claims of other areas, he proposes to allocate most of the resources available in 1971–72 to projects in urban areas of acute social need.'[26]

In November 1969 the Secretary of State was asked about progress in the priority areas—about pupil/teacher ratios, about the amount of money allocated and attempts to measure its effectiveness and about the number and proportion of children attending nursery schools or classes. Mr Short reported that 86 local education authorities had benefited from the £16 million special building allocation, the £75 allowance for teachers in schools of exceptional difficulty (£0·4 million per annum) and from the educational element in the Urban Programme (£3·4 million up to date). He pointed out that no areas were designated as EPAs as such. The Department's information related to those authorities which had qualified for a share of the £16 million building allocation or within which schools had been recognized as of exceptional difficulty or which had had schemes approved under the Urban Programme. Figures about pupil/teacher

[25] *Parliamentary Debates, Commons,* 24 April 1969, cols. 639-40; 17 July 1969, col. 874.
[26] Letter from the DES to local education authorities, 13 November 196

ratios and the proportion of children in nursery classes were available for the whole local authority areas and these were supplied. But the Secretary of State maintained it was too soon to attempt to measure the results of the expenditure. Further information about nursery education in the 86 authorities was provided in December.[27] The increase of 10,000 nursery school places under the Urban Programme meant that there would be a total of 107,000 places in these areas.

By January of 1971 further expenditure of £4·4 million was authorized under the Urban Programme for capital spending over the next two years with an additional £600,000 for non-capital projects. It was to cover an additional 5,219 places in nursery schools and classes, and other schemes for day nurseries, centres for the old and handicapped, community work, special facilities for immigrant children and housing advisory centres. The approved expenditure was in respect of 530 projects submitted by 107 local authorities. In all 135 local authorities had proposed 1,530 schemes. At the end of the year the government allocated a further £1·2 million to provide 3,000 more nursery places,[28] thus bringing the total of new places approved under the Urban Programme to over 18,000. Plowden recommended an increase of over 500,000 places for the country as a whole by 1975.

Conclusion

At the end of 1971, government interest in the EPA idea remained very uncertain with only one more year of the present Urban Programme to run and with a history of only half-hearted support by either political party for the proposals spelled out in the Plowden Report. On the hustings in 1970 both Mr Short and Mrs Thatcher promised priority for primary education; smaller classes, better buildings and more nursery provision. There had been some progress in the five years since 1966 but it had been slow.

The Plowden Committee aimed to improve the ratio of teachers to children in EPAs to a point at which no class in

[27] Parliamentary Debates, Commons, 11 December 1969, cols. 163-4.
[28] Parliamentary Debates, Commons, 18 November 1971, cols. 659-60.

those areas exceeded 30. By 1970 the Chief Education Officer of Manchester reported that in his 38 EPA schools there were 237 classes among which 107 were up to that standard with 29 children or less, 89 with between 30 and 40 children, and only 12 with 40 or more. Reporting from Wolverhampton in *The Times* (December 1971) Mrs Rene Short remarked that the borough had nearly 2,500 primary school children being taught in classes of 40 or more. She also complained that Wolverhampton was being allowed to build only 2 out of 11 primary projects in the period 1972–74. Again, while there had been some gesture towards a national building plan it fell short of the recommendation in the Plowden Report that approximately £5,000 be allocated for minor works for every EPA school. There had also been some move to increase nursery education against a background of total inactivity from 1944, but the majority of EPA children still had no such provision.

One of the first of the government's responses to the Plowden Report was to introduce a £75 a year increment for EPA teachers, which is now raised to £83, but the Committee had recommended £120. Meanwhile little or nothing has been heard of the proposal to add teachers' aides in the priority schools to a ratio of 1 to every 2 infant and junior classes. There were also proposals to link students in training with priority schools and to set up teachers' centres for in service training. Our study has shown that a very valuable contribution can be made by the colleges of education, but little has been done to develop such schemes nationally. Local projects have also concentrated on trying to develop the notion of the community school to which the Plowden Committee attached great significance, and enterprising and ingenious experiments have been introduced in efforts to establish the schools as centres of local interest and activity which form an essential part of the life of the neighbourhood.

In general, the efforts to turn the idea of the priority area into reality and to devise ways of following up the recommendations of the Plowden Committee have derived largely from the enthusiasm and commitment of a small group of people. Local experience has undoubtedly opened up a great range of possibilities and the Urban Aid Programme has allowed some significant advances. The question now is whether the British government is prepared to launch a full-scale national policy.

11

P. ARMITAGE

Planning in Practice: the Work and Legacy of the External Committee

It is a British tradition to protect the work of civil servant
from direct scrutiny and only a very small part of thei
labours is divulged in publications. Consequently, when mos
people are asked about educational planning they think firs
of the famous committees and commissions (usually know
by the names of their chairmen—Robbins, Plowden, Newson
Crowther, James) which have deliberated over particula
aspects of the educational system during the past two de
cades.

Any study of planning in practice could well begin b
examining the work of these committees in detail. Here w
will briefly look at the Robbins and James Reports as prim
and representative examples of the work of external com
mittees. We will be particularly interested in their contrastin
approaches and the different underlying conceptions of pla
ning revealed by the two reports. We will then look at th
method of Robbins in more detail as a prelude to notin
how planning is transformed when this work is assimilate
and taken over by the Department of Education and Scienc
A further example of this metamorphosis will be provided k
following the work of the National Advisory Council on th
Supply and Training of Teachers as it has subsequently bee
pursued by the DES. Finally we will look at the 1972 Whi
Paper on education as the latest stage in the evolution
planning since Robbins and conclude by considering tl
problems of 'open planning' and public involvement.

Robbins and James

As appointed committees, both Robbins and James were given terms of reference. Appointed by the Prime Minister, Robbins[1] was asked:

> to review the pattern of full-time higher education in Great Britain and in the light of national needs and resources to advise Her Majesty's Government on what principles its long-term development should be based. In particular, to advise, in the light of these principles, whether there should be any change in that pattern, whether any new types of institution are desirable and whether any modifications should be made in the present arrangements for planning and co-ordinating the development of the various types of institution.

A Committee of Inquiry appointed by the Secretary of State for Education and Science, James[2] was asked:

> In the light of the review currently being undertaken by by the Area Training Organizations, and of the evidence published by the Select Committee on Education and Science, to enquire into the present arrangements for the education, training and probation of teachers in England and Wales and in particular to examine:
> (i) what should be the content and organization of courses to be provided;
> (ii) whether a larger proportion of intending teachers should be educated with students who have not chosen their careers or chosen other careers;
> (iii) what, in the context of (i) and (ii) above, should be the role of the maintained and voluntary colleges of education, the polytechnics and other further education institutions maintained by local education authorities, and the universities and to make recommendations.

It should be noted that neither committee was asked to 'solve' a problem. They were invited to review, to inquire into and to examine areas of growing concern and to advise and make recommendations. The committees were not expected to per-

[1] *Higher Education*: Report of the Committee appointed by the Prime Minister under the Chairmanship of Lord Robbins, 1961–3. HMSO, Cmnd. 2154. Page 1.

[2] *Teacher Education and Training*. A Report by a Committee of Inquiry appointed by the Secretary of State for Education and Science, under the Chairmanship of Lord James of Rusholme. HMSO, 1972, p. iii.

form the role of management consultants and this was
reflected in their composition. The members were distinguished and possessed diverse educational experience, but the
overall character of the committee was dilettante rather than
technical.

Robbins and James set about their tasks in quite different
ways. With the whole of higher education in its sights, the
Robbins committee took nearly three years to report whereas
James, pressed to report urgently, managed to do so in
about one year. Whereas Robbins could be expansive and
entertain astonishment that there has 'never been a comprehensive survey of the field of higher education in the sense
in which we have decided to use that term',[3] James rushed
at its task and betrayed no lack of self-confidence. The main
virtue of Robbins was the recognition of higher education
as a system:

> Higher education has not been planned as a whole or
> developed within a framework consciously devised to
> promote harmonious evolution. What system there is has
> come about as the result of a series of particular initiatives
> concerned with particular needs and particular situations
> and there is no way of dealing conveniently with all the
> problems common to higher education as a whole.[4]

As a result, the review of the pattern of full-time higher
education led to a description which constituted a model that
played a vital role in the committee's reasoning. As we shall
see later, the principal expression of this model was the
calculation on the numbers of places needed in future in
various types of institutions. Although Robbins' deliberations
took many other forms as well, it was this pre-occupation
with numbers that characterized Robbins and gained it
reputation. Before and since other committees have been
vague in their formalizations. The conscious recognition of a
model as a necessary pre-requisite of any planning process
was an important step forward by Robbins.

In this respect, James was a regression, a throw-back of
the pre-Robbins style of report in which a model is so
implicit and so deeply buried for belief in its existence to
be a matter of faith. This did not impair the forceful expres-

[3] Robbins, p. 4.
[4] Robbins, p. 5.

sion of conclusions. The result of inquiry and examination was that the Committee upheld the widespread misgivings about the present pattern of teacher training and felt the need for a radical solution. Moved by the inadequacy of present arrangements and by the thought that a future surplus of teachers would necessitate the diversion of resources currently devoted to teacher training, James enunciated three propositions. First, 'the implicit standards of a key profession' require that entrants should have completed a full course of personal, higher education. Secondly, the distinctions between the training of graduate and non-graduate teachers should be abandoned. Thirdly, pre-service training is not enough. Consequently, James advocated a new three-cycle pattern consisting of a two-year general diploma, two years of teacher training and practice, and subsequently in-service training.

With a complete reorganization of teacher training in mind, there was no point in making a projection of the expected behaviour of the existing system in the manner of Robbins, and James either thought it impossible to make a projection of the proposed restructured system, or was discouraged from doing so by the Department of Education and Science.

There is a genuine difficulty here but, lacking a discernible model and Robbins' inclination towards statistical analysis, James's proposals were reached by a process of general propositions which left the Committee impotent to examine the consequence of its proposed system on the future supply of teachers or the costs of implementing the scheme. In place of such an examination, there are unsupported judgements such as the reassurance that the number of applicants qualified and willing to proceed to teacher training may be expected to exceed the number of second cycle places. Of course, James is not unique in appeals to expert opinion, and this assertion is not unlike Robbins' belief that there existed a pool of ability which could not be exhausted within twenty years. Time may prove that these views are correct but, no matter how vigorously they are stated, their speculative nature should not be forgotten.

The rather detached viewpoint of James is perhaps best revealed by the refusal to quantify costs because they would be based 'on a series of arbitrary assumptions (which, in any case, it would not be for us to make) ... too speculative to be worth presenting.'[5] Cost estimates, however unreliable, are likely to play a decisive role in whether any scheme is adopted or not, and to pretend otherwise is disingenuous. The attitude adopted by James either betrays some fundamental misconceptions about planning or some heel-dragging by the civil servants whose job it was to brief the Committee

Some element of forecasting is present in all planning and this involves assumptions which are inescapably arbitrary If some consideration is thought to be relevant or of importance, it cannot be dismissed on the grounds that it would require assumptions too speculative (or too politically sensitive) to be worth presenting. Sensible decisions cannot be reached by taking into account only those things which are thought to be 'reasonably' certain and by excluding those which are considered 'highly' uncertain. There is no point up to which speculation is worthwhile and beyond which it is worthless. What matters is whether something is relevant and likely to be important and this may have nothing to do with our certainty about it.

From our point of view, James might be cited as an example of anti-planning. Robbins would appear to be a much more rewarding source if only because of the emphasis upon statistical considerations. As we have already noted the Committee interpreted its task mainly in terms of how many places should be provided in future in the universities the colleges of education, and on courses of advanced further education. These provisions corresponded to decisions that had to be made.

In order to arrive at these decisions, it would seem necessary to consider the capacity of existing institutions and the consequences of providing various numbers of places in each of the sectors in future years. The Committee had to ask itself 'what the demand for places in higher education was likely to be' and 'what supply of different kinds of highly educated persons will be required to meet the needs of the nation'.[6] Robbins came to the conclusion that the forecasting of manpower needs was highly unreliable at that time and could only fall back on affirmations that a greatly increased stock of highly educated people was in the national interest

[5] James, p. 76.
[6] Robbins, p. 48.

The Committee laid down the famous guiding principle that 'all young persons qualified by ability and attainment to pursue a full-time course in higher education should have the opportunity to do so' but it did not specify the entry standards implied by this statement. At the time the information on demand and student motivation was highly inadequate, and Robbins was most concerned that the degree of competition for places, which had been seriously intensifying in the late fifties, should become no worse. Consequently, the Committee arrived at its estimate of how many places should be provided in future by assuming that the percentatages of school leavers with a given number of 'A' levels going to specific higher education destinations would be the same as they were in 1961. Later some improvement was hoped for and it was assumed that a 10 per cent increase would occur across the board by 1981. The whole of this increase was supposed to happen between 1967 and 1972 when the burden upon the system would be minimized.

It should be noted that the vagueness of the guiding principle did not mean that Robbins proposed to satisfy the qualified demand for places in each sector but only laid down that a place should be available somewhere in higher education. Since places had not been so freely available to those qualified by ability and attainment in 1961, the Committee was aware that it was under-estimating future demand. Robbins is usually regarded as having adopted a 'social demand' approach because the manpower approach was impracticable on the basis of evidence available at the time. This is erroneous because even the qualified demand could not be properly measured. A more correct label for the approach adopted would reflect the prime consideration that the degree of competition should become no worse and the secondary consideration that 'the organization of higher education must allow for free development of institutions'.[7]

In effect what happened was that Robbins prejudged the limits to which the government would go towards the satisfaction of qualified demand, avoided the need to examine the consequences of alternative decisions and then presented a single projection as its advice on the future scale of provision.

[7] Robbins, p. 9.

Robbins was concerned with many other things than the future number of places in higher education though its advice on provision was given pride of place at the top of a list of 178 recommendations. Many of these recommendations were accepted and from this point of view Robbins was probably the most successful educational committee to date. By comparison, James with a mere 133 recommendations was much less successful with the adoption of in-service training for teachers and a transformed version of its envisaged two-year diploma in higher education as its principal credits.

The acceptability of a committee's report depends upon many factors as well as its intrinsic merit. At least one critic has deflated the success of Robbins by asserting that the report 'no more than confirmed' the prospects already divined by the UGC and that all the vital decisions had been taken *before* the Committee was appointed.[8] Robbins was also lucky in timing. As Lord Boyle, who was Minister of Education when Robbins was presented, has noted: the Government had a bad conscience arising out of their decision early to 1962 to authorize a smaller sum of money for the 1962–67 quinquennium than the UGC had recommended' and 'echoes of this dispute were among the reasons that caused the government to accept Robbins with such alacrity'.[9] Lord Boyle also points out that the presentation of the Newsom and Robbins reports one after the other meant that 'after 1963 it was hardly controversial to say that you had massive evidence of the number of boys and girls who were being allowed to write themselves off below their true level of ability'.[10]

The value of a committee's work may not lie in its recommendations. Apart from the attraction that the establishment of a committee may put a troublesome topic on ice, their appeal to the Secretary of State could lie in the fact that he is under no obligation to accept the advice offered. Proposals may be rejected because of the intervention of considerations beyond the committee's terms of reference, while the airing of ideas is likely to be beneficial and demonstrates the Secre-

[8] Lord Boyle, 'Ministers and Educational Reports', Universities Quarterly Winter 1972, p. 8.

[9] *The Politics of Education,* Edward Boyle and Anthony Crosland in conversation with Maurice Kogan. Penguin, 1971, p. 93.

[10] Ibid., p. 91.

tary's concern. Even if no recommendations are adopted, it may be that the committee's work will stimulate a new policy in order to prevent some envisaged development.

The methodology of Robbins

Much praise and much criticism has been heaped upon Robbins. The criticism has concentrated on the definition of higher education used, the pre-occupation with full-time education and school leavers, the conservation of the existing structure of sectors, institutions and education opportunities.

Our present concern is with the underlying conception of planning revealed in the report. This was primitive and somewhat obscure. Excusably, because of the paucity of available information, the model of higher education used was crude and, consequently, dealt with the interplay of demand and supply inadequately. This conflict was avoided by equating the demand for places with the maximum supply which it was presumed the government would contemplate. This guesswork circumvented the need to consider the expected consequences of alternative decisions and the prob-lem of discriminating between them in order to choose the best decision. It led to a unique projection being offered as the sole basis of advice to the Minister.

Robbins was aware of some of its own shortcomings and of the weaknesses of the position it found itself in, and sug-gested improvements in models and their use and in planning arrangements. Better models would be achieved through the collection of better, more reliable data permitting more detailed descriptions. Of course better data is always desir-able but it should not be assumed that more data means better data. A more profound suggestion recognized that planning should not be carried out on an *ad hoc* basis. It can always be argued that consultants are unnecessary and it has been said that 'dependence on advice given by one-off groups of part-time, unpaid outsiders is evidence of some malfunction of the permanent bureaucracy'.[11] Partly in recognition of its own inadequacy and partly in recognition of the uncertainty of long-term estimates, Robbins envisaged a system of rolling planning in which detailed planning should

[11] 'An Anatomy of Commissions', W. Plowden, *New Society*, 15 July 1971.

be made for a period extending ten years ahead and those responsible for policy should also be provided with estimates covering the following decade. The Committee also went on to recommend 'a single Grants Commission should be responsible for advising the Government on the needs of all autonomous institutions of higher education in Great Britain and for distributing grants to them'.[12] Among the Commission's tasks was to be the setting up of 'standing committees to deal with areas of study and *ad hoc* committees to deal with topics of current interest'.[13]

These recommendations were not adopted but the DES did take on the task of up-dating calculations. Projections similar to those featured in the process of Robbins' argument began to appear frequently. However, it was not until 1970 that a total reappraisal along the lines of Robbins was published in *Educational Planning Paper No. 2* (hereafter referred to as EPP2). This consolidated, rather than advanced from, Robbins. There were minor variations but the same crude model was used and the computational procedures were almost identical. The basic simplicity of the method should be appreciated and is worthy of a brief description.

The whole calculation consists of six stages, each of which produces an interim projection that is necessary as an input for the stage that follows.

In stage 1, a projection is produced of the numbers of pupils by age expected to be in school in future years. This depends upon the size of the age groups as projected by the Government Actuary's Department and upon assumptions about the proportion of each age group who will be in school. These assumptions are based on trends in the past. For example, in 1955 8·9 per cent of the seventeen-year-old boys were in school. By 1960, this had risen to 12·4 per cent. The percentages from 1965 for each year up to 1971 were:

15·33   16·17   17·38   18·56   19·71   20·45   21·01

and it was assumed that the percentages would be 26·21 by 1975 and 21·40 by 1980. As the expected numbers of boys aged seventeen in 1975 are 365,000 and in 1980 are 418,000 these assumptions imply that the number of seventeen-year old boys in school in these years will be 95,000 and 131,200

12 Robbins, p. 241, para. 744.
13 Robbins, p. 241, para. 745.

respectively. A complete projection of the school population by age is built up in this way.

This is used in the second stage to produce a projection of school leavers of a given age in any year. For example, if there are 95,700 seventeen-year-olds in school in 1975 and 34,900 eighteen-year-old boys in school in 1976, it follows that 60,800 seventeen-year-old boys left school in 1975.

At the third stage this projection of school leavers is turned into a projection of leavers with given levels of qualifications. If we look at boys leaving school aged seventeen, we find that 97 per cent have at least one 'O' level, 91 per cent have at least three 'O' levels, 81 per cent have five or more 'O' levels, 69 per cent have at least one 'A' level, 58 per cent have at least two 'A' levels and 40 per cent have three or more 'A' levels. After examining variations in these achievement levels in the past, we can make assumptions about what they will be in the future, and so find how many boys aged seventeen will leave in any year with a given level of qualification. This can be done for all ages and for both boys and girls. We can then add up the leavers of all ages with a given level of qualification and find that our assumptions imply that there will be, say, 51,100 boys leaving with three or more 'A' levels in 1975–76 and that there will be 32,500 similarly qualified seventeen-year-old girl leavers at the same time.

The next stage produces the number of entrants to higher education. For example in EPP2 it was assumed that 28 per cent of the boys leaving with exactly two 'A' levels would currently go to university and another 10 per cent would go to colleges of education. The comparable percentages for girls were 15 and 42 respectively. Given the numbers of boys and girls projected to be leaving with two 'A' levels in 1976, this implied that there would be 6,200 boys and 3,000 girls with this qualification going to university in that year. When this process was repeated for all levels of qualification, it gave a total of 42,900 men and 23,300 women going to university from school in 1976. In determining the grand total of entrants to university, it is necessary to take into account entrants from further education, from overseas and from employment, as well as those from school. The assumptions made in EPP2 pushed the total number of men entrants to university in 1976 up to 55,500 and women up to 26,800.

The same procedures gave a complete projection of all the entrants to universities, colleges of education and advanced further education courses for every year up to 1981.

In the fifth stage of the calculation, the numbers of entrants to higher education are converted into numbers of places. Ideally this should be done by subjecting entrants to wastage and success rates every year and then adding up the numbers in higher education at any particular time. Because of the lack of data, Robbins and EPP2 resorted to notional 'effective lengths of course'. For example, in EPP2, it was assumed that the effective length of course for university undergraduates was 3·11 years for boys and 3·02 years for girls. Such assumptions produced an estimated 557,400 men and women in higher education in 1976 of whom 286,900 were in universities, 124,200 were in colleges of education and 146,300 were on advanced courses in further education.

In the final stage of the calculation unit costs are determined for a place in each sector of higher education, taking into account both recurrent and capital components, and used to multiply the projected numbers of places to provide the total public expenditure on higher education.

It will be appreciated that the whole calculation is essentially simple but requires a lot of arithmetic. It also embodies a considerable number of arbitrary assumptions. As we have already observed, Robbins deliberately understated the expected demand for places: 'we have been conservative in our assumptions and, if we had to guess at the probable direction of error, we think it more likely that we have set our sights too low'.[14] The Committee was aware that its estimates 'were inevitably attended by uncertainties and the possibility of error'[15] and that it had assumed 'criteria of selection that are capable of improvement'.[16]

When on the other hand a projection is produced within the DES (as in EPP2), the shift from a government submission to an official statement involves a retreat. Instead of the calculated understatement and firm recommendations expressed in modern, diplomatic language, there is even greater caution to the point of self effacement. The assumptions are supposed to be neutral with all speculation rigorously avoided

[14] Robbins, p. 265.
[15] Robbins, p. 66.
[16] Robbins, p. 265.

in case anything be construed as policy commitment. Thus EPP2 'is a working document intended to assist discussion ... and carries no implication whatever for future Government policy or finance'.[17] The assumptions adopted are described as 'reasonable premises in the light of information available at the time'.[18] Consequently the fallacy that the past is capable of unambiguous and neutral interpretation is repeated as are the Robbins assumptions about the proportions to be admitted to higher education. There is, of course, an awareness of other possibilities (some of which may even have been worked out by officials within the Department) but they are put aside for the purposes of publication: 'Different assumptions at any point in the calculation would have led to results differing to a greater or lesser extent from those presented here ... a considerable range of projections with differing scales of development could be devised. There are a considerable number of factors, both internal to the higher education system and external to it, which may have a significant impact on its future development. In many cases it is not practicable to assess their impact in quantitative terms.'[19]

This statement and the claim that the projection is not a prediction should deprive the exercise of much interest for significant factors, differing assumptions and alternative possibilities cannot be cheerfully dismissed. No convincing reason is offered for making this solitary projection the sole object of attention, worthy of setting all other possibilities aside. Any rational decision-maker would surely want to know, and would feel bound to consider, what the consequences of providing different numbers of places would be. We can only conjecture that the Department does perhaps consider the range of possibilities, but while these remain unpublished we are left to speculate on their policy implications. It may be that the DES was content to produce a facsimile of Robbins' public presentation. On the other hand it may be that, just as Robbins judged the extent to which the government would go towards meeting expected demand and so eliminated the need to look at alternatives, the Planning Paper involved a similar judgement balancing the pressure

---

[17] *Student Numbers in Higher Education in England and Wales.* Educational Planning Paper No. 2. HMSO, 1970, p. iii.
[18] Ibid., p. 8.
[19] Ibid., pp. 8–9.

from above in the form of the budgetary competition with other departments, against the pressure from below in the form of the buoyancy of demand and the proposals of educationalists. If this were true, it would be another flagrant example of decision by exclusion.

Certainly it is difficult to see how a single projection, presented with the disclaimer that it is not a prediction of the future and is free from all thought of new policies, can be the foundation of a debate having any sensible influence on actual decisions. As the agencies outside the DES do not produce independent projection and have no real vision of alternative future possibilities, it seems likely that the provisional and neutral nature of the DES estimates, and the arbitrariness of the assumptions upon which they are based, will soon be forgotten. There is the danger that the official estimates will dominate all argument and the minds of decision-makers to the point where they will tend to become self-fulfilling and the opportunities to develop the system in different ways will be neglected.

The Demand and Supply of Teachers

It would appear that the virtues of planning exercises being carried out regularly within the DES may be offset by the inhibitions upon the public expression of officials. Since we can expect planning functions to be more and more absorbed and developed within the DES, it is worth taking another example of the way in which the work of an external body has been modified by internal absorption. The National Advisory Council on the Training and Supply of Teachers was set up to advise the (then) Minister of Education in the late forties. Over the years the Council produced a number of reports, the last of which, the Ninth, appeared in 1965. For most of its later years, the Council was primarily concerned with making projections of the future demand and supply of teachers. The demand was projected by taking the number of teachers required to achieve specified aims in the distribution of class sizes by the use of pupil-teacher ratios. The supply was projected on the basis of the expected recruitment and the survival and wastage of the present stock of teachers. The differences between the projected demand and supply implied the future numbers of teachers to be trained.

The recommendations fluctuated over time. At the time of the fifth report it was thought that shortages were going to be substantially reduced and, in 1956, it was opportune to recommend the extension of training courses from two to three years. By 1965, when the ninth report appeared, the elimination of shortages was not foreseen until the late seventies or early eighties and the speeding-up of the expansion of the colleges of education was advocated.

A 'Note of Dissent' was appended to the Ninth Report by Eric Robinson (with the 'broad agreement' of Carter and Vaizey) which adopted the line that 'The Council has done competently what it set out to do but in my view it has undertaken the wrong task'. It went on:

> This Council has the reponsibility to make recommendations to the Secretary of State about the provisions and arrangements which should be made to ensure that the nation's schools are adequately staffed by suitable teachers. It has failed to make such recommendations. It has not asked the necessary questions 'What is the satisfactory level of teacher supply, in type, number and quality? How can we attain that level and how can we maintain it? How quickly can this be done and what will be the cost?' ... Instead of asking the questions I have enunciated the Council has asked 'What is the best that can be done about teacher supply if we assume the implementation of the Robbins Report?'[20]

The National Advisory Council was not reappointed and the (then) Secretary of State has since revealed that he had no intention of ever appointing it again:

> I thought that was a job that should be done inside the Department and not by an amorphous outside body. If the Department couldn't do that job, which was central to all its activities, it ought to pack up.[21]

At first, when DES took over the projections on the supply and demand of teachers, their form and style showed little difference from that adopted by the Council. Subsequently the pupil-teacher ratios upon which the demand projections

[20] *Ninth Report* of the National Advisory Council on the Training and Supply of Teachers. HMSO, 1965.
[21] *The Politics of Education*, Edward Boyle and Anthony Crosland in conversation with Maurice Kogan. Penguin, 1971, p. 173.

were heavily based, were brought into disrepute. With good reason it was pointed out that where extra teachers became available they were not always used to reduce class sizes and doubt was thrown on the 'continuing validity of this assumption, and indeed upon the practicability of equating any particular pupil-teacher ratio with a particular limit of class size'. The pupil-teacher ratios were not immediately abandoned but the following year the old-style shortages found by differencing supply and demand were shown only as far ahead as 1977 (previously they had been calculated to 1985) as a traditional measure, and a new concept was introduced. This was the simple quotient, the average number of pupils per teacher, and it had the attraction of putting a better gloss on prospects. As a result of the fast expansion of the colleges of education in the sixties, the supply of teachers was improving all the time, though no more so than had been expected previously. However, whereas the old method of presentation still showed shortages persisting until the late seventies, the new method simply showed things getting better without adding any notion of what was good enough. As a consequence, the concern over the shortage of teachers was dispelled immediately and replaced by the notion that the long-standing teacher problem had been overcome. No further projection has since appeared.

By 1972 the notion of a teacher shortage was now so deeply buried that James offered the threatening choice of dissipating the imminent surplus or of being deprived:

> To put it bluntly, the supply of new teachers is now increasing so rapidly that it must soon catch up with any likely assessment of future demand, and choices will have to be made very soon between various ways of using or diverting some of the resources at present involved in the education and training of teachers.[22]

James felt that there was no need to go into 'the failure of the National Advisory Council':

> Some of the reasons seem to be that it was too big: that it found itself advising on matters which fell solely within the discretion and responsibilities of the Government and was thus taking decisions that were essentially political;

[22] *Teacher Education and Training*, op. cit., p. 75.

and that it was hampered by working too much, in practice if not in theory on the principle of mandation.[23]

Nonetheless James did recommend the setting up of a National Council for Teacher Education and Training which was to have a variety of functions but 'would in some sense take the place of the former National Advisory Council'. The subsequent White Paper did not endorse this recommendation but stated that 'the Secretary of State has it in mind after consultation to establish an Advisory Committee on the Supply and Training of Teachers broadly on the model recommended by a 1970 Working Party'.[24] In view of the extension of nursery schooling, the introduction of wider in-service training and the moves towards a completely graduate teaching profession, clearly this will be a necessary step if the Secretary of State is to discharge 'her central responsibilities for teacher supply and training'. It remains to be seen whether the new Advisory Committee can be set up with sufficient independence from DES to be able to make a more positive contribution to planning than its predecessor.

The 1972 White Paper

The 1972 White Paper marks a further stage in the evolution of planning since Robbins. This statement of decisions and views by the Secretary of State was heralded as 'the first real look at full educational strategy', and 'the most comprehensive review of the educational system'[25] since the Butler Education Act of 1944. The justification for this claim was that the White Paper took into account five aspects at once—nursery education, school building, staffing standards in schools, teacher training and higher education—unlike the many commissions and committees which, during the intervening years, had studied one aspect at a time. This was an advance though the coverage seemed superficial and further progress will have to be made so that many more aspects can be considered simultaneously, e.g. non-advanced further education, adult education, special education, part-time

[23] Ibid., p. 57.
[24] *Education: A Framework for Expansion*. A White Paper presented to Parliament by the Secretary of State for Education and Science by Command of Her Majesty, December 1972. HMSO. Cmnd. 5174, p. 27.
[25] *Financial Times*, 7 December 1972.

education, curriculum reform, educational priority areas, etc. As a policy statement the White Paper was presented with negligible statistical backing and no promise that the basis of decisions would be revealed later. Even the parliamentary debate two months later failed to bring much clarification.

Like EPP2 and much of the argument since Robbins, the White Paper focussed on matters of scale, organization and cost rather than educational content. Unlike the earlier documents, however, it is characterized by tentativeness and an awareness of uncertainty and is lacking in any air of finality. The White Paper is put forward as

> a framework for future action. It indicates the general direction of a ten-year strategy for the education service but there is room for a good deal of tactical flexibility and for variation in timing in the later years and in the rate of progress. In each part of the programme, many points still remain for decision. The Government and their several partners in the provision of the service will be able to consider these and work out in consultation how the programme can best be carried through. This will call for a sustained coordination effort over a substantial period.[26]

Elsewhere there is the insistence that 'the Government must be free to vary the pace of development of these new measures according to the circumstances'[27] and at one point, there is the surprisingly modest proposition that 'the Government believe that they have a contribution to make to the current debate about the objectives of higher education'.[28]

The mixture of courage and doubt is best captured by the final paragraph of the White Paper. After contrasting the proposed rise in the schools sector from an annual rate of growth of $2\frac{1}{2}$ per cent for the decade 1961/2 to 1971/2 to a rate of 3 per cent for the decade 1971/2 to 1981/2 with a proposed decrease for the higher education sector from $6\frac{1}{2}$ per cent to 5 per cent, the White Paper closes:

> These percentage figures are very vulnerable to the uncertainties of longer-term forecasting, and are not of great significance in themselves. But taken together, they illustrate the Government's intention to continue the expansion

---

[26] *Education: A Framework for Expansion*, op. cit., p. 2.
[27] Ibid., p. 48.
[28] Ibid., p. 30.

of the education service; and, at the same time, reflect their judgement and intentions as to respective rates of expansion within the growing total. The Government believe that these constitute a balanced programme which builds upon the successes already achieved and will match, as they develop, the different requirements of the decade ahead.[29]

In some respects the White Paper marks a distinct break from all the previous post-Robbins pronouncements. It is frequently said that Robbins conclusions amounted to 'more of the same' rather than a change in the pattern of full-time higher education and the principles upon which it was based. The White Paper recasts the teacher training system, gives approval to the introduction of two-year Diploma of Higher Education courses and envisages that the universities will soon cease to be the major sector of higher education in terms of full-time places. Still there is no evidence that other possible developments of the system have been explored before reaching these decisions. The consequences of structural change present the planner with much more difficult problems than mere changes of scale. Whereas Robbins lacked information on what the demand for higher education had been, but otherwise tried to meet what it expected it would be, in the future, without disturbing the nature of demand, the White Paper makes changes which purport to offer a more diverse range of opportunities and must, if they have any effect at all, affect the attitudes and intentions of those who are eligible for higher education.

It is important that the prospects should be surveyed, but this is an exceedingly difficult task. In the two and a half years between EPP2 and the White Paper, there has been a trickle of statistical data from DES to suggest that some of the earlier assumptions needed revision. Although the proportions staying on in school were still rising, they were not rising quite so fast as had been expected. Similarly the percentages of school leavers with given levels of qualification were not quite up to EPP2 expectations, and in the early school years there was some alleviation of pressure as a result of the decline in the birth rate from mid-sixties to the present. Official comments have implied that later data, not yet published, will confirm these trends. However, this evidence was not marshalled to support the decisions in the

[29] Ibid., p. 49.

White Paper, and the lack of fresh information has frustrated the evaluation of both what has been happening and what might happen.

It is unfortunate that the basis upon which decisions have been reached is not disclosed. In consequence it seems as if changes have been dictated by the pressure of events and by wishful thinking rather than by reason. For example, the desire to reduce university costs leads to financing on the basis that the staff-student ratio will be modified from a current value of about 8:1 to about 10:1 by the end of the decade. This is backed by the hope that 'a gradual transition to this average figure should be possible without lowering standards'.[30] Similarly, although no decision emerges, there is an announcement that the Government 'are examining what steps might be taken to reverse the present trend and thus encourage many more students to base themselves at home while studying'.[31] This is accompanied by the observation that only 16 per cent of university students are home-based and by the admonishment that 'the Government share the frequently-expressed view that it is unrealistic and unnecessary for such a high proportion of students to reside and study at a distance if equally acceptable courses are available for them within travelling distance of their homes'.[32]

A more important example of the extent to which the success of policies rests heavily upon wishful thinking comes with the reaffirmation of the Robbins principles that courses of higher education should be available to all those qualified by ability and attainment who wish them. This is maintained despite the belief that 'there seems little doubt that the continuing expansion of higher education will more than match the likely expansion of graduate employment opportunities'.[33] The prospect of graduate unemployment is declared to be of minor relevance: 'Opportunities for higher education are not however to be determined primarily by reference to broad estimates of the country's future need for highly qualified people; ... The Government consider higher education valuable for its contribution to the personal development of those who pursue it; at the same time they

[30] Ibid., p. 37, para. 126.
[31] Ibid., p. 37, para. 128.
[32] Ibid., p. 37, para. 127.
[33] Ibid., p. 34, para. 116.

value its continued expansion as an investment in the nation's
human talent in a time of rapid social change and technological development.'[34] However 'the purposes and the nature
of higher education, in all its diversity, must be critically and
realistically examined ... The Government hope that those
who contemplate entering higher education—and those
advising them—will more carefully examine their motives
and their requirements; and be sure that they form their
judgement on a realistic assessment of its usefulness to their
interests and career intentions.'[35] The implication of this
section of the White Paper is that if demand is not moderated,
the 'limits of available resources and competing priorities'
will jeopardize the survival of the Robbins principle. On the
evidence of this argument, there has been very little progress
in the practice of planning since Robbins.

The Problems of Open Planning

In the decade since Robbins there has been much attention
to looking ahead and making calculations. These projections
are subject to great uncertainty and they embody many
arbitrary assumptions. Too much credence is given to these
numbers. They should not be treated as if they have some
independent validity but should be regarded as a minor
element in the apparatus of planning. Whether they are the
work of an external Committee or emanate from the DES,
the production of one set of numbers when a wide range of
developments is possible, corresponds to a lucky dip.

It has been a feature of the lucky dips so far that they
have all been low, and it would seem that there is always
some cause for a low bias. Robbins' anxiety to reach acceptable conclusions was so great that it made 'assumptions so
modest that no reasonable man could reject them'.[36] The
projections of DES aim at an impossible neutrality of assumption so that all speculation is ruthlessly shunned in case it
might be mistaken for policy commitment. When the UGC
makes judgements on what might be a reasonable basis for
planning, the figure is 'deliberately conservative' because 'It

[34] Ibid., p. 34, para. 117.
[35] Ibid., p. 35, para. 117.
[36] *The Impact of Robbins*, R. Layard, J. King and C. Moser, Penguin,
1969, p. 31.

would have been comparatively easy, if the Government were more generous to add to it' but 'more disturbing for universities to have to subtract substantially from it'.[37] Again the officials who prepare the public expenditure surveys 'do not try to agree upon any particular level of Government expenditure to be recommended to Ministers, nor upon its allocation. They confine themselves to the task of agreeing a factual report showing where present policies are likely to lead in terms of public expenditure at constant prices if they remain unchanged over the ensuing five years. ... The presentation of the material in this way does not prejudge the decisions which have to be reached.'[38]

There has been a recent tendency for planning activities to pass from the external committee and be carried out within the DES and this would seem to be right in so far as the Department possesses the full-time resources and technical competence to carry out the task. Unfortunately some experiences of the planning activities being brought within the orbit of the DES have not been satisfactory so far. The long civil service tradition of self-effacement and avoidance of 'sensitive areas' has meant that the exploration of possibilities has disappeared to vanishing point, and that the Secretary's assurance that a reasonable and balanced judgement has been reached carries no conviction.

Of course, educational planning is still emerging from the early stages of make-believe. It will take much more than improved techniques for tackling problems to realize the hoped-for advantages of open planning. It will require a new set-up with the planners inside the DES freed from the inhibitions of their traditional roles to ensure that their activities are no longer stunted to the point of absurdity. It will also require that those outside the DES, who participate in the planning process, have full and quick access to central information and intention. It will not be easy to achieve either of these necessities.

---

[37] *Second Report* from the Expenditure Committee together with the minutes of the evidence taken before the Education and Arts Sub-Committee and Appendices. Session 1970-71. HMSO, 1971, p. 201. 3.
[38] Ibid., p. 4.

12

R. LAYARD and J. KING[1]

The Impact of Robbins[*]

The explosion of higher education

Apart from electronics and natural gas, higher education has probably expanded faster than any other major industry in the 1960s. In the social histories of this period, it is certain to occupy a prominent place. From 1961–62 to 1966–67 the number of students in full-time higher education in Britain grew from 193,000 to 339,000. In these five years the increase in the absolute number of students was greater than in the preceding fifty and the percentage growth, of 76 per cent, was nearly twice as high as in the preceding five-year period (41 per cent). As Chart 12.1 shows, the proportional growth was highest in the colleges of education (126 per cent) and in the technical colleges and other institutions of further education (120 per cent). But the universities also grew though much slower (at 49 per cent)—a growth in which nearly all of them played a part.

How has this fantastic explosion come about? It has to be seen in terms of demand and supply for places. Demand has grown particularly sharply over the last five years owing to the coincidence of 'bulge' and 'trend'—the 'bulge' being the increase in the number of young people of the relevant age (due to the surge in births at the end of the War), and the 'trend' being the increase in the proportion of those who

[*] [From 'The Impact of Robbins' in *Higher Education Review*, Autumn 1968.]
[1] This article is based on a forthcoming Penguin Education Special by P. R. G. Layard and J. R. B. King, and the work has been carried out in the Unit for Economic and Statistical Studies on Higher Education at LSE. Details on the statistical sources for the article will be found there. [*The Impact of Robbins*. By Layard, Moser and King, Penguin, 1968.]

228   New Developments in Educational Planning

obtain school leaving qualifications. The 'trend' was already, by 1961, a well-established phenomenon and has continued, though at a sharper rate, since then. The bulge was, however, new and greatly boosted the output of well-qualified school leavers.

An increased demand for places need not of course produce a magic increase in supply. This depends on the response of the suppliers. How has the Government responded? Let us begin with university provision. Table 12.1 shows the growth in the numbers of young people having two or more GCE 'A' levels and the growth in university entry. From 1957 to 1962 the average increase in the numbers with two or more 'A' levels was relatively small compared with that experienced since. Yet the provision of university places grew a good deal less fast than the relevant group of school leavers and their opportunities declined proportionally. This was the context in which the Robbins Committee* was appointed.

There were of course many reasons for the Committee's appointment—the need for administrative co-ordination between the different sectors, the problems posed by the rising academic standards and aspirations of the colleges of advanced technology and colleges of education, the difficulty of having the Treasury directly responsible for the increasing volume of public expenditure taken by universities, and the widespread feeling that all the parts of the system of higher education should be planned as a whole. But in essence all these problems sprang from the growth in demand for higher education and the consequent inflation of the system. In particular there was increasing public feeling that university entry was becoming more difficult—a feeling borne out by our figures.

There was at the time no clear government philosophy on how to respond to the increasing flow of applicants. The Robbins Committee supplied a philosophy: the number of places should grow fast enough to accommodate a constant proportion of applicants. To be more precise, it recommended that the ratio of entrants to the output of those with two or

† [Committee on Higher Education, appointed by the Prime Minister, under the chairmanship of Lord Robbins. Established in 1961, the Committee reported in 1963. Note that unlike Plowden the Robbins Committee was not a reconstitution of the Central Advisory Council, which produced the Newsom Report at about the same time as Robbins himself reported.]

more 'A' levels should, over the period up to 1967, remain constant. As Table 12.1 shows, this is broadly speaking what has happened. Despite enormous increases in the number of well-qualified school leavers, the numbers of university entrants and of entrants to all forms of higher education have

Chart 12.1

Students in full-time education in Great Britain

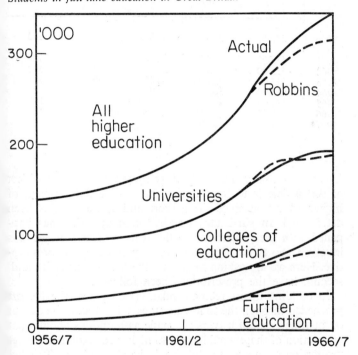

since 1962 broadly kept pace with them. By the combined efforts of the Government, the local authorities and the institutions themselves, the downward trend in entry rates over the previous five years has been halted and the crisis of the 'bulge' surmounted without any serious aggravation of pressure on places. This in essence is the quantitative impact of Robbins.

Table 12.1

Output of those with two or more 'A' levels and entrants to full-time higher education. Persons from England and Wales

	Numbers obtaining two or more 'A' levels (1)	University entrants (including) former CATs (2)	All entrants (3)	University entrants as % of two or more 'A' levels (4)	All entrants as % of two or more 'A' levels (5)
1956	27,000	21,400	36,300	79	133
1961	43,000	28,000	52,000	65	120
1962	51,000	30,000	57,000	59	112
1963	53,000	32,000	64,000	59	121
1964	61,000	36,000	74,000	59	121
1965	73,000	42,000	87,000	57	119
1966	75,000	43,000	95,000	57	126
1967*	79,000	46,000		58	

* Estimated.

It is not of course the whole story by any means. The object of this article is to look at the quantitative development of higher education since the Report and at how it has been determined. In particular, we shall compare what has happened with the projections in the Report. These projections involved two types of assumptions—predictive and prescriptive. Here we are asking first, were the predictions right, and, second, have the prescriptions been followed?

In building up its recommendations on places the Report proceeded through the following steps[2]: it forecast the output of 'qualified school leavers'; it made assumptions about what proportion of these would apply to higher education and what proportion of those who did should be given places. This led to an estimate of entrants. It made assumptions about length of course and overseas students, thus providing an estimate of places. It also made recommendations on staffing and finance. The blueprint which resulted was the first overall plan for higher education in this country.[3]

[2] See *Higher Education*, Cmnd. 2154, HMSO, 1963, Chapters 6 and 11.
[3] In what follows we shall continue ourselves to full-time higher education. On places, staffing and finance we deal with Britain and on school leavers and entrants with people from England and Wales, as the Scottish data provide no meaningful time series.

Before we look at how the plan has worked out, we shall take a look at the Government's immediate reception of the plan and at the public's reaction to the way in which it was constructed.

Reception of the Report

Few official reports in British history, and certainly in educational history, have led such immediate changes in Government policy. Many of the qualitative recommendations were, it is true, left in abeyance, but the quantitative recommendations up to 1973–74 were accepted in a White Paper published within 24 hours of the Report.[4] It is not cynical to compare the treatment received by the Crowther Report published months after a General Election and the Plowden Report published months after another one, with that received by Robbins which came out a year before one. However, there were other powerful reasons for the Government's favourable response. In the first place the crisis of the 'bulge' was so near that there was no time to waste. Moreover, the very setting up of a committee and the debate which follows often completely changes the whole climate of public opinion about the issue being investigated. This is certainly what happened with Robbins. When the Committee was set up there was probably a majority of educated opinion, in the Civil Service and outside, in favour of the view that there was some limit that would soon be approached in the proportion of people who could benefit from higher education. But during the two and a half years of the Committee's work, this 'pool of ability' school of thought was in progressive retreat. The Committee's foreign visits helped to remind people of the lengths to which things seemed to have gone in other countries without loss of quality; and when the Report was published the Committee's Survey of twenty-one-year-olds further strengthened the hands of those who believed in the importance of environment in determining intellectual attainment. Thus by 1963 it seemed quite acceptable to look forward to an endless upward trend

[4] *Higher Education, Government Statement on the Report of the Committee under the Chairmanship of Lord Robbins 1961–63*, Cmnd. 2165, HMSO, 1963.

in higher education in the foreseeable future, and not, as had been customary, to look for a plateau.[5]

The public reception of the Report was also on the whole enthusiastic. Of the major papers, *The Times* was noticeably hostile, and, although chided by Sir Geoffrey Crowther for intellectual 'Bourbonism',[6] its hostility did not diminish with time. A part of the trouble was based on a misunderstanding of the term 'qualified school leavers'. This term had been used in the Report in an entirely neutral sense to mean those holding particular qualifications (e.g. two or more 'A' levels) and not in a normative sense implying that such people were necessarily qualified for higher education. *The Times* in its leaders managed to imply that Robbins had said that all with two or more 'A' levels should go to university. This point was ultimately clarified[7] but for the avoidance of confusion we use here the term 'well-qualified leavers' to indicate the total output (from school and technical colleges) of those with whatever the qualifications concerned.

Other critics have questioned the relevance of numbers obtaining GCE as a variable from which to deduce numbers suitable for higher education. This criticism is only relevant on the hypothesis that past trends in GCE have not corresponded to past trends in numbers suitable for higher education. In fact we believe the trends have been broadly similar, and this was the reason for the claim in the Report[8] that what is being projected is some variable proportional to numbers suitable for higher education, and that for convenience we label this variable by familiar qualifications.

An annual signal for the 'pool of ability' school to show itself has been the publication of the figures of vacancies in university departments. It is true that these vacancies, which are almost entirely in science and technology, raise important issues of the balance between faculties, but they normally represent not more than 1 or 2 per cent of all places. Moreover the annual expansion in student numbers is always many

---

[5] It is also relevant that the Robbins figures for 1973–74 were not a great deal higher than for 1967–68, as the latter were swollen by the 'bulge'. This undoubtedly made the Government more willing to enter into a ten year commitment than it might otherwise have been.

[6] *The Times*, 28 October 1963.

[7] See *The Times*: Leaders of 28 September 1964 and 5 October 1964, and letters from G. A. Moser and P. R. G. Layard of 29 September 1964 and 8 October 1964.

[8] Appendix One, p. 97.

times the number of vacancies in the previous year. Though frictional under-utilization of capacity should be cut to the minimum, it is hardly a sign that the general philosophy of expansion is wrong. There is no shortage of well-qualified applicants overall, though there is a mis-balance between faculties.

A more fundamental criticism attacked the whole philosophy of basing provision on the demand of school leavers for places, rather than on the demand from the economy for the products of the system. The Robbins Committee rejected this latter basis, both because of their desire to meet the 'social' demand from boys and girls, and because of their doubts about techniques of manpower forecasting.

There is a strong case in principle for basing the provision of education on cost-benefit criteria—benefits being defined in the widest possible way to include psychic as well as more directly measurable effects.[9] This would involve calculating the current rates of return obtained by using current income differentials, and also attempting to estimate future shifts in the demand for educated manpower by isolating the variables which affect it. At present a good deal of work is proceeding on both these fronts in our Unit[10] and elsewhere, but it is not yet sufficiently advanced to form a basis for projections based directly on manpower requirements.

However, it is wrong to underestimate the link between the growth in numbers who would be justified on social cost-benefit grounds and the numbers which would arise on the Robbins criteria of demand for places. For the private demand for places depends, we think, largely on the private rate of return to be got from undertaking higher education, while the number of places justified on cost-benefit grounds depends on the social rate of return. On a number of quite plausible assumptions these two rates of return will move in step;[11]

---

[9] On general issues of objectives in educational planning see Moser and Layard, *Planning the Scale of Higher Education in Britain: Some Statistical Problems*, JRSS Series A, 4, 1964. M. Blaug, *Approaches to Educational Planning*, The Economic Journal, June 1967, and Alper, Armitage and Smith, *Models for Educational Decision Making* (forthcoming). Explicitly on social rate of return see Blaug, *The Rate of Return on Investment in Education in Great Britain*, The Manchester School, September, 1965.

[10] The Unit for Economic and Statistical Studies on Higher Education at LSE.

[11] The social rate of return depends on the pre-tax income differential between people with and without higher education and on the social cost

thus private demand will surge forward only when people with higher education can be productively employed and vice versa. One key assumption, however, is the continuation of present policies on subsidies to students. The Robbins Committee judged that, given prevailing attitudes to education, these ought to be maintained for a time on social grounds. It is clear, however, that if the private price were raised, the private demand would be lower than otherwise. The Robbins Committee have been wrongly charged with being unaware of the fact.[12]

A quite different line of criticism has come from those who think that, though there may be enough suitable students worth educating, there will not be enough staff. The Report contained the tautological statement that on certain assumptions a system expanding at a constant or declining rate

Table 12.2

Percentages of the age group at school at 17 and obtaining two or more 'A' levels

	1954	1961	1966	
			Actual	Robbins
At school aged 17				
Boys	8·6	13·1	16·2	16·2
Girls	7·1	10·2	13·2	12·2
Boys and girls	7·9	11·7	14·7	14·2
Obtaining two or more 'A' levels				
Boys	5·7	8·7	11·6	10·8
Girls	2·9	5·1	7·5	6·1
Boys and girls	4·3	6·9	9·6	8·4

of higher education. The private rate of return depends on the above together with the rates of taxation and the rates of subsidy of higher education. Thus the absolute level of private and social rates of return differ But suppose the demand for educated people, viewed as a function of their relative wages, grows at a given rate, that proportional tax rates are constant and that social costs and subsidies rise at the same rate as average wages per head. Then the shift in supply of educated people needed to keep the social rate of return constant will also maintain the private rate of return at its present level.

[12] For the influence of student grants on private demand, see the Robbins Report, para. 645 and Appendix One, p. 100, para. 15.

of compound interest could staff itself. This was admitted to be true, but critics argued that the steady state assumption was irrelevant and that short-run problems were formid- able.[13] Calculations in the Report had in fact explicitly pointed to these short-run problems. But events have on the whole disproved these fears, and student-staff ratios have even fallen in most faculties. At the same time teachers' salaries have not in general moved adversely to other salaries. The success of the expansion programme is thus due to the fact that in a general sense the Government not only willed the end but also willed the means.

Table 12.3

Annual increment in the percentage of the age group staying at school as percentage of its 1961 value England and Wales

	1954–61 Actual	1961–66 Actual	1961–66 Robbins
At school aged 17			
Boys	4·9	4·9	4·7
Girls	4·3	6·1	3·9
Boys and girls	4·6	5·4	4·3
Obtaining two or more 'A' levels			
Boys	4·9	6·7	4·8
Girls	6·1	9·4	4·1
Boys and girls	5·4	7·8	4·5

Trends in qualified school leavers

Now to the trends. As we explained, the Committee's recom- mendations for places were built up step by step starting with a projection of the output of well-qualified school leavers. As is well known, this projection has turned out to be too low. The position can be summarized in Tables 12.2 and 12.3.

Robbins forecast that the proportion of the age group con- taining two or more 'A' levels would rise from 6·9 per cent in 1961 to 8·4 per cent in 1966. In fact as Table 12.2 shows it rose to 9·6 per cent. The number of leavers with these quali- fications was thus (only 5 years from the base year) already

[13] See Professor Thwaites at The Home Universities Conference, Decem- ber 1963.

16·5 per cent higher than was forecast. If we look at the position in terms of growth rates the forecast annual increment (0·31 per cent of the age group) equalled 4·5 per cent of the percentage of the age group successful in 1961 (0·31 per cent is 4·5 per cent of 6·9 per cent). This forecast rate of 4·5 per cent simple interest growth is shown in Table 12.3 and compares with 7·8 per cent actually realized, and 5·4 per cent over the period 1954–61. The difference between forecast and actual rate of growth is much greater for girls (9·4 per cent compared with 4·1 per cent) than for boys (6·7 per cent compared with 4·8 per cent). These results have amply confirmed the warnings of the Robbins Committee that their projection of places needed should be regarded as a minimum, and their view that the projections were particularly conservative in the case of girls. We are not able to say, except in terms of arithmetic, why the trend in achievement has been so much higher since 1961 than before; but it may well be that the Report itself and the atmosphere it created has contributed to the outcome.

Arithmetically we can examine the two components in the forecast of output: first, the numbers staying on at school, and second, the proportion of these who get good qualifications. If we do this, we find that the Robbins estimates of the trend to stay at school have been relatively accurate (especially in 1965 and earlier)—the growth in the percentage staying on to each age being fairly well in line with that predicted by linear extrapolation of the experience of 1954–62. This illustrates an interesting fact about the British (and many other) educational systems. Suppose we want to predict the numbers of seventeen-year-olds at school at a given time. The simplest method would be to project the past trends in the absolute numbers, but in this particular period this would have produced hopelessly wrong results. For the size of the age group (which in this period fluctuated wildly) profoundly affected the numbers staying on in school. However if we take this as given, the proportion of people of a given age who stay at school shows an uncannily stable trend. The mechanism whereby this comes about must be complicated. One can imagine that in any particular year the pattern of attainments among a cohort is independent of its size, and that it is this pattern that determines, via its effect on attitudes of school teachers, parents and children, the proportion who stay on.

Even so, it is remarkable that the absolute number appears to be more or less irrelevant, considering that it is the absolute number who have to be provided with desks and teachers and the absolute number who have to find suitable jobs. The stability of these trends in staying on makes it clear that the adjustment of private educational behaviour to market opportunities is subject to important time-lags, and that other important long-term influences may also be at work.

Though the Robbins 'staying on' forecast was fairly successful, the 'A' level forecast went wrong; whereas the Robbins Committee assumed that the proportions of leavers of each age who obtain a given qualification would remain constant, they have in fact risen. The reasons are not too clear. The proportions clearly cannot go on rising above 100 per cent, and projections done at the Department of Education and Science since Robbins normally assume that their future rate of increase will be less than in the past. The result, as illustrated in Table 12.3, is that the projected growth in the percentage of the age group getting 'A' levels has tended to be smaller than that in the past.[14]

Universities

Granted the output of qualified school leavers, we can now examine the course of university expansion and see how opportunities of entry have been affected by government policy. As soon as the Government accepted the Robbins target of 197,000 places in universities (including former colleges of advanced technology) for 1967–68, the Chairman of the University Grants Committee wrote to all the universities asking them to say what they thought they could do to help to achieve this target and how much it would cost them. The required increase in places amounted to 40 per cent over four years, yet in their replies, the universities said they could provide some 20,000 places more than were needed—a magnificent response which considerably surprised those who hold

[14] This raises an important statistical question as to whether it is best to make separate projections for the two stages mentioned—first, 'staying on' and then the proportion of stayers on who qualify—or whether a more accurate answer might not be obtained by projecting the 'A' level proportions directly. For a number of reasons, we prefer the latter approach, even though it produces the statistical inconvenience of not being able directly to relate the 'A' level projection to that of school population.

a general belief that universities are impervious to social need. The response was undoubtedly influenced by the euphoric atmosphere induced by the publication of the Report, and also perhaps to some extent by the new opportunities offered by such an expansion. It did however dispel, one hopes for ever, the picture of universities as exclusive clubs which cannot bear to expand their membership. When we show (later) that other sectors have expanded faster than the universities, the reader should not forget that this is by the wish of the Government and not of the universities.

In the revision of the quinquennial settlement which followed, the universities, in receiving their new recurrent allocations, were asked to provide a total of places equal to the Robbins target. This they have done almost to the letter as Table 12.4 shows. The Robbins targets were based on the objective of maintaining the 1961 ratio between entrants and the output of well-qualified leavers. As we have seen in Table 12.1, the number of well-qualified leavers has been higher than Robbins forecast, by about 16 per cent by 1966. Since the number of entrants has been as Robbins recommended, the ratio of entrants to well-qualified leavers has fallen by about 12 per cent of itself, as Table 12.1 shows. But most of this fall occurred in 1962. It still seems desirable to aim at getting back to the 1961 position.

The recent quinquennial settlement for the years 1967–68 to 1971–72 does not achieve this. It provides for an increase of about 20,000 places over the Robbins targets for 1971–72: 220,000 to 225,000 places being the new official target.[15] But by that year we can expect (using the Department's latest projection) an output of people with two or more 'A' levels some 21 per cent higher than Robbins. This implies that the entry rate in 1971 will be only some 90 per cent of its 1961 value.

There remains however the critical problem of the subject balance in the intake.[16] In the late 1950s and early 1960s it was the policy of the UGC, reiterated by Robbins, that two-thirds of additional places in universities should be in science and technology. The point of view was that the total size of the universities should be based on a passive response to

[15] See Hansard, 27 October 1967, Cols. 591–2.
[16] On the issues discussed below see also Moser and Layard, op. cit. p. 510–11.

Table 12.4

Students in full-time higher education
Great Britain

	Universities (including former CATs)		Colleges of Education		Further Education		All full-time higher education		Percentage of places in universities	
	Actual	Robbins	Actual	Robbins	Actual	Robbins	Actual	Robbins	Actual	Robbins
1956–57	96	...	31	...	10	...	137	...	70	...
1961–62	123	...	42	...	27	...	192	...	64	...
1962–63	131	...	55	...	31	...	217	...	60	...
1963–64	140	142	62	59	36	36	238	238	59	60
1964–65	154	156	71	66	43	39	267	262	57	60
1965–66	169	173	82	74	51	42	302	290	56	60
1966–67	184	187	95	80	59	45	339	312	54	60
1967–68*	200	197	106	84	71	47	376	328	53	60
Percentage growth 1961–62 to 1966–67	49	51	126	89	120	67	76	62	...	...

* Estimated

popular demand, this demand being taken as relatively impervious to policy. On the other hand it was felt that the
subject balance within the resulting total could be based on
manpower considerations and that attempts to manage demand in this sense could be successful. They have proved a
complete failure. The swing away from science in the sixth
forms, that began in 1959 and was first noticed in the Robbins Report,[17] has continued; and the universities, faced with
a growing proportion of good candidates in arts, have responded in an essentially passive manner. Entry rates in arts
and science have moved roughly speaking together and
though it may have become marginally more difficult to find
a place in arts relative to science, the change does not come
out strongly in the statistics. As a result, instead of two-thirds
of the extra students in universities (excluding colleges of
advanced technology) being in science and technology, the
proportion of the extra places provided from 1961–62 to
1966–67 has been only 37 per cent. If we include colleges of

Table 12.5

*Places in universities (including former CATs) by faculty
Great Britain 1961–62 and 1966–67*

	Arts	Pure science	Applied science	Medicine	Agri-culture	Total
Number (thousands) Actual						
1961–62	49·3	31·4	24·1	16·6	2·1	123·4
1966–67	81·3	44·4	37·0	18·9	2·5	184·2
Robbins 1966–67	68·9	52·7	43·8	19·0	2·5	186·9
Percentage Actual						
1961–62	40·0	25·4	19·5	13·4	1·7	100
1966–67	44·1	24·1	20·1	10·3	1·4	100
Robbins 1966–67	36·9	28·2	23·4	10·2	1·3	100

[17] Robbins Report, pp. 163–4.

advanced technology in both years the proportion was 43 per cent. As Table 12.5 shows, the proportion of all places in arts subjects has risen from 40 to 44 per cent instead of falling to 37 per cent.

How are we to interpret this outcome? It is undoubtedly a failure of planning, since it implies that the capital investment in science has been higher relative to arts than it would have been if the ensuing teaching commitments had been foreseen. This debacle has arisen from the fact that, paradoxically, the universities, which are often thought to be outside social control, are in fact much more centrally planned than the schools. There is no advance planning of the size of sixth forms, still less of their subject balance. One reason for this is, of course, that the sixth forms constitute a small part of the school population and substantial changes in them can be fairly easily absorbed. The main instrument of planning in the educational system is via the control of capital expenditure, but most sixth forms have no specific buildings, and therefore those who sanction capital expenditure are not required to form a view about the sixth forms; nor, if they had a view, would they have any ready means of implementing it. There seems to be two ways out of this situation: to take an active manpower-orientated policy in the schools; or to stop taking one in the universities.

The UGC have now overtly opted for the latter. For the first time they issued (in November 1967) a 'Memorandum of general guidance explaining general ideas lying behind the allocations of the final quinquennial settlement announced in the same month.'[18] This is what the statement said about the subject balance: 'The Committee have taken the view that in the light of present "A" level trends the major increase must be in the number of arts-based, rather than science-based students.' Among the other paradoxical results this has had the effect of sharply restricting the prospective growth of the former colleges of advanced technology, which, had they not become universities, would now be a major focus of expansion.

A different approach informs the Report of the Dainton

[18] University Grants Committee, *Annual Survey, Academic Year, 1966–1967*, Cmnd. 3510, HMSO, 1968, Appendix C.

Committee.[19] They believe that the swing is a disaster which must be halted by an active policy in the schools. They base this argument on the demonstrable national demand for more engineers, technologists and scientists.[20] Unfortunately they do not themselves demonstrate the demand, and a respectable argument can be made that an accelerated production of scientists and engineers would require an over-investment in those sectors of education. We must after all ask ourselves about the economics of the swing. Unfortunately there are not yet usable statistics on the salaries of graduates in different subjects.[21] But common observation suggests that, if scientists and engineers command any premium, it is not large.[22]

Even if we suppose that scientists and engineers are paid less than the value of their (marginal) product, we have to remember that they cost society very much more to produce than their opposite numbers in arts. Unless arts graduates are paid a good deal more than their value, it seems very doubtful whether society's return on producing scientists and technologists can be higher than on producing arts graduates.

There is one other major point we should like to make on the question of university expansion. The Robbins Committee looked not only to 1973–74 but also to 1980–81. It estimated the places needed then and obtained from the UGC an estimate of the numbers who could be accommodated in existing universities. (This included the 'new' universities which, contrary to common impression, were planned for before Robbins.) After allowing for the upgrading of some non-university institutions, there was left a gap of 30,000 places which Committee said should be filled by six further universities, of which the one should be a so-called 'SISTER'— a Special Institution for Scientific and Technological Educa-

---

[19] Council for Scientific Policy, *Enquiry into the Flow of Candidates in Science and Technology into Higher Education*, Cmnd. 3541, HMSO, 1968 (The Dainton Report). See also C. M. Phillips, *Changes in Subject Choice at School and University* (forthcoming).

[20] Dainton Report, para. 3.

[21] A follow-up study of a sample of graduates from the 1966 Sample Census currently being undertaken on behalf of the Department of Education and Science will help here.

[22] The case of doctors is different and their high pay explains the still strong demand to study medicine better than the Dainton explanation that the subject is 'in touch with human and social affairs' (para. 162), which was equally true in the 1950s.

tion and Research, designed to strengthen the appeal of technology and to win for applied studies a proportion of the
bright lads who are now so predisposed to pure research. In
the event the 'overbidding' by the universities in their immediate response to the Report led the Government to think
that the UGC might have also underestimated the potential
capacity of existing universities in 1980–81. For this reason,
and because of its 'binary' philosophy (on which more below), the Government rejected the idea of the six further
universities. They also rejected the idea of SISTERS. The
higher trend in 'A' level output might however make them
think again, and the case is particularly compelling for a
brand new institution concentrating on really high level technological studies, to be founded in the early 1970s.

Finally, at a more detailed level, it is pleasing to note that
the proportion of graduates going on to postgraduate studies
has grown faster even than the Report suggested, by at least
4 per cent a year of its 1961 level as compared with $2\frac{1}{2}$ per
cent recommended. Unfortunately the UGC do not seem to
share the Robbins Committee's belief in the national importance of a rapid growth in the expertise which only
graduate studies can give. In their Memorandum of the
Quinquennial Settlement they explain that they 'have consciously taken the view that the undergraduate numbers are
a genuine priority'.

While postgraduate numbers have grown faster than Robbins recommended, the proportion of overseas students,
which Robbins recommended should remain constant, has
fallen from 11·5 per cent in 1961–62 to 9·4 per cent in 1966–
1967.[23] Overseas students have come to represent a much
smaller proportion of undergraduates, while remaining a
fairly constant (or a slightly declining) proportion of post-
graduates. This outcome is in line with the advice which the
Chairman of the UGC gave the universities in the letter which
he wrote to Vice-Chancellors after the publication of the
Robbins Report. In it he said: 'In the emergency period up
to 1967–68 the Committee feel that the universities will not
dissent from the view that priority should be given to the
increase in the home demand, on which the Robbins figures
now adopted were calculated; and that a corresponding pro-

[23] In further education too the proportion fell from 18·0 per cent in
1961–62 to 13·0 per cent in 1966–67.

portionate increase in the intake of overseas students could not be expected.' The advice caused some despondency among the protagonists of the underdeveloped countries, but appears in fact to have been broadly followed. The absolute number of overseas undergraduates had already been stable since 1961–62 and has continued so. The number of overseas postgraduates has risen, but as a proportion of the total they have slightly declined—the decline occurring mainly in humanities and social studies. Further growth in the number of overseas students will now be less than it otherwise would have been, owing to the decision of Mr Crosland in December 1966 to press the universities to raise their fees to overseas students to £250 a year as compared with the normal fee of £50.

Taken all in all, however, university development has followed fairly closely the lines proposed by Robbins. But the relationship between the universities and the rest of higher education has developed quite otherwise. As Table 12.4 showed, the universities provided 60 per cent of the places in higher education in 1962–63 and Robbins recommended the same proportion for 1966–67. But the actual proportion was 54 per cent. When the number of well qualified school leavers rose above the Robbins prediction, the Government abandoned the Robbins principle that a constant (1961) proportion should go to university and stuck to the Robbins number of places. The increased supply of students was channelled into the non-university sector. But behind this outcome lay a more fundamental divergence between the Government's and the Robbins Committee's view of the role of the universities in the system of higher education.

The binary system

This is not the place to dwell on the qualitative and administrative recommendations of the Robbins Report nor on the extent to which they have been implemented.[24] There is, however, the one issue of the 'binary system', which has major quantitative as well as administrative implications and must therefore be looked at.

As we said earlier, the quantitative aspects of the Robbins

[24] For a discussion of such questions see Lord Robbins, *The University in the Modern World*, Macmillan, 1966, esp. Chapter 8.

Report were accepted by the Government at the outset and have left a major impact on national history. A good number of the administrative recommendations were also accepted— for example the turning of the colleges of advanced technology into universities, the establishment of the Council for National Academic Awards, and the introduction of a B Ed in colleges of education.

But two of the most important administrative proposals were ultimately rejected. First, where Robbins had opted for two Ministries (one for universities and science, and another for the rest of education) the Conservative Government decided, after some months of deliberation and political infighting, to have a unified Department of Education and Science.[25] This decision must have affected the quantitative development of higher education, but it is impossible to tell whether it promoted or discouraged it.

The second major administrative decision going against the Robbins recommendations was left to the Labour Government and its Secretary of State, Michael Stewart. The Robbins Committee had recommended that the colleges of education should become parts of universities, being federated into university schools of education. Each school would be financed through its university and would be academically responsible to the senate. After over a year's discussion the colleges and the universities (or nearly all of them) came out in favour of the marriage, but the University Grants Committee raised an impediment and, on their recommendation, the Secretary of State decided that 'for the present the colleges should continue to be administered by the existing maintaining bodies'.[26] There were a number of weighty practical, as well as the more philosophical, arguments in favour of this decision—in particular the argument that, in a period of acute shortage of primary (and especially of infant) school teachers, it could be disastrous to remove the colleges from relatively direct Ministerial control.

But the period of acute shortage will pass and it was therefore encouraging to note the phrase 'for the present' in the official announcement. However, it was only months after this announcement that Mr Stewart's successor, Anthony Cros-

[25] This decision became effective on 1 April 1964.
[26] The decision was announced in the House of Commons on 11 December 1964.

land, enunciated in a speech at the Woolwich Polytechnic a new principle to underline future government policy, which implied that the divorce between the universities and the rest of higher education was to be regarded as permanent.[27]

This was the 'binary' principle, which said in essence that there should be two systems of higher education at degree level, one in the autonomous sector (the universities) and one in the publicly-controlled sector (the technical colleges, and, for B Ed courses, the colleges of education); and the second should be developed more rapidly than the first.

The issues involved here were, and remain, extremely complex, powerful arguments existing for and against the policy. This is not the place to do more than record them in summary form. The arguments in favour of the policy include the following.

> Universities are unwilling to develop applied studies at a high level on a large enough scale, and are correspondingly remote from industry and commerce.
> Universities provide little part-time education and it is vital for part-time students that they can be taught in institutions which also provide high quality full-time education.
> Bright young people from working-class homes are either put off by universities or have qualifications (such as ordinary national certificates) which universities will not accept as satisfying entry requirements.
> Universities are not sufficiently accessible to Government control for these evils to be remedied.
> The unit cost of producing a comparably educated student is less in a technical college than a university.

Some of the arguments against the policy are:

> Only the universities can give real status to applied studies.
> Students will continue to put universities as their first choice; the binary policy by restricting university places will intensify the unhealthy competition for university entry.
> A binary policy involves dispersion of resources on too many institutions and fails to reap the economies of placing large numbers of students in contact with the best brains, most of whom may want to work in universities.
> There is no evidence that it is cheaper on average to pro-

---

[27] The speech was given on 27 April 1965.

duce graduates in technical colleges than in universities, even if we include the cost of university research in the cost of producing graduates; in terms of marginal costs it may be less sensible to expand relatively small colleges with staffs appointed for lesser responsibilities, than to create new universities.

Without elaborating on the debate we cannot help saying we are convinced that the binary philosophy is wrong and that, insofar as it is implemented, it will involve a greater waste of national resources than a policy in which the universities were given a larger role.[28]

Happily the policy has only been implemented in part. Its main concrete expression so far is the plan to create 30 polytechnics of ultimately around 2,000 full-time students each. These will be based on existing technical and other colleges and their staffs, though it seems likely that a considerable number of them will in fact involve a physical change of site.[29] However, on top of this, further education and teacher training have already expanded a great deal faster than the universities. It is time to look at the remarkable developments in these sectors.

Teacher training

The Robbins Committee recommended that teacher training should grow faster in the 1960s than any other sector: the shortage of school teachers (especially in primary schools) demanded nothing less. While the Committee were sitting the Government had announced a programme for about 80,000 places in England and Wales by 1970-71.[30] The Committee were told by the Ministry that, given the constraints of buildings, staff and the adaptive capacity of the colleges, it would be impossible to go above this plan in any year before 1969. However, from that year onwards the Committee recommended a further steep increase to 111,000 places by 1973-74.

[28] For the Robbins Committee's arguments in favour of a central role for the universities see the Report, pp. 150-2 and 117-21.
[29] See Department of Education and Science, *A Plan for Polytechnics and Other Colleges*, Cmnd. 3006, HMSO, 1966.
[30] The plan was for 80,000 places in 'general' and 'specialist' colleges. If all colleges are included (technical teacher training colleges as well) about 82,000 places were implied.

In the event the Robbins recommendations, and by the same token the 80,000 place programme, have been greatly exceeded—by about 26 per cent by 1967–68. This is mainly the result of the efforts of the Ministry to increase the productivity of the colleges and of the colleges' splendid response. The Ministry's interest in achieving increased productivity was long-standing, but the real drive for it stemmed from Mr Crosland's request to the colleges early in 1965 that they should, with minor modifications, use their buildings (already existing and planned) to house 20 per cent more students than originally envisaged.[31] Their recurrent finance was however adjusted so that the staff-student ratio was maintained. As a result the entry to colleges of education in England and Wales in 1967 was 35,000 compared with 26,400 in Robbins. Whether an increase of this order would have been possible if the output of qualified school leavers had been as projected by Robbins is uncertain. It probably would have been, with some reduction in the average qualifications of entrants. But the actual increase has been accompanied by no such reduction. This is due to the increased output of qualified school leavers. Since the rate of university expansion has not increased *pari passu*, a growing proportion of qualified school leavers have applied to colleges of education and a growing proportion of these have been admitted.

Plans for the future are still (at the time of writing) officially the 111,000 places in Robbins. However, this number of places will be reached by 1969–70 with no further increase in entry over the present level. We can therefore be sure it will be exceeded.*

Further education

In further education too, the Robbins recommendations have been greatly exceeded, though by a quite different mechanism. This sector has always, since the war, acted as the safety valve for higher education, mopping up the demand not satisfied in the other sectors, and of course handling it in its own particular way. The Robbins Committee cast it in the same

[31] See College Letter No. 7/65 of 3 July 1965, following Mr Crosland's speech to the NUT at Douglas in April 1965.

* [In 1971–2 there were about 114,000 initial training places in colleges of education and polytechnic departments of education, of which some 3,000 were in the latter.]

light in the future, and since it envisaged a constant (and, later, rising) entry rate to universities and a rising entry rate to colleges of education, it recommended a slightly falling entry rate to further education. In the event further education seems to have performed exactly the pre-assigned role, but the magnitudes have been different. The university entry rate has fallen since 1961 and the entry rate to further education has risen, bringing the number of entrants high above the Robbins target. This has happened less because buildings have been more intensively used (since in further education buildings can fairly easily be switched from non-advanced to advanced work) than because of increased student demand. It is because the demand can be absorbed in this way that the overall entry rate to higher education as a whole has remained relatively stable.

Which courses have expanded fastest? As we should expect, it is the degree courses. In 1961-2 there were 5,500 students on these courses, if we include for comparability the Diploma in Technology courses, most of which have now been converted to degree courses of the Council for National Academic Awards. Five years later, as Table 12.6 shows, the number had risen to over 19,000. Higher National Diploma courses have also grown rapidly while art courses have been more or less static—it is noteworthy that where student unrest cannot be explained by expansion it has to be explained by stagnation.

Table 12.6

Students on full-time advanced further education: by type of course England and Wales, 1961–62 to 1966–67

	Thousands		Percentage growth
	1961–62	1966–67	
London degrees	4·2	12·3	190
CNAA degrees and Dip Tech	1·3	6·9	438
HND	4·0	11·9	200
National Diploma in Design	5·8	6·4	10
Professional qualifications	8·5	17·0	100
Total	23·8	54·5	129

Looking to the future, the plan for polytechnics will clearly encourage rapid expansion in further education. But, if we accept the safety-valve analogy, its expansion will also depend on the relation between the future growth in well-qualified leavers and the expansion of the universities.

The future

After a period of violent expansion, higher education is now moving into one of relative tranquillity, at least in terms of overall numbers. According to the latest projection by the Department of Education and Science the number of well-qualified leavers will be roughly static from 1967 to 1971, the continuance of the 'trend' being just sufficient to offset the declining numbers of eighteen-year-olds.

If this is correct, the present plans for universities will provide places roughly sufficient to maintain the entry rates of 1962 and after but not to revert to the 1961 rate, which would require a further 10 per cent or so of places. However, as we have seen, there seems to be a general mechanism which keeps the overall entry rate to higher education roughly constant. The Robbins Committee believed, moreover, that in a period when demographic pressures were suddenly relaxed there would be a tendency for the application rate to higher education as a whole to rise: the figure set on this was an overall rise of 10 per cent between 1967 to 1972; thus to keep the degree of competition constant would require an increase in entry rate of 10 per cent. The Robbins Committee envisaged that in the short-run this extra demand should be absorbed in teacher training and further education. It would certainly be consistent with present government policy if this were to happen.

At present the new Planning Branch at the Department is undertaking the first comprehensive reappraisal of policy in higher education since the Robbins Report; and, particularly in the present uncertainties about public expenditure, it is not possible to predict what policy measures will emerge. But, granted the current expansionary momentum in teacher training and further education, it seems likely that the overall provision of higher education in 1971 will be as high as the Robbins approach would require, though its composition would be somewhat biased against the universities.

Changes of the kind we have already experienced would have been inconceivable even five years ago. Doubts abounded not only about the availability of suitable students ('more means worse'), but also about the ability of the institutions to adapt to expansion. The performance of each of the sectors, and most of all perhaps of the colleges of education, have confounded the doubters. Though a period of ease is now around the corner, rapid expansion will be needed again from the mid-1970s. This is only daunting if the great achievements of the last five years are forgotten.

13

EDUCATION PLANNING PAPER
No. 2

Student Numbers in Higher Education in England and Wales*

The demand for higher education

The concept of demand for higher education has been expressed variously as meaning potential students' desire for it, or society's need for it as measured in terms of requirements for qualified manpower or of the total benefits expected from educational investment. A variety of factors, social, cultural and economic, may influence students' desire for higher education. There are direct benefits to individuals in the form of life-time earnings differentials greater than could be expected from innate ability alone. Other direct benefits to individuals may be of a less tangible nature, such as, in the short term, the attractions of student life, and in the longer term additional job satisfaction. Moreover, some of the economic benefits accrue not only to those who have received higher education but often to others also; the productive potential of those who are not highly educated may be increased by working with those who are. In these ways higher education may contribute directly to higher productivity and so to increased national prosperity. Of the wider social benefits, the Robbins Report[1] emphasized the transmission of a common culture and common standards of citizenship. To take full account of

---

* [From Department of Education and Science, Education Planning Paper No. 2. 'Student Numbers in Higher Education in England and Wales', HMSO, 1970. We print 2 extracts, pages 2–6 setting out the methodology used in the projection, and pages 36–37, giving the conclusions of the exercise.]

[1] Report of the Committee on Higher Education, HMSO, Cmnd 2154, 1963.

all potential gains from increased provision of higher education would require improved methods of assessment which are likely to be developed only gradually over time. The more immediate decisions on new provision must be made in the light of observed student trends, calculations of the more tangible benefits, and qualitative assessments of the less tangible.

Three main theoretical approaches to the provision of higher education have been enunciated:

(i)   the so-called 'social demand' approach of the Robbins Report (hereafter described more correctly as 'private demand');

(ii) the rate of return (or investment in human capital) approach;

(iii) the manpower approach.

Though conceptually distinguishable, these three strands are closely intertwined in reality and should not be regarded as independent approaches. The extent to which they can currently be applied in Government decision-making depends on the degree to which each approach has been developed in theoretical terms and on the availability of appropriate data and measurement techniques.

PRIVATE DEMAND

Private demand arises from the individual appreciation by each potential student (or his parents) of the benefits which he may obtain from higher education. Each individual may make his own appraisal, objective or subjective, compounding both intangible and tangible benefits. It may include an assessment of the economic gains in later life expected in return for income forgone while studying, as far as his knowledge of the labour market permits. What each individual takes into account cannot readily be ascertained and in general is not subject to government influence in a direct sense (though it may be influenced by improved careers guidance facilities). Private demand has therefore to be forecast mainly by projecting the aggregate demand pattern observed in the past, allowing for changes in numbers qualified to enter higher education. Where past opportunities to enter higher education have been greater than current opportunities, it will be natural to consider whether to revert to the earlier opportunity rates and apply them to the projected flow of people qualified to enter. The projection of past experience implicitly makes some allowance for the so-called 'generation effect', that is the tendency for parents' aspirations for their children's higher education to rise with the parents' own educational level. The projection necessarily reflects the influence on student demand of the existing structure and financing of the higher education system. While this approach does not make any explicit provision for the economy's requirement of trained manpower, it does make some implicit allowance in as much as private demand for higher education is influenced by impressions of employment opportunities for holders of particular qualifications.

RATE OF RETURN APPROACH

The rate of return approach is one application of the concept that education is a form of investment in human capital, improving the quality of labour resources and hence contributing to economic growth.[2] Attempts to estimate this educational contribution to economic growth in the aggregate have raised formidable technical problems.[3] Rather more directly applicable to educational provision is the disaggregate treatment which measures the rate of return to investment in particular educational qualifications. Such a rate of return may be calculated in either private or social terms. The former expresses the relationship between an individual's extra post-tax earnings arising from education and the costs incurred by the individual in obtaining this education (including income forgone while studying); it may be one of the factors affecting the private demand for higher education discussed above. The social rate of return expresses the relationship between benefits and costs for society as a whole. These two

---

[2] A concept developed in T. W. Schultz—'Investment in human capital' *American Economic Review*, Vol. 51, 1961, pages 1–17 and 'Sources of economic growth in the United States and the alternatives before us'— Supplementary Paper No. 13, Committee for Economic Development (New York, 1962).

[3] The aggregate method attributes to education that part of national income growth not explained by increases in physical capital and in labour force numbers. The estimates obtained thereby are indications of possibilities rather than precise calculations, for they are subject both to errors of attribution (as other causal factors may have been involved) and to the compounding of error margins entailed in any calculation involving residuals.

rates will not necessarily coincide[4] and it is the social rate of return which is more relevant to decisions about the public provision of higher education facilities.

Estimates of the social rate of return assume that workers are paid according to their contribution to production, so that the pre-tax earnings of an individual may be taken as representative of his contribution to national income. Differences in earnings attributable to education are thus taken as a measure of the economic benefit of education and compared with the total costs of that education (including forgone earnings), whether privately or publicly financed. To the extent that there are other gains from education besides the direct economic advantages, this approach under-estimates the total social benefits of education; allowances would need to be made for these non-economic benefits in any comparison of the rate of return on education with that on other forms of public investment. Within the education sector, the rate of return technique may be used to compare the benefits of different lengths of schooling,[5] or of different types and levels of qualification[6] or of different subjects of specialization. The use of rate of return analysis in Britain has hitherto been restricted by lack of data on the earnings associated with educational qualifications, except in a few specialized occupations. But the wide coverage of qualifications recorded in the 1966 Census of Population and the subsequent 'follow-up' enquiry to a sample of the qualified respondents asking for

[4] In Britain the public sector pays the larger part of the costs of educational provision; the student and his family the smaller part. The additional income received on account of higher qualifications (the economic return) is divided in the opposite way; the State (through tax) takes the smaller part, the former student (on average) the larger. Thus the private rate of return is likely to exceed the social rate. For example, one very tentative estimate for the returns to a three-year first degree in post-war Britain suggested a private return of 14 per cent per annum as against a social return of 8 per cent. (D. Henderson-Stewart, *Manchester School*, September 1965).

[5] As in various American studies, e.g., W. L. Hansen 'Total and private rates of return to investment in schooling', *Journal of Political Economy*, Vol. 81, 1963, pages 128–41, and G. S. Becker 'Human capital' (Princeton, 1964).

[6] As in M. Blaug, M. Peston and A. Ziderman 'The utilization of educated manpower in industry' (London, 1967) and L. Maglen and R. Layard 'How profitable is engineering education?', *Higher Education Review*, spring 1970, pages 51–67.

information on their incomes[7] have now begun to provide material for the fuller use of this technique in improving estimates of society's needs for higher education.

One of the difficulties in the use of rate of return analysis is to estimate the extent to which higher earnings result from education rather than from superior natural ability, family background or other advantages.[8] Another problem is to make allowance for the fact that earnings differentials reflect not only differences in productivity, but also conventional relativities, professional entry restrictions, and the relatively high proportion of qualified manpower employed in public sector occupations partly isolated from the competitive labour market. An important limitation is that information on earnings differentials is usually obtained by recording at a single date the earnings of qualified people of different ages and then inferring life-time earnings patterns for the holders of particular qualifications. Figures for individuals' past earnings are often difficult to establish, and for their future earnings non-existent, so that the calculated rates of return really reflect the state of the labour market at the time of the income survey. For guidance on educational provision, it is thus desirable to survey earnings over a period of time and to combine rate of return findings with estimates of future demand for particular kinds of educated manpower.

MANPOWER APPROACH

The manpower approach to society's need for higher education is thus complementary to the rate of return approach. Manpower forecasting in this country has begun with a number of unrelated projections of employment supply and demand for a few qualification or occupational groups—such as doctors, teachers, scientists and engineers—although

[7] See V. Morris and A. Ziderman 'The economic return to investmen in higher education in England and Wales', *Economic Trends*, May 197 (HMSO). Also *Education*, 1969, and April 1970 (HMSO).

[8] The difficulty arises because it is mainly the more able school leaver who are attracted to higher education. Some American studies have indi cated that about two-thirds of the earnings differential is attributable t education (G. S. Becker, op. cit.; E. F. Denison 'Proportion of incom differentials among education groups due to additional education' in J Vaizey (ed.) 'The residual factor and economic growth' (Paris, 1964)). / Swedish study, however, suggests that a lower figure is obtained whe adjustments are made for the socio-economic background of those in differ ent educational groups (T. Husen 'Talent, opportunity and career' (Stock holm, 1969)).

almost invariably without any reference to the price factor. Similar projections have yet to be made for other fields of qualification. All projections would then need to be reviewed to ensure consistency with each other, for example, to ensure that, on the supply side, projections for particular disciplines can be accommodated within the total qualified manpower supply. On the demand side, adjustment may also be needed for consistency with the expected growth in national income and total labour force and to eliminate distortions where employers have projected requirements without considering associated changes in pay scales.

In moving from manpower projections to estimates of the need for particular educational facilities, allowance must be made for the fact that the new supply emerging from the educational system is small by comparison with the total stock of qualified manpower: the latter is also affected by adult retraining, migration, changes in activity rates and mortality. Account should also be taken of changes in the composition of this stock resulting from workers' experience and movement between occupations, as well as of changes in patterns of utilization and deployment. More study would be needed of occupations where it is difficult to establish a close correlation between the nature of the work and educational qualifications, especially in many management-type posts where the possession of qualifications has often been regarded mainly as an indication of general ability. This means investigating the potential substitutability of various levels and subjects of qualification; guidance on this may be provided both by relative earnings data and by detailed job analysis in relation to qualification content. Where different qualifications are found to be of similar value to employers, the relative costs of acquiring them will tend to determine the rate of return on the respective educational investments.

THE SCOPE OF THE PAPER

Pending the fuller development of the rate of return approach and of techniques of manpower forecasting, the basis of projection adopted in this paper is, essentially, the extrapolation of trends in private demand. Future numbers entering the university and further education sectors of higher education have been related to the estimated increase in numbers staying on at school and reaching the academic standards hitherto required for entry. But places in colleges of education have been related to the projected requirement for teachers in primary and secondary schools. The approach adopted here has much in common with that of the Robbins Report, though there are many differences in the detail of the calculation.

The projection, which is confined to England and Wales, covers all full-time undergraduate and postgraduate studies in universities, all full-time advanced courses in the further education sector and all full-time courses of initial training in colleges of education. The term 'full-time' embraces sandwich courses. Advanced courses in further education are defined as postgraduate, post-diploma and research work; courses in preparation for first and higher degrees. CNAA degrees, the Higher National Diploma or Certificate, the Diploma in Management Studies, the National Diploma in Design and the Diploma in Art and Design; courses leading to final professional examinations or college Diplomas or Associateships if above the standard of instruction required for the ONC or for GCE 'A' level; and other courses of study of equivalent standard. Provision for 'refresher' courses (e.g. in-service teacher training) is outside the scope of this paper and is excluded from the projection.

The present calculations start from a projection of qualified school leavers which is based on data on school leavers up to the end of the session 1966–67 and on trends in staying on in school up to January 1968: so far as leavers at ages sixteen and over are concerned, the projection is a substantial upward revision of the one published in *Statistics of Education 1967, Volume 2*, which had assumed a slower long term growth in staying on. The school leavers projection adopted here was made before data became available on school leavers in the session 1967–68, and therefore will be superseded by the school leaver projection which appears in *Statistics of Education 1968, Volume 2*; the latter projection shows a rather greater number of future school leavers with 'A' level qualifications than the projection adopted in this paper. When the calculations in this paper were made, actual numbers of students in higher education were available only for years up to 1967. Some figures for 1968 and 1969 have subsequently become available and are shown for comparison where appropriate.

14

K. G. GANNICOT and M. BLAUG

Manpower Forecasting since Robbins—a Science Lobby in Action*

No one predicting the future of scientific manpower forecasting in the UK in the early 1960s could have foreseen the
wealth of papers and reports which have flowed from official
committees in the last few years. The Committee on Scientific
Manpower had been extremely successful during its fourteen
years of existence in persuading the Advisory Council on
Scientific Policy and the UGC to expand science and technology places in higher education. But its influence on policy
was out of all proportion to the quality of its forecasts, in
which almost everybody had lost confidence by 1964 or
thereabouts. Moser and Layard, in reviewing the work of this
Committee, expressed severe misgivings about its techniques
over both the medium and the long term and, in particular,
questioned the value of three-year forecasts based on unconditional estimates by employers.[1] Furthermore, the Robbins Report, in adopting a 'social demand' approach to the
planning of higher education in 1963, justified itself by noting
the primitive state of manpower forecasting in Britain. Indeed, one of the bases of its dismissal of manpower forecasting must have been the evidence of the Chairman of the
Scientific Manpower Committee, Sir Solly Zuckerman, who
placed himself in the curious position of defending both his
proposals for expanding the colleges of advanced technology
and the Committee's long term forecast which predicted a
surplus of scientists and engineers by 1970. In his oral evidence, Sir Solly not only abandoned all claims to faith in his

* [From *Higher Education Review*, Autumn 1969.]
[1] Moser and Layard, 1964, pp. 503–4.

own forecasts but also gave the strong impression that, despite the variety of techniques which had been tried since 1946, his Committee was really no nearer to developing a reliable forecasting technique for scientists and engineers. He said, for example:

> I must indicate again that I myself am not prepared to die in the ditch for any one of these figures. I could not agree with you more that the precision with which some of these figures are given seems rather remarkable when one remembers that we are predicting ten years ahead.

And again:

> I would like to re-emphasize that it (the 1961 forecast) was one of a series of four reports . . . in which different methods have been used. . . . Each time a different method has been used. No doubt, if there is a fifth report, yet another method would be used.[2]

Far from suffering a rapid demise, however, the Zuckerman Committee has since 1965 been transformed into the Committee on Manpower Resources for Science and Technology under the chairmanship of Sir Willis Jackson (now Lord Jackson of Burnley) and has vastly increased its scope and influence. In its first report, the Jackson Committee made it clear that it interpreted its brief 'to advise . . . on manpower resources for science and technology' in the widest sense, and boldly set out a programme of work covering 'such matters as statistical sources; factors affecting the choice of a scientific or technological career; preparation for employment in the context of a rapidly changing technology; (and) the better utilization of scientific and technological manpower' (Jackson Committee, 1965, paragraph 4). The Committee has fulfilled almost the whole of this programme: not only has it continued to conduct triennial surveys of manpower requirements, but its reports—on science study in schools (Dainton 1968), the 'brain drain' (Jones, 1967), the growth of postgraduate studies (Swann, 1968) and the proposals for industrial training schemes (Arthur, 1965; Bosworth, 1966)—have received wide publicity and favourable attention from both the popular and the scientific press. The Committee has in fact succeeded in erecting a comprehensive view of scientific

---

[2] Robbins Report, 1963, *Evidence*, Part One, Vol. B, pp. 431, 433.

manpower problems in the UK, a view which rests on four central propositions: (1) that the existence of a long term shortage of scientists, technologists and engineers in Britain has been empirically established; (2) that universities tend continuously to denude industry and school teaching of the best talent; (3) that there exists a high rate of emigration of scientific manpower; and (4) that there is a strong swing away from science study in secondary schools, foretelling even greater shortages in the future.

Now that the Jackson Committee has itself wound up, to be superseded by a new Committee for Manpower Resources, the time is ripe for a post mortem on its work. A similar attempt in the *Higher Education Review*, although critical of some aspects of the Committee's work, congratulated it for creating an atmosphere in which 'controversies on scientific and technological manpower have been frankly and ably ventilated'.[3] Our starting point is different. We contend that, instead of making out a convincing case for a shortage of scientists and technologists, with due attention to the 'swing from science' and the 'brain drain' which may have intensified it, the Jackson Committee's effort to develop an integrated picture of scientifically-qualified manpower is simply a mass of contradictions. Using no better forecasting techniques than those discredited a few years earlier, indeed the very same which Sir Solly had found wanting, the Committee has curtly dismissed reasonable criticism of its methods and has merely taken as an axiom that the country 'needs' more scientists and technologists. Considering the composition of the Jackson Committee (seven science and engineering professors and seven senior managers from science-based industries) it is remarkable that its doctrine of a chronic shortage should have been swallowed so uncritically by all concerned. Presumably, the Committee was so constituted on the grounds that academic scientists and business managers can be expected to know their own interests: in this respect at any rate all expectations have been fully borne out.

Methods of forecasting

We begin by examining the Committee's case for the existence of a shortage of scientists and technologists. The amount of space devoted in the 1965 Triennial Survey to 'Problems of Interpretation' leaves no doubt that the Jackson Committee was aware of some of the technical criticisms of the forecasts of the Zuckerman Committee. Whereas terms like 'demand', 'needs' and 'requirements' had been used interchangeably and confusingly in earlier forecasts, the Jackson Committee drew a distinction between 'demand', as defined 'with respect to the community's and in particular the employers' willingness and ability to pay', and 'needs' emphasizing that its surveys of employers' intentions measured the former (Triennial Survey, 1966, paragraph 35). We shall show in a moment that, despite this terminological distinction, the Jackson Committee continued to confuse 'demand' with 'needs'. Nevertheless, it is important to grasp the fact that its forecasts were intended to measure observable market demand, independently of anyone's normative judgement. That is to say, it is possible at least in principle to test the accuracy of the Committee's forecasts.

The method used to measure future demand was quite simple. The Ministry of Labour circulated a questionnaire to all educational establishments, government departments and a sample of industrial sectors, asking them to give, by discipline and type of work done, the numbers of qualified scientists and engineers employed, the number of vacancies and 'the number of persons you aim to have in your employment in three years' time', assuming 'that the required number of persons will be available'. (The questionnaire, the sectors surveyed and the definitions used can be seen in detail in the Appendix to the Report on the 1965 Triennial Survey. Thus, if we are given the actual employment in 1965 and the predicted demand for 1968, the net additional demand is simply a matter of arithmetic. Similarly, net additional supply is derived by adding the actual increments up to 1964 and the predicted net annual additions over the period 1964–68 to the total active stock (as given by the sample inquiry into scientific and technological qualifications in the 1961 census

Presumably the rationale for this method is that the three basic analytical problems of manpower forecasting—effect of the composition of demand, substitutability between inputs, and productivity changes—are solved implicitly by the employer who provides the estimates. But this is almost certainly wrong. Both Peacock and Moser and Layard have pointed out that an unconditional survey of employers' demand invites inconsistent replies.[4] Unless some target rate of output or a market share is specified, how can we be sure that a motor manufacturer's assumptions are consistent with those of the steel manufacturer who supplies him? Sir Solly Zuckerman, who had accumulated a good deal of experience with this type of survey, testified that 'we discovered in our successive inquiries that one of the least reliable ways for finding out what industry wants is to go and ask industry'.[5] Moreover, it is a fallacy to assume that employers can take account of 'foreseeable fluctuations arising from scientific and technological developments'.[6] Although one might think that businessmen are good at predicting the likely trend of technical developments in their own industry, there is abundant evidence that productivity improvements, in the form of the diffusion of 'best practice' techniques throughout an industry, are quite irregular, even in the short run (see Salter 1966). The Jackson Committee was aware of this: it conceded that 'the quality of employers' estimates is likely to depend on the size of the firms and on the degree of sophistication in their manpower planning'. But it simply assumed away all further doubts with the assertion that 'cumulatively these estimates are useful in giving guidance on short-term trends in demand'.[7]

Without further ado, the Committee drew extremely pessimistic conclusions from its survey for the period 1965–1968: 'Returns from employers in the sectors surveyed indicate that they expect to employ by 1968 a further 50,400 scientists, technologists and engineers than in 1965. This represents an increase of 24 per cent, or 7·4 per cent annually, and exceeds the expected rate of growth of stock estimated at some 14·6 per cent (or 4·6 per cent annually).'[8] The first table illustrates this: given the size of demand in the surveyed sectors, the predicted supply in 1968 would be sufficient to meet the forecast demand in these sectors only if employment in the *un*surveyed sectors decreased, an unlikely possibility given the trend between 1962 and 1965.

[4] Peacock, 1963, p. 10; Moser and Layard, 1964, p. 503.
[5] Robbins Report, op. cit., p. 432.
[6] Triennial Survey, 1966, paragraph 32.
[7] Triennial Survey, 1966, paragraphs 31, 32.
[8] Triennial Survey, 1966, paragraph 33.

This kind of comparison between stock and demand may make some sense if both are unambiguously defined in the same terms, but this is manifestly untrue in the case of the Triennial Survey. Despite the chapter on 'Terminology and Definitions', the survey got nowhere to grips with the fundamental problem that scientists, technologists and engineers

Table 14.1

Stock of and Demand for Scientists, Technologists and Engineers, 1962–68

	1962 '000s	1965 '000s	1968 '000s	Growth	
				1962/65 %	1965/68 %
Total Active Stock	273·2	313·0	358·7 (forecast)	14·6	14·6 (forecast)
Employment in Sectors covered by Surveys	183·2	211·2	261·7 (forecast)	15·3	23·9 (forecast)
Balance available for Employment in Unsurveyed Sectors	90·0	101·8	97·1 (residual forecast)	13·1	−4·6 (residual forecast)

Source: Triennial Survey, 1966, Table VI, p. 16.

can be classified either in terms of qualifications attained or of job carried out. Consider the following meaningless phrase intended to show how manpower should be classified: 'The technologist is frequently several steps ahead of the scientist in the breadth of his knowledge and in his awareness of the potentialities within his field of inquiry but he is likely to be less concerned with full understanding of the underlying scientific relationships.'[9]

Even the apparently quite straightforward method of adding annual increments to the 1961 census stock becomes seriously misleading when it is remembered that 'total active stock' represents a very mixed bag of age groups, new and outdated qualifications, and trained and untrained personnel. The Committee showed itself fully aware of this when it declared that a direct comparison with demand cannot 'reveal the kind of balance between supply and demand which has

[9] Triennial Survey, 1966, paragraph 10.

previously been inferred from it',[10] a statement apparently designed to disclaim the Zuckerman Committee's long-term forecast in 1961, predicting a surplus by 1970 on the grounds that total active stock would exceed predicted demand in that year (Zuckerman Committee, 1962). The Jackson Committee was right to be sceptical of such a naïve comparison, but apparently absolved its own forecast from taking account of the same criticism. If stock and demand cannot be directly compared, what possible meaning can we give to Table 14.1? If 'total active stock' is a thoroughly ambiguous notion in this context, then the third row, derived as a residual, is equally meaningless.

No less confused were the terms in which future demand was expressed. Respondents were asked in the questionnaire to indicate 'present and future requirements of qualified scientists, engineers and technologists, irrespective of the type of work done'.[11] Superficially, this provides a clear-cut forecast in terms of educational disciplines required, but a closer look suggests that the results are every bit as ambiguous as the forecasts of active stock. What the Committee's forecast really showed was, not that in 1968 industry expected to employ x numbers of extra mechanical engineers, but rather that by 1968 it expected to employ x people carrying out a mechanical engineering function, which is not at all the same thing. The two are identical only if no other educational discipline but mechanical engineering can adequately supply the demand for jobs with a mechanical engineering function, and if the occupational category of mechanical engineer is a technically indispensable input into production which cannot be contributed at any price by other job functions. In short, the Committee's method is a viable technique for forecasting the demand for educational disciplines only if there is a very low degree of substitutability both within and between occupations—an untenable assumption for a Report which admits that 'it is unrealistic to press distinctions between disciplines too far'.[12] The Committee nowhere drew the obvious conclusion from this admission: if industry's stated demand for 'mechanical engineers' can in fact be satisfied by people trained in a whole range of educational discip-

---

[10] Ibid., para. 41.
[11] Ibid., p. 44.
[12] Ibid., para. 53.

lines, it makes little sense to inquire into the demand for the educational discipline of 'mechanical engineering'.

None of these criticisms is new: they have all been made before by critics of the Zuckerman Committee. But whereas Sir Solly came in the end to recognize all the difficulties of surveying employers and attempting to fathom their intentions, the Jackson Committee refused to believe that 'technical problems in estimates of this type' affect the results more than marginally.[13] Indeed, so confident was the Jackson Committee of both its own results and those of the Zuckerman Committee that it simply linked together all the three-year forecasts made since 1956 to demonstrate that they formed part of a consistent long-term pattern of shortage. The graph opposite derived from Figure 1 of the 1965 survey summarizes this exercise.

It is easy to see from the graph how the Jackson Committee arrived at its alarmist conclusions about the employment of scientists and technologists in the UK. The implications of the graph would seem to be (1) that there has been a long-term failure of supply to meet demand and (2) that industry has suffered most from this shortage, whereas the education sector has much more nearly achieved its forecast. Apparently the fact that 'actual' employment has consistently been below 'forecast' employment constitutes sufficient evidence for a shortage. Incredibly, nowhere in any of the reports is there any suggestion of an alternative explanation: that the forecasts of shifts in the demand curve were simply mistaken. This possibility does not seem to have occurred to the committee because it defined 'shortage' in such a way as to preclude errors in forecasting. It will be recalled that employers were asked in the questionnaire to state the number of qualified people they would aim to employ in three years on the assumption 'that the required number of persons will be available'.[14] The very phrasing of this invites the interpretation that an employer ought to be able to hire as many people as he wants (at identical salaries?); if actual employment falls short of such aspirations, then by definition the cause is an overall shortage.

It is perfectly obvious that, in spite of assertions to the contrary, the Committee failed utterly to understand what

[13] Ibid., para. 31.
[14] Ibid., p. 44.

Chart 14.1

Growth of Employment and Demand 1956-68 Analysed by Sector of Employment

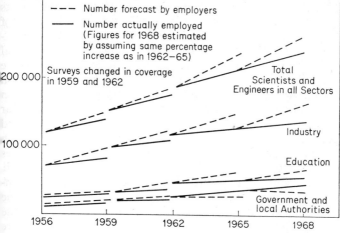

Source: Triennial Survey 1965, Figure 1, page 19.

is meant by 'demand' in the labour market: the uncritical acceptance of employers' estimates, the way the question of future demand is posed, and the talk of forecasts being 'achieved', all point to a prediction of future demand totally devoid of economic content. The concept of demand the Committee seems to have had in mind is one where relative prices play no part: earnings rate no mention in the questionnaire, and indeed any consideration of their role is emasculated by the assumption of 'available supply'. It is a concept of demand where, if the employer can predict his future output with some degree of accuracy, technical requirements dictate his demand for labour. On the supply side too, relative earnings play no part. As earnings are nowhere mentioned, the assumption must be that the supply of scientists and technologists is price-inelastic and is a function simply of the number of places made available for the study of scientific subjects. The costs of education may apparently be ignored: if it is 'required' by the technological nature of the output, the cost of producing it is irrelevant. In short, demand is fixed without regard to possible supply; supply is fixed independently of demand and there is no common, automatic mechanism for ever bringing the two into equilibrium.

A further reason why the Committee was loath to raise the possibility of an inaccurate forecast was its view that demand estimates represent only a minimum target: we ought really to try to produce enough scientists and technologists to meet the 'needs' of the country. The 1966 Triennial Report declared that 'the present output ... is still deficient in relation to ascertainable short-term demand, let alone to need', and the Swann Report in 1968 suggested that 'if we are to achieve new and more productive patterns of utilization and employment, manpower policy must attempt to cover long-term need as well as short-term demand'.[15] Indeed, one of the reasons why the Jackson Committee dismissed previous criticisms of manpower forecasts was its belief that all such criticism misses the point: the notion is that even if demand forecasts are unreliable, one cannot go far wrong in putting them forward as minimum estimates, since the real 'needs' must exceed them.

What precisely does it mean to assert that there is always an unsatisfied 'need' for scientists and technologists, even if there is no market shortage? The Committee evidently found it easier to state the problem than to solve it. The 1965 survey offers little guidance on this problem: all we get is an international comparison of the crudest type ('the combined technological resources of the European Economic Community are well ahead of our own'), without adducing any evidence that the EEC is actually being rational or efficient in allocating this proportion of its total resources to science and technology, together with a rag bag of objectives of such generality that no one could possibly disagree. We select an illustrative sentence: 'Some examples are the need for technological viability in our aircraft, ship-building machine-tool and computer industries, for better standards of design and means for the training of larger numbers with design skills, for better utilization of scientific knowledge of materials, for better standards of mensuration and calibration and for the more scientific exploitation and conservation of our limited national resources.'[16]

The only clue the Committee provides is the statement

[15] Triennial Survey, 1966, paragraph 94; Swann, 1968 paragraph 64.
[16] Triennial Survey, 1966, para. 49.

that '. . . at any time the scale and composition of a country's productive activity . . . give rise to a postulated need for highly qualified skills if economic, technological and cultural progress is to be sustained'.[17] But this, as we have seen, is precisely the belief underlying the Committee's concept of demand. Conceptually, therefore, 'demand' and 'need' are the same thing; the only difference is that 'demand' is what employers say they require, 'need' is what the Committee thinks employers ought to require.

A possible justification for the Committee's belief that 'need' always exceeds 'demand' is the notion that scientists and technologists in the UK are systematically underutilized. That is to say, employers are inefficiently utilizing them in occupations that could be just as effectively carried out by less educated individuals: if they were efficiently utilized, there would be a greater demand for them. This argument may well be correct but it has some far-reaching consequences for the rest of the Committee's work. If one really believes that employers malutilize educated manpower, one clearly cannot put much faith in forecasts of demand based on employers' opinion. Furthermore, malutilization of labour implies a high degree of substitutability between labour with different educational qualifications, albeit at a cost, in which case one must allow for the differential earnings that are associated with demand for different kinds of educated labour, something that the Committee has never done.

If this much is accepted, two things follow: (1) if employers fail to perceive optimum 'needs', it seems pointless to rely exclusively on their so-called estimates of demand as the basis for forecasting; and (2) if 'needs' as perceived by the Committee are so remote from the actual structure of job opportunities that employers cannot reasonably be expected to perceive them, any attempt to increase the supply up to this target will, in the absence of compulsory direction of labour, result in the unemployment or emigration of scientists and engineers. (It is, of course, possible that employers' demands are not a good guide to national needs, since the salary which employers are prepared to pay, and hence the numbers of scientists and technologists they are prepared to employ, may not reflect the external economies which result

[17] Ibid., para. 35.

from educating more of them. But this type of argument can be used to support an increase in the numbers of virtually any highly qualified skill: one could just as easily assert on these grounds that the recent economic performance of the UK indicates a 'need' for more economists. How do we choose between economists and scientists?)

Yet, so far from accepting the logic of these propositions, the Committee did not consider the first and expressly rejected the second with the statement that '... employers can be expected, when there is a better educational supply, to revise their views about the importance of employing new skills, and also because *the emergence of such skills duly creates its own demand*'.[18] It would be hard to find a more confused statement. If the supply of highly educated manpower creates its own demand—a modern version of Say's Law—there never can be a surplus of manpower. We cannot go wrong, the Committee is saying, by producing too much (Apparently, however, the argument is assymetrical: demand does not create its own supply, so there can be shortages. But how are all possible increments in supply absorbed into employment, if a given supply leads to a determined demand? Clearly, the Committee has suddenly ceased to believe in the low substitutability of educated manpower, in which case why worry about shortages? If demand and supply are not independent of each other, forecasts of demand are meaningless and in asserting Say's Law for scientists and technologists, the Committee has in fact abandoned its entire theoretical rationale.

All this adds up to the conclusion that the Committee has failed to make its case for a long-term shortage. Its measure of demand not only ignores the realities of the labour market but relies on dubious surveys and misleading classification techniques. 'Needs', the umbrella term under which the inadequate demand forecasts were supposed to take shelter turns out on examination to be nothing more than an assertion of a value judgement that more scientists and technologists would benefit the country. This has nothing to do with the art of manpower forecasting and is simply the special pleading of a science and engineering lobby.

[18] Ibid., para. 37.

Surveys of policy problems

If the Committee has failed to make a case for a chronic shortage of scientists and technologists, some of the alarmist talk about 'the swing from science' and the 'brain drain' looks a trifle misplaced. In the absence of a reliable criterion for judging where manpower 'ought' to go, there is no reason to assume that the 'swing' in secondary schools or the growth of postgraduate education represents a misallocation of resources. Even so, it is highly instructive to examine the policy reports dealing with these phenomena, for they illustrate the way in which the Committee's dependence on naïve forecasting left it without any analytical framework to explain the educational problems with which it concerned itself after the last triennial survey of 1965.

According to the Committee, the basic factor that ties together all the problems investigated by Dainton, Swann and Jones is the rigid and specialized nature of the British educational system and the irrelevance of science teaching in schools and universities. The result, it is alleged, is to produce a group of narrow specialists who 'emerge with little knowledge of ... the problems of the society in which they are to become responsible members', and who 'see little place for themselves except in the specialities in which they have been trained', 'Are they to be blamed', so the arguments run, 'for preferring the academic world here or abroad to industry or school-teaching in this country?'[19]

This type of explanation is most clearly seen in the Dainton Report on the 'swing from science' in schools. This report was concerned to explain why there had been a movement away from science subjects at 'O' and 'A' level in schools since 1960, with the consequence that entrants into science and technology faculties in universities had fallen from 45·9 per cent of total admissions in 1962 to 40·6 per cent in 1966. A corollary to this was 'a tendency towards acceptance of candidates for science and technology of lower grades of "A" level achievement than those applying for arts and social studies'.[20]

Much of the Report is an excellent analysis of the way in which specialized university entrance requirements percolate

[19] Swann, 1968, para. 158.
[20] Dainton, 1968, paras. 56, 31.

down and dictate a rigid pattern of specialization comparatively early in a secondary school career. In particular, the Report correctly demonstrates that the irreversible decision for or against specialized science study is made at the point in secondary schools when mathematics ceases to be taught. As a result, one of Dainton's central recommendations was that broad courses of sixth form study should replace the present emphasis on two or three specialized 'A' levels: mathematics, the key to increased flexibility, would be the norm for the majority of sixth formers, who would thus be able to postpone the fatal choice for or against science Universities in turn could assist this process by altering their entry requirements so as to encourage a broad span of studies in the sixth form.

Whatever the genuine merits of these proposals, it is absurd to suggest that an early choice of subject specialization is in itself a cause of the 'swing from science'. To be sure, the Report recognizes that its proposals will not necessarily influence pupils' preferences in the direction of science, but it goes on to imply that they are very likely to because older pupils will not fail to appreciate the glories of science: 'It is in the individual's interest that he should not be required to take these critical decisions at a relatively immature stage before he has had opportunity to appreciate something of the true significance of science and technology as intellectually satisfying pursuits in themselves, or to see them more roundly in their social context.'[21]

Even disregarding the unpleasant combination of condescension and self-interest in that statement, to imply that universities will thereby have a wider range of applicants for science study is totally to confuse necessary and sufficient conditions for an increase in the number of science and technology students. One of the most distressing features of the Dainton Report is the manner in which it is shot through with these wordy generalizations whose only purpose is to glorify science and technology: e.g. 'few students can be aware ... of the extent to which science ultimately unifies knowledge and makes learning easier by giving a structural framework of concepts that brings diverse facts into relationship' (paragraph 150); or 'the study of science requires inte

[21] Ibid., para. 174.

lectual rigour; indeed it is one of the cardinal characteristics which distinguish it from mere speculation and experiment. For the gifted pupil this can be a positive attraction. But most young people are now able to choose apparently less rigorous alternatives and have to be encouraged, if not persuaded, to face the discipline of science' (paragraph 149).

After thoroughly exploring and conclusively rejecting the hypothesis that the quality of science teachers is responsible for the 'swing', the main influence the Report identified was the school science curriculum; it called for an urgent move '. . . to infuse breadth, humanity and up-to-dateness into the science curriculum' so that something of that 'satisfying and regenerating intellectual curiosity along ever-widening boundaries' can be transmitted to children.[22] There is little question that the science curriculum *is* out of date: as early as 1960, the Advisory Council for Scientific Manpower commenting on the Crowther Report, said that 'school sciences curricula were in need of a thorough re-examination' (Advisory Council, 1961). But this can hardly be the main explanation of the 'swing', since the Dainton Report itself pointed out that 'science, engineering and technology gained ground in school and higher education from about 1945 to the late fifties',[23] and presumably much the same curriculum was in use then.

Specialized education and an ossified curriculum may be bad for all sorts of reasons, but they do not explain what is essentially a change during the last few years: vast generalizations about educational structure and the 'public image' of science are hardly convincing when what one is trying to explain is a movement of very recent origins. Dainton's long-term projections of what might happen if the trend continues should not blind readers to the fact that the acute pessimism of the Final Report represents a complete turnaround from the 'qualified optimism' of the Interim Report a mere two years earlier. Nowhere is the alarm and desperation with which the Jackson Committee approached its task better seen than in its attitude to science teachers. Even after Dainton had rejected the hypothesis that the quality of science teaching is responsible for the 'swing', the Swann Report recommended that 'local authorities should consider re-employing

---

[22] Ibid., para. 181.
[23] Ibid., para. 145

specialist teachers who have recently retired'.[24] If the curriculum is really as important a factor in the 'swing' as Dainton contends, how can Swann think that to employ teachers with obsolete qualifications would improve the swing? Perhaps such inconsistency is only to be expected from a report which is capable of asserting that '... the demand for graduate scientists and technologists of high academic ability to teach in schools cannot at present be quantified, though there is evidence of acute shortage'; or again: 'we have no means of saying how many (top-level graduates) the schools ought to have, (but) ... the evidence of shortage is indisputable'.[25]

The Swann Report saw an exactly analogous process, for similar reasons, occurring at the higher educational level. The main theme of the Report was the apparently worrying trend that graduates and postgraduates were preferring to remain in the 'higher education and research' sector rather than seeking employment in industry or in schoolteaching. Even more worrying was the tendency of this sector to cream off the more able graduates: 'almost three-quarters of scientists and half of technologists obtaining "firsts" have proceeded to postgraduate work, together with substantial proportions of those gaining "upper seconds" ... industry and schools (including teacher training colleges) recruit less than one-tenth of science "firsts", and the proportion entering Schools has declined over the last five years.'[26] The Report was in no doubt about the cause: university degrees were not oriented to the real 'needs' of industry, and graduates were being produced who believed that the only worthwhile activity was academic research. Reinforcing this trend was a PhD system which was even more remote from the vocational training which industry required.[27]

One feature of Swann's analysis is immediately obvious: by focusing attention exclusively on trends among *university* graduates, the report completely neglects the fact that almost one half of engineers qualify through CNAA awards or through membership of professional institutions. Since industrial experience is a requirement for the qualifications of professonal institutions, the supply of these engineers is

[24] Swann, 1968, para. 141.
[25] Ibid., paras. 63, 82.
[26] Ibid., para. 104.
[27] Ibid., Chapter VII.

related very closely to industrial demands. Therefore, even if Swann's analysis of the trends among university graduates is correct, it follows that what Dainton identified is not necessarily a general 'swing from science'. Although Swann quoted Dainton approvingly in support of his own analysis, it makes little sense to accept both explanations at face value. If the uninteresting curriculum, the early specialization and the poor image of science add up to a swing away from science study among fifth and sixth formers, why do we observe such high proportions of scientists at university level only too keen to remain active in specialized scientific research? Is it that science becomes interesting only after it has been studied up to first degree level? If the trends noted by Swann and Dainton do have a common cause, that cause is certainly not a general social drift away from science. If it lies in the structure of the educational system, then apparently it has to do with the appalling teaching of science in secondary schools and the superb teaching of science in universities and technical colleges. This may be the right explanation, but, if so, it still awaits demonstration.

The failure of the Committee to provide a comprehensive explanation of these phenomena is nowhere better seen than in the Jones Report on the Brain Drain. This Committee was charged with explaining the specific problem of 'an increasing net loss in recent years of qualified manpower arising from an upsurge in emigration with no marked change in immigration . . ., from a near numerical balance in 1961 . . . to a position in 1966 which represented a net loss equivalent to nineteen per cent of the 1963 output of newly qualified engineers and technologists and nine per cent of the scientists'.[28]

The Jones Committee professed to be unperturbed by the upward trend for scientists, since 'most scientists who go abroad do so on a temporary basis for further research and study', but took fright at the emigration of engineers and technologists, since these groups were seeking permanent employment abroad.[29] Nowhere does the report offer an analytic resolution of these differences in the behaviour of scientists and of engineers. Part of the answer lies in figures which the Report itself presents, showing that a substantial

[28] Jones, 1969, paragraph 34.
[29] Jones, 1967, paragraph 28.

proportion of emigrant engineers and technologists came from the aircraft and associated industries, which at this time were going through an acute phase of uncertainty, provoked by doubts about the future of Concorde, the cancellation of the TSR-2, HS1154 and HS681, and the heavy redundancies at Bristol, Preston and Luton. These figures were supplied to the Ministry of Technology by a North American recruiting agency, and although not comprehensive, give an illustrative picture of those registered and those hired by subject of qualification. The Jones Report concluded that 'three-quarters of those hired were under thirty-five, and that most of them come from design and development jobs in aeronautical engineering, electronics and control systems'.[30] The report noted that 'the uncertainty of the aircraft industry ... can be held responsible for much of the loss of aeronautical and allied engineers in late 1965 and 1966', but failed to recognize that such essentially short-term problems have to be carefully distinguished in an assessment of long-term trends. It preferred to write emotively about the 'loss of seed-corn' and the 'disastrous consequences for British industry and the economy within ten or twenty years if it were to continue at the present rate' in a way that suggests that the UK's prime shortage is not of engineers but of competent economists.[31]

Not surprisingly the result of this exercise is another airing of the explanation we have seen before: The UK educational system produces graduates who are biased against employment in industry and who in turn have received such a specialized, theoretical education that they are of little use to industry. The fault for this 'lies as much with university curricula in science as with those who do the teaching, and we must look for the solution here in a change of emphasis in the curricula towards the needs of industry'.[32] If the curriculum really does produce narrow specialists, imbued with the ideal of pure research and biased against employment in industry, one wonders why the bias apparently disappears when contemplating employment in America; nor is American industry complaining that the skills produced by British education do not match its 'needs'. And even if

[30] Ibid., para. 33.
[31] Ibid., paras. 143, 36.
[32] Ibid., para. 177.

the allegations about the nature of the curriculum and of the graduates produced are true, these long-term factors manifestly cannot explain such a recent phenomenon as the upsurge in emigration since 1964. If a key role in this turn-around is assigned to the demands of the space programme and the defence industry, it still has to be shown how these 'pull' factors alone could operate so successfully in a situation of alleged shortage of scientists and technologists in the UK.

The policy recommendations are inevitably as mixed as the analysis. And if to emphasize that it has not really mastered the problem it was discussing, the Committee placed under 'non-acceptable remedies' the very key to the problem. It was scornful of the idea that 'since the rate of emigration of certain types of specialist can be held to imply their over-production, the educational system should be adjusted to match the annual output more closely to the immediate national demand. This argument may well hold true in the case of some specialist disciplines which may be fading into obsolescence ... but it is fallacious as a general proposition in the face of large domestic demand for talented engineers, technologists and scientists.'[33] What *is* fallacious is the Report's abrupt dismissal of this line of argument: it provides yet another example of the way in which reliance on man-power forecasting, together with a bogus concept of 'shortage', leads to the complete inability to analyse labour market adjustments: the brain drain is precisely one indicator of behaviour which can support or refute a manpower forecast.

An economic analysis of manpower shortages

The subject of this paper has been the lack of intellectual substance in the work of the Jackson Committee. We go on now to show that economics suggest a radically different method of measuring manpower shortages which at the same time seems to provide a unifying explanation of the associated phenomena of the 'swing' and of 'brain drain'. In so doing, we shall sketch an outline of the ways in which the new Committee for Manpower Resources might direct its work.

The essence of our criticism of the Jackson Committee was that it ignored the operations of the labour market:

[33] Ibid., para. 137.

relative earnings, prices, and costs were not even mentioned, much less analysed. Even the Jones Report, which came nearest to an assessment of the role of earnings and costs failed to integrate them in its examination of the 'brain drain'. Two recent articles have attempted to examine the hypothesis of a shortage of scientists and technologists in Britain in terms of changes in vacancy rates and relative earnings (Peck, 1968; Richardson, 1969), but both attempts founder on the use of *median* salary levels, which are known to conceal continual adjustments by age and so fail to bring out the impact of short-run changes on starting salaries.

A much more satisfactory measure of shortages of highly qualified manpower is that pioneered by Hansen in his use of rate of return analysis, comparing rates of return on investment in different educational qualifications in the USA (Hansen, 1965, 1967 and see Blaug 1966). Rates of return are a summary statistic combining those variables of earnings and costs which the Jackson Committee consistently ignored in assessing manpower shortages. This is not an over-simple rejection of all non-economic factors: the assumption is simply that, on the margin, students implicitly calculate the net financial advantage of choosing one career rather than another.

Armed with this tool, the problems which Dainton, Swann and Jones failed to explain satisfactorily fall neatly into place. The behaviour they noted is precisely what would be predicted from a relatively low or declining rate of return, or a *surplus* of scientists and technologists. The essence of the 'swing' is a decline in the relative number and quality of entrants into science and technology. While many factors can help to explain this, one of the most obvious is that the yield on this training has declined, and this decline in turn indicates the appearance of a surplus. Similarly the preference for lengthier postgraduate research by scientists and technologists may be motivated not by the 'academically-oriented values' of the students but by their perception that they will now have to undergo a lengthier training period than colleagues in relatively scarcer disciplines in order to secure equally remunerative employment. Dainton pointed out that 'in chemistry ... we are already moving towards the situation where the PhD is the professional qualification pursued by nearly half of those attaining a first degree' but merely noted that 'if a degree course in science or technology took much longer than in other subjects this would act as a discouragement'.[34] He failed to realize that the lengthier training period for chemists raises the private costs and so lowers the rate of return to chemistry education. The alternatives to this, in a situation of a surplus of chemists, are for the BSc chemist either to accept an offer of employment unrelated to his skill as a chemist, or to take a job at a lower level of skill than his training fits him for.

Such an interpretation sheds an entirely different light on the other problems that worried Swann. In these circumstances, of course it is the lower quality of graduates who will go into industry immediately after their BSc, and of course the curriculum, both in schools and in universities, will remain oriented to academic values. Swann's recommendation to shift postgraduate education from the traditional types of courses to something more 'vocational' misses the point that the undergraduate curriculum and the structure of the PhD *are* vocational: they are vocational just as long as students perceive that the rational choice is to undertake research for a higher degree.

The most recent data from OECD yield an interesting perspective on this analysis. The report on *Gaps in Technology between Member Countries* demonstrates that the UK is training 40 per cent more technologists in relation to the size of the age group than the USA, and a higher proportion of pure scientists than any OECD country but the USA (OECD 1968). In the light of the Jackson Committee's belief that we cannot have too many, the question posed by OECD is apposite: 'in view of her low rate of economic growth and her low levels of physical investment, is the United Kingdom investing too much in the production of expensive high level scientists and technologists and producing more than the economy can absorb at present rates of investment in physical capital and with present management capacity?'[35]

In the earlier analysis we assumed that pupils and students were acting as if they were making perfectly rational decisions in a world where they are well informed and where demand for educated manpower is transmitted smoothly through the

[34] Dainton, paragraphs 191, 192.
[35] OECD, 1968, paragraph 12.

price mechanism. Ultimately, we should expect to see a change in the pattern of research work and emigration for scientists and technologists as the recent 'swing' in the schools works its way through the education system and out into the labour market. That is to say, Dainton, Swann and Jones were witnessing nothing more disturbing than the operation of a supply/demand adjustment process. This is not to imply that we can simply rely on this process to bring us to equilibrium in the near future. Arrow and Capron discuss all the factors on the demand side which inhibit a rapid labour market clearance (Arrow and Capron, 1959) and in the UK this process is considerably worsened by the slow response on the supply side. The result is that although the market is functioning, it is not necessarily completely clearing the market in any one period. Thus, by the time the 'swing' has worked itself through the schools, the labour market may well be attempting to employ more scientists and technologists. The fear of cobweb cycles is the classic justification for manpower forecasting, but these very imperfections in the education and labour markets mean that the outcome of an inaccurate forecast, as the OECD Report implies, can be a disastrous misallocation of resources.

The new Committee can best addresss itself to analysing the operation of the labour market for highly qualified manpower in Britain. What is needed is not more employers' surveys, but an analysis of the nature of market responses. We list below some of the questions it should attempt to answer.

What changes in earnings and numbers of entrants are likely to occur in the short and long term, given shifts in the demand curve for different types of qualified manpower?

What factors account for the lags between the short and long term?

How might government policy help to reduce these lags and what are the costs of doing so?

What are the alternative methods of increasing the supply of qualified manpower?

What are the costs and benefits of these alternatives?

What is the cost to the economy of a shortage of any particular skill?

The adoption of this agenda for research will not have an immediate pay-off in the kind of dramatic conclusions to which we have become accustomed after fourteen years of the Zuckerman Committee and four years of the Jackson Committee. But it may mean that manpower policies can at least be conducted in an atmosphere free from partisan prejudice.

Fortunately, there are already signs of an official change of heart. The UGC, so long persuaded by manpower forecasts to expand science and technology places and restrict those in the arts and social sciences, has reluctantly bowed to the probability that 'pressure of demand for places in undergraduate courses requiring science-based entry qualifications was unlikely to increase', while 'on the other hand, pressure of demand for undergraduate places in arts and social studies ... would continue to increase'; in the circumstances, it was 'these two considerations (which) largely determined our planning figures for the distribution of undergraduate places during the quinquennium'.[36]

However, the UGC has not entirely lost faith in the Jackson Committee. Although individual preferences are to be the guideline for undergraduate places, at postgraduate level it proposes to implement Bosworth 'matching sections', in spite of Arthur's evidence of little industrial interest in that type of course (Arthur, 1965), and in spite of the fact that postgraduates have shown themselves to be in favour of more academic research. ('Matching sections' are short bridging courses, designed to expunge 'academically oriented values' from the graduate and convert him into an effective industrial technologist.) If we are right in our supposition that individual preferences for research have reflected the existence of a surplus of scientists and technologists, we can almost guarantee the failure of Bosworth's scheme: postgraduates are almost certain to seek to convert 'matching sections' into more academic type courses. If individual preferences can be allowed to guide undergraduate places, why is it that postgraduates cannot be allowed the same choice?

This plea for individual choice is not a plea for *laissez-faire*. On the contrary, it implies a massive increase in vocational counselling, counselling that is, firmly rooted in actual job opportunities, not in the metaphysical world of 'needs'. Clearly the Government has to take a look into the

[36] UGC, 1968, paragraphs 331–5.

future, since the provision of science and technology places means that specialized and indivisible investment decisions have to be made, but forecasting with a view to providing for likely trends in enrolment is a very different matter from persisting in the fiction that a forecast of 'manpower requirements' can tell us how many scientists, technologists and engineers the educational system ought to produce.

REFERENCES

Advisory Council on Scientific Policy, *Annual Report 1959–60*: HMSO, 1961.

Advisory Council on Scientific Policy, Committee on Scientific Manpower, *The Long-term Demand for Scientific Manpower*: HMSO, 1961, Cmnd. 1490.

Kenneth J. Arrow and William M. Capron, 'Dynamic Shortages and Price Rises: the Engineer-Scientist Case', *QJE*, Vol. 73, May 1959.

H. Arthur, *Enquiry into Longer-term Postgraduate Courses for Engineers and Technologists 1964–65*: HMSO, 1965.

M. Blaug, 'An Economic Interpretation of the Private Demand for Education', *Economica*, May 1966.

Committee on Higher Education, *Higher Education, Report of the Committee under the Chairmanship of Lord Robbins 1961–63*: HMSO, 1963, Cmnd. 2154.

Committee on Manpower Resources for Science and Technology, *A Review of the Scope and Problems of Scientific and Technological Manpower Policy*: HMSO, 1965, Cmnd. 2800.

Committee on Manpower Resources for Science and Technology, *Report on the 1965 Triennial Manpower Survey of Engineers, Technologists, Scientists and Technical Supporting Staff*: HMSO, 1966, Cmnd, 3103 (Cited as the Triennial Survey 1966.)

Committee on Manpower Resources for Science and Technology, *The Brain Drain, Report of the Working Group on Migration*: HMSO, 1967, Cmnd. 3417. (Cited as the Jones Report.)

Committee on Manpower Resources for Science and Technology, *The Flow into Employment of Scientists, Engineers and Technologists, Report of the Working Group on Manpower for Scientific Growth*: HMSO, 1968, Cmnd. 3760. (Cited as the Swann Report.)

Council for Scientific Policy, *Enquiry into the Flow of Candidates in Science and Technology into Higher Education*: HMSO, 1968, Cmnd 3541. (Cited as the Dainton Report.)

Michael Hall, 'Research v Industry', *Higher Education Review*, Spring 1969.

W. Lee Hansen, ' "Shortages" and Investment in Health Manpower' *The Economics of Health and Medical Care*: the University of Michigan 1965.

W. Lee Hansen, 'The Economics of Scientific and Engineering Manpower' *Journal of Human Resources*, Vol. II, No. 2, Spring 1967.

C. A. Moser and P. R. G. Layard, 'Planning the Scale of Higher Education in Britain: Some Statistical Problems'. *JRSS*, Vol. 127, 1964, reprinted in *Penguin Modern Economics; Economics of Education, I*, edited by M. Blaug, Penguin Books, 1968.

Organization for Economic Co-operation and Development, *Gaps i*

Technology between Member Countries: An Analytical Report. (To be published.)

A. T. Peacock, 'Economic Growth and the Demand for Qualified Manpower', *District Bank Review*, No. 146, June 1963.

Merton J. Peck, 'Science and Technology', *Britain's Economic Prospects*, Richard E. Caves and Associates, The Brookings Institution, 1968.

V. A. Richardson, 'A Measurement of Demand for Professional Engineers', *British Journal of Industrial Relations*, Vol. VII, No. 1, March 1969.

W. E. G. Salter, *Productivity and Technical Change*, University of Cambridge, Department of Applied Economics, Monographs No. 6: Cambridge University Press, 1966.

University Grants Committee, *University Development 1962–67*: HMSO, 1968, Cmnd. 3820.

15

V. M O R R I S*

Investment in Higher Education in England and Wales: the Human Capital Approach to Educational Planning

The last ten years have seen considerable developments in various approaches to educational planning, which have been accompanied by an increasing activity and involvement of successive Governments in the whole planning process. Certainly part of the explanation for this activity lies in the very considerable growth in educational expenditure, now taking a major share of the public sector budget and reflecting the importance attached to education by politicians and social scientists as well as educationalists. Over the past decade Governments in this country have also come under increasing pressure to both contain the scale and rate of growth in public expenditure, and to scrutinize plans affecting the allocation of public funds between departments. The main spending departments (amongst which the Department of Education and Science ranks high) have therefore had to justify their budgets in terms of other competing demands. It is these kind of pressures which have encouraged Government Departments to take a more positive role in setting up planning machinery to assess and review basic needs and priorities. The outcome may not yet be judged satisfactory but at least the planning process has begun.

The machinery set up by the Department of Education and Science to undertake this planning has undergone several changes over the past ten years: first there has been a shift

* [The author is a Lecturer at the Open University and Research Fellow at the Centre for Studies in Social Policy.]

away from the essentially external advisory committee structure of the early and mid-sixties, such as the Robbins, Crowther and Plowden committees, towards planning undertaken within the Department itself, starting with the Planning Unit set up in 1967, leading onto the Programme Budgeting analysis of 1969 (Education Planning Paper No. 1) and *Student Numbers in Higher Education* (Education Planning Paper No. 2), then continuing with the Policy Analysis and Review (PAR) which partly contributed to the White Paper *Education: A Framework for Expansion* 1972. There has also been a shift in the issues covered; whereas the advisory committees of the early and mid-sixties tended to investigate specific and separate problems such as nursery or higher education, the work being undertaken more recently by the Department in the late sixties and early seventies has included programmes encompassing the educational system as a whole. For example *Education: A Framework for Expansion* reviews plans and targets for both the compulsory school age group and the higher education sector in the same document. The Department therefore seems to be moving away from its fragmented approach to planning, towards a more comprehensive approach involving the consideration of alternative policy options within a general framework. However it is not yet clear whether the Department is also evaluating the long-term implications and impact of these options. Nevertheless it is now an appropriate moment to ask what planning methods are available and to question whether these are really being used effectively by the Department. Although this article investigates only one method in detail, any successful planning must depend on the Department's willingness to explore all the available methods.

It is perhaps not surprising that most of the work on educational planning has until recently been concentrated on higher education; provision of additional education beyond compulsory schooling is after all very costly, particularly all forms of higher education. This means that the scale and scope of higher education must be carefully planned to achieve appropriate balances between it and other demands on public expenditure, both within the education sector and in relation to other sectors of the economy. Higher education encompasses a wide variety of courses, subject disciplines, and levels of study in the different institutions—universities, polytechnics, colleges of education, thereby offering policy-makers a wide range of choice in considering alternative policy options.

There are several approaches at present available to government for the analysis of these problems, and briefly outlined in the DES Education Planning Paper *Student Numbers in Higher Education in England and Wales*; social demand, manpower forecasting requirements and the human capital approach. Of these three approaches, social demand has been the one most frequently adopted by the Department for policy purposes over the past ten years. It was originally developed by the Robbins Committee on Higher Education, and subsequently used to project *Student Numbers in Higher Education* (EPP2). More recently, this approach has been implicitly used in *Education: A Framework for Expansion* (indeed there have been official denials of any departure from the 'Robbins' principle' in the White Paper). Use of the manpower forecasting approach has, on the other hand, been very much more limited, and confined to a few professions such as engineers, scientists, doctors and teachers. Nevertheless during the sixties a number of official committees, notably the Committee on Manpower Resources for Science and Technology, produced several forecasts indicating substantial shortages of qualified scientists and technologists which have led certainly to policy decisions. But more recently the work of this Committee has been heavily (and correctly) criticized for being both partial and incomplete at no point including concepts of either price or cost in the demand forecasts (Gannicot and Blaug: *Manpower Forecasting since Robbins*).[1]

The third, human capital or cost-benefit, approach to educational planning has only recently been explored by government, so it is still too early to assess any impact of this approach on policy. Nevertheless both Educational Planning Papers Nos 1 and 2 refer to the initial work being undertaken by the Department of Education and Science; it is therefore appropriate to trace some implications of adopting this approach.

This article therefore concentrates on some of the issues and policy implications of using a human capital approach to educational planning. It presents the results of a cost

[1] Pp. 259–83.

benefit analysis where expenditure on education is treated as a form of investment from which benefits accrue in the future both to individuals receiving the education, and to society as a whole. The method involves a systematic comparison of the monetary values of the benefits, reflected in the individual earnings differentials associated with additional education, and the costs of this provision. By using discounted cash flow techniques it is possible to estimate the rates of returns to the individual (private rates of return), and to society (social rates of return). The private rates of return are estimated by the economic benefits of the post-tax earning differentials, and the costs incurred by the student in undertaking additional education such as tuition fees and foregone earnings. The social rates of return measure the direct economic benefits to society from additional education provision beyond compulsory schooling, estimated by the increase in national production resulting from having more qualified manpower (as reflected in the pre-tax earning differentials associated with additional education); the costs include the monetary value of resources used by the teaching institution in making this educational provision, and the production forgone by students not in the labour force.

Private and social rate of return may be useful to policy makers in different ways: private rates of return would be most useful in providing some guide to the direction in which student demand for additional education could move, for example in choice of course and subject, as well as occupation. Private rates of return could therefore be used as supportive evidence for the assumptions underlying the so-called social demand' projections. But it is the social rates of return which are most relevant to the resource problems of central government.

For this reason the present article concentrates on the return to society, and discusses some policy implications of the results relating to the allocation of scarce resources between different levels of qualifications, different subjects and type of training, and between men and women. Although the results do not provide the decision-maker with conclusive answers to questions of resource allocation they do nevertheless help to identify several major policy issues which might otherwise remain concealed, and indicate the relative magnitudes in reallocating resources.

A full social cost-benefit study would, of course, include the direct economic benefits, the consumption benefits which people enjoy from greater education, and the indirect spill-over benefits (or externalities) which accrue to future genera-tions from a better educated present generation (for example, research evidence suggests that parental attitudes play a significant part in children's school performance), or affect increased levels of individual productivity indirectly through the additional education of others. However the scope of this present study is less ambitious, and more narrowly confined to measuring the direct economic benefits, so in many ways it resembles an investment appraisal, rather than a full social cost-benefit study.

Since the consumption and indirect spillover benefits can almost certainly be assumed positive the rates of return shown here probably under-estimate the yield on educational expenditures. But as there is little evidence of the variance in spillovers between qualification levels it is not possible to estimate the amount by which comparisons between these levels could be affected. On the other hand, to the extent that part of the extra production of highly qualified persons may be attributed to non-educational factors such as family background, natural talent and motivation, taking the whole value of earning differentials tends to over-estimate the return on educational expenditure. Nevertheless it is extremely difficult to disentangle the causal relationship between these factors, so only an illustrative adjustment has been made.

In order to estimate these direct economic benefits, age specific earnings data for different educational qualification are needed. The benefits are measured by the earnings dif-ferentials of those with additional education, taken a approximations for future life-time earnings. In identifying the direct economic benefits of education accruing to society as a whole with the increased production of educated persons and taking differential pre-tax earnings of the educated as measure of this increased production, the implicit assumption is made that relative wages closely conform to relative mar ginal productivities. While recognizing that labour market imperfections do exist, the assumption made here is that the labour market remains sufficiently competitive to validate the rates of return calculations. However certain groups were provisionally excluded where extra-educational influence were judged sufficiently important to affect relative earning levels. The main grounds for exclusion were that additional but non-educational costs might be incurred in obtaining some qualifications through for example on-the-job training, that significant non-monetary advantages or disadvantages may be associated with certain occupations, and that monopoly or monopsony powers might be exerted in certain occupations. The groups excluded were those with professional qualifications in medicine, dentistry, accountancy, law, architecture, librarianship, the armed forces and clergy. School teachers were treated separately so rates of return are shown including and excluding teachers.

The Age Earning Profiles

The data on the earnings of qualified manpower were obtained from a postal survey carried out for the Department of Education and Science by the General Register Office in April 1968 as a follow-up sub-sample to the economically active persons enumerated in the 1966 10 per cent Sample Census of Population for England and Wales. The data excludes pension income, and the earnings of those ceasing to work during 1966–67, but includes the income of the self-employed, and the actual earnings of those recording breaks in employment.[2]

This survey is both the most comprehensive and recent source of information on the earnings of qualified manpower in England and Wales. It is also the first survey of earnings to be analysed for subject of qualification. The data was obtained by questionnaire sent to 15,000 qualified men and women in England and Wales, but the effective sample, with a 69 per cent response rate, and after the exclusion of the groups noted above, was only 2,474. Inevitably this limited the amount of detailed processing to groups where sufficient numbers of observations were obtained, so that some subject disciplines have had to be grouped together, and certain qualifications such as the Higher National Diploma could not be included in the analyses. Nevertheless sufficient infor-

---

[2] As the details were not recorded no allowance has been made in the subsequent rate of return estimate, but the effect of including pension benefits would be to increase the returns where pensions are positively correlated with earnings resulting from additional education.

mation was obtained to cover the following qualifications. Subjects were analysed in four main groups: arts, social science, science and technology. The qualifications analysed for men were: Higher National Certificate—HNC (science and technology); Higher National Certificate with professional qualifications[3]—HNC,PQ (technology only); first degree—BA, BSc (arts, social science, science and technology). Fewer observations were obtained for post-graduates so that the following further groupings were used; master's degree—MA, MSc (combined science and technology); doctorate—PhD (combined science and technology); master and doctorate together (combined arts and social science). Only first degree qualifications were analysed for women. Finally where there was more than one qualification the highest was taken, and where two similar qualifications in different subjects that most recently obtained was taken. This data was analysed to obtain age specific mean annual earnings for each of these groups: some of the results are summarized in Tables 15.1 and 15.2; for purposes of simplification the charts of graduates and post-graduates show only a two-way subject split into arts (including social science) and science (including technology).

The most obvious features shown in the tables and charts are the consistent rise in earnings with age, and the close association of mean earnings with qualifications; the profiles for higher qualifications lie above the lower ones and the qualification differentials increase with age: persons with post-graduate qualifications tend to earn more on average than graduates, who in turn earn more than those with part-time vocational qualifications. It is noticeable that a person with a degree still earns more on average than one with a Higher National Certificate followed by professional training (although these two qualifications are generally described as equivalent).

Comparisons between the subject disciplines are equally interesting. In general these confirm the close association between level of qualification and mean annual earnings. Thus subject by subject those with post-graduate qualifications earn more than graduates. But it is also noticeable that within each qualification starting salaries by subject are similar with

[3] HNC with endorsements obtained by part-time study and qualifying the holder for membership of major professional institutions.

Table 15.1

Mean Annual Earnings by Age Group of Part-time Vocational Qualifications 1966–67

Age	Higher National Certificate (HNC)			HNC with Professional Qualifications	
	All Subjects	Science	Tech-nology	All Subjects	Tech-nology
	Mean Annual Earnings	Mean Annual Earnings	Mean Annual Earnings	Mean Annual Earnings	Mean Annual Earnings
	£	£	£	£	£
20–24	1,112	1,019	1,133	1,339	1,394
25–29	1,386	1,253	1,412	1,510	1,587
30–34	1,562	1,587	1,560	1,720	1,733
35–39	1,759	1,625	1,782	2,034	2,018
40–44	1,862	1,746	1,870	2,335	2,336
45–49	1,788	1,472	1,842	2,515	2,489
50–54	2,023	2,150	2,017	2,315	2,315
55–59	1,857	—	1,857	2,467	2,467
60–64	2,060	—	2,060	1,521	1,521
65 & over	2,875	—	2,875	—	—
Overall average	1,593	1,440	1,619	2,017	2,047
Number in sample	707	81	614	305	282

Source: Survey of Earnings of Qualified Manpower in England and Wales 1966-67.
DES Statistics of Education 1971.

fairly narrow differentials in the years up to forty, the profiles tend to widen with age thereafter. One interpretation of this data might be that there is little substitution between the markets for graduate and non-graduate labour, employers showing a strong preference for graduates. On the other hand the differentials are smaller between graduates and post-graduates suggesting more ready substitution between these two markets. The similarity in starting salaries and relatively narrow differentials between subject disciplines within each qualification level (at least up to forty years) suggest some fairly ready substitution between

Table 15.2

Mean Annual Earnings by Age Group of First Degree by Subject* 1966-67

Age	All Subjects	Arts	Social Science	Science	Tech-nology
	Mean Annual Earnings	Mean Annual Earnings	Mean Annual Earnings	Mean Annual Earnings	Mean Annual Earnings
MEN	£	£	£	£	£
20-24	1,132	1,159	1,038	1,115	1,201
25-29	1,555	1,502	1,536	1,508	1,675
30-34	2,092	2,026	2,425	1,959	2,082
35-39	2,563	2,725	2,437	2,292	2,825
40-44	3,122	2,731	3,508	2,981	3,189
45-49	3,536	3,159	3,493	4,128	3,352
50-54	3,083	2,491	3,284	3,430	2,934
55-59	3,719	4,514	2,949	3,493	3,808
60-64	4,134	5,263	4,825	2,814	3,264
65 & over	2,359	3,935	2,197	1,416	2,019
Overall average	2,547	2,651	2,681	2,365	2,559
Number in sample	1,053	208	205	318	322
WOMEN†					
20-24	1,017	992	978	1,088	—
25-29	1,092	1,025	1,277	1,094	—
30-34	1,355	1,095	1,613	1,554	—
35-39	1,417	1,421	1,696	1,171	—
40-44	1,222	1,099	1,377	1,454	—
45-49	1,767	2,318	1,217	—	—
50-54	1,474	1,134	2,166	1,349	—
55-59	1,752	1,541	3,842	1,549	—
60-64	1,867	2,171	1,900	416	—
65 & over	556			—	—
Overall average	1,321	1,259	1,532	1,250	—
Number in sample	152	80	36	36	—

Source: Survey of Earnings of Qualified Manpower in England and Wales 1966-67. DES Statistics of Education 1971.

* Definition of these subjects is given in 'CSO Qualified Manpower in Great Britain'. The 1966 Census of Population. Annex 3. The subject groups used here are: Arts, (combined arts, language studies, vocational studies, music and visual arts); Social Science (including economics and geography); Science (including mathematics); and Technology (including all engineering subjects).

† The analysis shows 232 women graduates in school teaching; giving by subject, 134 in arts, 28 in social science, 60 in science, and 1 in technology. Their inclusion would result in the following overall average earnings: arts £1,488, social sciences £1,406, science £1,585.

subject disciplines. On the other hand, in the later years graduates in arts and social science seem to earn more than those in science and technology, which may be attributable to the employment pattern of graduates in higher management. Clearly the level of qualification accounts for greater difference in earnings than the subject discipline.

These subject profiles are especially relevant to some of the main policy issues concerning higher education in the sixties, particularly the controversy surrounding the shortage of scientists and technologists referred to earlier. In general evidence of such a shortage might be reflected in the relative earnings of science and arts graduates: those for scientists being on average higher than those of arts graduates,

Chart 15.1

Age earning profiles of first degrees by subject (men)
(mean annual earnings 1966-67)

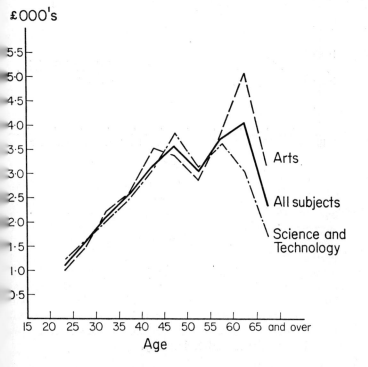

Chart 15.2

Age earning profiles of combined Masters & Doctorate degrees by subject (men)
(mean annual earnings 1966-67)

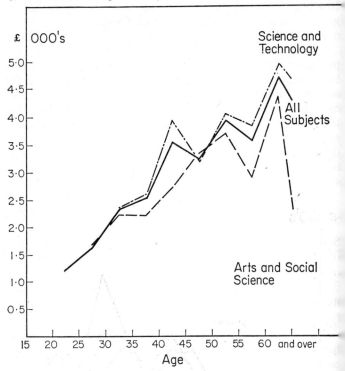

but the profiles shown here indicate no such difference. However, as this data relates to one year only it is far from conclusive; still, the narrow subject differentials do not lend support to the argument of critical manpower shortages of scientists. The whole question of shortage is especially pertinent to problems surrounding the allocation of university places between science and arts faculties by the University Grants Committee and this allocation was almost certainly influenced by the science lobby during the sixties—a lobby whose conclusions may have been ill founded. This could provide at least a partial explanation of the later surplus capacity in science and technology.

Turning to women graduates: their earnings are well below those for men, partly attributable to the kind of occupations and career patterns followed by qualified women and partly because the earnings from part-time employment are included. Nevertheless their average earnings tend to increase when graduate women teachers are included in the data (see footnote, table 15.2).

So far the discussion has concentrated on the age earning profiles, but it is the economic benefits to society, measured by the earning differentials which are used in this cost-benefit analysis. These benefits and the associated costs can be estimated by the use of the internal rate of return, conventionally known as the social rate of return. The following section presents the results of this cost-benefit analysis and discusses some of the policy implications, which are relevant to questions concerning the allocation of resources between sectors.

Social Rates of Return

Social rates of return measure the economic benefits to society of additional education. The analysis involves a comparison of the costs and benefits, the benefits being measured by the cross-sectional age earning profiles of those persons with higher education qualifications, taken as proxy measures for future life-time earnings.

In order to calculate these returns the following procedure has been adopted: first, the life-time stream of mean annual earnings associated with each subject and qualification were discounted year by year by a selection of interest rates to obtain the gross present values at age fifteen. Since it is the differential between any two earnings streams which are taken to measure economic benefits, the gross present values were subtracted from each other to obtain net present value differentials. Second, the resource costs associated with each subject and qualification were discounted by the same set of interest rates. Finally present value differentials net of costs at each discount rate were obtained by subtraction for each comparison. The internal rate of return is then established by that rate of discount which renders the present value of the benefits equal to the present value of the costs—i.e. equal to zero.[4] The three stages in estimating the social rates of return are discussed in turn in each of the sections which follow.

The Benefits

Investment in education involves society in uncertainties and risks, so recorded annual earnings need to be corrected for the probability of inactivity, unemployment and mortality. These corrections were made on the basis of the following information: activity (or participation in the labour force), by rates appropriate for each educational qualification based on the 1966 Sample Census of Population; unemployment (and part-time employment), by including actual annual earnings from the Earnings Survey; survival, by General Registrar Office life-expectancy tables. The effect of these corrections is to reduce the expected benefits stream.

On the other hand students may also obtain some earnings before qualifying, thereby increasing the benefits stream. These are added to the relevant early years of training or study. For part-time vocational qualifications such as the Higher National Certificate, the earnings for the preceeding qualification were taken.[5] The earnings of full-time students were assumed to accrue mainly from vacation and other casual employment: an average figure of £80 was therefore added to each year prior to graduation.

Present values of these corrected age earning profiles were calculated by summing over 15–69 years after discounting the mean annual earnings of the benefit streams at a variety of interest rates, these were then used to measure the economic benefits of additional education.

---

[4] The expression solving the internal rate of return

$$\sum_{t=15}^{69} \frac{Bt - Ct}{(1+i)^{t-15}} = 0$$

Bt is the earnings differential between two streams.
Ct is the resource cost of additional education and training
i is the internal rate of return.

[5] For the HNC, the earnings associated with holders of the Ordinary National Certificate were taken.

The Resource Costs

The costs incurred by society in educational provision beyond the minimum school-leaving age are estimated by the total monetary value of goods and services withdrawn from alternative uses or investments. They include the direct educational expenditure consisting of recurrent institutional costs and the annual value of capital and equipment; they also include the value of production lost by students not in the labour force. Transfers of income, such as student grants, are not included because they are not resource costs.

For the purposes of this study, each qualification was separately costed, based on 1967–68 data,[6] and shown in Table 15.3. The recurrent costs were estimated on two different assumptions: first, only teaching costs were included, on the grounds that the personal research of academic staff does not incur necessary expenditure on student education. The second estimate is based on the opposite assumption that academic research does benefit students, thereby forming a necessary element in expenditure (in fact it is probable that some research costs are incurred in postgraduate teaching, but are not necessary for all undergraduate teaching, so that an overall average of the two separate cost figures may give a realistic approximation). The capital costs include research because of complications involved in separating research from the teaching costs: these figures were converted to annual capital charges by amortizing at an assumed rate of 8 per cent over sixty years. Since it is the costs of obtaining a qualification which are relevant to this analysis, the average annual recurrent and capital costs were adjusted for each year of study by appropriate rates for examination failure, wastage, repetition, and length of course.

The total resource costs also include estimates of production foregone by society while students are in higher education. These costs are represented by the earnings which might have been paid, after deduction of remuneration from vacation employment. These imputed costs[7] are likewise

[6] Adjusted for 1966–67 prices. Details of the calculations are available in a mimeographed paper by the author.

[7] These earnings are those obtained with the preceding qualification: or 'A' level costs—two years 'O' level earnings; for first degrees costs—three years 'A' level earnings (less vacation earnings); and for master or

adjusted for factors such as examination failure by rates similar to those used for recurrent and capital expenditures.

The resource costs of each individual qualification can be derived from Table 15·3 by summing columns 4 or 5 (recurrent costs, excluding, or including research), with 6 (capital costs) and 7 (forgone earnings). But is it also possible to estimate the cumulative costs incurred in post-compulsory schooling, for example from 'O' levels through to master or doctorate degrees. This can be done by simply adding the resource costs associated for each individual qualification. The final cost estimates used for each qualification are given in Table 15.3, column 8 (excluding research costs) and column 9 (including research costs). The present values of these resource costs are obtained by discounting at a set of interest rates similar to those used to obtain the present values of the benefit streams.

The Rates of Return

The gross present values of the differential benefits and of the costs are now brought together to derive net present values at each discount rate: the present value of the costs being subtracted from the present value of the benefits to give the net present values of investing in education. The rate of return on any particular educational investment therefore lies between the two rates of discount where the net present value of the benefits turns from positive to negative.

The social rates of return presented in Table 15.4 show a wide range of the investment opportunities available to governments in deciding the appropriate scale and type of educational provision, and are especially relevant to decisions affecting increases or decreases in expenditure. They illustrate the relationship between the costs and economic benefits associated with various educational programmes and bring home the important point that returns may be high either because the costs are great or the benefits small. These

doctorate qualifications—two and three year first degree earnings are taken respectively (less employment income). It is arguable whether any production is lost by students on part-time HNC courses; but it is here assumed that some production is foregone, measured by one day a week in a thirty-six week academic year. The measure is 0·15 of annual earnings—i.e. for the ONC, 0·15 of one year's 'O' level earnings are taken, and for the HNC 0·15 of two years' ONC earnings.

social rates of return help to demonstrate the implications of some policy options open to governments in allocating resources between educational sectors, for example between universities and advanced further education colleges; between different types of course, such as full-time and part-time training; and between subject disciplines. Comparison of successive levels also show the economic benefits associated with each additional qualification, illustrating options to provide university education after a first degree to master or doctorate levels.

From the point of view of planning educational expansion it is probably most useful to consider adjacent qualification levels in each sector; it is these which are likely to be most relevant to the way in which policy is actually formulated (rather than by overall comparisons starting from post-compulsory schooling). These comparisons, which are referred to in Table 15.4 as the 'incremental comparison', cover the following qualifications and subjects for men, and women where sufficient data was available: postgraduate, master and doctorate degrees in science (including technology) and arts (including social science) are compared with first degrees in these same subject groups; first degrees in science, technology, art and social science are each compared with 'A' levels;[8] 'A' levels are compared with minimum schooling (at fifteen years);[9] Higher National Certificate with professional qualifications are compared with HNC; Higher National Certificates in science and technology are compared with Ordinary National Certificates;[10] and the ONC is compared with minimum schooling. These measure the return to society

---

[8] The Qualified Manpower Earnings Survey, 1966, only obtained data on those with higher qualifications: to complete the comparisons it was therefore necessary to draw on data from the following alternative sources: the 'A' level profile is derived from salary scales of the Civil Service executive class, assuming average promotion patterns; it may for this reason be somewhat unrepresentative and over-estimate earnings associated with 'A' level qualifications—thereby reducing the first degree differential, and perhaps lowering the rate of return estimates.

[9] The profile for men with minimum schooling is based on DHSS data of one-half per cent of persons registered under the National Insurance Act. The profile for women with minimum schooling is based on the Department of Employment New Earnings Survey 1968.

[10] The ONC profile relates to those persons with this qualification in the electrical engineering industry, and is probably fairly realistic. It is based on a survey reported in P. R. G. Layard, J. D. Sargan, M. E. Ager, and D. J. Jones, *Qualified Manpower and Economic Performance*, Allen Lane, 1971.

Table 15.3

Average Annual Costs, Recurrent, Capital and Forgone Earning Costs(£) of Each Qualification 1967–68

Educational Qualifications	Recurrent and Capital costs			Costs per successful student				Total resource costs per successful student	
	Average annual recurrent costs		Capital cost per new student place (i)	Recurrent costs		Capital costs	Forgone earnings	Excluding research	Including research
	Excluding research	Including research		Excluding research	Including research				
	1	2	3	4	5	6	7	8	9
FULL-TIME EDUCATION									
'O' level (4 passes)	155	155	571	196	196	58	366	620	620
'A' level (3 passes)	239	239	771	744	744	195	1,050	1,989	1,989
First degree: (ii)									
All subjects	459	694	2,408	1,477	2,234	626	1,805	3,908	4,665
Art	413	597	1,702	1,314	1,900	439	1,784	3,537	4,123
Social Science	334	487	1,702	1,058	1,541	435	1,778	3,271	3,754
Science	492	790	3,136	1,580	2,536	814	1,800	4,194	5,150
Technology	662	977	3,757	2,192	3,235	1,005	1,853	5,050	6,093
Master's degree:									
All subjects	905	1,385	3,538	2,412	3,691	761	2,400	5,573	6,852
Art and Social Science	630	903	2,034	1,723	2,472	451	2,607	4,781	5,530
Science and Technology	1,104	1,723	5,516	2,840	4,433	1,147	2,234	6,221	7,814

All subjects	905	1,385	3,538	3,507	5,363	1,107	3,992	8,606	10,464
Art and Social Science	630	903	2,034	2,571	3,685	670	4,320	7,561	8,675
Science and Technology	1,104	1,723	5,516	4,222	6,593	1,706	3,875	9,805	12,174
PART-TIME VOCATIONAL EDUCATION: (iv)									
'O' level (3 passes)	155	155	571	188	188	56	366	610	610
ONC:									
All subjects	90	91	528	279	283	133	186	598	602
Science	79	81	528	244	251	133	186	563	570
Technology	93	94	528	286	291	133	186	605	610
HNC:									
All subjects	118	123	727	355	371	177	258	790	806
Science	140	154	727	427	470	179	258	864	907
Technology	113	116	727	339	351	177	258	774	786
HNC PQ:									
All subjects	139	145	727	491	513	208	—	699	721
Technology	124	128	727	430	445	216	—	646	661

Table notes

(i) Capital costs per new place in school and part-time education relate to 1968–69 and exclude residential costs. No separate estimates are made for capital costs excluding research.

(ii) University costs exclude the following: Medicine, dentistry, agriculture, veterinary science, forestry, architecture, other vocational studies and education (ATO expenditure). Science includes mathematics.

(iii) The same postgraduate unit cost has to be used for master and doctorate qualifications.

(iv) Part-time costs are based on one day and on evening study with institutional costs weighted, according to student numbers.

Table 15.4

Rates of Return (%) *to Society from Investment in Education, Incremental Comparison 1966–67*

Educational qualifications	With no ability adjustment		With an ability adjustment	
	Excluding research costs 1	Including research costs 2	Excluding research costs 3	Incl. res. c.
FULL-TIME EDUCATION (men)				
'A' level/non-qualified	7·5	7·5	7·0	
First degree/'A' level:				
All subjects	12·0	11·0	10·5	
Arts	13·5	12·5	10·5	
Social Science	13·0	12·0	10·0	
Science	11·0	9·5	8·5	
Technology	11·5	10·0	8·5	
Master's/first degrees:				
All subjects	2·0	1·0	<0·0	<
Science and Technology	4·0	3·0	2·5	
Doctorate/first degree:				
All subjects	2·5	1·5	1·0	◂
Science and Technology	2·0	1·0	1·0	
Postgraduate/first degree:				
Arts and Social Science	1·0	<0·0	<0·0	◂
FULL-TIME EDUCATION (women)				
First degree/'A' level:				
All subjects	6·5	5·5	5·0	
Arts	7·0	6·0	4·0	
Social Science	10·5	9·0	6·5	
Science	<0·0	<0·0	<0·0	◂
VOCATIONAL EDUCATION (men)				
ONC/non-qualified	7·5	7·5	6·5	
HNC/ONC:				
All subjects	>20·0	>20·0	>20·0	>
Science	16·5	16·0	13·5	
Technology	>20·0	>20·0	20·0	
HNC.PQ/HNC:				
All subjects	20·0	20.0	16·0	
Technology	>20·0	>20·0	>20·0	>

* Benefits have been adjusted for ability by reducing earning differentials by 0 from investment in an extra qualification over the preceding one: they also measure returns from alternative subject investments at the same qualification level.

The most noticeable aspects of the results are the very low returns on all the postgraduate qualifications and, by contrast, the very high returns on the part-time vocational qualifications. These results reflect high postgraduate costs not being offset by extra earnings, and the smaller part-time vocational training costs being more than offset by the earnings levels, even though these are relatively low. The fairly high returns on first degrees illustrate the effect of a substantial drop in costs accompanied by only a slight movement in earnings (first degree costs fall well below those of postgraduates, but earning levels remain fairly close). The returns on 'A' levels and Ordinary National Certificate, are similar but lower than those on first degrees or Higher National Certificates. In general the results indicate that at first returns to additional education increase, but subsequently decrease or tail off. In other words the returns to society on persons entering the labour force after 'A' levels, or ONC, are below the benefits which could be obtained by higher education provision up to first degree or HNC, but thereafter the economic benefits associated with extra educational investment such as postgraduate drop very substantially.

The outstanding and somewhat unexpected results are the relatively small differences shown by the subject comparisons within each qualification level. This helps to confirm the general conclusion which is of some significance, namely that differences in returns on investment in additional education are greater between qualification levels than between alternative subjects at the same level. Nevertheless there are still a number of subject differences which, though not very great, are both extremely relevant to policy and useful in the whole process of educational planning. Thus the returns on first degrees are higher in arts and social science than in science and technology, reflecting the fact that higher science costs are not met by extra earnings. Indeed an even greater difference might have been anticipated since not only do arts subjects cost less, but overall average earnings are also slightly higher than in science. On the other hand this pattern is reversed for postgraduate qualifications with higher returns on science than arts subjects (at this level extra earnings do offset the higher costs). The returns to part-time vocational qualifications show fairly marked subject differences: the smaller return on science compared with technology reflecting the lower earnings and higher costs of science at this level.

The subject rates of return can therefore be seen as highly sensitive to costs—a feature which is further illustrated by comparing the effect of the alternative cost estimates, excluding and including research expenditure: although all the returns are reduced by including research costs, the effects are unevenly spread. The returns on first degrees show the most marked effect: the higher research cost of science and technology causing a sharper reduction in these subjects than in arts or social science. The returns on postgraduate qualifications are also noticeably reduced because research forms a large part of the total costs. By contrast the returns on part-time vocational qualifications remain practically unaltered because the research element is extremely small.

Some rate of return results are given for women, but these may be somewhat unreliable because there are few observations in subjects other than arts, and the 'A' level earning estimates are almost certainly too high. Nevertheless the returns for women are, not unexpectedly, lower than for men, due partly to the effect of part-time working and lower participation. Since teaching accounts for over half the employed women graduates in this sample, some separate estimates

Table 15.5

Rates of Return (%) *to Society for Men and Women Graduate Teachers 1966–67*

Graduates	Men Graduate Teachers	Women Graduate Teachers
All subjects	11·5	8·0
Art	11·0	7·0
Social Science	12·0	10·0
Science	—	7·5
Technology	11·0	—

including teachers are illustrated in Table 15.5 for men and women. These estimates exclude research and postgraduate diploma costs.

The inclusion of teachers in the results therefore has the general effect of increasing the return on women's education, but reducing it for men.[11] This reflects the higher earnings of women graduates in teaching compared with other employment, and the lower earnings of men graduates in teaching compared with other employment.

At this stage a second set of estimates could be included in the analysis based on a comparison of those with and without higher education, and derived from the cumulative cost and benefit differentials for each qualification. They would show the overall rate of return on post-compulsory schooling through higher education to the last qualification obtained. However this further analysis seemed unnecessary as the general pattern of such estimates would be similar to the incremental comparisons showing lower returns and narrower differences.

So far the calculation of subject returns has included the full monetary value of the lifetime earning differentials. However it may be objected that higher earnings could also be associated with such factors as natural ability or talent and family background. There is no adequate evidence for the UK on what proportion of differential earnings may be attributed solely to the additional education expenditure: indeed different proportions may be appropriate for different qualifications. Multi-variate analysis and cohort studies may help in elucidating these issues, but it would still be difficult to disentangle the cause and effect, and the American evidence does so only imperfectly. Some alternative estimates of the fraction of the earnings differentials due to educational provision range from 0·5 to 0·75. The most frequently adopted has been 0·66 (G. S. Becker, 1964, USA), and in the absence of any comparable estimate for Britain this figure has been adopted here. A series of proportions could be used, but none would be any more realistic. The effects of allowing for these other, non-educational causal factors in the social returns are shown in Table 15.4 (columns 3 and 4): all the returns are of course reduced.

[11] Teachers account for less than a quarter of all employed men graduates.

There is a further adjustment which can be made to increase the validity of the results—that is an adjustment for growth. As the results so far relate to a cross-section of individuals at a single point in time an adjustment can be made for an assumed growth in real average earnings over time. Real earnings may of course increase at separate rates for different qualification levels or subject disciplines, but if it can be assumed for simplification that all earnings rise by the same annual percentage rate, an adjustment for this secular growth in real income can be made by the addition of any assumed average rate of growth in earnings (G. S. Becker, 1964, USA). The effect of an illustrative two per cent adjustment is shown in Table 15.6. It is worth noting that were some real average earnings to fall, while others remained constant, absolute earning differentials would narrow and the rates of return decrease.

This table helps to illustrate the main results of the study: the returns on educational investment tend at first to increase with each successive level of qualification (the returns on

Table 15.6

Summary of Selected Subject Rates of Return (%)* 1966–67 (including a 2 per cent growth adjustment)

Educational Qualification	All Subjects	Arts	Social Science	Science	Tech
FULL-TIME EDUCATION (men)					
'A' levels	9·0	—	—	—	
First degree	12·5	12·5	12·0	10·5	
Master degree	2·0	2·0		4·5	
Doctorate degree	3·0			3·0	
FULL-TIME EDUCATION (women)					
First degree	7·0	6·0	8·5	2·0	
PART-TIME VOCATIONAL EDUCATION (men)					
ONC	8·5	—	—	—	
HNC	>22·0	—	—	15·0	
HNC-PQ	18·0	—	—	—	>?

* Excluding research costs, but including an ability adjustment from Table 15.4, column 3.

first degrees are higher than 'A' levels) but subsequently either decrease or tail-off; the differences in return are greater between qualifications than between subjects, although investment in science and arts subjects do not produce equal benefits; the returns on part-time vocational courses are substantially greater than on full-time university courses; finally investment in women gives a lower return than similar investment in men's education. In general, differences in rates of return arise less from the benefits or earnings differentials, and more from costs.

These returns represent an evaluation of a wide range of the investment opportunities open to Government; they illustrate the costs and benefits associated with alternative policy options and different expenditure programmes. Although the results are tentative, and need to be interpreted carefully, they are nevertheless significant economic indicators with a number of relevant policy implications. Thus, the increasing returns up to first degree or HNC level suggest room for expansion, while the decrease on subsequent levels such as postgraduate qualifications suggests some reduction in expenditure might be appropriate. Certainly the benefits from investments in part-time advanced further education are greater than in universities, and were this pattern to persist with the inclusion of full-time courses there might well be some justification for expanding advanced further education more rapidly than universities. The returns on science and art subjects would argue for some re-allocation of resources while the exclusion of research costs would produce even greater benefits. These results are especially interesting in the context of the DES' most recent White Paper, *Education: A Framework for Expansion*, the effect of which almost certainly, will be to encourage a rapid expansion of advanced further education and cause some reduction of university postgraduate provision, while leaving the allocation of university places between arts and science almost unchanged.

However it is the relative rather than the absolute magnitude of the returns which may be interpreted as indicators of the economic value to society of investment in higher education. Changes in the supply of or demand for qualified manpower may be expected to alter relative earnings differentials so affecting the rates of return estimates and for these reasons this human capital approach would be usefully combined with supply and demand forecasts for qualified persons, as well as the social demand approach.

This article has explored the human capital, or cost-benefit, approach to education, but it has only dealt with the economic benefits to society from investment in post-compulsory schooling: it has not included all the other diverse and extensive social or cultural benefits that the community may derive from extra education, and which may be equally if not more relevant to decisions about educational expansion. These non-monetary benefits may be assumed positive, so that the results presented here almost certainly understate the total social benefits of additional education.

REFERENCES

G. S. Becker (1964), *Human Capital*, National Bureau of Economic Research, New York, 1964.

M. Blaug (1965), *The Rate of Return on Investment in Education in Great Britain*, The Manchester School, September 1965.

M. Blaug, M. H. Peston and A. Ziderman (1967), *The Utilization of Educated Manpower in Industry*, Oliver and Boyd, 1967.

E. F. Denison (1964) 'Proportion of Income Differentials among Education Groups' in *The Residual Factor and Economic Growth* (ed. J Vaizey), Paris OECD, 1964.

DES (1970) Education Planning Paper No. 1: Output Budgeting for the Department of Education and Science, HMSO, 1970.

DES (1970), Education Planning Paper No. 2: Student Numbers in Higher Education in England and Wales, HMSO, 1970.

DES (1972), Education: A Framework for Expansion, Cmnd 5174, HMSO December 1972.

DES Statistics of Education (1971), Special Volume, No. 3. Survey of Earnings of Qualified Manpower in England and Wales, 1966–67, HMSO 1971.

K. G. Gannicott and M. Blaug (1969), 'Manpower Forecasting Since Robbins: A Science Lobby in Action'. *Higher Education Review*, Corn market, Autumn 1969.

L. Maglen and P. R. G. Layard (1970), 'How Profitable is Engineering Education?' *The Higher Education Review*, Spring, 1970 (or Chapter 1 of the subsequent book—P. R. G. Layard, J. D. Sargan, M. E. Ager and D. J. Jones. *Qualified Manpower and Economic Performance*, Allen Lane, 1971).

Vera Morris and A. Ziderman (1971), 'The Economic Return on Investment' in *Higher Education in England and Wales' Economic Trends* HMSO, May 1971.

16

Output Budgeting for the Department of Education and Science[*]

What is Output Budgeting

Output budgeting is one of a number of tools which have been developed to help in the planning, management and control of public expenditure and of the resources used by the public sector. There is no universally accepted definition of the terminology used, and in particular 'output budgeting' has been used with different meanings in different contexts. This section therefore sets out to explain the essentials of the output budgeting approach and to define the sense in which particular terms are used.

Output budgeting is in fact a general approach rather than a particular technique. Its specific contribution is to bring together the objectives of a particular service and the resources being devoted to them, and to provide a framework within which the costs and advantages of possible policy choices are examined side by side. An output budgeting system is a policy tool, and as such is naturally concerned mainly with future expenditure. As the then Joint Permanent Secretary to the Treasury wrote when he first suggested that some departments might consider output budgeting:

> When Governments took less of the country's resources than now, the main question was whether they should do more. As they have taken more and more resources, that question has been changing into one of making choices, rejecting one thing in order to be able to do another. Governmental arrangements for deploying and using information for major decisions and choices have been de-

[*] [From Education Planning Paper No. 1, HMSO, 1970.]

veloping correspondingly in the same general direction, through long-term forward costings, the Public Expenditure Survey Committee and forward planning limits on main programmes. The more that the nature of decisions becomes that of choice, the more important it is for the Government and for departments in their own interest to have their information deployed to make the implications of choices clear; and the more important it is to have the information in a form which is suitable for considering what value is obtained for the outlay.

Traditionally, budgets have categorized expenditure by the type of resource on which it is to be spent—staff, buildings, materials and so on—rather than by the purpose for which it is to be spent. The aims of an output budgeting system may briefly be stated as being to analyse expenditure by the purpose for which it is to be spent and to relate it to the results achieved. It is a formal system for establishing:

(i) what a department is aiming to achieve—what its objectives are—in the areas of policy for which it is responsible;
(ii) which activities are contributing to these objectives;
(iii) what resources, or inputs, are being devoted to these activities;
(iv) what is actually being achieved, or what the outputs are.

The introduction of output budgeting is one way of carrying further, within a block of expenditure, the ideas implicit in the annual work for the Public Expenditure Survey Committee (PESC).[1] By international standards the PESC survey is already a sophisticated method of examining public expenditure, at least in some respects: it looks forward for five years, deals generally with all public expenditure rather than central government expenditure, and groups expenditure into functional blocks. The PESC forecasts are considered in conjunction with annual assessments of the economic prospect over the same period. Output budgeting can take this further in particular areas by relating expenditure to objectives, rather than simply to functions, by looking at what is

[1] See the Green Paper 'Public Expenditure: A New Presentation', Cmnd 4017, April 1969, for an account of these surveys.

being achieved, and by taking into account, where appropriate, costs other than public expenditure costs.

Output budgeting has to be considered as a system, and not just as a new way of setting out the table of figures in respect of public expenditure. The whole system is intended to ensure that the objectives underlying the programmes are reviewed regularly, that the necessary studies are carried out to establish the effectiveness of what is being done, and that alternative policies are properly examined and costed. The nature of the system is perhaps better described by the name used in the United States, with Canada the only country which has applied the technique on a significant scale outside the defence field, a 'planning-programming-budgeting system'. The name emphasizes that it links expenditure with the planning process and with the attainment of objectives. In some ways it conveys the flavour of what is useful in the technique better than 'output budgeting' if the latter term is taken to imply that all outputs must be specifically forecast in advance and measured after the event.

There are three essential elements in output budgeting:

(a) the allocation of expenditure to programmes which are as closely identified as is practicable with objectives. This is the programme budget which shows, for each programme, expenditure—proposed, forecast or actual —and whatever quantitative measures of output can be meaningfully constructed and used on a regular basis;

(b) the systematic review of programmes on a regular basis.[2] This includes the questioning of the continued validity of the objectives as well as consideration of alternative ways of achieving them and of the progress so far made;

(c) special studies, either to establish the value for money of alternative ways of achieving the given objectives, or to evaluate the progress made towards achieving

[2] The PESC system, including the 'costed options', at present performs an analogous role for public expenditure as a whole. The programme reviews would do the same for a block of expenditure in greater depth. In the USA and Canada annual submissions are made to the Bureau of the Budget in Washington and the Treasury Board in Ottawa, on a programme basis, supported by programme review documents which survey the whole field and argue the case for the particular appropriations proposed.

particular objectives if this information is not available on a regular basis.

Output budgeting in its early years will naturally concentrate on the construction and discussion of programme budgets, since in many, if not all, areas of activity the measurement of final output presents formidable conceptual and practical difficulties. A programme budget constructed as part of an output budgeting system will be similar to what has hitherto been known as 'functional costing'; the essential difference will be that the functions are related to objectives rather than to the institutional pattern as is the functional costing at present used in the PESC education block.[3] An output budgeting system could however be progressively developed as and when assessment of output was carried further and new measures of output were devised; the extent and speed of this development would depend on the field of application.

Setting up an Output Budgeting System

In preparing an output budgeting system for a government department (or for a field of activity spanning more than one department) the first step is a general survey of the area of activity and the identification of the relevant objectives.[4] These objectives should, so far as possible, be ends and not means.

The next steps are an analysis of the existing activities of Government, local authorities, in order to identify their contribution to the various objectives; and the identification of the outputs, that is to say, of what counts as success or failure in achieving the objectives. It is often found that the

[3] The present PESC classification is considerably more 'objective-oriented' than was the US expenditure classification before the introduction of programme budgeting. The classification of objectives in the US programme budget for education is still closely linked to types of educational institutions.

[4] The activities contributing to an objective may be the responsibility of different parts of a department, and sometimes of different departments. An example of the former is given by some of the work of the children's services and probation services in the Home Office. An example of the latter is the work of the Board of Trade and the Overseas Departments in export promotion.

identification of outputs leads to a refinement of the statement of some of the objectives. There is no unique approach to the identification of objectives: two chief considerations should guide the way in which they are stated:

   (i) They should be meaningful in terms of policy purposes; that is to say, they should be drawn up in a way which makes policy options clear;

   (ii) they should have regard to what is practicable in terms of the allocation of inputs and the assessment of outputs.

The statement of objectives should strike a balance between these two, sometimes conflicting, aims.

A hierarchy of programmes can then be defined. Major programmes will be those groups of activities which contribute to a particular major objective or set of objectives. The programmes should be comprehensive in the sense that they should cover all the activities for which the Department is responsible and should be related to all its objectives. Ideally they should also be mutually exclusive in the sense that they do not overlap; in practice this cannot always be achieved.

The framework having thus been established, the inputs have to be allocated to the programmes. Quantitative measures of the success of the various programmes in contributing to their objectives are also made so far as is practicable on a regular basis. At this stage the programme budget is ready for use in considering policy choices. When new policy decisions are taken, any changes in the inputs have to be allocated as appropriate to the various programmes.

The operation of an output budgeting system will generally require information additional to, or in a form different from, that already available. The information system should be able to cater for changes in objectives or options and for alternative classifications. The special studies will be able to draw to some extent on the information collected for the programme budgets, but will generally need to be supplemented by further enquiries.

The steps in setting up a programme budget can be conveniently summarized in the following diagram:

Fig. 16.1

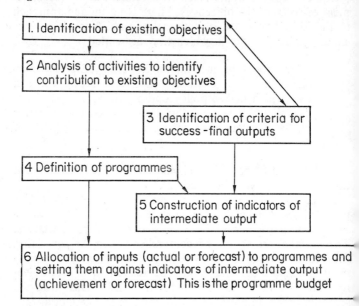

The Value of Output Budgeting

Output budgeting is a useful tool even without the measurement of final output. The chief advantages which have been claimed for it are that by directing attention to final objectives, even where success in achieving them cannot be measured, it can suggest improved methods of assessing the success of a programme of expenditure; that it provides a framework for assessing systematically how resources are being used; and that it crosses institutional boundaries, so illuminating policy choices which might otherwise have been obscured. In most fields of Government activity the assessment of final output poses severe problems, progress in solving which will be slow and difficult. While measurement of final output would clearly be a valuable part of an output budgeting system, there are clear advantages in using such a system before this stage has been reached.

The General Approach to Output Budgeting for the Department of Education and Science

The starting point for the present study was an examination of all the activities either which the Department finances, directly or indirectly, or for which it assumes some kind of policy responsibility. It appeared, on analysing the objectives of those activities, that most of the activities could be regarded as contributing to one or more of the following three main objectives:

*(1) to meet the needs of the community for education, including both the individual's need and desire for it and the requirements of the community for educated manpower;

 (2) to increase human knowledge, either so that it may be applied sooner or later, or to improve the intellectual and cultural environment, or both;

 (3) to enrich the quality of people's cultural and recreational activities, and to increase opportunities for such activities.

The Planning of Educational Expenditure

Output budgeting has hitherto, in the United States and this country,[5] been discussed, and so far implemented, in relation to decision-making structures which are broadly centralized. The existence of a structure of this kind facilitates the tasks of allocating resources between objectives and of making choices between alternative ways of achieving them. The activities for which the Department is responsible do not have this structure. But it is necessary to ask not only by whom money is spent, but, more importantly, what influences are exercised on the way in which resources are used. The extent and the nature of the involvement of the Department

[5] The interaction between education and society is such that it is scarcely possible to conceive our society without education, nor therefore to say what has been the effect of having education as a whole. The fact that the question cannot be answered hardly matters however, since stopping all education is not a conceivable policy option.

* [The education block ((1) above) includes all the activities of nursery, primary and secondary schools, and special schools. It mentions most of the work of the establishments of further education, although a small part of this work is best considered under (3), and it includes the teaching (as opposed to the research) activities of the universities.—Ed.]

in particular, and the Government in general, in the three areas of education, research, and cultural and recreational activities vary markedly, and this will inevitably be reflected in the scope and form of the respective output budgeting systems.

In the case of education, it would be meaningless to confine the system to the Department's voted expenditure, the coverage of which is the result largely of historical accidents and does not correspond to the objectives either of the education system or of the Department. The education system is almost wholly composed of public sector institutions, if universities may be included within that term, and the bulk of the costs of those institutions is financed by central or local Government. Moreover, the Department has certain statutory duties in respect of both public and private education. In the first instance, because of the limited availability of data about the private sector institutions, it is suggested that the programme budget should be confined to the public sector, including universities and direct grant schools. But in principle it probably ought to embrace the private sector as well, both because of the interaction between the two sectors and because government decisions can affect in various ways the volume of national resources devoted to the private sector.

The Government is concerned with the costs of its policies, not only in terms of public expenditure, but with the full consequences in terms of resource use. Moreover, if one is to look at the total outputs of education, one ought logically also to look at the total inputs. Hence the programme budget should from the outset provide the data from which it is possible to calculate the resource implications of the Department's activities as well as showing the public expenditure which is involved.

The programme budget will not however attempt to show the total effect on society of having an educational system. The provision of certain resources for the educational system (as for research) will have second and third order effects. Students will probably have a different personal consumption pattern from what they would have had if they were employed, and this will affect the employment, profitability and export performance of certain consumer goods industries. This in its turn may affect the consumption pattern of workers in those industries and the demands of firms for investment goods, and so on and so on. The same applies to output; the availability of trained manpower at various levels will affect the economic performance of various industries and so of the economy as a whole.

The conceivable policy choices all relate to changes which are small in relation to the total of educational expenditure, although they may be significant in absolute terms; whether more or less resources should be devoted to particular parts of education, whether the pattern of resource inputs should be changed, and so on. It is suggested that in general it should be confined to showing the direct costs and outputs, and ignore the second and third order effects referred to above. This would not, of course, rule considering such effects in subsequent detailed studies of particular choices, or showing in the programme budget an alternative set of figures to bring out particular effects which may be relevant in a policy choice. A possible example would be to show, alongside the public expenditure figures for particular programmes, the taxation which would be needed to offset the effect of that expenditure on the overall level of demand in the economy.

In education, there is much diffusion of authority and decision-making to different parts of the system. This is more than simply delegation of central authority, since to a considerable extent initiative rests in the hands of the local authorities. The Department referred in its evidence to the Royal Commission on Local Government to 'the basic role of the elected authority in making policy, deciding priorities and controlling finance' (para. 83). Moreover, to a very real extent the allocation of resources is a matter for decision by those in charge of individual institutions: a headmaster, for instance, determines how his staff are deployed and whether he is prepared to accept over-size classes among the younger children in order to widen the range of options available in the sixth form. This devolution is mirrored in the fact that a very small proportion of total expenditure on education is financed directly by the Department: some 80 per cent is financed by 163 local education authorities of widely varying sizes and standards, drawing on local revenue and on the Rate Support Grant; the greater part of the remainder is financed through the University Grants Committee. Local authorities can vary their expenditure on education from that assumed for purposes of Rate Support Grant by switching funds from or to other purposes and by changing the rates.

However, the Department has a strong, if indirect, influence on the pattern of educational expenditure. It exercises a close control over capital expenditure for schools, further education and colleges of education. Formally this is a negative control in the sense that the Department cannot initiate proposals. But in practice it can stimulate them by circulars (such as those on secondary reorganization and educational priority area schemes), and can generally ensure that what is done conforms to the Government's priorities. The pattern of capital expenditure will, over the years, have an effect on such current expenditure as maintenance, heating and lighting. In some cases the Department has used its controls over capital expenditure as an indirect way of achieving other ends: for instance, it has restricted capital expenditure on nursery schools in order to prevent a diversion of teachers from infant schools.

The largest single element in local authorities' current expenditure, teachers' pay, is also subject to a considerable extent to the influence of the Department which is responsible, mainly through the capital investment programme, for planning the numbers of student teachers in colleges of education, the most important source of supply of school teachers for many years in advance. The number of teachers in service at any one time is also affected by several other factors, including the wastage rates at different ages, the extent to which married women return to teaching, the recruitment of graduates and the age distribution of the teaching force. The first, second and third of these facts can be affected through pay and conditions of service. The Department is represented on the Burnham Committee and thus has a voice in the determination of teachers' salaries.

The Department can also influence the development of education by less direct means and in the longer term. It has guided important policy developments such as the elimination of all-age schools, the process of secondary reorganization, and the establishment of polytechnics. H.M. Inspectorate has had a considerable influence on what is generally accepted to be good educational practice. Such actions are not explicitly related either to the control or to the planning of resources; but because of the stand which the Department and H.M. Inspectorate have taken up over these matters, it has followed that resources are now being, and will in the future be, used in certain ways. The extent of influences of this kind on resource use has never been quantified.

In the university field, the Department's main influence lies in determining the size of the quinquennial grant. The final settlement is made with targets expressed in terms of 'weighted' student numbers in mind, although the 'target' figure has been consistently exceeded. Expenditure decisions are thus implicitly or explicitly related to assumptions about what the appropriate standard of qualification for entrants should be in the future. The Government has not attempted to influence explicitly either the cost per student or the relative proportions of research and teaching expenditure in universities.

These considerations would appear to lead to three main conclusions for the form of the output budgeting system and the kind of use to which it would be put. First, because the Department's influence is on the whole long-term rather than short-term, general rather than detailed, the system for education should be conceived of essentially as an instrument of planning rather than of detailed control. It should be designed to illuminate the likely resource implications of various policies open to the Department, and to provide a framework for them by forecasting the likely resource consequences of factors exogenous to the Department, such as changes in numbers in the population in various age groups.

Second, although many of the decisions which will determine the pattern of resource use are not directly within the control of the Department, the duties laid upon the Secretary of State by Section 1 of the 1944 Education Act imply that the Department needs to be aware of developments in the educational system, and in particular of the policy choices that may arise. Even in the areas where it deliberately leaves decisions to others it will wish to be aware of the broad pattern of development, not only because of the general statutory responsibility, but also because of any implications that there may be for the total of public expenditure on education. For this purpose it needs to monitor the way in which resources are in fact used in education, and an output budgeting system could form a useful part of such a monitoring process. If, for example, it were observed that in secondary schools a significant proportion of the increased supply of teachers, who were provided in order to meet the objective of reducing the number of over-size classes, were instead being diverted to sixth form work, the Department might wish either to reconsider its objective on the grounds that it did not accord with the priorities of a significant group of educationists—in this case headmasters—or to seek compliance with it. The latter could be done either through the familiar method of exhortation, or through the use of existing control mechanisms, or by changing the existing control mechanisms, or by changing the existing pattern of control.

Finally, output budgeting may, by the way in which it indicates alternative means of obtaining the same end, itself raise questions about the structure of decision-taking. Increasing the number of teachers and increasing expenditure on educational technology may be alternative ways of improving the educational provision of certain age groups. But the Department has considerably more control over the number of teachers than over the rate of introduction of educational technology in schools. It might be that where the present structure does not permit an effective choice to be made between the two because the decisions on each are taken in different parts of the system, the structure needs to be changed to enable the alternatives to be balanced against each other.

The Objectives of Education

The objectives of education have, of course, always been a subject for debate. They are inextricably bound up with the objectives of society as a whole; and it will be recognized that our society has no clear consensus of opinion on its own objectives, or, therefore, on the objectives of education.[6]

It is clear that education at each level serves a number of

[6] The Plowden Council attempted to obtain formulations of general objectives from head teachers. The Report commented: 'This list shows that general statements of aims, even by those engaged in teaching, tend to be little more than expressions of benevolent aspiration which may provide a rough guide to the general climate of a school, but which may have rather tenuous relationship to the educational practices that actually go on there. It was interesting that some of the head teachers who were considered by HM Inspectors to be most successful in practice were least able to formulate their aims clearly and convincingly' (paragraph 497).

objectives: educational, economic, cultural and social. The educational objectives are concerned with a child's development, with the acquisition of basic skills such as literacy, numeracy and oral communication, with the fostering of individual talents, and so on. The economic objectives are chiefly concerned with increasing the country's productive capacity by providing a more skilled, more flexible and better motivated labour force. Economic returns will accrue both to individuals who have received education, for example in the form of higher incomes, and to the rest of the community —for example, the effectiveness with which the community uses the resources available to it will depend to some extent on the standard of education in management in both the public and private sectors. Other objectives are social (such as preparing young people, both generally and in specific ways, for the society in which they are going to live), and cultural (such as increasing young people's sensitivity to the arts). In these fields also benefits may accrue both to individuals and to the rest of the community in which they live. Other objectives do not fall exclusively into any category: for instance, the reduction of inequalities in the distribution of income by providing equality of opportunity, or even positive discrimination, in education, or specific measures to increase the cultural awareness of children from culturally deprived backgrounds. The educational and other objectives are to some degree interdependent, in the sense that the successful achievement of some of the former is a precondition of achieving some of the latter, and in some instances *vice versa*. Reading, writing, oral communication and numeracy are necessary in order to play a part in our society. It may, in principle, be possible to assess whether the educational objectives are being achieved or not, either during, or at the end of, the educational process, at least in some respects; but it is not generally possible to determine whether the other objectives are being achieved until some time, in some cases many years, after the end of the educational process. This has implications for the practicability of assessing success, or measuring output.

The objectives of the education system are related not only to the general aims of education referred to above, but also to the needs and aspirations of the individuals who are to receive it. It must, in the words of the 1944 Education Act, be related to their age, aptitude and ability: there would be no sense in aiming at university education for all, even if the country could afford it. Indeed, a useful way of making the aims of education more specific is to ask what the education system is trying to achieve for a particular (and reasonably homogeneous) group of individuals, for instance those who have reached a certain standard in their 'A' levels and are now seeking higher education, or children who are still below the age of compulsory schooling. There is a special complication in regard to nursery education, which contributes towards two quite separate objectives: helping the educational development and social adjustment of children below the compulsory school age, and releasing mothers with scarce skills for work. These objectives may conflict: a development of nursery education in an area where it will be essentially for the benefit of the children may not release many skilled mothers for work; while the areas where its expansion will release for work mothers who have scarce skills will often be areas in which the children's needs for nursery education are less and there may already be a significant amount of private nursery provision.

The discussion so far has primarily been concerned with those benefits that accrue after some time lag—what economists refer to as 'investment' benefits. There are also benefits which accrue at the same time as the educational activity which confers them—what economists refer to as consumption benefits. One example is the enjoyment which pupils and students derive from being educated (not necessarily positive). The desire to raise the quality of the environment in schools and colleges, so that it bears some kind of relationship with the general environment, is probably a significant objective of much educational expenditure. Another example is the availability of married women for teaching as a result of the provision of nursery education for their children.

It can also be argued that another objective of educational expenditure might be that teachers' working conditions should rise in line with the general improvement in working conditions in other forms of employment. The standard of working conditions is not necessarily confined to physical conditions: for instance, teachers might argue that reductions in class size are an important way in which working conditions can be improved. Such increases in consumption benefits can be regarded as an alternative to additional pay: this fact is recognized in the Burnham Committee's decision to award a special allowance to teachers in particularly difficult areas.

The Division into Major Programmes

There is no unique approach to the devising of a structure of objectives, and the related programmes, which contribute to the overall objective. The structure has to be meaningful in terms of policy choice and should have regard to the practicalities of input allocation. One approach might be to try to associate major programmes either with the individual educational objectives of the kind referred to above, or with the main groups of economic, social and cultural objectives. But this is not possible. There is no unique identification between the various activities which go on in, say, a secondary school and the achievement of these objectives. Clearly some activities will contribute more to some objectives than to others: a course in the history of architecture is more likely to contribute to a school's cultural objectives than is the teaching of mathematics. By changing the balance of the various activities, it is possible to change the balance of the extent to which the various objectives are achieved. But in general it is the totality of the educational process at each level which achieves the objectives for that level. It is not practicable to define uniquely in a sixth form which activities, and so which inputs, have gone to achieving good 'A' level results, which to broadening the pupils' general knowledge and which to developing their abilities in creative thinking. It would be even harder to define which activities in a man's education contributed to his earning potential at the age of, say, thirty or forty, although by comparing the earning potential of people with his educational background with that of people with a different one it may be possible to assess the difference which was caused by the difference between the two levels or types of education.

Three possible ways have been considered of structuring the objectives of education which might prove practicable for the allocation of activities to those objectives and so of inputs to them. These are to structure by subject, or by institution, or by the groups at which education is aimed. The first would involve subdividing education into a series of constituent activities, for example, in a secondary school the teaching of English, mathematics, religious instruction, physical education and so on. The second, a structure based on the types of institution providing education, has certain attractions. It is what is done at present for the purpose of PESC. Any additional data collection required would be relatively simple and the programmes would correspond with the present organizational structure in the Department, in local authorities and among the educational institutions themselves. But the educational system aims to meet the needs of individuals and, through individuals, the needs of society for particular types of education rather than to provide education through certain institutions. An institutional structure of objectives and programmes would obscure the fact that to a significant extent different institutions provide alternative means to the same end—at one end of the spectrum both nursery schools and nursery classes in primary schools provide nursery education for children below the age of compulsory schooling, and at the other end universities and establishments of further education provide alternative routes to a first degree. Such a structure would also imply that the provision of education through certain institutions is an end in itself.

A division into major programmes by the groups at which the education is directed has the advantage of being more nearly related to the objectives of the system. It does seem meaningful to ask what are the objectives in providing education for the sixteen to nineteen age group, what resources are being devoted to it, what success is being achieved, whether more or less emphasis should be put on this particular group, and whether the present balance between the different types of institution providing education for this group is the right one. Further, because the leavers from such a group, for example those completing (successfully or unsuccessfully) 'A' level courses, are more homogeneous than are the leavers from a particular institution, for instance those from an establishment of further education, it is more practicable to make assessments about what has been achieved in their education.

It is therefore proposed that the division into major programmes should be by the groups at which the education is directed. The first division is by age at the lower end, for instance those below and those within the age range of compulsory schooling and by educational level at the higher end, for instance first degree level courses and postgraduate work. Such a division would involve regarding the totality of education given to a group as producing a 'package' of results corresponding to the various objectives of education.

A major advantage of the division of the system into major programmes corresponding with different levels of education is that the programme budget could be closely linked with a flow model of the whole educational system, should one be developed. Models of this kind are of great value in examining the consequences, in terms of student and pupil numbers, of different patterns of development of the educational system. They can also, as does the model being developed in the Department for students in higher education, show the expenditure consequences of different patterns, in a way which fits well into the structure of major programmes recommended in this report.

THE MAJOR PROGRAMMES

The major programmes suggested, and their associated objectives are:

A.1 **Compulsory Education**
   To provide the highest possible standards of education, according to the child's age, aptitude and ability, during the present years of compulsory schooling.

A.2 **Nursery Education**
   (i) to help the educational development and social adjustment of children below the compulsory school age;
   (ii) to release mothers for work, especially those with scarce skills.

A.3 **Education for the 15-year-old**
   To provide education suited to the age, aptitude and ability of the 15-year-old to the highest possible standard and for as high a proportion of the age group as possible.

A.4 **Education for the 16- to 19-year-old**
   (i) to provide education and/or vocational training for all those between the ages of 16 and 19 who wish to receive it and could profit from it;
   (ii) to meet the requirements of society for people

> with educational training to this level, either to
> be employed directly or to go forward for higher
> education or vocational training.

A.5 **Higher Education (courses not leading to a degree or equivalent)**
>   (i) to provide higher education for those who could
>   benefit from it but who are not qualified for, or
>   do not want, a degree course;
>   (ii) to meet the requirements of society for qualified
>   manpower.

A.6 **Higher Education (courses leading to a first degree or equivalent)**
>   (i) to provide degree level courses for those who
>   could benefit from them and desire them;
>   (ii) to meet the requirements of society for qualified
>   manpower.

A.7 **Postgraduate Education**
> To meet the requirements of society for highly quali-
> fied manpower with particular qualifications or with
> research experience.

The following paragraphs describe briefly the coverage of the
individual major programmes. Major programme A.1 includes
the work of ordinary primary and secondary schools up to
the statutory school leaving age, it also includes special
schools for children of compulsory school age. It provides
a convenient framework in which different 'ages and stages'
may be considered. The objectives of the various stages of
compulsory education are very much the same, and there
is considerable interaction between them. The policy choices
which arise at the various stages are so similar, and differ
in important respects from those in other major programmes
principally because compulsory education covers the area
in which the whole population in the revelant age-group
is within the educational system. It would not, for the same
reason, in general be practicable to distinguish the various
economic, social and cultural 'outputs' of different stages of
the compulsory system in the same way as it may be practicable to do between the output of compulsory education as a
whole and that of, say, education for the sixteen to nineteen
age-group.

Major programme A.2 covers both nursery schools and

nursery classes in primary schools. Major programme A.3 has been separated out because of the particular problems associated with the raising of the school-leaving age in 1973. It includes the work in secondary schools and further education for those who are above the existing compulsory leaving age but who would be in compulsory education if the leaving age were now sixteen.*

Major programme A.4 marks an intermediate position. A.1 to A.3 are based on a grouping by age, while A.5 to A.7 are based on a grouping by educational level. It is in A.4 that the transition between these two principles may best be effected, since A.3 is a temporary programme and a grouping by level is needed for A.5 and subsequent programmes. Major programme A.4 therefore covers the level of work in secondary schools and in establishments of further education usually considered appropriate for the sixteen to nineteen age-group; it also, however, includes work for a lower standard done by pupils and students of sixteen plus; and work of a comparable standard done by older pupils and students.[7]

Major programme A.5 covers the work of colleges of education and the higher education work of establishments of further education which is below first degree level. A.6 covers the work of universities and that work in colleges of education and establishments of further education which leads to a first degree. The coverage of major programme A.7 is essentially work in universities, including departments of education and business schools.[8]

It is almost inevitable that whatever structure is adopted there will be some interaction between the major programmes, since the pupils who are the 'input' into one part of the educational system are generally an 'output' from an earlier part. It is probable that children who receive nursery education are more prepared for the beginning of their life in primary schools. The standards in sixth forms clearly depend on those achieved during compulsory schooling.

[7] It could be argued that A4 should also include work of a comparable standard done by pupils under sixteen. It is, however, more consistent, and incidentally more in accord with the way in which statistics are currently collected, to include these pupils under A1 and A3.

[8] The work of UDE and some other work generally classified as postgraduate work, is not in fact at a higher level than that of a first degree and has generally been classified for manpower purposes as roughly equivalent to the level of major programme.

* [Note; this was published in 1970, before ROSLA.]

It is therefore not possible to think of any of the major programmes completely in isolation and, indeed, it is important that the possibility of interaction should not be ignored when considering a policy choice within the major programme categories. Where the interaction takes the form of a change in the numbers, either qualified or wanting to move from one section of the system to the next, it would be possible to trace it using an educational flow model: for instance, such a model might be used to trace through the effects of raising the school leaving age on the numbers staying on in sixth forms, and on the numbers of the latter who wish to go to university. But the fact of this interdependence does not invalidate the basic programme structure which is suggested.

The Structure within Major Programmes

The classical view of an output budgeting system requires that each major programme should be subdivided into a series of programmes corresponding to the intermediate objectives which contribute to the objectives in the major programme. But this form of structure does not really fit the circumstances of the educational system. It is true that many of the Department's particular objectives clearly fall within the objectives of a particular major programme—for example to raise the school leaving age in 1973, to provide 'roofs over heads', to improve staffing ratios in schools—and so would fit into a 'classical' structure. But other changes in the allocation of resources are taking place, not as the result of particular objectives of the Department, but as the result of numerous decisions in individual local authorities and institutions, and in some cases as the result of the pressures of 'demand', rather than as a result of changes in policy: the growth of expenditure on advanced further education is an example. Moreover, the main calls on the total resources devoted to education are the maintenance of the existing standards and provision for increases in the child population.

It is therefore suggested that the structure within major programmes would best be devised to show how far resources are required to provide for the continuation of existing activities with the present standards and the present numbers of pupils and students, to cope with increased numbers, either resulting from changes in the size of the population or from changes in 'participation rates', to meet changes in the proportion of students at a given level of education going to different types of institution, or studying different subjects, and to provide for other changes such as improvements in the standards of education or the scale of provision of teachers. Such a structure would focus attention on the variables which determine changes in the level of educational expenditure, ranging from those which were exogenous, such as population growth, to those which were the subject of specific policy decisions by the Department, such as the capital investment programmes.

The structure within major programmes, and in particular the degree of detail that is necessary, will clearly vary from major programme to major programme, depending on the intrinsic nature of the programme, the range of institutions involved it in, and the particular problems and policy concerns current at any time. But it is possible to have a common basic structure within each of the major programmes, which can then be adapted and developed to meet the particular needs. The basic structure suggested is brought out by a common numbering system for the programmes within each major programme—all but two of the programmes have the same character in each of the seven major programmes. The common ones are:

1. Maintenance of existing pattern and scale of provision.
2. Reduction of the cost of provision while maintaining existing standards of output.
3. Changes in the proportion of the age group receiving education.
4. Changes in the proportion in different types of institution or taking different subjects.
5. Changes in the standards and quality of accommodation (including residence).
8. Other changes in the pattern of inputs.
9. Changes in the incidence of costs.
10. Other (i.e. inputs allocable to objectives in the major programme, but not to particular programmes within it).

The two remaining programmes differ slightly between the three higher education major programmes and the remainder. For major programmes A.1 to A.4 they are:

6. Changes in the availability and training of teachers.

7. Improvement of teaching methods and curricula.

For the three higher education major programmes, they are:

6. Changes in staffing ratios and standards.
7. Changes in the length of courses.

To sum up, the suggested common structure is intended to be flexible and to be capable of development in accordance with the needs of policy-makers and the availability of information. It is capable of showing separately the implications for resources of the various exogenous factors affecting the education system, and the various policies of the Department.

The Assessment of Educational Output

It was suggested above that at each level of education there is a 'package' of objectives which it is not meaningful to attempt to differentiate when inputs are being analysed. Individual programmes should be assessed by the contribution which they make to the objectives of the whole programme. Inevitably it will be easier to make progress with assessment and measurement of some objectives than with others. The objectives chosen should be as 'final' as possible, but the final outputs of education, associated with its basic objectives are often very difficult to measure, although some attempts have been made, primarily in the United States, on the economic side. Some means of assessment of performance within the educational system exist already, such as the series of tests of reading ability (which might be extended to other fields), examinations and objective tests. Equally important will be the judgements of HM Inspectorate and other educationalists. Different types of assessments will not always be comparable with each other: those assessments which are precisely quantifiable should not be preferred to those which are not simply because the latter are more difficult to cope with. Some assessment of educational output is already implicit in the decisions which are now taken within the education system: an output budgeting system would provide a framework within which such assessments could be made explicit.

Much of this section is concerned with the measurement of the 'investment' benefits of education, which may be either monetary or non-monetary or both. But some measurement of 'consumption' benefits might be possible. The standard of living of school-children is probably related more to standards of buildings than to anything else. If the standard of educational buildings could be successfully measured changes in such standards could be related to the rise in general living standards.

What is at issue is not the measurement of gross output, but what may be termed, in economists' shorthand, the 'value added' by education. This introduces two problems. First, the native quality and abilities of pupils vary enormously and careful allowance must always be made for this. Moreover, their performance at successive stages is conditional on their success at earlier stages. Second, the return to a particular stage of education may not be measured simply in terms of the benefits accruing to that process itself, since they also enable pupils to go on to a further stage. All this adds to the difficulty of estimating the returns to particular pieces of educational expenditure.

The investment benefits may, for purposes of assessment, be divided broadly into two groups, described in the following paragraphs as extra-educational and intra-educational. The extra-educational outputs, relating to the performance of pupils and students outside the educational system, fall into three main categories—economic, social and cultural. Measurement should be concerned with the benefits to society as a whole, as well as the benefits to educated individuals; however, it is more difficult to measure the former than the latter.

Existing measures of final output are neither adequate in themselves nor sufficiently comprehensive to figure in the programme budget itself. It is proposed that intermediate measures of output, which may be in the nature of targets or numerical estimates of policy commitments, should be formally integrated into the programme budget. The Department is already using some targets of this kind, e.g. for the improvement of staffing ratios; they could be extended to cover other areas of activity, and perhaps developed to the point where target dates and time paths could be set and alternative target dates costed. Measures of intermediate output need to be validated by means of special studies to establish the relationship between them and the final outputs.

Much of the information needed for a programme budget on the lines suggested is already available to the Department: in many cases, although there are important exceptions, all that would be necessary would be the bringing together of this information. Special studies, including those already proposed in the Department, would help to develop the methodology of allocation.

Measurement of Final Output

Although the measurement of educational performance is at an early stage of development, there has been considerable progress in certain directions in recent years. Much work has been carried out in the United States in attempting to measure the economic return to education. This work, allowing for all the difficulties inherent in the approach, has suggested that in the United States education has a high rate of return and that human capital and the growth of knowledge are becoming more important than physical capital in expanding economic growth. The Department is currently collecting information on the relationship between earnings and qualifications in England and Wales and it is hoped that this will provide some indication of the economic return to different types of higher education in this country.

Work of this nature could be supplemented by employers' assessments of the quality of school leavers; such assessments would have value in particular for pupils leaving the education system at or a little above the compulsory leaving age, where the differential earnings measure is not really applicable. Such evidence may be a useful way of distinguishing between the quality of school leavers at any point in time, but this kind of assessment over a period of time will probably not be of much value as the development of educational opportunity affects the type of school leaver seeking particular jobs, and the general ability of those leaving at fifteen is affected by the increased numbers of more able pupils staying on in school.

Less work has been done on the non-economic returns to education. There is a clear case for encouraging other social scientists, sociologists, social psychologists, etc., to develop appropriate measures in their fields. It is to be expected that progress will be fairly slow, but some progress is clearly possible. For example, some form of social adjustment indicator is clearly needed, it being indubitably one extra-educational objective of the education system to prepare young people for the society in which they live.

Measurement of the cultural returns to education is likely to be even more difficult. It is not only a matter of 'the transmission of a common culture and common standards of citizenship' of which the Robbins Committee spoke—these anyway relate partly to what will be described by many as social objectives. Education also has objectives in the field of the arts, in developing children's sensitivity to the arts and sometimes in fostering creative talents.

The intra-educational benefits, corresponding to the intra-educational objectives, concern the performance of individuals within the educational system. Like measures of extra-educational output, any measures of performance within the system will be multi-dimensional, but by contrast with extra-educational assessments of performance there will generally be a shorter time-lag between a change in policy or a change in inputs and a resultant change in the school performance of pupils. Yet if such intra-educational measures are to have their full value, it is important to attempt to establish some connection between intra- and extra-educational performance.

To some extent, progress in assessing intra-educational output involves the development of existing means of assessment. One means which has been in existence since 1948 is the series of tests of reading ability which have been carried out (except for the first one) by HM Inspectorate. These tests provide an indicator over time of the success of the educational system in one aspect: they measure reading ability over a wide range and appear to be acceptable to the educational world generally. Extension to any of these fields would pose problems, if only because of the existence of different views about the appropriate method and content

[9] In regard to mathematics, there would, particularly at the present time, be marked disagreement about what skills children should be able to perform and what knowledge they should have at any stage. In regard to foreign languages, there is at present a divergence of opinion between those who believe that a second language, at least in the early stages, should mainly be developed orally, and those who believe that accurate written work and attention to sound grammar are important. Some work on creativity testing (or, more strictly, on 'divergent thinking'), of varying quality, has been carried out in the United States, there is certainly scope for further study in this field.

of teaching in these fields.[9] Some other aspects of educational performance in the schools have been quantified for a considerable time. The examination system, imperfect though it is, remains an indispensable tool of appraisal. However, examination standards may not remain constant through time. Objective tests still have a very useful role to play in a variety of contexts.

As explained above, subjective judgements may be ordered and categorized even where they cannot be placed on a calibrated scale. HM Inspectorate assessed the educational quality of primary schools for the Plowden Council, on an objective basis in the sense that 'the idiosyncracies of individual judgements were eliminated as far as possible', without being prepared to treat these assessments as readings on a common scale.

There are other intra-educational objectives, success in which is not at present, and probably never will be, susceptible of any kind of measurement in the strict sense. Here the judgements of educational experts, HM Inspectors, teachers and others—are crucial. HM Inspectors already take matters of this kind into account when making judgements about schools—the relationship between teachers and pupils, the extent to which younger children's play is constructive, the way in which pupils are encouraged to think for themselves, to mention but three examples. The relationship between the home and the school, although only in part 'intra-educational' rather than 'extra-educational', is a matter of increasing importance for educationalists. It is important to recognize that the judgements of experts will often differ: a familiar example is the difference in judgements made about sixth form leavers by their schools and by the universities which they enter.

In this report it is possible only to suggest lines along which further thought might be given to this problem of the assessment of output. Broadly it may be said that the assessment of intra-educational output is essentially a matter for educationalists, whereas extra-educational output falls to be assessed by people less immediately concerned with the educational system, such as employers, sociologists, economists. Different types of assessment may not always be comparable one with another: it will be difficult to relate a measurement of increased equality of opportunity with a measurement of the contribution of an educational activity to the Gross National Product. Yet it is useful to relate the assessment of different kinds of output as far as it is possible to do so. What is important is that assessments which are precisely quantifiable should not take precedence over those which are not just because it is more difficult to take the latter type readily into account.

The Use of Indicators of Intermediate Output

Although it should be possible to make progress in assessing final output through special studies, existing measures of final output are neither adequate in themselves nor sufficiently comprehensive to figure in the programme budget. But measures of intermediate output which are to some extent already used by the Department, could be developed and formally integrated into the programme budget. Some of these measures of intermediate output are in the nature of targets or paths towards targets (for example, the plans for the improvement of staffing ratios), and some are numerical estimates of general commitments (for example, forecasts of the numbers staying on after the school leaving age). These targets' could be extended in scope: the Department could decide to set a target date and a time path for reaching the target, e.g. for a programme of improvements in primary school accommodation; for the completion of secondary reorganization; for the universal provision of day release facilities; for a continuation of present trends in the proportion of qualified school leavers going on to higher education. Such targets need not involve the spending of additional money: the UGC could decide to adopt a policy which involved a progressive increase in the utilization of the university capacity. Many of these 'targets' may originate from the recommendations of advisory bodies or from an accumulation of pieces of research like research into the equality of educational opportunity.

The cost of achieving these intermediate outputs can, in principle, be forecast, although the information may have to be specially assembled or collected. So can the costs of achieving different levels of intermediate output, for example conducting a more or a less ambitious programme for the improvement of staffing ratios or alternative dates for the raising of the school-leaving age. The costs of different target can be compared in order to bring out the implications o alternative policy choices.

But these measures of intermediate output, because they relate only to intermediate objectives, need to be judged against the final objectives and assessments of final output For example, any target for the proportion of science student in universities should, at appropriate intervals, be checked against some study of the costs and benefits of a change in the supply of scientific manpower. Any changes in target relating to staffing standards should be checked against studies showing pupils' performance in reading, mathematics etc., compared with class sizes and pupil/teacher ratios These studies, which should be carried out on a regular basis would vary greatly in scope and sophistication. Where there are accepted measures of performance, as in the case o reading ability, such studies will be very much simpler than in the case of scientific manpower where measures of benefi are not yet agreed upon. The effort which it is worth devoting to such studies and the frequency with which they are under taken will depend partly on the scale of resources at stake i relation to the availability of resources for such studies an partly on the inherent complexity of the subject matter Studies could be carried out internally or by commissioned research. In many cases full scale enquiries will have to b made at infrequent intervals, both to examine existing target and perhaps to set new ones, while simpler *ad hoc* researc studies could be made more frequently to validate the target in existence.

There have in recent years been significant changes in th scale and scope of the Department's interest in education chiefly, of course, its assumption in 1964 of responsibility fc the universities. The major policy choices facing the Depart ment are increasingly becoming choices which cross institu tional boundaries. The substantial time-lags between decision and their effects in the education system imply a need (whic is already recognized) for long-term planning. The output budgeting system has been designed to highlight these polic choices, and to provide a means of reviewing systematicall the resource implications of long-term plans.

The whole of the argument in this report has to be see in the wider context of the general prospect for public ex penditure in relation to the resources likely to be available. In education particularly the sheer pressure of increasing numbers coming forward, in the next decade or so, implies a rate of expansion greater than any of the rates of growth of the Gross National Product envisaged in the Green Paper 'The Task Ahead'.[10] Further, these numbers have important implications for the proportions of skilled manpower to which the education service may lay claim. All this will make it increasingly necessary to analyse areas of choice, to understand the full implications of such choices and to develop systematic ways of deciding on priorities. If an output budgeting system were in existence, much of the basic information and the understanding of choices which would be required would already be available both for regular surveys and any *ad hoc* reviews of policy which might be made from time to time. This availability of the basic data would also make it possible to work out more fully, within the time available for such reviews, the implications of the various choices, both in the long and the short term. An output budgeting system should enable the Department both to allocate more effectively the resources made available to it, and to argue more cogently for its share of public expenditure.

[10] HMSO, February 1969.

17

LESLIE WAGNER†

The Economics of the Open University *

The Open University began teaching its first 25,000 students in January 1971. The main interest in the University has focused on its role as an educational experiment providing part-time tuition to unqualified mature students through the use of a range of media. However, thoughts have also turned to how the University might help to meet the growing demand for full-time higher education. The Secretary of State for Education and Science has already asked the University to examine 'the contribution it can make to the development of higher education provision in the future'.[1] An analysis of the costs of the Open University and the effect of its unique method of production would, therefore, seem appropriate both as a contribution to the economics of higher education and to an informed debate about the future provision of higher education.

The main purpose of this paper is to provide some figures for the Open University. To give these figures some significance, however, I have calculated comparable figures for conventional universities wherever possible. Some formidable problems arise however in comparing the Open University and conventional universities, and these will be discussed in the next section. These problems should be borne in mind when the results are compared, and the figures should be regarded as giving only a broad indication of the cost differences between the two types of institution.

The University Grants Committee (UGC) in 1964 (see refs.

* [From *Higher Education*, Vol. 1, No. 2, 1972.]

† [Leslie Wagner is a Lecturer at the Open University.]

[1] Letter from the Department of Education and Science to the Open University, 12 August 1970.

frowned on exercises designed to compare the costs of education in different kinds of institutions, on the grounds that
they were likely to be misleading. The Robbins Committee
(1963) had already carried out such an exercise a year earlier,
and a recent educational planning paper by the Department
of Education and Science (DES, 1970) contains a chapter
and appendix on the costs of higher education. Most economists would agree with Professor Carter's statement (1965)
that he would be concerned 'if people did *not* compare the
"costs" of education in different institutions. This is the
analogue of the inter-firm comparison, a process which has
shown many industrialists the way to ask searching questions
about their own activities.' It is in that spirit that the present
paper has been written.

The next section will discuss some of the problems of
comparing the Open University and conventional universities,
after which the Open University and its cost breakdown will
be explained. The paper then moves onto four calculations of
the Open University teaching system, and compares these
with similar calculations made for conventional universities.
The four calculations are:

(a) the average recurrent cost per equivalent undergraduate;
(b) the capital cost per new student place;
(c) the average recurrent cost per graduate;
(d) the resource cost per equivalent undergraduate.

Two other calculations which are usually relevant have not
been made, namely the cost to the individual and the cost to
the public sector. The Open University fee structure is under
constant review and any figures given are likely to be outdated very quickly. The paper therefore concentrates on the
costs of the institution and not on whom these costs fall.

Some Problems of Comparison

1. COSTS AND BENEFITS

Ideally a paper on the economics of higher education should
include calculations on both the costs and benefits sides.
Calculations on the private and social benefits of higher education in conventional universities have been made by Blaug
(1965). A recent attempt to estimate the rate of return to

higher education is given in *Economic Trends* (Morris & Ziderman, 1971). Similar calculations for the Open University cannot be made until the University has been operating for some considerable time. In any event the Open University has set its academic standards to be equivalent to those of conventional universities and it would be invidious to assume anything else until evidence is available. The output of the Open University is planned to be similar to that of conventional universities. It is the raw material and the techniques of production which are different. It seems appropriate therefore to assume, for the time being, that the private and social benefits of the two types of institutions will be the same, and to concentrate the analysis on the costs side of the equation.

There is the point, however, that as the average Open University student is older than the average conventional university student, even if the benefits are similar, they are cumulatively less over the older student's lifetime than over the younger's. In fact the mean age of the Open University student on the evidence of the first two years' applications is between twenty-six and twenty-seven, although of course the dispersion is quite large. This is some seven years older than the average conventional university student, and when discounting is allowed for, the difference is not likely to be significant.

2. TEACHING AND RESEARCH

There are some difficult statistical problems to be overcome before a fair comparison can be made between the Open University and conventional universities. As Professor Carter (1965) has pointed out, 'A University is a multi-product firm with three main classes of product,' *viz.,*

(a) men and women with degrees;
(b) research;
(c) the storage of knowledge and maintenance of cultural standards.

This paper is concerned with inter-university comparisons on the first of these—namely the cost of teaching and producing a graduate. The other two must be considered as well; for if the ratio of expenditure on the first to the other two is different at the different types of institution, the comparison will not be a fair one.

The central academic staff at the Open University have similar conditions of service to their colleagues at conventional universities. They are expected to devote half of their time to research. However, the central academic staff at the Open University form a smaller proportion of total teaching costs than they do at conventional universities. At the Open University, the BBC, media production, and regional part-time tuition staff all play a part in the teaching process. None of these carry out research functions as well. At conventional universities, almost the entire teaching load falls on the academic staff. Because the Open University proportion of central academic staff to total teaching staff is relatively small, the proportion of its total expenditure allocated to research will also be smaller relative to conventional universities. It is difficult to make an allowance for this, but a rough estimate would be that whereas in conventional universities about 35 per cent of total recurrent expenditure could be allocated to research, at the Open University the figure might be a little less than 10 per cent.[2]

These figures are of course only a very rough guide, and many university teachers would argue that research and teaching functions cannot be separated, certainly not in terms of expenditure. Unfortunately the effect of teaching on research, and vice versa, cannot be measured in any meaningful way. It is difficult to be precise in this area. Whenever this consideration is relevant in the calculations, it will be allowed for by making two separate calculations. One will assume no difference in the proportion of expenditure going to research in the two types of institution and will therefore take total expenditure as a reliable guide to teaching costs. A second calculation will attempt to allow for research costs more explicitly by reducing the Open University recurrent expenditure figure by 10 per cent and the conventional universities figure by 35 per cent.

As regards the 'storage of knowledge and maintenance of cultural standards', the Vice-Chancellor of the Open University has gone on record as stating that he regards his academic staff as of equal standing with those in conventional universities (Perry, 1970). In this sense the Open University

[2] A rough calculation can be made by halving the total teaching and research costs figure at conventional universities and halving the faculty and Institute of Education Technology costs at the Open University.

contribution is not likely to be proportionately less than the contribution of conventional universities. There is, however, the question of library facilities. The Open University library is meant to be a teaching library rather than a research library, and the expenditure on library facilities is about 1 per cent of total expenditures, whereas in conventional universities it amounts to between 3–4 per cent of the total. While this distinction might be borne in mind, it is not significant in terms of the overall expenditure figures. The central calculations, therefore, will assume that the recurrent expenditure of the two types of institution reflects the same proportionate expenditure on the production of men and women with degrees, but where relevant, separate calculations will be made to allow for the different research costs ratios.

3. STANDARDIZED INPUT

A further problem is that while Open University in its earlier years will be working with a standardized input, i.e. undergraduates, conventional universities have an input mix that includes both undergraduates and post-graduates. These must be standardized to enable a valid comparison to be undertaken. The University Grants Committee (1969) calculates that education diploma students are worth 1 unit of undergraduate load,[3] arts and social science post-graduates are worth 2 units of undergraduate load, and science-based post-graduates are worth 3 units of undergraduate load. The number of students at conventional universities can therefore be weighted to produce a figure for equivalent undergraduates.

4. EX-POST AND EX-ANTE

The latest reported financial figures for conventional universities are for the academic year 1968–69, although student numbers figures are available for a year later (UGC, 1969). These have to be compared with the Open University's projected expenditure for some years in the future. A comparison of ex-post costs of the two types of institution cannot be made for some considerable time until the Open University is fully established with a flow of students entering and leaving the system each year. This situation will not arise until 1973 at the earliest.

[3] Load is defined as staff effort, library facilities and laboratory and equipment resources.

However, the Open University budget until 1973 has been agreed with the DES, which provides the resources directly at present, and not through the UGC. There is, of course, no guarantee that the budget will not change or that a budgeted figure for 1973 will not be exceeded when actual expenditure occurs. Experience so far has shown that the overall budgetary figure is unlikely to change, although funds may be transferred from one spending head to another. Moreover, the total budget is related to a given number of students. If the number of students changes then the budget will also change, although, because the average cost curve is not linear, the change will not be proportional. The present estimates are a reliable guide for the purpose of calculating the average cost per student, or per graduate. In any event these are the only figures available, and there will be no conclusive evidence to challenge them until 1974–75. It seems unnecessarily long to wait until then before carrying out a comparative exercise, despite the limitations of the existing figures.

So the basic data available are the Open University budgetary estimates for 1973 which are at 1971 prices. These will be compared with the conventional universities figures for 1968–69 at current prices. Two adjustments are necessary to bring these figures into line. First a price index adjustment to convert the conventional universities' figures into 1971 prices, and secondly an allowance for any productivity changes in conventional universities between 1968/69 and 1973.

5. PRICE INDEX
An index of 'university costs' is maintained by the UGC, and this has been used to convert figures for 1968–69 into 1971 prices.[4] This index shows that between July 1969 and July 1971 conventional universities' costs rose by about 22 per cent. Accordingly the conventional universities' recurrent costs figures for 1968–69 will be increased by 22 per cent to convert them into 1971 prices.

6. PRODUCTIVITY CHANGES
The figures for conventional universities give their recurrent expenditure and student numbers in 1968/69. An assumption

---

[4] I am grateful to Professor A. J. Brown for his help in this matter.

needs to be made as to whether this ratio will change by 1973. The Robbins Committee (1963) assumed constant costs per student over time. Woodhall and Blaug (1965), however, found a decrease in university productivity over the period 1938 to 1962. This has been disputed by Carter (1969), and with the increasing use of capital-embodied technological aids to teaching, it seems plausible that any declining trend in productivity has at least been arrested. Accordingly, it would seem most reasonable to assume that no change in productivity will occur over the period 1969 to 1973.

It can be seen that some concrete problems of comparison exist, and this section has attempted to find the best method of dealing with them. As far as is possible, the figures have been standardized to refer to similar periods at similar prices and measuring similar variables. It is likely that any discrepancies that still exist will be significant only if there are small differences in the costs of the respective institutions.

The Open University Teaching System

Before comparing the costs of the two types of institution, it is necessary to describe the Open University teaching system and the implications of this for its cost structure.

There are five components to the Open University teaching system, namely correspondence material, television and radio programmes, class tuition at local study centres and summer schools. The first three items are impersonal, whereas the last two involve direct student–teacher contact. An additional form of student–teacher contact is through the provision of counsellors whose function it is to advise the student on any non-academic problems he may be encountering.

The student receives at regular intervals a block package of correspondence materials containing written material, and where relevant, slides, films, records or science kits for home experiments. The written material includes references to other reading, some self-test questions, and a guide to the relevant radio and television programmes. The student is given assignments at regular intervals to be marked either by a tutor or by a computer.

This system determines the cost structure. The expense of the impersonal components is in effect a fixed cost. A television programme costs as much to produce for one student as it does for 50,000. The only variable element in the correspondence package is the cost of printing and postage, and this is regarded as a variable cost in the University's budget. The ancillary material that might be sent with the packages (slides, records, etc.) is also regarded as a variable cost. Besides these, the only major cost that varies with the number of students is that concerned with the provision of personal tuition services. Various provisions which could be allocated to either overhead costs or direct costs, such as the hire of study centres, are in fact allocated to overhead costs within the University budget. This high ratio of fixed-to-variable costs is in contrast to conventional universities, where the largest single item in recurrent expenditure—academic salaries—is directly linked to the number of students.

The fixed costs budgeted for in 1973 are shown in Table 17.1. These figures should be regarded only as a general guide to the allocation between different items of fixed costs and between fixed costs and direct student costs. As has already been mentioned, the University allocates some border-line costs to fixed costs. It is quite possible that changes will be made in the allocation between spending heads between the writing of this paper (1971) and 1973.

One of the points that emerges is that BBC costs are higher than faculty and library costs. It would be wrong to deduce from this, however, that the broadcasting component of the teaching function costs more than the other elements. The correspondence element involves not only faculty costs but printing, paper and postage costs. The latter are classified as direct costs and, of course, will vary with the number of students. Nevertheless, the large size of the BBC budget, even with the limited broadcast component of the Open University system, indicates why the original idea of the 'University of the Air', by which the majority of teaching would be through the broadcasting medium, had to be changed.

Direct student costs are a little more complicated. Basically they are calculated by working out a cost figure for each item of direct cost in relation to total output. These total figures for such items as printing, postage, audio-visual aids, science home experimental kits and the provision of tuition and counselling services, are divided by the total number of students to provide a unit direct cost figure. This average figure will depend on the mix of total student numbers, sub-

Table 17.1

Fixed Element in the Open University's Recurrent Costs in 1973 at 1971 Prices*

Item	Cost (£000)
Central Administration	1,093
Regional Administration	1,244
Faculties and Library	1,588
BBC	1,647
Funds not yet allocated to specific heads	519
Miscellaneous, e.g. Operations, Educational Technology, Staff–Student Facilities, Maintenance, etc.	854
Total	6,945

* Source: Open University Budgetary Estimates.

jects studied and level of courses taken. For example, the print costs of the correspondence element will depend on the number of students; equally, the larger the number taking science the greater will be the expenditure on the relatively expensive home experimental kits;[5] and as the tuition and counselling services are required more in the foundation year than in other years, the tuition costs will vary with the proportion of students in each year. With the mix expected in 1973, the average direct cost per student at the Open University is likely to be in the region of £61 per student per year. If a greater proportion of students than is thought likely wish to take science subjects or if the foundation year proportion is higher than is budgeted for (possibly through dropouts), then the average figure will be higher. If the opposite occurs or students take more courses per year, then, correspondingly, it will be lower.

In 1973 with fixed costs of £6·945 million and an average direct cost per student of £61 per year, the average recurrent cost per student is given by the equation

[5] Home experimental kits are in fact very cheap compared to the usual costs of laboratory experiments. They are expensive, however, in relation to the other items in direct student cost.

$$C = \frac{6945}{n} + 0 \cdot 061$$

where C=average cost per student,
        n=the number of students,
and the units are in £000.

There is some divergence between the notion of direct student costs and the economists' concept of marginal cost. Some costs such as the hire of regional study centres and of examinations, which might be classified as marginal costs, come under the fixed costs allocation at the Open University. Even if allowance is made for this, the equation indicates that the marginal cost of each extra student is relatively small and that average recurrent costs per student decline as the number of students increases. Some increase in fixed costs may occur to cover increased administrative expenditure when student numbers reach a particular size (possibly 60,000), but this will be relatively small and the long-run curve of average cost per student will continue to fall. It is more likely to be the sheer physical and administrative problem of dealing with large numbers of students rather than cost considerations that will limit the expansion of the University. It is interesting to note that the Government has limited the University to a total student population of between 36,000 and 42,000. The University is planning for 36,500 students in 1973. This figure does not fully exploit the economics of scale in the Open University system that clearly exist. In the next section the cost implication of increasing student numbers above 36,500 will be shown.

Average Recurrent Cost per Equivalent Undergraduate

OPEN UNIVERSITY

The recurrent costs of the Open University in 1973 are given in its budgetary estimates. As explained previously the important variable is that of direct student costs, which has been calculated on the basis of a total student population in 1973 of 36,500. At an average direct student cost of £61 this produces a total of £2·23 million for variable costs. With a fixed cost of £6·95 million this produces a total recurrent cost figure for the Open University of £9·18 million as is shown in Table 17·2.

Table 17.2
Recurrent Costs of the Open University in 1973 at 1971 Prices*

	(£)
Fixed costs	6,945,000
Variable costs (based on 36,500 students)	2,232,000
Total recurrent costs	9,177,000

* Source : Open University Budgetary Estimates.

With a total recurrent expenditure of £9·18 million and 36,500 students, all of whom are undergraduates, the average recurrent cost per equivalent undergraduate at the Open University is

$$£\frac{9,177,000}{36,500}=£251·0$$

CONVENTIONAL UNIVERSITIES
Student numbers at conventional universities have to be converted into undergraduate equivalents. This is done in Table 17.3 by the method described earlier which indicates a total of 302,920 undergraduate equivalents in 1968/69. Recurrent expenditure in that year was £233·4 million. Allowing for the 22 per cent rise in prices between July 1969 and July 1971 this figure becomes £284·7 million at 1971 prices. Thus the average recurrent cost per equivalent undergraduate in conventional universities[6] in 1968/69 was

$$£\frac{284,748,000}{302,920}=£940·0$$

[6] An attempt at an explicit allowance for research costs can be made, as explained earlier, by reducing the Open University recurrent costs figures by 10 per cent and the conventional universities' figures by 35 per cent. The result is as follows:
Open University—recurrent costs=£8,259,300 ;

average recurrent cost per equivalent undergraduate=$\frac{£8,259,300}{36,500}$=£226.

Conventional Universities—recurrent costs=£185,086,200 ;

average recurrent cost per equivalent undergraduate=$\frac{£185,086,200}{302,920}$=£611.

So even when an explicit allowance for research costs is made the Open University costs are a little over 35 per cent of conventional universities' costs for teaching an equivalent undergraduate.

Table 17.3

Conventional Universities
Conversion of figures for total students into a figure for equivalent undergraduates 1968–69*

	Number	Weighting	Weighted number
Undergraduates	178,125	1	178,125
Post-graduates			
Education	9,525	1	9,525
Science (incl. Medicine)	26,296	2	78,888
Arts (incl. Social Science)	18,191	2	36,382
Total	232,137		302,920

* Source: UGC (1968). *UGC Statistics of Education (1968)*, Vol. 6. London, HMSO.

The DES planning paper 'Student numbers in higher education' calculates a recurrent cost per student year in 1967/68 of £1,045 in 1969 prices. If the weighting system used in Table 17.1 to take account of post-graduate students—which raises the number of equivalent undergraduates—and the conversion to 1971 prices are allowed for, the results are broadly similar.

It would seem, therefore, that the average recurrent cost per equivalent undergraduate at the Open University is little more than a quarter of that at conventional universities. The essential difference in costs between the two types of institution is in the nature of the input (part-time as opposed to full-time students) and the techniques of production. It would be interesting to have some indication of the relative importance of these two differences. An attempt can be made by allowing for the cost differences between part-time and full-time students. Any cost differences remaining may then be attributed to the difference in production techniques.

The *Robbins Report* (1963, p. 108) states that 'two part-time students are counted as being equivalent, for costing purposes, to one full-time student'. No reason is given for this assumption and intuitively it seems a little exaggerated. The ratio may arise as a result of part-time students being costed at short-run marginal cost filling spare capacity within the present conventional university system which is predominantly organized to cater for full-time students. It may not be appropriate on the basis of long-run marginal cost for a wholly part-time institute. If the 2:1 ratio is adopted, a calculation can be made in terms of *full-time* equivalent undergraduates. The Open University figure is simply half the number of part-time undergraduates—namely 18,250. The conventional university figure is shown in Table 17.4.

The Open University number of full-time equivalent undergraduates is half the part-time number so the average recurrent cost per equivalent undergraduate is doubled to produce a figure of £502.

For conventional universities the recurrent expenditure in 1968/69 is divided by the weighted number of full-time equivalent undergraduates shown in Table 17.4 to produce the following:

$$£\frac{284,748,000}{281,927} = £1,010 \text{ at } 1971 \text{ prices}[7]$$

So even when allowance is made for the cheaper costs of part-time tuition the average recurrent cost per full-time equivalent undergraduate at the Open University is about half of that at conventional universities. The production techniques used would seem to be the more important element in the cost differential. The use of broadcasting and correspondence media as the major element in the system clearly allows economies of large-scale operation to be exploited.

In fact, as was mentioned earlier, the larger the number of students at the Open University, the lower is the average

[7] If the research costs allowance explained earlier is made the figures are as follows:

Open University—recurrent costs = £8,259,300;
average recurrent cost per equivalent full-time undergraduate =
$$\frac{£8,259,300}{18,250} = £453.$$

Conventional Universities—recurrent costs = £185,086,200;
average recurrent cost per equivalent full-time undergraduate =
$$\frac{£185,086,200}{281,927} = £656.$$

Open University costs are 70 per cent of conventional universities' costs, even when (a somewhat exaggerated?) allowance for research costs and the nature of the students at the respective institutions is made.

recurrent cost per student. Table 17.5 indicates how average recurrent costs fall as student numbers rise from 36,500 to 60,000. Above this latter level higher administration costs are likely to be incurred and there may be administrative and educational difficulties in dealing with more than 60,000 students in one institution. The figures are calculated on the basis of each student involving an extra cost of £61. It would seem to be a false economy to limit the number of students at the Open University to a relatively low level on the basis of total cost calculations when there are substantial economies to be reaped at relatively high numbers and a clear demand from prospective students for the University to a higher number.

Table 17.4

Conventional Universities

Conversion of figures for total students into a figure for full-time equivalent undergraduates in 1968–69*

	Number	Weighting	Weighted number
Full-time			
Undergraduates	173,510	1	173,510
Post-graduates			
Education	6,841	1	6,841
Science (incl. Medicine)	18,695	3	56,085
Arts (incl. Social Science)	12,248	2	24,496
Part-time			
Undergraduates	4,615	0·5	2,308
Post-graduates			
Education	2,684	0·5	1,342
Science (incl. Medicine)	7,601	1·5	11,402
Arts (incl. Social Science)	5,943	1	5,943
Total	232,137		281,927

* Sources: UGC (1969) *Statistics of Education 1969*, Vol. 6; Committee on Higher Education under the Chairmanship of Lord Robbins (1936). Cmnd. 2154, Appendix IV.

Table 17.5

Average Recurrent Cost per Full-Time and Part-Time Undergraduate at the Open University as Student Numbers Increase*

(1) Student Numbers	(2) Full-Time Equivalent Students	(3) Average Recurrent Cost £000	(4) Average Recurrent Cost per Student (3/1) £	(5) Average Recurrent Cost per Equivalent Full-Time Undergraduate (3/2) £
36,500	18,250	9,177	251	502
40,000	20,000	9,385	235	470
45,000	22,500	9,690	215	430
50,000	25,000	9,995	199	398
55,000	27,500	10,300	187	374
60,000	30,000	10,605	177	354

* Source: Open University Budgetary Estimates.

Capital Cost per Student Place

Universities also require a large expenditure on capital resources. For conventional universities the DES (1970, Table 14) recently calculated that the capital cost per new teaching place was £3,000 at 1969 prices. This figure includes the cost of land and equipment, but not the cost of residence. The average figure depends to a large extent on the ratio of arts-based places to science-based places. The Robbins Committee (1963, Table 22, p. 113) produced figures for different subjects as shown in Table 17.6. Column A in Table 17.6 gives the Robbins figures in 1963 prices. Column B gives the figures in 1970 prices using the index of building costs as given in the figures for new construction prices in the index of wholesale prices.

K. L. Stretch (1964) calculated capital costs by differentiating between building costs on different sites. On the assumption that 40 per cent of places were allocated to Science and Technology, he calculated capital costs (excluding equipment) per student place as shown in Table 17.7. Column A is in 1963 prices; Column B gives the same costs in 1970

Table 17.6

*Capital Cost per Student Place**

Subject	Capital costs per student place (£)	
	A. 1963 prices	B. 1970 prices
Arts	1,320	1,729
Science and Medicine	2,640	3,458
Technology	3,850	5,044

* Source: *Robbins Report*, Appendix IV.

prices, calculated by means of the same index as in Table 17.6.

Professor Carter (1965) thought these figures might be too low, and calculated some provisional figures for the University of Lancaster, covering the period of its growth to 4,170 students and assuming that 61 per cent would be students of science and technology. These figures exclude the cost of site, fees and equipment, and are given in Table 17.8. Column A gives 1963 prices, and Column B 1970 prices.

On the basis of these figures, the average capital cost per student place (including land and equipment but excluding residence) at conventional universities is likely to be in the region of £2,500 to £3,000 at 1970 prices, depending on the particular site and the proportion of science and technology places.

The capital costs of the Open University are given in its

Table 17.7

*Capital Cost per Student Place**

Area	Capital cost per student place (£)	
	A. 1963 prices	B. 1970 prices
Large city	2,580	3,380
Medium town	1,820	2,384
Small town	1,640	2,148

* Source: Stretch, K. L. (1964), *Minerva* (Spring).

Table 17.8

Capital Cost per Student Place at Lancaster University*

Subject	Capital cost per student place (£)	
	A. 1963 prices	B. 1970 prices
Arts, Social Science and Mathematics	1,850	2,424
Science and Technology	2,711	3,551
Weighted average	2,338	3,063

* Source: Carter, C. F. (1965). 'The economics of higher education', *Manchester School of Economic and Social Studies* (January).

budget at 1970 prices, and this expenditure is expected to be its total capital costs in the foreseeable future. At conventional universities there is some scope for economies of scale in capital expenditure as a certain proportion of capital costs is independent of the number of students. At the Open University almost all capital expenditure is independent of the number of students. The main items of capital expenditure, such as site, office and catering accommodation, and scientific laboratories, are geared to the number of staff; and as has already been mentioned, the number of staff is independent of the number of students. The major capital item which is dependent on the number of students is the correspondence section, which is in charge of collating, packaging and mailing material to students and which is likely to comprise about 15 per cent of total capital costs.

So the capital cost per student place at the Open University depends crucially on how many student places are allowed. The present figure is 36,500 student places, but many more could be enrolled with only a marginal increase in capital costs. Nevertheless, even with only 36,500 students the total capital costs of the Open University are expected to be about £6 million in 1970 prices, producing a capital cost per student place of £165. On present estimates, therefore, the capital cost per student place at the Open University is about 6 per cent of the cost at conventional universities. Moreover, student numbers can be increased substantially with only a marginal increase in capital costs. Open University student numbers would have to fall to 2,000 before capital costs per student place became equal to those at conventional universities.

It should be remembered that these costs exclude residential costs which, if the Robbins Committee figures are updated to 1970 prices, are in excess of £2,000 per student place at conventional universities. The Open University has virtually no residential costs; a few research students will live on the campus, but the great mass of students are undergraduates who study in their own homes and if this is taken into account the average capital cost per student place at the Open University is about 3 per cent of that at conventional universities.

It is important to appreciate just how this Open University advantage arises. The residential factor has just been mentioned, but even if all students at conventional universities studied at home or in lodgings, the capital costs per student place at the Open University would still only be 6 per cent of those at conventional universities.

The crucial difference is that students at the Open University are not physically on the campus. This means, for example, that student cultural, recreational, library and miscellaneous facilities together with catering accommodation do not have to be provided. To obtain all these facilities the Open University student will use existing capacity in the economy at an extremely low marginal cost. A similar situation exists with regard to teaching accommodation. In conventional universities, arts subjects require only classrooms, but it is in the science subjects that the main burden of expenditure occurs. The cost of scientific laboratories at the Open University is for staff facilities for research and the preparation of correspondence material. Students' work is undertaken at home, with the use of the ingenious experimental kits which each student hires from the University, and in the laboratories of existing institutions.

These items are in fact part of the recurrent costs of the Open University. So in effect the Open University's capital estimates benefit at the expense of the recurrent estimates in comparison with conventional universities. It will be remembered, however, that even with this transfer of some capital items to recurrent expenditure, the Open University's recurrent expenditure is less than a third of that at conventional universities.

It would seem, therefore, that the Open University has a recurrent cost equivalent to about 30 per cent of conventional universities recurrent cost per equivalent undergraduate, and a capital cost per student place some 6 per cent of conventional universities cost, even when residential costs of conventional universities are excluded.

Cost per Graduate

It is of course true that these seemingly advantageous figures for the Open University are of little use if the University produces very few graduates because of a high drop-out rate. This section, therefore, calculates the cost per graduate at conventional universities and at the Open University.

CONVENTIONAL UNIVERSITIES

The cost per graduate is measured by the average recurrent cost divided by the number of graduates. However, there are difficulties in making this calculation. A large expansion in University entrance boosts the figures for recurrent cost in the early years and the figure for the number of graduates in later years. In order to avoid this, a series of figures over the period 1965/66 to 1968/69 is used.

A second problem is to differentiate between degrees and diplomas, and between first degrees and post-graduate degrees. As recurrent expenditure is incurred in producing these various types of graduates, they must all be included. The difficulty is finding the correct weighting in terms of first-degree equivalents.

Most part-time students will be taking diplomas, which are likely to involve less expenditure than degree work. So the assumption is made that all diplomas count as half a first degree. Post-graduate degrees are a little more difficult. In any one year a post-graduate costs more to teach than an undergraduate, but the time taken to obtain a post-graduate degree is often less than for a first degree. The cost also varies between subjects. Accordingly, two different assumptions will be made, first that post-graduate degrees are

quivalent to first degrees, and second, that each is equiva-
ent to two first degrees. This will produce a range of figures
or the cost per graduate depending on which assumption
s regarded as the most appropriate. The calculations are
hown in Tables 17.9 and 17.10 below.

The tables show that the cost per graduate is in excess of
3,000 in conventional universities even when the most
avourable assumptions with regard to post-graduate degrees
re made. Allowing for the adjustment to 1971 prices, the
ost per equivalent first degree graduate in conventional uni-
ersities is likely to be near to £4,000 at 1971 prices, with the
gure nearer £4,500 if post-graduate degrees are assumed to
ost as much to produce as first degrees.

able 17.9

irst-Degree Equivalent Graduates in Conventional Universities*

Year	First-degree graduates	Diplomas +2	Post Graduates		Total	
			× 1	× 2	PG × 1	PG × 2
965–66	31,887	5,961	6,453	12,906	44,301	50,754
966–67	36,256	6,293	7,910	15,820	50,459	58,369
967–68	41,685	6,680	9,713	19,426	58,078	67,791
968–69	44,820	6,736	10,245	20,490	61,801	72,046

* Source: *UGC Statistics of Education 1966, 1967, 1968, 1969.*

able 17.10

ost per Equivalent First-Degree Graduate in Conventional
niversities at Current Prices*

Year	(£) Recurrent costs (2)	Total graduates cost per graduate (£)			
		PG × 1 (3)	PG × 2 (4)	PG × 1 (2)+(3)	PG × 2 (2)+(4)
65–66	161,005,638	44,301	50,754	3,634	3,172
66–67	188,605,450	50,459	58,369	3,738	3,231
67–68	211,099,284	58,078	67,791	3,635	3,114
68–69	233,363,000	61,801	72,046	3,776	3,239

* Source: *UGC Statistics of Education 1966, 1967, 1968, 1969.*

OPEN UNIVERSITY

The Open University calculation involves problematical assumptions about the future total student population and annual number of graduates. There is, at least, a stated University and Governmental policy on the number of students, namely that the figure should be within the range of 36,000 to 42,000. The number of students entering the system each year will depend on the number of people leaving the system either through graduation or drop-out. The University has itself assumed that with an eventual stable total student population of 37,500, in the long run it should be able to offer about 15,000 new places each year. A student population of 37,500 is likely to involve the University in recurrent costs of about £9·235 million.

There is no reliable information on the number of likely graduates each year. The Open University is an innovation and drop-out figures from existing correspondence schools are little guide. The Open University is much more than a correspondence college, since it offers an integrated system of teaching in which television, radio, personal tuition and correspondence all play a part. The most useful procedure would seem to be to estimate the cost per graduate at different possible drop-out rates and thereby find the drop-out rate at

Table 17.11

Cost per Graduate at the Open University*

Assumption: Annual student intake of 15,000

Drop-out rate	Graduates	Recurrent Cost (£m)	Cost per graduate (£)
40%	9,000	9.235	1,026
50%	7,500	9.235	1,231
60%	6,000	9.235	1,539
70%	4,500	9.235	2,052
80%	3,000	9.235	3,078
85%	2,250	9.235	4,104
90%	1,500	9.235	6,157

* Source: Open University Budgetary Estimates.

which the cost per graduate at the two types of institution is equal. This will at least provide some guide by which to judge future performance. The assumptions are that the total student population is 37,500, involving a recurrent cost of £9·235 million, and that the annual student intake is 15,000. All Open University graduates in the foreseeable future will be first-degree graduates. The results are shown in Table 17.11 below.

It is clear from Table 17.11 that the drop-out rate at the Open University—measured by the percentage of annual entrants failing to graduate—must reach about 85 per cent before the cost per graduate at the two institutions is equal.[8]

Total Resource Cost per Equivalent Undergraduate

The total 'resources cost' of a University is its opportunity cost. The Robbins Committee (1963, Annex E) included four elements in the resource cost of universities. They are calculated below for conventional universities and for the Open University.

CONVENTIONAL UNIVERSITIES
(a) Recurrent expenditure on teaching and research
The 1968/69 figure at 1971 prices as calculated previously.

(b) Resources used in the use of existing buildings
The Robbins Committee (1963, Annex E) calculated an imputed rent on existing buildings of over £2 per student, per week, but did not provide enough figures for this calculation to be checked.[9] This figure included teacher training and advanced further education, and the figure might be higher for universities which have a larger element of research and scientific work. In any event the rise in building costs since 1962/63, and a higher rate of interest, might be expected to raise the imputed rent on recent buildings, and a figure of £150 per student year for 1968/69 has been assumed. With

---

[8] Allowing for research costs, as explained previously, changes the picture only marginally. The *teaching* cost per graduate at conventional universities is reduced to about £2,700 at 1971 prices, and the Open University drop-out rate would have to be about 80 per cent for the *teaching* cost per graduate at the Open University to be of an equal amount.

[9] The figure is based on a depreciation period of 60 years and a 6 per cent rate of interest.

a total student population of 232,137 (the weighted figure for post-graduates is not relevant here), this produces an imputed annual rental figure of nearly £35 million. The figure does not include residential accommodation, as this would still have to be provided whether people were students or not.

(c) Capital cost of new buildings

Robbins simply uses the capital expenditure figures for any given year as an indication of the capital resources used in that year. However, these resources will yield capital services over a number of future years. The previous paragraph attempted to convert a capital stock figure into a flow of capital services per annum. Similarly the capital expenditure figure must be converted into an 'opportunity cost of capital' figure for one particular year. This opportunity cost is measured by the cost of borrowing capital (the rate of interest) and the cost of wasting capital (the rate of depreciation) in any one year.

The capital expenditure figure for 1968–69 was £7·0 million. Revaluing this by the rise in the index of building costs (15 per cent) produces a figure of £83 million in 1971 prices. Applying the annual depreciation rate of $1\frac{1}{2}$ per cent used by the Robbins Committee yields an annual depreciation charge on a replacement cost basis of £1·25 million. The appropriate rate of interest at present would seem to be 10 per cent which on the historic cost yields a figure of £7·2 million, and a total annual resource figure of £8·45 million.

(d) Cost of output foregone through students not being in employment

The DES (1970, Table 14) recently estimated the foregone earnings of post-graduates in 1969 as £955 each and of undergraduates as £755 each. Allowing for a 15 per cent increase to 1971 prices the figures are as follows: post-graduates, £1,100, and undergraduates, £870. These calculations take into account vacation earnings.

The calculations for conventional universities in 1968/69 are therefore as follows:

Full-time undergraduates $173,510 \times £870$ = £150,953,700

Full-time post-graduates $37,784 \times £1,100$ = £ 41,562,400

Total earnings foregone £192,516,100

Part-time students are assumed to be in full or near full-time employment, and are therefore assumed not to forego any earnings while they are studying.

The resource cost of conventional universities in 1968/69 is summarized as follows:

(a) Current expenditure on teaching and research £284·7M̄
(b) Annual services of existing buildings   £ 34·8M̄
(c) Annual services of new buildings in 1968/9   £ 8·5M̄
(d) Output foregone   £192·5M̄

         Total   £520·5M̄

Total equivalent undergraduates—302,920. Therefore, the resource cost per equivalent full-time undergraduate in 1968/1969 is

$$£\frac{520 \cdot 5M̄}{302,920} = £1,577$$

OPEN UNIVERSITY

(a) *Recurrent expenditure on teaching and research*
In 1973 recurrent expenditure for 36,500 students will be £9,018,000 at 1971 prices.

(b) *and* (c) *Resources used in the use of existing buildings and capital cost of new buildings*
The Open University has a capital expenditure programme which is due to be completed in 1973. This will provide the entire capital provisions of the Open University for the foreseeable future and will cost £6 million at 1970 prices (or £6·5M̄ at 1971 prices.) Using a 1½ per cent depreciation rate and a 10 per cent interest rate gives an annual depreciation cost of £97,500 and an annual interest cost of £650,000, giving a total annual cost of capital services of £747,500.

(d) *Cost of output foregone through students not being in productive employment*
Students at the Open University are all either in full-time employment or else not seeking employment (e.g. housewives). No output is thereforegone as a result of their studying. There might conceivably be some marginal reduction in productivity as a result of students working instead

of relaxing in the evenings, but this has been ignored.

The resource cost of the Open University in 1973 is summarized as follows:

(a) Recurrent expenditure on teaching and
    research   £9,018,000
(b) and (c) Resource cost of capital expenditure £ 747,500
(d) Cost of output foregone   £   Nil

                    Total   £9,765,500

Total equivalent undergraduates 36,500. Therefore the resource cost per equivalent undergraduate at the Open University is

$$£\frac{9,765,500}{36,500} = £268$$

The resource cost of the Open University is thus about a sixth of conventional universities. A large element of this advantage is due to the part-time nature of the students. If all students at conventional universities were part-time, a resource cost of £193 million a year, in terms of output foregone, would be saved. This amounts to about 37 per cent of the total resource costs of conventional universities.

There would be other savings, but it is only possible to give a crude estimate of these. Recurrent costs would be substantially reduced if the *Robbins Report* statement (1963) that 'two part-time students are counted as being equivalent, for costing purposes, to one full-time student' is supported. The figure would not be exactly halved as the existing recurrent expenditure figure includes expenditure on some 21,000 part-time students. Taking this into account and following the Robbins Report recommendation, the recurrent expenditure of conventional universities might be reduced to about £152 million if all their students were part-time. This may be misleading because, as has been mentioned previously, the Robbins estimate may have referred to marginal rather than average cost. Costing calculations which may be appropriate when part-time students are a small proportion of the total may not be valid when all students are part-time.

However, if recurrent expenditure was reduced to £152 million and no output was foregone in the economy, the total resource costs of conventional universities would be in the region of £190 million. With a total equivalent under-graduate population of 302,920 the resource cost per equivalent undergraduate at conventional universities would be reduced to about £630 if all students were part-time. This figure, however, is still nearly $2\frac{1}{2}$ times the Open University resource cost figure of £268 per equivalent undergraduate

Summary

Table 17.12 summarizes the main results for the Open University and compares these with the figures for conventional universities.[10]

Table 17.12

Cost of the Open University and Conventional Universities

Calculation	Open university	Conventional universities
A. Average recurrent cost per equivalent undergraduate	£251	£ 940
B. Capital cost per student place	£165	£3000
C. Average recurrent cost per graduate	£4000 at 85 per cent drop-out rate	£4000+
D. Resource cost per equivalent undergraduate	£268	£1577

It would be imprudent to draw any very definite conclusions from these figures. There are too many conceptual and statistical problems for that sort of exercise. Nevertheless, the gap between the Open University and the conventional universities' figures is too large to be ignored, and is unlikely to disappear when ex-post figures become available. The Open University would seem to have a substantial cost advantage over conventional universities, particularly when

[10] The figures for 'teaching' costs are not summarized.

capital costs are taken into account. Moreover, even when a possibly exaggerated allowance for the part-time nature of Open University students and the possible lower research ratio in the University's costs are made, conventional university costs are still significantly greater than those of the Open University.

A substantial element of the Open University advantage would seem to be in its production techniques. The use of correspondence media, radio and television produces economies of scale and, above a certain minimum number, allows more students per £ to be taught. In a period when severe constraints on resources for higher education are likely, this is a method of teaching which will demand increasing attention.

REFERENCES

Blaug, M. (1965), 'Rate of return on investment in education in Great Britain', *Manchester School of Economic and Social Studies* (September).

Carter, C. F. (1965), 'The economics of higher education', *Manchester School of Economic and Social Studies* (January).

Carter, C. F. (1969), 'Can we get British higher education cheaper?' Manchester: Manchester Statistical Society.

Committee on Higher Education under the Chairmanship of Lord Robbins (1963). Cmnd. 2267 (*Robbins Report*), Appendix (October).

DES (1970), 'Student numbers in higher education in England and Wales', *Educational Planning Paper No. 2*. London: HMSO. See also Chapter 13.

Morris, V. and Ziderman, A. (1971), 'The economic return on investment in higher education in England and Wales', *Economic Trends* (May).

Perry, W. (1970), Lecture to Royal Society of Arts, 4 February. Reprinted in *Journal of the Royal Society of Arts* (April).

Stretch, K. L. (1964), *Minerva* (Spring).

UGC (1964), 'University development 1957–62', Cmnd. 2267, Para. 180.

UGC (1969), *Statistics of Education*, Vol. 6. London: HMSO.

Woodhall and Blaug, M. (1965), 'Productivity trends in British university education', *Minerva*, 3:4.

18

P. ARMITAGE

An Introduction to some Educational Models and their Applications

In order to understand or anticipate some phenomenon or event, we often construct circumstances or develop theories and contrive to experiment. One particular form of this activity is the building of models. It is an ancient method but its conscious use in the social sciences has come into vogue only in recent years.

When we construct an educational model, we attempt to find an abstract representation that corresponds sufficiently well with the real system to satisfy the purposes we have in mind. The basic idea is that the similarity between the real and the abstract can be exploited, and the model manipulated much more conveniently and quickly. If the correspondence with the actual system is good enough, we will reap great advantage from being able to draw useful inferences about the possible behaviour of the real system.

What does an educational model look like and how do we go about constructing one? Normally the model builder will be motivated by having issues and a whole range of problems in mind, and this will shape how he goes about things. Whatever the aim may be, it is probable that the model will be initially constructed from personal knowledge and experience of the educational system; first primary school and then secondary school. Since this is compulsory, it will be true of everybody. Personal variations will begin to appear after the minimum school-leaving age has been reached, for example school may be left at the first opportunity and only returned to for a course at a much later time, alternatively school may be left after the 'O' or 'A' Level examinations. Subsequently some kind of higher education may be undertaken, such as a degree, or professional training. Many may spend all, or part of, their working lives as teachers and so have remained in contact with the educational system but as 'providers' rather than as 'consumers'.

If a description of the system were attempted which fitted with personal experience, or that of friends, as well as many of the educational life-cycles which may exist, the result might be set out as in the block diagram of Figure 18.1. This identifies several parts of the world inside and outside education, and these parts are shown as boxes. The lines and arrows show how anyone may move between these recognized parts. In addition, it is possible to remain in the same box.

What has been done in this description is to identify com-

Figure 18.1

Block diagram showing movements into, through and out of the educational system

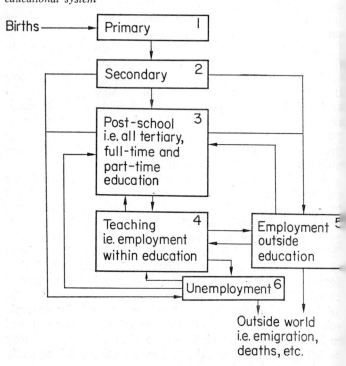

ponents of the real world that are of interest, or, to put it another way, we have identified the educational and non-educational states that a person may be in at any particular time. The connections between these states or parts of the system have also been defined. These inter-connections are vital to the design and it is worth emphasizing this by summarizing them in a different form. Figure 18.2 shows that a child in primary school this year may still be there next year or may have moved to secondary school. Anyone in secondary school this year may still be there next year or may have moved on to some form of post-school education or have left school either for employment or unemployment.

In effect, the tableau shows the movement possible from one period to the next and by repeated application we see

Figure 18.2

Possible movements in the model shown in Figure 1

Y = movement possible
N = movement not possible

From Box Number	To Box Number (see rows for code) 1 2 3 4 5 6 *						
– Births	Y	N	N	N	N	N	N
1 Primary	Y	Y	N	N	N	N	N
2 Secondary	N	Y	Y	N	Y	Y	N
3 Post –school	N	N	Y	Y	Y	Y	N
4 Teaching	N	N	Y	Y	Y	Y	N
5 Outside Employment	N	N	Y	Y	Y	Y	Y
6 Unemployment	N	N	Y	Y	Y	Y	Y

* Outside world

the paths that can be traced through the system over time. These paths correspond to the educational case histories which were our starting point. One possible path would be to spend several years in primary education, several more in secondary education, followed by a shorter period in post-school education and thereafter periods alternating between education and employment. This is a pattern that is expected to become much more common in future and is covered by the term 'recurrent education'.

The identified parts of the real world and the stated interconnections between them constitute the model. It can be thought of as a set of statements such as:

The number of pupils in primary school next year	=	The number of pupils in primary school this year who stay in primary next year	+	The number of five-year-olds starting school next year

or, to take another example, as:

Number in post-school sector next year	=	number in post-school sector this year who 'repeat' next year	+	number in secondary this year who move to post-school next year	+	number of teachers this year who go to post-school as a student next year

		+ number employed outside education this year who go to post-school as a student next year	+ number unemployed this year who go to post-school as a student next year

In general the form of such statements is:

The stock of students in a given sector next year	=	The sum of all the flows of students and others into the sector next year from all the sectors connected *to* it (in which they are to be found this year)	+	New entrants who are outside the system this year but who will be in the given sector next year

The model consists of a complete set of statements of this kind covering all the parts of the system that have been identified. If these verbal statements are expressed in the equivalent shorthand of algebra, we have a mathematical model.

We can now go ahead and make calculations. Suppose that we know that there are 5 million pupils in primary school this year. Some will be transferring to secondary school next year, and we may be prepared to assume that only four out of five will still be in primary school next year. This would mean that 4 million primary pupils will still be in primary next year. Suppose we also know that there are 800,000 four-year-olds this year and we assume that they will all have started school by next year. Adding these two numbers together as indicated in the statement above, we now have an estimate of 4,800,000 pupils in primary school next year. If we now assume that four out of five of this number will stay in primary the next year and that all the 850,000 three-year-olds at present will be in school in two years' time, then there is an estimated total of 4,690,000 in the primary population in the following year. We can go on projecting estimated totals into the future for so long as rational and reasonable alternative assumptions can be made. The projection produced in this way gives some notion of the possible future.

At this point the model may appear too crude or wrong in some other important respect. Further, new entrants may not only come into the model through births or people leave only by employment or unemployment: immigrants can enter any part of the system and therefore new entrants are possible in every sector. It is also possible to leave the system by emigration or death at any age. But it is important to realize that every model is a simplification and it is a good working rule to try to make any model as simple as possible in terms of the job in hand. The introduction of 'redundant' detail makes a model cumbersome and much more difficult to handle and the temptation to include detail for detail's sake is to be resisted. What is relevant and what is redundant can only be prejudged by the model builder. A new model needs only be built when the correspondence between the model and reality is no longer good enough to fulfil the purpose.

Other criticisms can be made of the model we have constructed so far. Perhaps the most striking is that it has very little to do with education in terms of its content and classroom conditions and very little to do with people and their motivations. Apart from the labelling of the boxes, the model is without any distinctively educational character. Remove the labels and the flow diagram of Figure 18.1 might represent any physical system in which particles move from state to state. The generality of the abstraction is one of the virtues of model building, but the point can be taken that the enrolment model described fails to reflect important aspects of the actual world. We could, of course, begin to remedy these deficiencies. The progress of students could be made to depend upon their educational achievement at the time and this could be influenced by innovations in teaching methods and curricular developments.

Some other faults are not so easily dealt with. So far our description makes it appear that movement just happens and is in no way limited. In practice, movement is not always free; for example, the qualifications which meet university entry standards may not necessarily guarantee a place, and even a qualified teacher may be unable to get a teaching post of the kind he wishes. Selection procedures of this kind can be modelled but the result is much more complicated than our previous descriptions. Another serious objection on a more abstract level is that the model assumes a rigid structure which it tends to perpetuate. It is ill-suited to a future which involves much structural change and innovation. Again this can be overcome but only at the cost of making the model more complex.

Further criticisms will appear as we proceed but let us return to the use of the model. When we decide to make a projection, we have to make assumptions about many of the elements of the model and their future behaviour. How are these assumptions made?

Suppose, for example, that the calculation requires that we make assumptions about how many pupils will stay on at school beyond the minimum leaving age. It would seem sensible to start by looking at what has happened in the past and the proportion staying on could be examined over the last twenty years. This would show a strong trend towards a rising proportion staying on, though there will be some variation about this trend. In the absence of any other knowledge this trend could be assumed to continue into the future for as long as we were interested. Of course the data will not tell us all that we want to know and we may be unsure that our interpretation of the available data is correct. Furthermore, even if it is correct, it will not be an adequate guide to the future. To go back to our example, the pupils staying on will be changed by the raising of the school-leaving age and, since this situation is entirely new, the past offers no proper evidence. In such cases, and particularly where known decisions have not yet been implemented, the fact that speculation is necessary for projection cannot be concealed by burying ourselves in past data.

Even with relatively crude models, it is necessary to make a great many assumptions, but if we can bring ourselves to do this for every variable, then it is possible to calculate what will happen if all our assumptions are exactly fulfilled. An administrator might then look at the projection and register it as evidence when thinking about his subsequent actions. If he regards the picture painted as a desirable future development of the system, he may feel that no special action is called for and that he can carry on in the line of his past decisions. He may accept the projection but want to prevent the foreseen development by making new decisions. He may be competent to argue a decision on the basis of the projection already provided or he may call for an alternative projection, just as if he rejected the first one offered to him.

Producing further projections presents no difficulties. So many different assumptions can be made that it is virtually possible to come up with an infinite number of sets, each of which would lead to a projection. Given a number of projections, an administrator will begin to worry about whether one outcome is more likely or desirable than another and he will find it increasingly difficult to assimilate and choose as he is offered more and more alternatives. For the person making the calculations, producing one projection after another is highly monotonous and diminishing returns soon set in. If the model builder has been content to work in this way, he will now become disturbed and start to ask why he is making projections and what use the administrator is making of them.

It will become apparent that the administrator is either trying to solve a problem or to influence the system by his decisions in such a way that it will be free from avoidable problems. He may also be striving to persuade the system to reach targets or states which he sees as desirable. Of course his notions may well be vague but he is likely to need some basis for discriminating between his conjectures and the views that are presented to him by a variety of projections. It will be clear that the policy-maker's prime interest is in assessing the consequences of various options because it is this which determines his power to influence the system.

Two important consequences follow. As we have described a model so far, it consists of relationships in which the variables are tenuously linked with actual decisions. We now need to change our approach and create decision models, that is models where the emphasis is upon casting the assumptions in a form which is as directly related as possible to the actions that are open to the decision-maker. Even with this shift in emphasis and outlook, the model would still be merely a mapping device for producing projections, so it must be linked to a discriminator where evaluation takes place leading to revisions in the assumptions about the decision variables with the whole process being repeated until a satisfactory result has been produced. The view of the model may now be enlarged to become a loop as visualized in Figure 18.3.

Figure 18.3

The model as a loop for searching out policies with desirable results

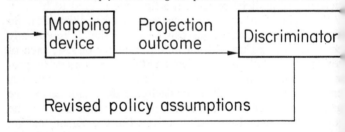

As the model ceases to be a totem and becomes a part of the decision-making process, it holds out the prospect of practical use, but we have much further to go before any confidence will be inspired. We may not make much progress by endlessly cycling round the loop of Figure 18.3 and we badly need some method of searching efficiently through all the policy options open to us. There is little evidence that anything approaching a passable search is ever made in practice and, indeed, it often seems that the search is virtually non-existent. It is usual in official publications to refer only to one projection which is normally based on the assumption of the continuation of present policy and that existing commitment will be fully realized. Possible government policy changes are specifically excluded from consideration as being entirely the responsibility of the politicians. Consequently though the politician may wish to alter present policy, or he may otherwise feel the need to act, he would appear to be without the benefit of any guidance on the possible effects of changed policies.

It seems reasonable to hope that something better is possible. If it is, it will lie in an improvement of what was called the discriminator in Figure 18.3. What is needed is a much clearer understanding of the objectives of education. It might be thought that this clarification is an easy, straightforward task, but it is not. The objectives are many, conflicting and confused. The basic dichotomy is usually presented that the educational system can either be set up to provide everybody with the maximum opportunity to fulfil their intellectual capabilities or to produce that distribution of qualified manpower most suited to the further development of the economy. The dilemma presented is that the educational system should either cope with the push of student demand or the pull of the needs of employers.

This simplistic view has been the source of protracted argument, and some economists have attempted a resolution through the adjustments of the market mechanism. In contemplating what path to pursue, the student may consider what he expects to gain by following each of the alternatives open to him, and to choose the one which gives him the greatest reward. The administrator deciding how many places to provide in particular sectors of education, may take into account the value of different distributions of qualified manpower as reflected by earnings, and to set the number of places so that the maximum value is obtained. In these ways demand and supply can be matched, the conflict resolved and an equilibrium established. While it is true that the system must respond to both push and pull, this argument is incomplete for both the student and the administrator will always have highly imperfect and uncertain information and will want to take many other considerations into account.

The pre-occupation with social and economic objectives is partly due to the fact that educational planning has so far been led by social reformers, politicians and economists. Clearly other aspects exist, and they should not be left out of account. Education is now a well-established activity with a long history and it has its own internal drive for change. This can take such forms as the development of nursery or higher education, the reform of secondary education including comprehensivization, and the development of teaching methods and new curricula. Such changes as the raising of the school-leaving age would be unlikely to occur if only social and economic objectives were recognized. The apparatus of education that has been built up also conditions the changes which can or should take place. Institutions, like individuals, have aspirations and self-awareness. No government would dare to advocate changes which directly called for the abandonment of existing academic standards or intervention in staff appointments, and in making a proposal such as the introduction of two-year diplomas in higher education, the government is dependent upon the institutions regarding this as an acceptable proposal. Many other pressures can come into play such as the internal political demand for equality of opportunity or the consequences of external political developments such as the reform of local government or entry into the European Economic Community. Most successful movements will pass through some final stage of political endorsement and if we try to characterize a change as either economic, social, institutional or political, we will often feel that it cannot be placed under one head but springs from a combination of sources.

Planning will not rise above the level of black magic unless planners can devise models that have the potential to embrace all the major forces and take into account qualitative as well as quantitative factors. (Most of the early approaches to educational planning should be rejected for concentrating only on those things that can be readily quantified.) An attempt is made in Figure 18.4 to draw up a scheme which, in principle, would go some way towards meeting many of the requirements. The educational, economic, social and political systems are shown as fully interrelated, though no detail is shown outside education. It is expected that signals will be transmitted from the other systems which demand a response from the educational system and what happens in education will stimulate responses from the other systems. The projection device that originally constituted the total model is now embedded in the 'decision centre' of the educational system. Its use depends upon a supply of specifications of policies to be investigated and this is the function of a 'policy generator'. When a projection is produced it is subjected to an analysis intended to provide comprehensive recognition of the multiplicity of objectives, constraints and criteria. It is imagined that this will consist of a mixture of performance indices and batteries of statements, both quantitative and qualitative. Any policy investigated would receive a number of 'scores' and pass or fail the qualitative criteria. In some cases the performance would be so poor that there would be no argument about rejecting the policy. If the policy led to good all-round performance—high scores and a few failures—it would be stored as worthy of further consideration. In effect the mesh of statements and criteria would resemble a series of filters leading to a policy being rejected or classified as nominally acceptable. It is possible that no policy satisfied all statements or was considered nominally acceptable but this procedure would tell us which criteria were having the most ruthless effects and would suggest how they might be relaxed or redefined. In Figure 18.4, the arrangement of the criteria within the box marked objectives is not intended to suggest any priority, though if such priority could be established to any degree, it could be utilized in making the search procedure more efficient.

This scheme does no more than identify a number of acceptable policies without providing any means of choosing between them. These supposedly viable policies would be displayed to administrators so that they might be better informed. Their comments and preferences would reveal hidden criteria and suggest how criteria already recognized should be made more explicit and sharpened. The main attraction of the scheme is that it would be both a monitoring procedure and a learning process.

The adoption of a method similar to that summarized in Figure 18.4 has much to recommend it but only as a starting point rather than as the ultimate stage in educational planning. Some outstanding problems still remain. First there is the problem of uncertainty. We have talked so far as if we can work out the certain consequences of a policy once it has been stated. It is unrealistic to think that this can ever be achieved. Taking decisions on the pretence that you are choosing between policies giving certain and distinctly dif-

Figure 18.4

A scheme for investigating policy alternatives

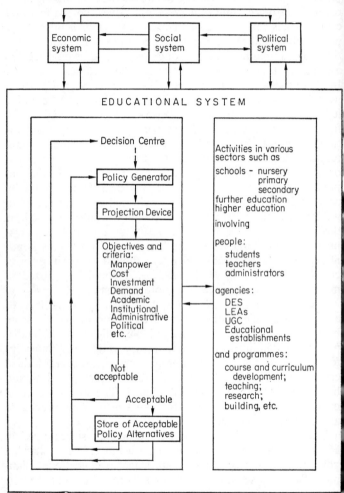

ferent outcomes, is likely to be highly fallacious. Facing uncertainty makes planning much more difficult but the problem cannot be avoided.

Secondly, all that has been said so far presupposes the existence of one central decision-maker, presumably the Secretary of State, who considers everything and acts on behalf of everybody. However, there are many participants in the educational system, all of whom have a part in the decision-making process. The student chooses what he wants to do but whether he achieves it depends upon the decisions of others. The Secretary of State may announce a policy though whether it is carried out precisely will depend upon the reactions and behaviour of numerous bodies and individuals. Decisions may be taken by Department officials, the officers of local authorities, the Universities Grants Commission, chancellors, principals, headmasters, professors, lecturers, teachers and students. If we built models from the viewpoint of each of these decision-makers, as they must do for themselves at least unwittingly, we would find that everyone has different perceptions of the system as it involves them, of their interrelationships, of the constraints upon their actions and of their objectives. It will probably be necessary to construct some models with the problems of particular decision-makers in mind if the theory of planning is to come closer to the realities of practice and if we are to unravel some of our confusions, particularly about objectives.

This has not been a success story with educational planning finally revealed as a highly advanced activity. It should not be surprising that this planning activity is still in its infancy for it has only attracted much attention in the last generation. On average, we spend about one-fifth of our lives in education as receivers and currently education absorbs over half a million of the most highly qualified members of the working force as well as annually consuming about £3,000 million with the expectation that this figure will rise to £5,000 million in the next decade. The enterprise of education is so vast that the need to press on is obvious and imperative.

III

The Administration of the School

19

S. BENNETT and R. WILKIE*

The School and Organization Theory

The aim of this paper is to indicate some of the interest that an organization theorist has in the school. The paper is divided into eight parts. First of all, there is a short introduction describing some of the reasons why one studies organizations. Then there is a section indicating some of the difficulties involved in seeing the school as organizations are sometimes seen. This is followed by five sections examining the subjects of membership, goals, structures, technology and environment of a school. The last section makes a plea for the development of organization theory based on research into schools. A short bibliography is appended to suggest ways in which students of organizations and educational administration might pursue topics of interest raised in this paper.

* [In this article frequent reference is made to the 'guidance' system in Scottish secondary schools. The Scottish Education Department (SED) introduced a system of pupil guidance based on a combination of ideas drawn from the English 'House' system and (to a lesser extent) from American pupil-counselling techniques. (See 'Guidance in Scottish Secondary Schools', HMSO, 1968.)

The main points to note in the context of this article are:

(a) guidance teachers are appointed at the level of principal teacher (head of department);

(b) principal teachers are traditionally honours graduates in an 'established' academic subject, whereas guidance staff may have ordinary degrees or qualifications other than a university degree;

(c) the guidance teacher is expected to respect the confidentiality of information given to him by pupils seeking help, but he may thus possess knowledge about a pupil which will lead to opposition to other members of staff;

(d) the guidance teacher, who is also a member of the *teaching* staff, may be a member of department under a principal (subject) teacher with whom he has equal formal status.

—Ed.]

I

There are many reasons for studying organizations. In the first place, some organizations have the power to determine events in ways which have critical consequences for the quality of people's lives. At the time of writing, the British Steel Corporation had just announced that one of its aims in the next decade is to reduce drastically the number of people it employs. At least one important consequence will be that thousands of human beings will be forced out of the steel industry to find employment in other occupations in other industries. The loss of a job is usually a harrowing personal experience. When it occurs on a large scale as the direct result of the deliberate strategy of a single organization it becomes a matter of public concern.

Examples of the ways in which the interests of organizations can come to produce traumatic peaks and depressions in the private lives of individuals are presented to us almost as a matter of course by the public media. There are questions that need to be asked about this. How is it that organizations manage to be powerful? What sorts of things contribute to the successful generation and exercise of power by organizations? What kinds of considerations shape the directions in which organizations make things happen? What kinds of power do they have? Are there other kinds of power?

Another reason for studying organizations follows directly from the first. We ought to concern ourselves with the nature and extent of that power. Are there rules that regulate organizational acts? What are these rules? How closely do they underpin and shape organizational power? Where do they come from? Who makes them? If organizations fail to abide by the rules, what follows in the way of sanctions against them? What means are available for challenging organizational decision? What are the conditions which allow for the effective criticism of organizations?

These questions focus attention on the degree to which organizations are accountable for what they do. Taking organizations to task for what they do is often a problematic business. One of the aims of a democratic political process is to constrain the ability of interest groups to act on their own behalf without due consideration for the interests of others. Attention to organizations in this respect will be necessary. Such study will produce systematically collected information about organizational aims, the procedures through which they create their policies, the managerial processes through which they are implemented, the intended and unintended consequences of such activities.

When organizational policies are in fact questioned, it is interesting to note their responses. When Ralph Nader, an American lawyer, criticized a motor-car manufacturing company for its evasion of car safety measures, one response of the organization was to discredit the critic by trying to find out nasty things about his private life. Whether it is the British Steel Corporation, the British Broadcasting Corporation, the Open University, or the local public authority, the issue remains the same—what curbs against arbitrary organizational action exist? How desirable is it to involve all members of the organization in the decision-making process? If it is desirable, what procedures will be needed to make such involvement effective?

Yet another reason for studying organizations is that there is overwhelming evidence that they shape the way in which people behave. Human beings as members of an organization do not act in a private capacity but more or less in conformity with the requirements of their organizational positions. They follow orders, comply with rules, fulfil obligations. How much discretion, we would want to know, do individuals have when acting in their organizational roles? How applicable is the notion of moral responsibility when human beings act as members of organizations? Sometimes people get dragged into organizations and become captives. Sometimes they queue to get in. Sometimes the situation is all mixed-up. Take a university where a student may not feel that he is consciously deciding to join it in the way that a person might do when he joins a political party. He may be at university for a qualification for a good career, social status or the happiness of his parents. The actual activities he will be required to engage in as a student may not be very attractive to him; he may feel more like a captive of 'the system' than a willing member of an academic community.

But organizations shape people in other ways. Some organizations are in fact termed 'people-changing'—schools, universities, psychiatric hospitals and churches—but often organizations, while not intending to obtain more than an outward conformity from their members, will still influence and mark their general ways of behaving. It is this permanent effect on the way people are, whether deliberate or not, which is of importance to the student of organizations. We are all familiar with examples of the ways in which people become characteristically affected through their association with particular types of organizations. The army officer may act more like a soldier towards his family than as a husband and father. The politically minded university teacher may carry on all his activities according to a bargaining model. There is evidence that taking on organizational roles, whether voluntary or not, may be more like being tattooed than putting on an overcoat. The one is more difficult to take off than the other.

If, then, an organization can inform our attitudes and values, and our behaviour generally, there is a strong case for a careful examination of this claim. How does an organization affect the behaviour of its members? Is this influence intended or unintended? What are the conditions which encourage such influence? If it is meaningful to talk of the behaviour of students, and civil servants, miners and seamen as if they had had their behaviour shaped by universities, the Civil Service, coal mines, and ships, in what ways has this come about? Are there significant variations within the behaviour of such groups of people? If there is, why is this so? Is it because of significant differences between firms, universities, and so on, or for other sorts of reasons?

A fourth reason for studying organizations arises from the concern of senior personnel in organizations towards a more problem-free and less costly-run organization that is relatively effective in achieving its ends. They have a practical desire to make their organizations operate more successfully; in fact, the most powerful encouragement for the study of organizations has come from managers of organizations. As a means by which some managerial problems may be eased or solved, the study of organizations has grown into a veritable industry in itself, both within and outside universities. This study might be split into two. First of all, managers will be concerned with what types of activities will be conducive to the organization's greater success. The study of organizations may allow for the evaluation of different types of activities and so lead to the inclusion or growth of some types and the exclusion or reduction of others. Should the university have a public relations officer? Should the engineering company retain its operational research unit? And so on. Secondly, managers will be concerned about the ways in which people perform their activities in the organization. This will usually depend upon the skills of the person recruited, the degree of enthusiasm he has for exercising those skills and upon the presence of certain favourable conditions within the organization. But whatever the activities required by the organization of its members, desirable standards of performance, whether from car workers, students, prisoners, or priests, do not automatically follow from the decisions by managers to specify that certain activities will take place. Whether or not such standards will be reached will depend upon a variety of circumstances, some of which in varying degrees will be amenable to control through managerial action. Moral, political, legal, economic and technical considerations amongst others may inform such action, as also will consideration about just what it is the organization is in business for.

II

The question, why study organizations, has been raised and briefly answered. Organizations are, to the organization theorist, Chinese boxes of problems and difficulties. They are never self-contained and must rely on their environments for the people who work in them, the material they work on and the buyers of their products and services. Even a monastery makes certain calls on its environment. With the school, however, the problem is even wider. For a start, definition is difficult:

> Organizations are social units (or human groupings) deliberately constructed and reconstructed to seek specific goals. Corporations, armies, schools, hospitals, churches and prisons are included; tribes, classes, ethnic groups, friendship groups, and families are excluded. Organizations are characterized by: (1) divisions of labour, power, and communication responsibilities, divisions which are not random or traditionally patterned, but deliberately planned to enhance the realization of certain goals: (2) the presence of one or more power centres which control the concerted

386 The Administration of the School

efforts of the organization and direct them towards its
goals; these power centres also review continuously the
organization's performance and re-pattern its structure,
where necessary, to increase its efficiency; (3) substitution
of personnel, i.e., unsatisfactory persons can be removed
and others assigned their tasks. The organization can also
re-combine its personnel through transfer and promotion.[1]

This well-known formulation of an organization by Etzioni
can be criticized at a number of points but the only ones relevant here are those which refer to the difficulties of applying
these characteristics to the school, or, to be more precise, to
the local authority-maintained secondary school in Scotland.
First of all, it is not true to maintain that schools are not
traditionally patterned. The system of principal teachers, for
example, has grown up over a long period of time and the
resultant pattern of principal teachers as heads of departments with a number of 'assistants' was certainly not deliberately planned. Secondly, if we accept that the headmaster
and his immediate assistants constitute one of the power
centres of the organization, then we must also point to at
least two power centres which are located outside the organization—the Local Education Authority (LEA) and the Scottish Education Department (SED). This, then, is not simply
a matter of senior personnel having to take account of environmental influences. In this case these outside influences
are decisive, and certain significant issues have to be referred
to them.

Thirdly, these outside bodies 're-pattern its structure' in
significant ways. Of course, the head can set up all sorts of
committee structures within the school to help in the running
of the school but the basic structure of the school is determined by outside bodies. For example, the total number of
staff of the school, the number and type of promoted posts
and the salaries which go with them are all decided outside
the school. Fourthly, substitution of personnel is another
matter not in the hands of the school personnel. Fifthly,
neither can they re-combine personnel through transfer and
promotion. These powers are all held by the local authority.

One could point to other ways in which the school as an
organization does not conform to the ways in which we
normally think of organizations. For example, the school may

[1] A. Etzioni, *Modern Organizations*, Prentice-Hall, New Jersey, 1964, p. 3.

cease to exist at a time to be decided by others and the staff and pupils dispersed to other schools or educational establishments.[2] The staff, of course, have the choice of moving to another authority or of leaving the profession. It should also be noted that the products of the school—the pupils— are rated and graded in a decisive manner by an outside body: in Scotland this is the Scottish Certification of Education Examination Board (SCEEB).

III

There are further questions about the people in the organization. There appear to be three different kinds of participants in the school. There are the teaching staff, including the headmaster although he may not teach, the pupils, and other auxiliary staff such as janitors, catering staff, technicians, secretaries and so on. Teaching staff may well be included in some of the decisions made in the school and in some schools pupils are also included in some decisions. Auxiliary staff, on the other hand, are unlikely to be included in decisions other than those within their sphere of competence. In the following discussion 'staff' refers to the teaching staff of the school.

Staff are seen as members of the school. They have a contract with the local authority which specifies the school but may also refer to the possibility of transfer to another school. They have a salary, terms and conditions of appointment, holiday entitlements, duties and responsibilities (fixed by the LEA and the headmaster). They may belong to a professional organization which may negotiate salaries and conditions with the employing or regulating bodies (the LEA or the SED), and which may intervene on their behalf with the employing body. They hold meetings, working parties and conferences to decide on common approaches to both employing and regulating bodies and to discuss matters relating to pupils. They may be promoted out of the schools to either employing or regulating bodies. None of this is true of pupils who are in general compulsorily recruited to the school. Therefore, if the pupils are to be regarded as members of the school then it is apparent that we have two different kinds

[2] L. Berg, *Risinghill: Death of a Comprehensive School*, Penguin Books, Middlesex, 1968.

of membership. This is not simply the difference between higher and lower organizational participants as, for example, in a business firm. It is a difference in kind.

Staff participation in decisions made in the school varies greatly from school to school. It may also differ between local authorities. In some schools the head may hold regular meetings with his staff although he may stress that these are for the purpose of giving information to the staff and that they are not decision-making meetings. In other schools staff meetings may be held only very occasionally. (Only the head, of course, or one of his authorized staff, may call a staff meeting.) Some headmasters, including not only those who distrust large staff meetings, work through smaller committees of staff. The obvious example is the meeting of principal teachers (heads of departments) to discuss matters such as examination dates, report dates, requisition allowances and the like. There may be a finance committee in some form or other which looks after the non-academic expenditure. There may also be *ad hoc* committees set up for specific purposes. Alternatively, the head may prefer to work with individual members of staff. He may hold meetings only very rarely, preferring the 'one-to-one' relationship. Whatever the case, it is a safe assumption that there are times when the head must seek the co-operation of members of his staff. It is not at all a safe assumption, however, that the head at times must seek the co-operation of his pupils, although he may do so from personal inclination or from a belief that that is the best way of attaining his objective. There may be some form or institutionalized co-option of the pupils as in the case of prefects, form captains, class leaders and so on, but the headmaster does not have to seek their co-operation and does not have to consult them.

Staff members, in general, have a choice of school. Although contracts may specify the right of the employing authority to transfer them to any other school, generally speaking teachers apply for a particular job in a particular school. Apart from the possibility of private schooling, pupils have no choice of school. In a situation where a grammar school and a comprehensive school co-exist and where a competitive exam controls entry to the grammar school, it may be possible to choose the comprehensive school whatever the result of the exam. However, in most cases, particularly where one comprehensive school serves an area, there is no pupil or parental choice of school. Pupils live in zones or catchment areas drawn up by the local authority and it is extremely difficult to go outside these except to private schools.

Pupils are, then, in general, compulsory members of the school. Even allowing for those cases where 'choice' may be exercised it is parental choice which in most cases will be the deciding factor. In this sense—of compulsory membership for one category of participants—schools may be compared with prisons, conscript armies and mental asylums. There are, of course, significant differences. Children are compulsory members of schools because of an Act of Parliament which requires all parents to ensure that their children are educated. Schools are the easiest way for most people to do this and public schools (public in the proper sense of the word) are the only possibility for most. They are compulsory members of a particular school largely as a consequence of an administrative decision or series of decisions. It is also a consequence of the fact that their parents have chosen to live in that particular area, but since few people would move house to ensure the attendance of their children at a particular school, this consideration is of little importance.

What happens to children in schools is partly influenced by legislation and partly by decisions made by local education committees, but largely by administrative decisions. For example, the SED has recently brought in new regulations which affect the staffing structure in Scottish schools, and the SCEEB has decided to change certain aspects of the O-grade structure. Staff members are also affected by administrative decisions, but they have recourse to their professional organization (in theory at least) and they can resign and move to another school or another authority. To say this is not to minimize the difficulties involved in such actions. Nevertheless, these possibilities exist. No such possibility exists for the pupils. The first efforts are however being made to form a pupils' union in order to mitigate the effects of what are seen as arbitrary administrative decisions.

Administrative decisions affect not only what is to be taught, when, how, where, under what conditions, and by whom, but also matters such as standards of dress, aspects of behaviour which may occur outside school and outside school hours, for example, smoking and drinking alcohol, eating lollipops in school uniform, and long hair. Some of these decisions may be justified by claiming that the school or the teachers are *in loco parentis*, others by reference to the good name of the school in the community. Occasionally, there may be no attempt to justify, it being simply stated that, for example, certain clothes are 'not suitable' for school.

IV

Another area of enquiry that fascinates the organization theorist is that of goal analysis. It is usually much more difficult an operation to tie down the goals than is normally assumed. First of all, there is the difficulty involved in making sense of the sentence 'Manchester Grammar School is trying to achieve X' or 'Cathkin High School is trying to achieve Y'. Some organization theorists have laid off such sentences on the grounds that in using them one is in danger of attributing to the organization characteristics, which, they would claim, should be more accurately attributed to individuals or groups of individuals in the organization. But such dangers can be exaggerated. In ordinary language situations, no one can be confused about sentences which assert that International Business Machines is marketing a new computer or the British Broadcasting Corporation is hostile to jazz music or Birmingham University is going to be reorganized. Attempts to translate such sentences about the school into other sentences describing the activities of Headmaster Brown, gym teacher Smith or janitor Jones would be misleading. Two logics would be mixed up.

Secondly, even assuming that we can meaningfully talk about the goals of a school, there is the added difficulty of trying to locate what these goals actually are. It is not very informative to be told that the school is 'trying to educate pupils'. It sounds a little like being told that the aim of a business firm is 'to make a profit' or the aim of a hospital is 'to cure patients'—phrases which are almost locked into the meanings of a business firm or hospital. 'Trying to educate pupils' would be not so much the goal of a school as a necessary condition in the sense that the school would not exist in the absence of that goal. Thirdly, once one digs below this almost trivial statement of the goals of a school, into the harder, empirical ground of what particular schools have what particular goals, then a virtual Pandora's box is opened. For it is quite meaningful to claim that the one school is trying to specialize in good university potential, trying to become more efficient, trying to establish itself as the leading school in the district, trying to improve parent-teacher relations in the neighbourhood, and so on. Another school might not have any of these goals but instead have others. The problem here is to create a useful way of categorizing such diverse goals. We might then be in a position to prepare a profile of the priority placed upon certain types of activity by the school, to assess their value to the school, to begin to understand why some activities are authorized and so on.

Moreover, the complexity of goal analysis often masks contradictory or competing goals. Just as a supermarket may install a security system of internal television and patrolling security personnel which could cost more to maintain than the value of the goods stolen which the security system is introduced to rectify, so resources may be invested in equipment for overtly cultural activities in a school—stage facilities, musical instruments, art equipment—but at the same time there may be no, or little, place in the time-table for such activity. Bullshine is not the prerogative of the army. The complexity of goal analysis is further compounded by the fact that we have to examine the behaviour of particular people in a particular school to discover quite what the goals of the school actually are. We have to scrutinize people's behaviour as well as the relevant educational documents to discover what exactly are the goals of the organization. This is because we cannot take at face value the various formal statements there are in existence, not only because, as we have suggested, they may be too general and vague or may mask a whole number of activities but because of the fact that, in schools, as in most organizations, there often is a discrepancy between the so-called formal or stated goals and the actual or real or operative goals that people are pursuing in the name of the school.

We referred earlier to the decisive influence which certain outside bodies have on the school, even to the extent of re-patterning its structure in significant ways. We should also point to the significant influence of these bodies on the goals of the school. An SED memorandum published in 1968 referred to the 'growing awareness of the need to make more systematic provision for pupil guidance in Scottish secondary schools'.[3] The term 'guidance' was used to denote

> the taking of that personal interest in pupils as individuals which makes it possible to assist them in making choices or decisions. The choices which pupils will have to face involve situations of various kinds: deciding which school subjects to continue or to take up or to drop, selecting one type of career as a vocational aim in preference to another, weighing up the merits of different courses of action.

The memorandum points out that many teachers have always taken a personal interest in their pupils, but

> many claims are ... made on a teacher's time and in the stress of other work even the most sympathetic teacher may fail to notice that a particular pupil would benefit from advice or help.

Following comprehensive reorganization there will be more large schools. 'Consequently the problem of ensuring adequate personal attention to every pupil has become more acute.'

Other reasons are given why guidance 'has become essential at the present time'.

> As has frequently been pointed out, young people are now subjected to stresses which did not affect their predecessors. They have to face the increasing complexity of modern life. Television, radio, films, books, newspapers have made them aware of matters of which they would formerly have known little or nothing. Many have a measure of financial independence which makes them a natural target for commercial propaganda, often before they are ready to deal objectively with it. The removal of certain fears and sanctions has made it easier for young people to assert themselves and challenge authority. The natural tendency of young people to rebel is aggravated by the gap between the generations, which has resulted largely from the rapidity of technological advance and social change. Finally, despite their apparent self-assurance, young people often experience a feeling of general insecurity and uncertainty and need help and support in their search for satisfying criteria on which to base the conduct of their daily life.

[3] Scottish Education Department, *Guidance in Scottish Secondary Schools*, HMSO, 1968.

The authors of the memorandum point out that 'this is really a problem for society as a whole, but it is right and inevitable that the schools should play a major part in helping to solve it'. Furthermore, since 'the responsibility is not theirs alone, they should be prepared to co-operate with other agencies'. Finally, having said that schools should 'enlist the help of the parents', they say that parents themselves may not be able to cope with their children or may not be interested.

> In cases such as these it is particularly important that the school should be able to offer young people the guidance they might otherwise lack and should do its utmost to compensate for any inadequacy in the advice and support given by the home.

Four distinct goals are clearly being advocated for schools; pupil guidance, helping in the solution of a social problem, co-operation with 'other agencies', and compensation for parents who are defined as inadequate. Local authorities were already experimenting with various forms of guidance systems, whether as year groupings or house groupings. Since that time new regulations have provided for the appointment of staff at principal teacher level responsible for guidance in schools. The number of such staff varies with the size of the school.

Some teachers have reacted to these developments on the grounds that the school is being over-extended and that much of this activity should be the province of social work agencies. Alternatively, some say that individual teachers did the sort of job that was necessary in cases of, for example, lateness or maltreatment, without the necessity for new structures which may detract energy from what should be the school's major task, that of teaching.

V

When people talk about organizational structure they often mean two-dimensional charts with, for example, the headmaster at the top, and various boxes labelled with job titles or names underneath. Lines usually link up the boxes indicating the communication or authority systems within the school. An acceptable, if commonplace, definition of organization structure would be the established patterns of relationships among the parts of the organization. Even if your school does not have an organization chart, one could quickly be drawn up. Such organization charts have their uses. They are useful introductions into the structure of the school for they are able to suggest the size of the school as well as its major activities and the degree of hierarchical levels. But they have limitations. In the first place, they do not usually indicate the scale of the power of each box. Secondly, they cannot indicate how the people represented by the boxes are supposed to relate to one another. Thirdly, of course, they cannot tell us how the school is perceived by its members, far less inform us how the school will work in practice.

When we speak of the structure of a school, a great deal more than a two-dimensional chart is intended. We have to find out the habits of the school, its rules and procedures, its policies and regular arrangements before we can draw out the school's complete organizational anatomy. We have, in other words, to find out how the school's rules and procedures really work as well as how members of the school assume they work or how the school prescribes how they should work. This is another Pandora's box. For example, the different types of staff have different types of authority. Both heads of departments and guidance staff have an authority based on their position in the hierarchy but the office of principal teacher (head of teaching department) is traditionally an important one in Scottish schools. It has existed for a long time and perhaps particularly before the advent of large schools and the appointment of staff senior to them or equal in formal status, principal teachers seemed to have regarded themselves as being in a *primus inter pares* relationship with the headmaster. It was a relationship among professionals each respecting the professional competence of the others. Stress is laid on academic achievement and most principal teachers, especially those in schools which present pupils for Highers, will have an Honours degree if theirs is an 'academic' subject. Guidance staff, on the other hand, frequently do not have Honours degrees. They may have Ordinary degrees or else qualifications in subjects in which degrees are not awarded. Consequently, there was some friction between guidance staff and heads of departments when the former were made equivalent in formal status to the latter.

The guidance staff, then, have no element of traditional

authority, and no academic authority in comparison with the principal teachers. What is often the case is that guidance staff develop a personal authority of their own. Individuals who do a competent job within the school and who manage to maintain good relationships with principals and others are accorded a status which is not derived from their hierarchical position. Furthermore, these individuals are noted as exceptions. Principals may think in terms of the school 'being lucky' with its guidance staff. It is feasible to assume that over time, and perhaps quite quickly, the picture will alter considerably as the guidance staff gain in competence and acquire their own specialized professional skills. It is important to note, however, that what we are dealing with is a conflict situation and that the structural causes of the conflict will not go away simply because one of the sides in the situation becomes more expert. What may happen, however, is that the symptoms of conflict might change and that less emphasis will be put on the lack of academic qualifications of the teachers concerned. Perhaps more will be put onto the interference with teaching caused by the guidance functions of the guidance staff.

A further aspect of the structure of the school which is not brought out well in the organization chart and which may also lead to conflict, is that guidance staff, although equal in formal status with principal teachers in the hierarchy of the school are also members of the departments which are headed by the principals. They must theoretically, therefore, accept direction from the principals on academic matters. Principals may also object if the teaching in 'their' departments is interrupted by a member of 'their' staff who is engaged on other duties. Furthermore, in some schools at least, all staff are attached to houses (guidance units) and are theoretically subordinate to the guidance staff in that capacity. Clearly, there is a degree of structural complexity here. It should also be noted that with the establishment of the guidance staff as principal teachers in their own right and with the opportunity to apply for more senior posts such as headships, they may be seen to present a threat to the heads of departments in terms of career opportunity.

The new systems of guidance can be seen as an attempt to increase control over the environment of the school, in the sense that they are designed to counteract what are seen as undesirable environmental influences on the pupils (although it should be noted that the guidance systems were imposed by the wider educational system). Attempts at increasing control over their environments have been seen as characteristic of bureaucratic organizations. By the term 'bureaucratic' we refer to a marked degree of differentiation between tasks with specialist personnel performing them. According to this formulation the new systems of specialist guidance personnel can be seen as indications of increasing bureaucratization in schools.

Another aspect of the increasing differentiation and specialization in schools has occurred with the splitting of departments, as, for example, in the case of Science, which has broken down into Physics, Chemistry, and Biology. (It is worth pointing out, however, that what appear to be opposing tendencies occur with the growth of co-operation between subject departments in the setting up of integrated courses and the creation of subjects such as 'Modern Studies'.)

A third aspect of this tendency can be seen in the administrative side of Scottish schools where there are now assistant headmasters as well as deputy headmasters to help the headmaster discharge his functions. These assistant heads may, for example, have responsibility for lower schools (first and second years), middle school (third and fourth years) and upper school (fifth and sixth years); or else they may be differentiated according to their responsibility for curriculum development, guidance, administration or leisure activities. The impression, then, is one of a proliferation of specialized organizational roles—in other words increased bureaucratization.

Bureaucratization, however, may also manifest itself in a system of rules. Here we come closest to the popular use of the word 'bureaucracy' as referring to 'red tape' and restrictions which are seen as unnecessary. It is here also that there is perhaps the greatest likelihood of conflict with the professionalism of the teacher, particularly if the headmaster emphasizes points of procedure which teachers may regard as within their discretion. Headmasters, of course, have always emphasized the rules of procedure. Not very long ago, the headmaster of one school issued written instructions to his staff to the effect that classes should remain seated until the bell rings; that staff were authorized to leave their classes one minute (emphasized) early if they were on, for example, cloakroom duty, provided that the pupils had been lined up for dismissal and left with appropriate instructions; that teachers' records of work should be sent to him on a particular day each month; that class tests as well as term examinations should be held on dates specified by him.

The staff may see this sort of rule-making as unnecessarily restrictive. From the head's point of view he has the safety of the pupils to consider and their educational well-being. He may be held responsible to the director of education and the education committee if accidents occur in his school and if examination results are not up to expectations. This kind of pressure may lead him to attempt to exert control over as many activities as possible in order to avert undesirable occurrences. Equally, of course, an emphasis on orderly movement and action against 'unseemly' behaviour may reflect the headmaster's own conservative outlook on life.

VI

Many organization theorists have speculated about the relationship between structure and technology. Some have taken the view that, in this relationship, technology is the independent variable and structure the dependent one—in other words, the technology used by an organization in the performance of its activities will have a direct bearing on the structure of that organization. Technology is often taken to mean the physical tools or plant used in an organization's operations. We think this a restrictive use of the term and prefer the definition offered by Robert Dubin.

> There are two major phases of the technology of any work: (a) the tools, instruments, machines and technical formulas whose employment is necessary to its perform-ance; and (b) the body of ideas which express the goals of the work, its functional importance, and the rationale of the methods employed. Technology, then, is composed of the tools used and the specialized ideas needed in getting particular kinds of work done.[4]

At the present time, the technology of schools is changing

[4] R. Dubin (ed), *Human Relations in Administration*, Prentice-Hall, New Jersey, 1968, p. 467.

at a faster rate than ever before. There is an emphasis on curriculum development and changes in teaching techniques; there is a greater recognition of individual differences between pupils and consequently there is more differentiation among them with more emphasis on courses 'tailor-made' for the individual pupil; and, of course, there have been advances in machine technology for use in schools. Michael Apter has written about the importance of new physical technology for the organization of the school. One of the barriers in the way of widespread adoption of the new techniques:

> is the fact that they cannot be fitted easily into normal school organization. Use of television in its broadcast form or as part of a closed-circuit network, for example, necessitates the school timetable being drawn up around the set times of the programmes. Use of a language laboratory with a standard number of booths (usually sixteen for some obscure reason) means that class-size must be made to conform to the number of booths available. Use of student-paced programmed instructions means that the organization of the school must allow for the fact that students will finish given programmed courses at different times.[5]

Henry Ruark also states:

> newly programmed capabilities of the new media force a reformulation of the conventional role of the teacher in the classroom. . . . The teacher will no longer be principally a communicator, presenting facts, constructing concepts, and guiding skill development; increasingly the teacher will work with individual pupils on a tutorial basis, directing their learning and using machines for which presentation and routine exposition, pointing out further resources, and encouraging the student to accept increasingly higher levels of responsibility for his own educational growth.[6]

These indications of a more rapidly changing technology will lead us to look for changes in a system developed when technological innovation was almost non-existent. There are differences of view as to the kind of influence which tech-

[5] M. J. Apter, *The New Technology of Education*, Macmillan, London, 1969, p. 113.

[6] H. C. Ruark, Jr., 'Technology and Education' in W. E. Drake (ed), *Sources for Intellectual Foundations of Modern Education*, Charles E. Merrill, Columbus, Ohio, 1967, p. 268.

nology has on structure. Some people believe that the technology determines the structure of the organization. Others have pointed out the importance of the senior personnel of an organization in deciding the kind of structure they wish to adopt or the ways in which they wish to modify their existing structures. This argument throws light on the importance of the head and his associates regarding decisions about the use to be made of new techniques or technologies, and the structural changes, if any, that will be made to accommodate them. The judgement of the headmaster is, in any case, an important factor in the structure adopted in the school, regardless of any changes which may be consequent upon new techniques or technologies. Although the basic staffing structure may be laid down by the employing and regulating bodies, there is a large area of what might be called 'discretionary structure' and this is one of the things which differentiates one school from another. By discretionary structure we may refer, for example, to the academic organization of the pupils and the structure of staff committees which may take a large part in the day-to-day running of the school.

VII

The school, like most organizations, has to engage in the environment at a number of levels. At one level, the environment provides the legitimizing context for the school. Parliamentary legislation, for example, provides the authority under which most schools are built, staffed and financed. In Scotland, the Secretary of State is responsible to Parliament for Scottish education, supervises this responsibility through the Scottish Education Department, and concerns himself with legislative, judicial, financial and administrative matters. This fourth category covers the day-to-day work of the Scottish Education Department which:

> ... as the central supervisory authority, guides the development of Scottish education in almost all its aspects. For example, the Department supervises the provision by educational authorities of primary, secondary and further education; approves various educational authority schemes —building projects, plans for further education, schemes for the transfer of pupils from primary to secondary educa-

tion, and so on; maintains a general oversight of staffing, curricula and methods; supervises the development of the schools meals service, though not the school health service, which is the responsibility of the Scottish Home and Health Department; and is responsible for the certification and superannuation of teachers (functions with regard to certification have been transferred to the General Teaching Council).[7]

The Scottish Education Department's influence, it can be seen from this, falls mainly on the local authorities. As the same observer puts it, the Scottish Education Department regulates and supervises the provision which is in fact made by the local education authorities. The powers and duties of the local education authorities are described as follows:

... the adequate and efficient provision of all forms of primary, secondary, and further education; the provision of adequate facilities for recreation and social and physical training; the provision of special education for handicapped pupils; the provision of a child guidance service; provision for religious observance and instruction in schools; provision, free of charge, of books, writing materials, stationery, mathematical instruments and other necessary articles; the enforcement of attendance at school; provision, in the case of a county, of books for general reading; provision and maintenance of hostels for pupils attending day schools; the payment of bursaries and other allowances to persons over age fifteen attending schools and further education centres; the granting in certain cases of exemption from the obligation to attend school to pupils over fourteen years of age; the payment of fees of pupils attending schools at which fees are payable; provision of milk and a midday meal; provision of clothing for pupils inadequately clad; provision for the medical inspection and treatment of pupils; the appointment and dismissal of teachers; the making of by-laws with regard to the employment of children.[8]

It may be agreed, then, that the legitimizing authorities for the school are the Scottish Education Department and the local authorities. Other organizations, however, affect the

[7] S. Leslie Hunter, *The Scottish Educational System*, Pergamon Press, Oxford, 1970, pp. 29-30.
[8] Ibid., p. 39.

legitimation process. The Scottish Certificate of Education Examination Board, for example, controls the major aspects of the public examination system in Scotland. This means that it has a substantial influence on what is taught in schools, at least in certificate courses. Examinations, and thereby the content of courses, are standardized and individual schools have no say in this standardization, except in so far as individual staff members may act as members of subject panels of the SCEEB or as examiners. Arrangements for sitting examinations are as rigorously controlled as are the contents of the examination papers. Invigilators from outside the school are brought in; lists of pupils to be presented by the school are sent to the Board, together with proposed arrangements for pupils who find that their examinations clash, orders of merit of pupils, examination attendance registers and other information. In addition to the SCEEB, there are other, less direct influences. Universities, colleges of education, teachers' professional organizations and so on, will all be involved in legitimizing schools.

The school, however, is not only at the receiving end of its environment; it also utilizes it. Individuals give talks to pupils, doctors lecture on drugs or sex education, policemen discuss crime, representatives of firms talk about their work and the work of their firms, monks talk about their way of life. Meetings, too, may be arranged between the staff of different schools, particularly where the schools are linked in some way as in a primary-secondary school relationship, or where a four-year school and a six-year school operate in the same area with the latter taking pupils at certain stages from the former. The purposes of these meetings will vary, but might include in some way the collaboration of teaching and the exchange of ideas on new developments. In making use of sectors in its environment in this way, schools may also be attempting to neutralize them. In this connection, headmasters often believe it important to maintain good relations with the communities in which their schools are situated. Public relations activities may thus be seen as part of the neutralization process.

Yet another connection the school has with its environment is with the cultural background of its members. For example, the social milieu of the children in a school will influence the ways in which they are or should be taught. Again, the background of the children will effect the responses of the teaching staff to them. In this connection, the change to comprehensive education is important, as many of the teachers who teach in comprehensive schools will have been trained and have received their early experience in a system of senior and junior secondary schools (as they are known in Scotland). Former senior secondary school teachers may in some cases be apprehensive and even hostile to children who would, under the old system, have gone to a junior secondary school. Complaints, for example, may be made about 'rough kids' who come from an area from which most children previously went to a junior secondary school.

Parents will also have a variety of responses to the new comprehensive schools based for the most part on their own school experiences and the hearsay experiences of others. Parents of 'bright' children may, in consequence, be hostile to the comprehensive school, fearing a lowering of standards and a substandard education for their children. Another factor to be taken into account is the increased geographical mobility of both pupils' families and teachers themselves. In areas where families are more mobile, the school may experience greater difficulties because teachers may have no personal knowledge of the families. Again, a high teacher turnover rate creates its own problems for the staffing of departments and the continuity of teaching.

VIII

Organization theory is a new discipline of the social sciences. In the last decade or so, social scientists from a number of disciplines, notably political science, social psychology, sociology and economics, have come to recognize that organizations, large and small, represent a 'natural' strategic site for testing their ideas. This essentially methodological claim has been reinforced by a theoretical one—the promise of contributing to the development of each separate discipline through the cross fertilization of ideas from other fields and the opportunity to create a multi-disciplinary subject of organization theory.

This theoretical impetus has in its turn, been buttressed by an increasing awareness of the social and political importance of organizations. Understanding organizations is widely ecognized as crucial to an understanding of modernity itself.)rganization theory has, as a result of these—and other— levelopments, emerged from its earlier 'parasitic' relation to ther disciplines to a more clearly symbiotic one, a process hat has only assumed significant proportion in the last four r five years.

Organizational analysis in the United Kingdom is devoted argely to industrial organizations, to the inculcation of echniques and to problems defined as managerially relevant. These are quite legitimate concerns but they are in danger, n Dorothy Parker's phrase, of being milked until they moo. uch a curtailment of both the subject's empirical range and he problems to be considered cannot be justified on methodo- ogical, theoretical or social grounds. Non-industrial organi- ations such as hospitals, universities, theatres can also be he foci of a teaching and research programme in organization heory. The school should not be an exception to this more nclusive approach.

This can be justified methodologically by pointing to the elative accessibility of the participants of the school. There also a greater likelihood of cultural similarities between esearchers and some (at least) of the researched, as well as he presence of social values supportive of the research. The najor justification, however, is theoretical. First of all, theory nat is developed largely from the study of industry is not ecessarily valid for the school. If it is valid, then it is not ecessarily salient. Secondly, theory that focuses on the roblems of innovative and creative organizations and people- hanging organizations will ultimately be much more relevant r the understanding of all organizations where such roblems are increasingly inevitable.

This theoretical development is at once the most practical. or whether the concern is to facilitate innovation in the :hool, slow it down, or prevent it, it has become a crucial olicy problem. In the absence of relevant guidelines, the :hool might be in danger of being encouraged to employ rategies derived from quite different and possibly inappro- riate organizational circumstances. The point of this essay to indicate these characteristics of the school that have be taken into account in an organizational analysis, and, y implication, to suggest that some of the problems that urrently beset the school could be more fully comprehended

(and ultimately solved) through adopting an organizationa
perspective.

BIBLIOGRAPHY

Students who wish to pursue the subject of organization theory may fin
the following useful:
C. Perrow, *Organisational Analysis: A Sociological View*, Tavistock Pub
    lications, London, 1970.
D. Silverman, *The Theory of Organizations*, Heinemann, London, 197(
A. Etzioni (ed), *Complex Organizations: A Sociological Reader*, Hol
    Rinehart and Winston, New York, 2 editions, 1961 and 1969. Majc
    changes were made for the second edition. Both are valuable.
J. G. March (ed), *Handbook of Organizations*, Rand McNally, Chicagc
    1965.
W. G. Bennis & J. Thomas, *The Management of Change and Conflic*
    Penguin Modern Management Readings, 1972.

Those interested in organization theory as applied to the school shoul
consult the following:
M. G. Hughes (ed), *Secondary School Administration: A Managemer
    Approach*, Pergamon Press, Oxford, 1970.
A. V. Cicourel & J. I. Kitsuse, *The Educational Decision-Maker*, Bobb
    Merrill, New York, 1963.
M. D. Shipman, *The Sociology of the School*, Longmans, Green, Londor
    1968.
C. E. Bidwell, 'The School as a Formal Organization' in J. G. March (ed
    Handbook of Organizations, Rand McNally, Chicago, 1965.
O. Banks, *The Sociology of Education*, Batsford, 1968.

20

L. E. WATSON[1]

Office and Expertise in the Secondary School[*]

A number of changes in secondary schools are leading to consequences which can usefully be understood by reference to certain notions current in organization theory. Specifically, we shall in this article trace some of the consequences of increasing school complexity and specialization.

The trend at present is towards the larger school, with a continuing reduction in the number of smaller secondary schools. This is being influenced by the increase in school population, especially in the numbers of children remaining at school beyond the minimum leaving age, and through secondary reorganization and schemes of consolidation. Barker and Gump (1964) is one of the very small number of studies concerned with the consequences of size in schools, although many sociologists are interested in the increasing size of organizations. As schools grow larger, there is less and less likelihood that any one person will know everyone, even by sight. The 'span of control' of senior staff and the need for intermediate positions of responsibility also increase. Where one teacher comprised a department in a small grammar school, the large comprehensive may have a dozen or more teachers within a department. These are not simply small schools physically enlarged. They are likely to include children varying widely in academic attainments, and are expected to provide a wide variety of curricular and extra-curricular activities.

[*] [From *Educational Research*, Vol. II, No. 2, 1962.]
[1] The author wishes to acknowledge with thanks the assistance of Dr (now Prof.) D. F. Swift, who read an earlier draft of this paper.

406   The Administration of the School

Conflicting pressures in the secondary school

As formal organizations, schools are set up to achieve certain objectives—broadly covered by the term 'the education of children'. Those who have the effective power to set up schools and, broadly, to order their form, are generally agreed upon at least verbal specifications of what ought to happen within these schools, and they have sanctions available to make such expectations more or less effective.

Scott (1964, p. 488) defines organizations as 'collectivities that have been established for the pursuit of relatively specific objectives on a more or less continuous basis'. For Gouldner (1959, p. 404) 'the organization is conceived as an "instrument"—that is, as a rationally conceived means of realizing group goals'. The components of the *rationality of action* were defined by Mannheim (1950, p. 53) as 'a series of actions ... organized in such a way that it leads to a previously defined goal', and clearly may take different forms. Thus, one can see wide differences between the administration of the Sultanates of the Ottoman Empire, the hereditary nature of the office of tax-collector in eighteenth-century France, and the hierarchy of offices characteristic of a large modern government department. Maintaining effective structures is a problem for schools also: local education authorities, boards of governors, parents, teachers and others have expectations (commonly stated as goals) for schools, which they desire to see realized.

Max Weber, in his studies of the legitimacy of authority (1946, 1947, 1961) elaborated three bases of legitimacy associated with three 'pure types' of authority: the charismatic, the traditional, and the legal-rational or bureaucratic. For him, bureaucracy was the most efficient means of exercising authority and realizing goals in organizations. The official operates impartially within a framework of law. His authority is that of his office; he is subordinate to his superiors, and has authority over his subordinates by virtue of his office.

It is clear that there are many bureaucratic elements in the secondary school, and many bureaucratic pressures. Offices, such as those of headmaster, head of department and assistant master, are ranked in order, with the superordinate to a large degree responsible for the actions of the subordinate. Salaries are paid according to fixed scales and tenure is according to stated contractual obligations. There is at least some attempt to ensure that the most competent are promoted to higher positions.

Similarly, there are considerable pressures towards standardization of the system. Bigger schools have accentuated problems of co-ordination; rapid changes in the technical and technological aspects of teaching have led to a need for more and more planned changes, and supervision of those involved in the change; while there is an increased demand for audit and other checks. All these result in more centralization of control, and a greater emphasis on bureaucracy.

But the school is not organized completely as an 'ideal' bureaucracy. It is not characterized by a single hierarchy of authority, complete subordination of individual judgement to rules and regulations, and so on. No organization, however apparently bureaucratized, can continue to function unless non-bureaucratic elements are present. If organizations have goals to fulfil, so have the individual people who work within them. The informal interaction characteristic of workplaces arises, partly from the psychological and social needs of the workers, partly because the regulations governing their behaviour are never complete in themselves; and partly because of the need for communication, discussion, consultation and other activities involving people. However important these informal factors may be—and there is no doubt that they are of crucial importance in understanding the operation of organizations—we will concentrate upon only one aspect of schools which runs counter to the bureaucratic element: professionalism.

We are familiar with the growth of 'professional' orientations among occupational groups which have not always been classified as 'professional'. This term has been variously defined, and there is indeed some doubt as to its utility as a sociological concept (Vollmer, 1966; Habenstein, 1963). The trend at present is to see occupations, not as divided into 'professions' and 'non-professions', but rather as variously involved in the general process of professionalization (Vollmer and Mills, 1966). When seen in this way, the appropriate question is not, 'Is this occupation a profession?' but 'What are the dimensions of professionalization, and where does this occupational group lie upon each of these, in relation to other occupations?' Thus Greenwood (1957) suggests that professionalism tends to emphasize expertise, the autonomy of the occupational group, and an organizational structure emphasizing a minimal hierarchy of authority. These are not the only characteristics, but are the most important for our purpose.

When applied to teachers, we can see that the 'professional orientation', with its emphasis upon the autonomy of the individual teacher, tends to be reinforced by certain structural aspects of the job. Classroom teaching is almost always conducted in isolation from colleagues—an isolation much appreciated by many teachers, who value the freedom they find within the four walls of the classroom. Lack of widely agreed criteria as to what constitutes good teaching, and the difficulty of providing behavioural definitions of educational objectives, makes standardization of teaching hazardous. Improved qualifications and training of teachers reinforces their self-confidence. But increased specialization is perhaps the most significant factor to encourage their claims for independence.

'Reference groups' of teachers

Under what circumstances do subordinates recognize the authority of others? Not all orders or instructions are obeyed; and some are obeyed only because of fear of the consequences of not doing so. It is also clear, however, that many people feel that their subordinate position is appropriate, and that he who commands has a right to command, that he who holds the higher office does so legitimately.

The notion of *reference group* has been used extensively to refer to 'those groups to which the individual relates himself as a part or to which he aspires to relate himself psychologically'. These reference groups may also be seen as sources of authority, of sets of norms which serve to validate or justify the behaviour or authority claims of those who recognize these norms. Gouldner (1957) has developed a taxonomy of 'latent social roles' in organizations, suggesting that people, and especially professionals, may tend to identify with, and accept the authority of, the organization to which they belong (the 'locals') or the wider professional group of which they are members, or to the membership of which they aspire (the 'cosmopolitans'). A scientist working in an industrial company may feel that his primary loyalty is to his organization, or to the fraternity of chemists. Teachers' attitudes could be classified into three categories. Loyalty to the school, its traditions, structure, rules and leadership, may identify the 'locals'. Another group may feel primary identity with those who share the same academic subject and training—these we might label the 'academics'. Such a teacher of physics would tend to identify with his fellow physicists, wherever they were working. Others again would identify with the profession of teaching, emphasizing a set of values and an ideology which refers to the 'how', the 'technology' of teaching, to the child and other values, irrespective of the subject being taught. These we may refer to as the 'craftsmen'. These three groups of attitudes represent different modes of recognizing and ascribing authority, all three of which may overlap in any one teacher.

At present we have little evidence to clarify the area of authority and teacher response. Predominantly 'academic' teachers, however, will probably be subject-centred and will resist supervision (which they may define as 'interference') in this area. The 'craftsmen' will probably emphasize the importance of pedagogical matters, and the 'locals' will stress organizational and administrative commitments. Bidwell (1955, 1956) has suggested that teachers are most likely to accept the supervision of administrators who seem to conform to their prescriptions about what administrators should do. Thus the advice or instructions of a headmaster or head of department is much more likely to be regarded as legitimate if he is thought to have the same reference group as the teacher. Some teachers, of course, rather than being primarily 'locals', 'academics' or 'craftsmen' may well be 'indifferents'. It has been suggested by some observers that the domination by occupationally 'indifferent' women teachers of some teacher organizations may help to explain their relative ineffectiveness.

So far we have distinguished between authority of office (bureaucratic orientation) and of expertise (professional orientation), and have classified modes of identification with the organization, the profession of teaching and the academic tradition. We will now look at the pyramids of authority within the school with their implications for the encouragement and supervision of teachers and for the role of the headmaster.

The pyramids of authority

In looking at any organization, it is important to examine any division of labour and the ways in which the varying offices are hierarchically arranged. In the secondary school, teacher specialization varies considerably according to task. Since most secondary school teachers teach only one or two subjects, the teacher is to this extent a specialist. Where size of school or lack of suitably qualified staff make it impossible to teach only one or two subjects the lack of specialization is usually considered undesirable. One consequence of the division of labour of teachers by subject taught is the characteristic class-subject basis of time-tabling and the exposure of all classes to a number of different teachers during the school week.

There is a large degree of non-specialization in general pedagogical matters. Classroom teachers are expected (and expect themselves) to decide individually questions of classroom organization and teaching method. However, this pattern appears to be changing, with increased emphasis on the role of department head responsible for the teaching in his department and for the professional guidance of his teachers, or in the development of team teaching groups. Again, on general questions of child handling and child welfare, the typical teacher in England tends to assume that he has a general 'pastoral' responsibility for all his pupils, and especially for those for whom he is 'form-master'. However, the existence of housemasters, year-tutors and especially of school counsellors implies a division of labour which concentrates the responsibility for certain aspects of the school programme into their hands.

There has always been some division of labour in administrative and organizational matters because of the need for consultation and co-ordination. The headmaster is the final formal authority in many matters. As schools grow larger, however, many administrative concerns are delegated to specific officials, such as bursars, secretaries, clerks, school lunch supervisors, caretaking personnel and even pupils, who handle the routine work. In some cases they may make significant decisions affecting the teaching staff. Thus the school secretary will have authority to require teachers to complete pupil attendance returns, and will function bureaucratically (i.e. by virtue of office, and delegated authority from the headmaster) in making these demands.

To speak of a single hierarchy of formal authority in the secondary school staff is to oversimplify the picture. Rather we must have in mind a structure of triangles each having at its apex the headmaster, who is usually the formal superordinate of each authority system. One can distinguish several authority systems—subject teacher, head of department, headmaster—classroom teacher, form-master, housemaster, headmaster (with the school counsellor, if the school has one, playing a specialized and often ambivalent role)—classroom teacher, school secretary, headteacher—classroom teacher, cleaner, caretaker, headmaster—and so on. A single person might well occupy different positions in several of the authority sub-systems. Thus a particular mistress may be a teacher of physics (and therefore responsible for certain purposes to the head of the physics department); a teacher of mathematics responsible to the head of mathematics; a form-mistress; a house-mistress; and, as a classroom teacher, responsible to the school office for certain of her functions. To complicate matters further, as a housemistress, she might have authority over heads of department (even the heads of physics or mathematics) in house activities or some aspects of pupil guidance.

The secondary school, then, is organized with a considerable but not always clear division of labour. It is a complex arrangement of specialized officials holding offices and exercising authority by virtue of this appointment but presumably having been appointed to the office by virtue of their expertise. The roles which they fulfil, however, are not necessarily clear, and the nature of their authority is frequently in doubt, especially when challenged by the 'academics'. The creation of superordinate offices (a tendency reinforced by the system of allowances within the Burnham scale) of itself does not necessarily create the conditions which encourage subordinates to accept the instructions or guidance of the superior official.

The encouragement and supervision of teachers

As schools become more complex, as the pupils and teachers they recruit become more diverse and the goals of the organization more varied, maintenance of standards, of planning change and of co-ordinating activity become more pressing. The response is often increased centralization and bureaucratization, with greater supervision of teachers. This seldom causes concern to the 'indifferent' teachers, for they are not firmly committed to any particular professional principle, and are likely to respond to increased pressure without enthusiasm, but without rebellion. The 'local' orientation of teachers is most conducive to the smooth bureaucratic operation of schools. Schools frequently encourage this attitude, emphasizing loyalty to the school, and tending to promote staff who remain with the school. It is the 'cosmopolitan' teacher who is most likely to be in conflict with bureaucratic elements within the school setting.

Blau and Scott (1963, p. 63) make clear the two sources of professional control:

> First, as a result of the long period of training undergone by the practitioner, he is expected to have acquired a body of expert knowledge and to have internalized a code of ethics which governs his professional conduct. Second, this self control is supported by the external surveillance of his conduct by peers, who are in a position to see his work, who have the skills to judge his performance, and who, since they have personal stake in the reputation of their profession, are motivated to exercise the necessary sanctions. Professionals in a given field constitute a colleague group of equals. Every member of the group, but nobody else, is assumed to be qualified to make professional judgements.

This situation implies an essentially flat control system. The problems that arise when professionals and those professionally oriented (the 'cosmopolitans') work within organizations which are to some extent bureaucratically controlled, have been studied in a number of contexts.[2] Con-

[2] See, for example, for trade unions, Wilensky (1956, 1961); hospitals, Corwin (1961), Goss (1961, 1963), Hughes, Hughes and Deutscher (1958), Perrow (1965), Smith 1958, Stanton and Schwartz (1954); universities, Clark (1963), Davis (1961), Gross (1965); military units, Bidwell (1961), Janowitz (1961); and social welfare agencies, Blau and Scott (1963), Peabody (1964).

cerning the problem of supervision of 'experts' within organizations, Gouldner (1959, p. 415) writes:

> Often, not only is the expert's immediate superior unqualified to judge him, but there are only one or a few qualified judges in the entire organization. Even if there are a few, they may be close friends or fierce competitors, whose judgement about one another will, in either event, be unreliable. This means that administrative superiors must depend upon persons outside the organization to select experts or to judge the performance of those already employed. This in turn means that the technical expert himself is often dependent on persons outside his organization to validate his position within it. Consequently his work must manifest a high degree of concern for the maintenance of technical standards. This not only disposes the expert to resist imperative pressures for 'results' coming from his superiors, but it also makes him less vulnerable to control from those within and in command of his organization.

Gouldner implies that the highly-qualified expert is potentially mobile and therefore independent of a particular organization. The situation in schools is less extreme, but the teacher who is well qualified in his subject often demands that his subject-knowledge competence be judged by his equals—a typically 'professional' approach. Similarly, when matters of teaching method are discussed, these cannot validly be divorced from a knowledge of the subject-matter to be taught. If the headmaster is not qualified in the same field, or if the 'cosmopolitan' thinks his head of department is incompetent, he is unlikely to accept their judgement. In such cases, however much he may conform for the sake of expediency, he is unlikely to be committed to the course of action he feels forced to take. He tends either to become apathetic—showing conformity without commitment—to subvert the policies of his superiors, to come into open revolt, or to leave. Occasionally he might change to a less 'cosmopolitan' orientation.

What, then, are the situations most likely to irk the 'academic' teacher? He tends to be resistant to rules. In a bureaucratic organization, the individual worker has no basis for making rational judgements on the choice of objectives or methods. They are selected and assigned to him. He is expected to follow rules and procedures. The tendency to follow this *rationale* of action is even present in schools. Decisions which will influence the work of the individual teacher are frequently made by a small group of senior teachers, or the headmaster himself. These are teachers, therefore, who must live with the occupational hazard of believing that they, by virtue of office, know what is best for the school and are thereby entitled to make decisions for their subordinates. Such an attitude is not always appreciated by the 'unco-operative' teachers who may be 'academics'. Such teachers tend to be intolerant of rules or conventions which interfere with their freedom of action.

Conflict can arise over the criteria used in evaluating the teacher's performance. In schools the problems can be acute because objectives are so hard to measure and the relationship between ends and means is so indeterminate. The young teacher, when criticized for teaching in some particular way or using some particular method, can deny that the method has the undesirable consequences attributed to it. This situation can easily give rise to a clash which raises the question of the legitimacy of the superordinate's authority.

These tensions are especially likely to occur when non-teaching staff make demands of the teacher which he thinks interfere with his 'proper' work. In most cases the authority of the non-teacher is that of his office, delegated by the headmaster. If such a dispute comes to the attention of the headmaster, it can pose a difficult situation; as, for instance, when a cleaner (who might be difficult to replace) is in conflict with one of the teaching staff.

Heads of department, who usually encourage and supervise classroom teachers, are among the better qualified of teachers in the school and continue their roles as classroom teachers. But once recruited, they tend to become more concerned with organizational and administrative matters. Many duties bring them into conflict with teachers: not only supervisory functions, but those concerned with co-ordinating syllabuses and allocating resources within the department. Assistants are less likely than the department head to have an overall view of the needs of the department and of its place within the total school programme. Thus he tends to become more concerned with organizational values which emphasize order, co-ordination and other aspects of the needs of the organization. He becomes more bureaucratic, while many of his teachers remain academically and professionally oriented. A common consequence is the development of considerable role strain (Goode, 1960). On the one hand, the departmental head probably understands and sympathizes with the orientation of his subordinates, from whose ranks he was himself recruited. On the other hand, he is faced with organizational demands which press him towards bureaucratic procedures, especially in the larger department. Although responsible to the headmaster for the conduct of his department, he cannot accomplish his work without the co-operation of his subordinates—he is the 'man in the middle' (Whyte and Gardner, 1945). Consequently, with the conflicts and tensions characteristic of the classroom teacher (Kob, 1961; Wilson, 1962) the head of department combines those of the middle-level administrator.

The authority and role of the headmaster

In many ways these problems are complicated for the non-teaching headmaster and in some ways they are simplified. Generally the head of the larger secondary school does little if any teaching. Certainly he finds an increasing amount of his time taken up with administrative matters, as well as working with parents, teachers and difficult children. His definition of the significance of his office tends to be a hierarchial one—this is 'his' school; he is its 'head'; and even when these attitudes are accompanied by reference to the attitudes of teachers and the importance of delegation, there is rarely any doubt in his mind but that his is the final responsibility. As headmasters are fully aware, they are held accountable for the school to its governors.

Something is known of the dynamics of organizational tension-reduction in some settings (Orzack, 1961; Blau and Scott, 1963), but we have very little knowledge of how schools adapt to the conflicts inherent in their structure. There is a need for well-conducted case studies of educational organizations, focusing upon this question. We may, however, suggest how tensions are sometimes reduced. In highly rational and technically specialized organizations, authority tends to be legitimated on strictly legal grounds, and this is certainly so for the headship of the school. The head usually feels entitled to command. Even if his staff feel that he ought not to occupy his position he has strong controls over them through his central position in the promotion system and through his ability to make life difficult for the deviant (Becker, 1953). Thus, along with an appeal to the authority of office, there may well be an appeal to the expedience of compliance, although few headmasters would carry these requirements to dangerous lengths. It is a characteristic of the school, along with other organizations, that it cannot be maintained for long with any real effectiveness without the co-operation and involvement of those who participate in its operation.

Headmasters faced with the problem of exercising authority over specialists may give adequately qualified subordinates control of the procedures (especially the content and method of teaching) adopted in the classroom. This is part of the significance of the role and position of the department head, and increasingly of other specialists carrying special responsibility for the work of teachers. However, while this removes strain from the headmaster, it can create a new organizational tension. Now, the relationship which the headmaster establishes with his deputy, heads of department and other officials becomes crucial. Unless he can carry them with him on matters of policy, it is unlikely that he will be very effective. By creating these offices, he insulates the ordinary classroom teacher from direct communication and pressure from himself. If he wishes to influence a teacher directly he has to work through delegated authority, or risk the departmental head's resentment at being by-passed.

Heads may emphasize the extent to which they share the teachers' attitudes and orientations, their ideologies and values. They may point to years spent in the classroom and to active participation in professional bodies. While this strategy can be effective where the head and staff *do* have these elements in common, it tends to break down when the positions taken by head and staff are fundamentally incompatible.

A further strategy often centres upon the role of the deputy headmaster, who is increasingly being seen as central to the communication and authority structure of the school, and who may play a vital supplementary role (Burnham, 1965). Especially in sensitive areas where the autonomy of the teacher is concerned, many headteachers are likely to suggest or advise rather than makes rules. A 'collegial' relationship makes it much easier for teachers to accept innovations or guidance when they are resistant to what they define as 'interference'. This pattern is often found where a significant number of professionally-oriented personnel work, as in hospitals. Even where there is a formally defined medical hierarchy, 'orders' are often given in the form of 'consultative advice' (Goss, 1963).

Increasingly, headmasters think, like management in business, that their occupation needs experience and training, specialized skills and a systematic body of principles. This belief has been strong for some decades now in the USA where many universities confer advanced degrees in educational administration. The English headmaster is increasingly professional, seeing himself as an 'expert', not in particular subject area nor even in subject teaching, but in school management and administration. Alongside his traditional role as leader, then, we are seeing a simultaneous tendency towards both the bureaucratization of the professional, and the professionalization of the bureaucrat.

Headmasters also attempt to strengthen their authority by increasing the professional stature and competence of their staff. The school is a powerful socializing agency for teachers as well as pupils (Brim and Wheeler, 1966). Informal pressures for conformity upon the newer staff; appeals to professional values and behaviour; the use of myths, symbols and rituals; all may work towards increased commitment of the teacher, and all are used by headmasters. In so far as appropriate values are internalized and appropriate skills developed, teachers become less and less in need of close supervision and the efforts of senior teachers can be concentrated upon the more acceptable aspects of leadership. However, many factors—the lack of consistency and clarity in the normative structure of the teaching profession, the large percentage of those with a low professional commitment (Colombotos, 1963; Mason, Dressel and Bain, 1959), the high turnover of staff, and the brevity and nature of much professional training—tend to reduce the effectiveness of the college and school as a learning environment for teachers. Simultaneously, many aspects of school life lead to the reinforcement of retrogressive attitudes and practices.

Conclusion

Although the study of industrial and other organizations has been proceeding for many decades, and despite the outstanding early work of Waller (1932), the study of the school as a complex organization has been relatively neglected both by educationists and by theorists of organizations. This neglect has operated to the disadvantage of both those who are interested in the nature and dynamics of complex organizations, and those whose concern is for the understanding of educational processes. Nevertheless, in the last few years more research and writing has focused on the characteristics of the school as an organization. I have suggested that the tensions shown to exist in other organizations between hierarchial structure and professional teacher attitude should also be studied in the secondary school.

I make no claims that my statements are anything more than informed guesses, based upon reasoning by analogy from research conducted in organizations other than schools. As such they emphasize the need for carefully conducted studies into the structure and functioning of schools as organizations. Some questions for investigation are:

> To what extent can one usefully interpret specific schools in terms of the suggestions made above?
>
> Do the majority of teachers tend to fall into one of the categories suggested? If so, do they behave in the ways predicted?
>
> What factors are associated with the strategies adopted by headmasters and heads of departments in the face of challenges to their authority, and with what functional consequences for the school?
>
> Are there consistent patterns in the reference-group characteristics of those promoted to senior positions within schools?
>
> What behavioural differences occur as a result of the promotion of people with differing orientations?
>
> How do the careers of cosmopolitans and locals within teaching vary and with what consequences for the schools?

These questions, along with many others, would appear to bear promise of a fruitful yield.

REFERENCES

Abrahamson, M. (1967). *The Professional in the Organization*. Chicago: Rand McNally.

Anderson, J. G. (1967). 'The teacher: bureaucrat or professional?', *Educ. Admin. Quart.*, iii, 3, pp. 291-300.

Barker, R. C. and Gump, P. V. (1964). *Big School, Small School: High School Size and Student Behaviour*. Stanford: Stanford University Press.

Becker, H. S. (1953). 'The teacher in the authority system of the public school', *Jour. Educ. Soc.*, 27, pp. 128-44. Reprinted in: Etzioni, A. ed. (1965). *Complex Organizations: A Sociological Reader*. New York: Holt.

Bidwell, C. E. (1955). 'The administrative role and satisfaction in teaching', *Jour. Educ. Soc.*, 29, pp. 41-7.

Bidwell, C. E. (1956). 'Administrative and teacher satisfaction'. *Phi Delta Kappan*, 37, pp. 285-8.

Bidwell, C. E. (1961). 'The young professional in the army: a study of occupational identity', *Amer. Sociol. Rev.*, 26, 3, pp. 360-72.

Bidwell, C. E. (1965). 'The school as a formal organization'. In: March, J. G. ed. *Handbook of Orginizations*. Chicago: Rand McNally; pp. 972-1022.

Blau, P. M. and Scott, W. R. (1963). *Formal Organizations*. London: Routledge & Kegan Paul.

Brim, O. G. and Wheeler, S. (1966). *Socialization After Childhood: Two Essays*. New York: Wiley.

Burnham, P. S. (1965). 'The role of the deputy head in secondary schools'. M.Ed. thesis, Leicester University.

Clark, B. R. (1963). 'Faculty organization and authority'. In: Lunsford, T. F. ed. *The Study of Academic Administration*. Boulder, Colorado: Western Interstate Commission for Higher Education; pp. 37-51. Reprinted in: Vollmer, H. M. and Mills, D. L. eds. *Professionalization*. Englewood Cliffs, N.J. Prentice-Hall; pp. 283-91.

Colombotos, J. (1963). 'Sex role and professionalism: a study of high school teachers (1)', *School Rev.*, LXXI, 1, pp. 27-40.

Corwin, R. G. (1961). 'The professional employee: a study of conflict in the nursing roles', *Amer. Jour. Soc.*, LXVI, pp. 604-15.

Dalton, M. (1961). 'Conflict between staff and line managerial officers'. In: Etzioni, A. ed. *Complex Organizations: A Sociological Reader*. New York: Holt; pp. 212-21.

Davis, J. A. (1961). 'Locals and cosmopolitans in American graduate schools', *Int. Jour. Comp. Soc.*, 2, 2, pp. 212-23.

Goode, W. J. (1960). 'A theory of role strain', *Amer. Sociol. Rev.*, 25, pp. 483-96.

Goss, M. E. W. (1961). 'Influence and authority among physicians in an outpatient clinic', *Amer. Sociol. Rev.*, 26, 1, pp. 39-50.

Goss, M. E. W. (1963). 'Patterns of bureaucracy among hospital staff physicians'. In: Freidson, E. ed. *The Hospital in Modern Society*. New York: Free Press; pp. 170-94.

Gouldner, A. W. (1957). 'Cosmopolitans and locals: towards an analysis of latent social roles', *Admin. Science Quart.*, 2, pp. 281-306; 2, pp. 444-80.

Gouldner, A. W. (1959). 'Organizational analysis'. In: Merton, R. K. et al. eds. *Sociology Today: Problems and Prospects*. New York: Basic Books; pp. 400-28.

Greenwood, E. (1957). 'Attributes of a profession', *Social Work*, 2, 3. pp. 44-55.

Gross, Ll. (1965). 'Hierarchial authority in educational institutions'. In:

420 The Administration of the School

Hartley, H. J. and Holloway, G. E. eds. *Focus on Change and the School Administrator*. New York: School of Education, Program in Educational Administration, State University of New York at Buffalo; pp. 23-36.

Habenstein, R. W. (1963). 'Critique of "profession" as a sociological category', *Sociol. Quart.*, iv, 4, pp. 291-300.

Hall, R. H. (1968). 'Professionalization and bureaucratization', *Amer. Sociol. Rev.*, 33, 1, pp. 92-103.

Hargreaves, D. (1966). *Social Relations in a Secondary School*. London: Routledge & Kegan Paul.

Hughes, E. C., Hughes, H. McG. and Deutscher, I. (1958). *Twenty Thousand Nurses Tell Their Story*. Philadelphia: Lippincot.

Janowitz, M. (1961). 'Hierarchy and authority in the military establishment'. In: Etzioni, A. ed. *Complex Organizations: A Sociological Reader*. New York: Holt; pp. 198-212.

Kob, J. (1961). 'Definition of the teacher's role'. In: Halsey, A. H. Floud, J. and Anderson, C. A. eds. *Education, Economy and Society* New York: Free Press.

Mannheim, K. (1950). *Man and Society in an Age of Reconstruction* New York: Harcourt, Brace.

Mason, W., Dressel, R. J. and Bain, R. K. (1959). 'Sex role and the career orientations of beginning teachers', *Harvard Educ. Rev.*, 29 pp. 370-83.

Orzack, L. H. (1961). 'Issues underlying role dilemmas of professionals' In: Abramavitz, A. B. ed. *Emotional Factors in Public Health Nursing. A Casebook*. Madison, Wisconsin: Wisconsin University Press; pp 140-59.

Peabody, R. L. (1964). *Organizational Authority*. New York: Atherton Press.

Perrow, C. (1965). 'Hospitals: technology, structure and goals'. In: March, J. G. ed. *Handbook of Organizations*. Chicago: Rand McNally pp. 910-71.

Scott, W. R. (1964). 'Theory of organizations'. In: Faris, R. E. L. ed *Handbook of Modern Sociology*. Chicago: Rand McNally; pp. 485-529

Smith, H. L. (1958). 'Two lines of authority: the hospital's dilemma'. In Jaco, E. G. ed. *Patients, Physicians and Illness*. Glencoe, Illinois: Free Press.

Solomon, B. (1967). 'A comment on "The authority structure of the school"', *Educ. Admin. Quart.*, 3, 3, pp. 281-90.

Stanton, A. H. and Schwartz, M. S. (1954). *The Mental Hospital*. New York: Basic Books.

Vollmer, H. M. (1966). 'Entrepreneurship and professional productivity among research scientists'. In: Vollmer, H. M. and Mills, D. L. eds *Professionalization*. Englewood Cliffs, N.J. Prentice-Hall; pp. 276-82

Vollmer, H. M. and Mills, D. (1962). 'Nuclear technology and the professionalization of labour', *Amer. Jour. Soc.* LXVII, 6, pp. 690-6.

Vollmer, H. M. and Mills, D. ed. (1966). *Professionalization*. Englewood Cliffs, N.J. Prentice-Hall.

Waller, W. (1932). *The Sociology of Teaching*. Wiley paperbacks, 1965 New York: Wiley.

Weber, M. (1946). *From Max Weber: Essays in Sociology*. Edited and translated by H. H. Gerth and C. W. Mills. New York: Oxford University Press.

Weber, M. (1947). *The Theory of Social and Economic Organization* Translated by A. M. Henderson and T. Parsons. Glencoe, Illinois: Free Press.

Weber, M. (1961). 'Three types of legitimate rule'. In: Etzioni, A. ed

Complex Organizations: A Sociological Reader. New York: Holt;
pp. 4-14.

Whyte, W. F. and Gardner, B. B. (1945). 'Facing the foreman's problems',
Appl. Anthrop., 4, pp. 1-28.

Wilensky, H. L. (1956). *Intellectuals in the Labour Unions.* Glencoe,
Illinois: Free Press.

Wilensky, H. L. (1961). 'The trade union as a bureaucracy'. In: Etzioni, A.
ed. *Complex Organizations: A Sociological Reader.* New York: Holt;
pp. 221-34.

Wilson, B. R. (1962). 'The teacher's role—a sociological analysis', *Brit.
Jour. Soc.*, 13, pp. 15-32.

21

R. KING

The Head Teacher and his Authority*

It is part of the English notion of the school that the position of head teacher should be associated with considerable authority.[1] It is the purpose of this discussion to analyse the nature and extent of that authority. This discussion is a fairly speculative one, because there have been few empirical studies of the role, status or authority of head teachers in Britain.[2] This lack of objective data is in itself a reflection of the nature and extent of the head teacher's authority. It has been suggested that our general lack of knowledge of the sociology of the school may be associated with the mistrust of research workers by teachers and head teachers.[3] Perhaps they are unaware of the sociologists' value-free objective approach, and feel that they are being judged rather than studied. More specifically, it may be the fear of a head teacher that his authority may be effectively reduced when its nature is exposed.

Empirical studies have been made of organizational role in American schools[4] However the equivalent office of head teacher is rare in American schools, and studies of school

* [From *Headship in the 1970s*, ed. Bryan Allen, Blackwell, 1970.]
[1] See G. Baron, University of London Institute of Education, 'The English Notion of the School' (*Unpublished paper*); and P. W. Musgrave *Sociology of Education* (Methuen, 1965), Chapter 14, Section A, p. 224 'The British Idea of the School', which Musgrave acknowledges '... owe much to Dr G. Baron. . . .' p. 223.
[2] For a review of some of the problems in this area of study see L. J Westwood, 'Reassessing the Role of the Head', *Education for Teaching*, No. 71, November, 1966.
[3] K. E. Shaw, 'Why no Sociology of Schools?' *Education for Teaching* No. 69, February, 1966.
[4] A well known example is N. Gross, W. S. Mason and A. W. McEachern *Explorations in Role Analysis: Studies of the School Superintendency Role* Wiley, 1958.

principals and superintendents, although interesting, are not particularly useful to the purpose of this discussion. Cross-cultural comparisons of the English and American school systems may reveal significant differences between the two systems, but they do not adequately account for the special features of each separate system. Because of the different concepts of the school held in the two societies and the different histories of their school systems, the results of American studies must be regarded as having only a limited potential validity in the English setting.[5]

One important point that does emerge from the American studies of organizational roles in the schools is that any investigation of authority within a school must be related to the formal social structure of the school. The head teacher is, to a large extent, responsible for devising and maintaining his school as a formal organization, and so, in a most revealing way, his school becomes the expression of his authority. Thus this discussion will draw upon some of the recent studies of organizations, with special reference to those few studies of the sociology of the school.

Even the most casual of observations of head teachers show that the extent of their authority is enormously variable, and that it can take many different forms. These variations are reflected in the wide diversity of schools in our society. This diversity is merely sketched by the use of such dichotomous classifications as, primary/secondary, selective/non-selective, day/boarding, private/maintained. Clearly there is little profit in discussing the authority of 'the head teacher'. Such a discussion would have to be made at such a high level of generality as to make it of very limited value. Thus this discussion will attempt to account for these variabilities in the authority of head teachers, and it will do so mainly by looking at the variability in the formal organization of schools.

The concepts used in this discussion are not new; they are some of the long established concepts in sociology. Most of them are large-scale unitary concepts, for example, the con-

---

[5] Some aspects of the differences between English and American schools are discussed in George Baron and Asher Tropp's chapter, 'Teachers in England and America', in *Education, Economy and Society: A Reader in the Sociology of Education*, edited by A. H. Halsey, Jean Floud and C. Arnold Anderson, Free Press, 1961.

cept of *authority* itself.[6] This means that the conceptual scheme presented here, cannot be regarded as being, what has been called, a 'theory of approach'.[7] That is, it could not be used, as it stands, as the design for an empirical investigation. The purpose of the discussion, and its scheme of concepts, is to bring some clarity to an area of interest, not, as yet, systematically investigated.

Power, Authority and Legitimation

The concepts of power, authority and legitimation are good examples of constructive concepts, in that they are defined, partly, in terms of one another.[8] *Power* refers to the ability to control the actions of others. *Legitimation*, in very general terms, refers to social approval. *Authority* is legitimized power.[9] An examination of the sources of the legitimation of the head teacher's authority gives an insight into the roots of his power over others.

In his typology of authority, Weber distinguished three important sources of legitimation. These were, legal/rational legitimation, affective legitimation, and legitimation by tradition.[10]

Legality of action is what is ordinarily implied by legitimacy. Much of the head teacher's power is legitimized in this way. Head teachers of maintained schools are bound by articles of government, which define, in a very general way, their duties.[11] Guidance in drawing up these articles was given in a White Paper, and most local education authorities have followed this guidance.[12] The head teacher is given control of the internal organization, management and discipline of the school. Any challenge to his authority in these

[6] Other examples of unitary concepts are, *class, role* and *bureaucracy.*

[7] Eric Hoyle, 'Organizational Analysis in the Field of Education', *Educational Research*, 7, 1965.

[8] F. Kerlinger, *Foundations of Behavioural Research*, Holt, Rinehart and Winston, 1964.

[9] *From Max Weber: Essays in Sociology*, translated, edited and introduced by H. H. Gerth and C. Wright Mills, Routledge, 1948.

[10] Op. cit., 9.

[11] M. M. Wells and P. S. Taylor, *The New Law of Education*, Sixth Edition, Butterworths, 1965.

[12] *Principles of Government in Maintained Secondary Schools*, HMSO, 1944.

spheres from subordinates within the school, or, indeed, from outsiders, may be met by reference to the legal establishment of that authority. Head teachers in non-maintained schools usually have a similar set of legal roots to their authority, in articles of government, contracts, covenants and foundations. In addition, head teachers, particularly those in maintained schools, may draw legal legitimation from the many circulars, reports and recommendations which come to them from the local authority administration, the inspectorate, the Department of Education and Science, and from the consultative committees of the Department. Some of these documents make imperative demands that the head teacher should take a particular course of action, e.g. to issue official permits to pupils who wish to cycle to school. Many more however merely recommend courses of action. The head teacher may choose to ignore many of these recommendations, but if he does begin to implement any of them in his school, he then may draw upon the original official document in support of his action.

Rationality is implied in legal legitimation. However, a rational belief in the value of an action can be an important source of legitimation for that action, without an accompanying legal or official codification. *Rational legitimation* of this kind usually derives from higher order social systems.[13] Thus the legitimation of a head teacher's arrangement of sixth-form studies derives, in part, from the universities and other forms of higher education, which many of the sixth formers eventually enter. The universities do not directly control the organization of the sixth form, but in drawing up their entrance requirements for various courses, impose a pattern on the schools that they draw their students from. Similar interactions may be observed between primary schools and grammar schools, between preparatory schools and public schools, between all secondary schools and the occupational structure. In general the head teacher of a lower order institution may refer to the expectations of the higher order institutions, as a justification for many of his actions.

Rational legitimation of the head teacher's authority may also be derived from other sources including the teachers in the school, and the parents of the pupils. Often this legiti-

[13] Talcott Parsons, *The Social System*, Free Press, 1952.

mation is latent and only manifests itself when a head teacher tries to introduce unacceptable changes. For example, it could be claimed that there is a rational belief in the value of mathematics as a subject for pupils to learn. Although a head teacher in a maintained school is legally authorized to arrange his own curriculum (with the exception of religious education, which must be included), he would be most unwise to run down or abolish the teaching of mathematics, because this action would not be legitimized by either teachers or parents.

Affective legitimation refers to the incidence of favourable sentiments, often of a non-rational nature, towards a certain course of action. Clearly the parents of pupils form an important source of this kind of legitimation. It is probable, for example, that the poor provision of sex education in this country is because there is little consensus of sentiments among parents towards this subject.[14] Although many official publications exist that urge the introduction of the studies on head teachers, it is significant that they do not compel him to do so.[15] This is an interesting instance of the relationship between legal and affective legitimation. A head teacher who wishes to introduce anything other than a concealed scheme of sex education, usually takes care to consult and inform the parents first.[16]

The importance of parental legitimation varies among schools. In general, the more the entry of pupils into the school is governed by parental choice, the more important this parental legitimation is to the head teacher. Thus it is very important in private schools, where parental disapproval could lead to the withdrawal of pupils, and possible economic ruin to a school without a protective trust or covenant, or a guaranteed proportion of pupils sponsored by the local education authority.

Among maintained schools, parental legitimation is likely to be important where the school has no formal mechanism for pupil entry, i.e. those that are usually called 'non-selective'.

[14] Michael Schofield, *The Sexual Behaviour of Young People*, Longmans, 1965.

[15] For example, 'Health in Education', *Educational Pamphlet* No. 49, HMSO, 1966.

[16] See for example, Albert Chanter, *Sex Education in the Primary School*, Macmillan, 1966.

A grammar school selects its pupils and then gives the parents the opportunity to accept or reject a place offered to their child. Since most parents accept, such selective schools may, to a large extent, assume that they also accept the means and ends of the school, although with differing degrees of understanding and knowledge of those means and ends.[17]

For the head teacher of a primary school, parental approval is usually more important. The esteem that a primary school receives from parents is based partly on its eleven-plus examination results. Many studies have shown that, keeping measured intelligence constant, the chances of success at eleven-plus are higher for children from middle-class homes, compared with those from working-class homes.[18] Thus a head teacher anxious to maintain and improve the esteem his school receives, must pay regard to the class-pattern of his recruitment of pupils. Many studies have shown that middle-class parents show more interest in their children's schools, and use their power of selectivity more often than working class parents.[19] A head teacher whose school is attractive to middle-class parents has his academic achievement problem well in hand. However, a head teacher who allows an active and articulate group of parents to decisively influence his organizational decisions, is in danger of suffering a reduction in esteem for his professional standing. This may be one of the reasons why some head teachers resist the formation of parent-teacher associations. (The head teachers of maintained schools appear to have the right to refuse the formation of such associations.) It is possible to envisage

[17] The rarity of refusing a grammar school place is reported in J. W. B. Douglas, *The Home and the School*, Macgibbon and Kee, 1964.

[18] J. E. Floud and A. H. Halsey, 'Intelligence Tests, Social Class, and Selection for Secondary Schools', *British Journal of Sociology*, 8, 1957.

J. W. B. Douglas, op. cit., 17.

Central Advisory Council Report, *15 to 18* (Crowther), HMSO, 1959 and 1960.

Prime Minister's Committee, *Higher Education* (Robbins), HMSO, 1963.

[19] Recent studies include: Jean Jones, 'Social Class and the Under Fives', *New Society*, No. 221, December, 1966, a report of the work of the University of London Institute of Education, Sociological Research Unit; and Roma Morton-Williams, Government Social Survey, 'Survey Among Parents of Primary School Children', Vol. 2, Central Advisory Council for Education, *Children and their Primary Schools* (Plowden), HMSO, 1967. It should be noted that no evidence exists to suggest that working class parents are less interested in their children; only in their children's schools.

the paradox of a school which is satisfactory from the point of view of the parents of its pupils, but where the authority of the head teacher is severely reduced, because effective power has passed into the hands of a small group of activist parents. Such a situation might exist in a favoured primary school in a mixed social area, or a University town.

Secondary modern schools in urban areas often compete among themselves for the same pupils. A head teacher whose school receives the approval of the middle-class and aspiring working-class parents in the area, will be able to recruit pupils who have a favourable chance of taking the educational opportunities offered by the school. To a large extent the situation is a self-fulfilling one, in that the 'good' school will recruit such pupils as will maintain, and even enhance, that reputation. This could be the situation in a system of non-selective comprehensive schools, if parental choice of schools were retained. Hence the action on the part of some local education authorities to constrain the recruitment procedure for their comprehensive schools by the use of the even distribution of ability cohorts.

The *traditional legitimation* of the head teacher's authority derives largely from the notions of the functions of the head teacher, which emerged during the second half of the nineteenth century, with the resurgence of the public schools and the emergence of a maintained system of secondary schools.[20] Even if parts of the traditional prescription of the head teacher's role are now being questioned, much of it is still retained since it has a congruence with the notion of the school we hold in our society. Thus the traditional expectation remains, that the head teacher should know all of his pupils. With the coming of larger schools, and the increasing difficulty of this ideal—expectation being met, there has been evolved a reformed house system and tutorial groups, in which this traditional head teacher function (however mythical its origins), has been fragmented and delegated to house-teachers and tutors concerned with the 'pastoral care' of groups of pupils.

Many more of the generally accepted activities of the school are legitimized by tradition. School uniforms, inter-school

[20] G. Baron, 'Some Aspects of the Headmaster Tradition', University of Leeds Institute of Education, *Researches and Studies*, 1956.

games competitions and house systems, are all good examples of such activities. Even where they are but poorly legitimated by favourable sentiments from pupils and even teachers, head teachers may insist on their continuing, by evoking tradition as legitimation. Traditional legitimation is essentially non-rational and is therefore not easily susceptible to modification by logical argument. An example there is the traditional insistence that small boys in primary schools wear short trousers even in very cold weather, despite their obvious discomfort and a significant incidence of cyanosis of the legs.

It is clear that the office of head teacher is one that is associated with a great deal of potential power. It is also clear that the use of this power is legitimized in diverse ways. The extent and diversity of this legitimation are usually effective constraints on the head teacher in the use of his power, so that his actions are mainly authoritative, and not simply exercises in pure power. Quite apart from these sources of legitimation, the power of the head teacher is constrained by some of the formal authority relationships he enters into with officials outside of the school. The precise authority relationships existing between a head teacher and his local authority, his governors and the inspectorate, are not often well defined. It is often the case that the nature of the relationship only becomes clear when the head teacher's actions do not receive official approval. Official sanctions against a head teacher are difficult to make because of the possibility of their affecting his staff and pupils. Any official sanction is likely to weaken the head teacher's authority within the school, and exacerbate the situation that first evoked the sanction. Mechanisms do exist to dismiss head teachers in maintained schools, but the incidence of such dismissals is very low. The existence of an appeal procedure against such a dismissal probably constrains local authorities, in that they do not welcome unfavourable publicity. Furthermore, the dismissal of a head teacher is the admission of a faulty selection procedure.

Whilst it is correct to refer to the head teacher as possessing a great deal of *autonomy*, it is not correct to refer to the head teacher as an *autocrat*. *Autonomy* refers to the ability to control one's own actions, and this head teachers clearly have. *Autocracy* refers to rule, controlling the behaviour of others, which does not relate to a higher or external authority.

This, head teachers do not have. Even they are not above the law with respect to their relationships with their pupils as children, or their teachers as men and women. Even those powerful headmasters of the late nineteenth century whom Cyril Norwood referred to as 'autocrats of autocrats', were ultimately responsible to someone for their actions.[21]

The Subordinates to the Head Teacher's Authority

The principal subordinates to the head teacher's authority are his teaching staff and his pupils. The extent of his authority not only enables him to possess a high degree of personal autonomy, but also to define the degree of autonomy of those subordinates. To this extent the head teacher may be said to make formal prescriptions of the organizational roles of his teachers and pupils. Of course the prescriptions may not be observed and the enacted roles be quite contrary to his expectations.[22]

The head teacher's control over his assistant teachers extends through time and space. He may decide which teacher takes which group of pupils at a particular time in a particular place. He usually has a most important part in selecting his staff. He may initiate the proceedings that lead to the dismissal of a teacher. No such formal mechanism exists in maintained schools for teachers to initiate a movement to get rid of a head teacher. Even the official route for communications with the governors or managers is through the head teacher. He may affect the pupil/teacher relationship in the formal learning situation by the way he allocates money for books and apparatus. In this way he may encourage or discourage educational experiments which require some capital outlay. He may directly affect the pupil/teacher relationship by actually entering classrooms, interrupting and taking over lessons. He may sit silently at the back of the classroom, or simply look through the door.

Not only does the head teacher play a decisive part in the appointment and dismissal of his teachers, he is also in a

[21] C. Norwood and A. H. Hope, *The Higher Education of Boys in England*, 1909.
[22] See D. J. Levinson, 'Role, Personality and Social Structure in the Organisational Setting', *Journal of Abnormal and Social Psychology*, 58, 1959.

position to influence a teacher's career prospects. This not only refers to his distribution of allowances for special responsibility and positions of heads of department, but also to the influence he has on the careers of his teachers when they leave, or attempt to leave, for other schools. A testimonial from the teacher's present head is sometimes obligatory when seeking a new post. The contents of that testimonial, however accurate, can be a critical factor in success.

Much of the power that head teachers have over their teaching staff is legitimized legally, by contracts and articles of government. Tradition has a contribution to make as well. But some things that a head teacher wishes his staff to do can only be accomplished if he receives their rational and affective approval. This certainly applies to any actions of the teachers within the classroom, where, in our society, the teacher is traditionally allowed a great deal of freedom. A head teacher who gets his way with an unwilling staff is really exercising power over them. In these circumstances teachers may resign. More often there is a compliance with the orders. The orders are carried out, but the teachers may do this in such a way as to signal their disposition towards their own forced actions, and the head teacher. These signals of role-distance will be quickly interpreted by the pupils, who may then undergo a changed orientation towards the head teacher.[23] Thus it is important for the head teacher to bear in mind the nice distinction between power and authority in his relations with his teaching staff. Ultimately, the exercise of power, without their legitimation, becomes dysfunctional.

The most numerous of the head teacher's role-relations are his pupils. His authority over them is wide in scope and very pervasive. He may control their actions in most spheres of their activities, at any time they are within the school, and anywhere within the school. He may use his power to regulate the length of their hair, where they may whistle or walk, even the colour of their underwear. His control may extend beyond the school, and outside of school hours. He may forbid the use of certain bus stops, purchases from certain shops, the removal of the school cap until a pupil reaches his front door.

[22] Erving Goffmann, *Encounters,* Bobs-Merrill, 1961, and 'Role-Distance', in *Sociological Theory: A Book of Readings*, edited by L. A. Coser and B. Rosenberg, Macmillan, 1964.

The powerful legal legitimation of the principle of *in loco parentis* creates the head teacher's authority over his pupils. There are few activities of a child that are not the concern of the 'wise parent', as we idealize this fictional role, in our society. In addition, the head teacher who gets on well with his pupils will receive their affective approval of his authority. The affective approval of pupils may also be influenced by their perceptions of their teachers' and their parents' orientations towards the head teacher. With older pupils the head teacher may receive a rational legitimation of his authority, when such pupils recognize the important influence the head may have on their educational and occupational destinies. The use of the head teacher's recommendations in the selection of jobs and places in further education, is a clear demonstration of his authority to such pupils. They may comply with his wishes, joining school clubs, doing what they perceive to be 'right things' to do, in order to secure a favourable recommendation.

There are a number of role-relations that the head teacher has within the school, where the authority relationship is not all well defined. In maintained schools, caretakers, and other plant-staff such as cleaners and visiting maintenance workers, are not appointed by the head teacher.[24] In their activities they have a kind of functional autonomy, but there are times when the head teacher must interact with them. In these circumstances, suggestions, rather than orders, often produce compliance more readily. Some caretakers will be well aware of the power they have over the head teacher. By wrongly arranging some chairs they could ruin a particular school function. Hence a situation found in some schools where access to the head teacher is guaranteed to the caretaker, even above senior teaching staff. In the extreme, the situation may arise where the head teacher actually goes to the caretaker for a consultation.

The head teacher's authority over the parents of his pupils is often latent and intermittent. The head teacher has the power to arrange his school to have different degrees of permeability to parents. The junior school head may request

---

[24] The authority relationship between the head teacher and the school secretary is not at all well defined either. This may contribute to the fantasies that gather around the relationship between the head teacher of a boys' school and his female secretary.

that they do not enter the playground when meeting their children from school. The Open Day may be used as a device to keep parents away from the school on every other day of the school year. In addition, the head teacher's authority over the parents may be mediated through the pupils. The imposition of a school uniform means that the head teacher effectively controls the parents' actions in the choice of their own children's clothing. The head teacher may transmit to his pupils concepts of behaviour and standards of taste which come into operation in the home. He may recommend certain television programmes, or urge that his pupils should go to Sunday school. Parents may unwillingly comply with his recommendations as relayed to them by their children, who are caught between the authority of the home and the school. A head teacher may also try to influence parents directly through a parent-teacher association. Here it should be recognized that his power is limited to influence, and does not become imperative.

There are, of course, limitations to the head teacher's authority over his role-relations, which preserve some autonomy for them. These limitations have been referred to already; the constraints of the sources of legitimation of his office and the operation of the common law. Over a period of years privately initiated court cases have helped to define the head teacher's authority, particularly his relationship with parents, and these have given some clarity to the concept of *in loco parentis*.[25]

Modes of Authority

Head teachers have the power to define, within very wide limits, their own role. They also have the power to define the roles of their subordinates, the teachers and pupils. The propagation of these prescribed roles is made through the formal social structure of the school, and the modes of social control used within the school. Since the head teacher is responsible for both the formal social structure of the school and the social control associated with the maintenance of that structure, a study of these becomes an examination of

[25] Several interesting cases are reported in *Teachers and the Law*, by G. Barrell, Methuen, 1966.

his mode of authority. The school in action is an expression of the head teacher's authority.

It is possible to distinguish three modes of the head teacher's authority, which express themselves in different kinds of social structures. These are, *bureaucratic authority*, *ritualistic authority*, and *charismatic authority*.[26] The role of any actual individual head teacher will probably contain elements of all three kinds of authority but it is convenient here to refer to the bureaucratic, ritualistic and charismatic head teachers as ideal-types.[27]

Bureaucratic Authority

The technical use of the term *bureaucracy* is in no sense pejorative. The common connotations of red tape and officialdom are not to be ignored, but the concept is used to describe much more.[28] Bureaucracies are organizations whose social structures are arranged for the rational distribution of time, space and resources, to accomplish certain rational functions.

Many elements of the school's organization are clearly bureaucratic. The time-table is an excellent example of the rational distribution of time, space and human resources. Syllabuses, curriculum, registers, official forms, school rules, tests and examinations and all modified written procedures, are essentially bureaucratic. Insofar as they subserve and organize such a structure, teachers and head teachers may be regarded as bureaucrats. Their careers certainly have many of the attributes of the career of the ideal-type bureaucrat. They are appointed to their positions, not elected or nominated. Appointment is dependent on the possession of specialized, technical qualifications. Their careers are full-time, life long and pensionable.

The authority structure within bureaucracies is hierarchical, and tends to be pyramidical. Clearly the head teacher is at the top of this power-pyramid. He is responsible for the

[26] These are derived from the discussion of authority by Max Weber, op. cit., 9.

[27] The Weberian concept of ideal-type is non-evaluative. It refers to a collection of features of an entity that are logically consistent and which render its existence possible. It does not refer to what is thought ought to be.

[28] See 'Bureaucracy', in *From Max Weber*, op. cit., 9.

official actions of his teaching staff, and through them the activities of the pupils. He has the responsibility for defining the official duties of his teachers and the allocation of responsibility. He may arrange a hierarchical stratum of heads of departments with some degree of control over the activities of members of their departments. The more specialized he expects his staff to be, the more bureaucratic his school is likely to become.

Clearly, the organization of a school in this bureaucratic way requires a technical, executive or managerial competence. The dysfunctions of bureaucracies arise when the rules and codes are not properly formulated or lack flexibility.[29] The hierarchical power structure may lead to distortion in the flow of communications. If a head of department is given some degree of responsibility for the competence of his departmental members, then he will tend to report their activities in a way that does not unfavourably reflect on his own competence in his duty.

The larger an organization grows, the more highly bureaucratized it tends to become.[30] The increase in the number of large schools in recent years has been accompanied by the emergence of the head teacher as an executive. Planning and clear decision-making are vital in a large school, whereas a tolerable degree of inefficiency is possible in a small school. In a small school a flow of less distorted information is possible, and it may be supplemented by a very efficient informal system of communication.

The bureaucratic authority of the head teacher clearly controls the activities of his teachers, but the bureaucratic social structure, and the system of social control it generates, functions primarily to regulate the behaviour of the pupils. In particular it regulates the social conditions of their formal learning processes; what they are taught, by whom they are taught, where and when they are taught. To a lesser extent a bureaucratic head teacher may regulate his pupils' behaviour outside the classroom by clearly formulated school rules, codified procedures relating to absence and lateness, the use of forms and written methods of communication. The breaking of rules or failure to follow a correct procedure may

[29] Peter M. Blau, *Bureaucracy in Modern Society*, Random House, 1956.
[30] Theodore R. Anderson and Seymour Warkov, 'Organizational Size and Functional Complexity', *American Sociological Review*, 26, 1961.

result in the operation of a set of codified sanctions, for example, being late may entail automatic detention, being late three times may bring an automatic caning.

In the school as a bureaucracy, the pupils may be regarded as the clients of the teachers and head teacher, acting as officials. The relationship between pupils and teachers will be, in certain respects, rather impersonal. In the operation of an efficient bureaucratic organization it is not possible to break rules and change procedures on the basis of the nature of the personal relationship between unequals in authority. A head teacher who allows certain pupils or teachers to flout rules on the basis of some special personal relationship they have with him, may find his bureaucratic authority no longer legitimized by other pupils and teachers, and that the whole elaborate structure of his school is seized with dysfunction.

The legitimation for the head teacher's bureaucratic authority is very powerful and is principally of the legal/rational type. It is possible for a head teacher to give fairly rational, explicit reasons for most of the bureaucratic procedures he uses. Often he may be able to produce official syllabuses and suggestions to support his actions. In maintained schools the salary structure of teachers, with its provision for head of department and special responsibility allowances, implies teacher-specialists and an attendant hierarchical authority structure. With the possible exception of the small private school that rejects examinations, and, so-called, 'formal learning', all schools have some bureaucratic features, and the authority of all head teachers has a bureaucratic component.

Ritualistic Authority

The term ritual is not necessarily used to refer to religious observance. Ritual refers to the use of rites, ceremonies, emblems and other symbolic devices.[31] Ritual has its own aesthetic and may be perpetuated and observed on this account only. However, the function of ritual is more often to be the symbolic representation of certain sacred things. Three important inter-related things are usually symbolized

[31] Emile Durkeheim, *The Elementary Forms of Religious Life*, translated by Joseph Ward Swain, Free Press, 1915.

in the ritual of the school.[32] Firstly, the ritual symbolizes those modes of behaviour that the school attempts to induct its pupils into. The use of distinctive ties and badges for members of school teams symbolizes the importance the school places on those activities and modes of behaviour implied in 'sportsmanship' and 'team-spirit'. Secondly, ritual may symbolize those cultural values the school attempts to transmit to its pupils. The plaques of scholarship winners' names in the hall symbolize the value the school places on learning and academic achievement. Thirdly, and perhaps most importantly, rituals symbolize the essential authority relationships within the school, and so act as a system of social control.

The traditional morning assembly may subserve certain religious functions and may be part of an essentially bureaucratic chain of communication, but more importantly, from the point of view of the school as an organization, it is a daily display of the authority relationships within the school. The head teacher, the holder of most authority, is on prominent display, often wearing the regalia of his office—his gown. Teachers and pupils stand in his presence unless permitted to sit. Teachers are placed separate but distinct, as are prefects. The pupils with the lower organizational status, the youngest, are placed at the front. Within age groups, the lower stream pupils stand in front of their more esteemed age-mates of the upper stream. The whole ceremony takes place in the school hall, saved, if possible, at great expense, exclusively for this daily ten-minute ritual. The routinized pattern of the ceremony emphasizes the continuity of the authority pattern on display from day to day. It is significant that in maintained schools the school assembly must usually begin the school day. It would be of little use to remind pupils of the authority relationships within the school at the end of the day. In the day school the morning assembly is a daily reminder to the child that he is now a pupil.

The school assembly illustrates both the consensual and differentiating functions of ritual. The assembly is an attempt to weld the pupils and teachers into a single moral community, distinct from other parts of society. The assembly

[32] Willard Waller, *The Sociology of Teaching*, Science Editions, 1965—first published 1932.

Basil Bernstein et al., 'Ritual in Education', *Philosophical Transactions of the Royal Society of London*, Series B. No. 772, Vol. 251, 1966.

may have varying degrees of success in achieving this consensus and differentiation. The very sacredness of the ceremony, some of which is borrowed from its religious content, may prevent pupils questioning the authority relationships it symbolizes. However, for pupils who already question that authority, the daily reminder of its power is likely to exacerbate the situation, reducing their involvement in the school and their compliance with the school's standards of behaviour.

The head teacher who relies upon ritualistic control is likely to have a system of prefects, to act as general models of school-accepted behaviour and agents of social control. He may induct them in a ceremony in which the passing of some of his authority to them is symbolized by his shaking hands with them, and the award of a distinctive tie or badge. The ritualized head teacher can delegate authority in this way. Even teachers may use the threat of such a head teacher to exercise social control in the classroom.

Ritualistic head teachers are likely to support a house system even where the basis of the pupils' allegiance to the house is largely fictional. Such head teachers are likely to impose a carefully defined school uniform so that the acceptance of his authority is symbolically enacted when the pupil dresses at home in the morning. It may of course be emphatically rejected at the end of the school day. The authority of the ritualistic head is often expressed in the use of *coercive control*. Coercive control has been defined as control by the deprivation of 'basic needs'. However, it is clear that the definition of basic needs depends on the *pain threshold* of the individual in question.[33] For a pupil who is highly involved in the school, a mere word of disapproval from a teacher may be a painful experience. It is also clear that although corporal punishment may have a coercive element it is also heavily ritualized. It is administered by the head teacher, or a delegate of his authority, using a ritual instrument on a ceremonial part of the pupil's body. The number of strokes is ritually defined; one, two, four or six, never three or five. The whole ceremony is usually carried out in the head teacher's sacred study. It may end with a moral sermon and pious exhortation.

The ritualistic head teacher is likely to be rather formal in

[33] Amitai Etzioni, *A Comparative Analysis of Complex Organisations*, Free Press, 1961.

his face-to-face relationships with his staff and pupils, practising a great deal of *social distance*.[34] In many ways he tries to conceal the *self* within his role.[35] Any hint that such a head was fallible and 'human' might detract from his ritualistic authority. To take morning assembly with odd socks on might be disastrous. Such a head teacher is likely to eat his meals alone and to suffer much role-isolation. He may emphasize the sacred quality of his authority by making sixth-form religious education his only teaching commitment. He is likely to be all the more effective in being so little seen.

Ritualistic authority is likely to be found in schools that are highly stratified. Virtually all British schools are *age-stratified*, that is, the pupils are arranged in chronological age groups. Many are also *ability-stratified*, usually by forms of streaming. In the stratified school, rituals will be used to mark off age and learning groups, differentiating these groups, creating consensus within them. The distribution of symbolic privileges and organizational status are the commonest devices used.[36] Older pupils may be allowed into dinner first; the A stream before the B stream. Older pupils may be allowed in their form-rooms at break times, older girls may be allowed to wear nylon stockings. Informal variations on the school uniform and minor violations of the school rules may be officially ignored in older pupils. A boy's patterned shirt or suede shoes, a little discreet make-up on a girl never seen. Individually these privileges, often really alleviations of deprivation, may seem trivial, but as they are perpetuated every day they often assume great significance for some pupils.

Rituals are used to mark off groups of persons on the basis of their imputed similarities. It is necessary to ignore or deny the differences that exist within a ritually maintained group if consensus is to be obtained. The ritualistic head teacher is likely to take the view that the cognitive ability of his pupils is relatively fixed and not easily susceptible to change. He may also believe that their other qualities have only a limited plasticity. Clearly, a head teacher of a selective school must accept the general validity and reliability of the pupil selection

[34] See Waller, op. cit., 32.

[35] For the conception of the 'self', see C. H. Cooley, *Human Nature and the Social Order*, Scribners, 1902.

[36] The distribution of privilege is discussed by Erving Goffman, 'The Characteristics of Total Institutions', in *Complex Organisations*, edited by Amitai Etzioni, Holt, Rinehart and Winston, 1965.

procedure used by the school. Thus ritualistic authority is more likely to be found in grammar schools rather than secondary modern schools. Since the legitimation of ritualistic authority is largely traditional, it is also more likely to be found in the older established schools, including public schools. Head teachers of new schools may try to establish a spurious set of traditions by the imposition of an elaborate system of empty rituals. Here the attempt is to create a separate identity for the school, and to imply that although the authority of the head teacher is new its continuance is assured.

Charismatic Authority

Charismatic authority refers to the use of the power of personal qualities to influence the actions of others. These personal qualities are supposed to exist independently of the office of the person exercising *charisma*. In the case of a charismatic head teacher, the accession of office may allow these special qualities to be recognized.[37] Charismatic authority is limited in that its influence must be direct, between 'leader' and 'follower', and cannot be mediated by others, unlike ritualistic or bureaucratic authority. Charismatic head teachers are therefore likely to be most effective in small schools. In a large school such a head teacher will find it difficult to exert his influence on all of his pupils. He may therefore try to convert his teachers to his own particular ideology. He may select new staff on the basis of their agreement with that ideology.

The ideologies of head teachers may be widely variable. The ideology may be one that relates to a social philosophy which entails the propagation of certain organizational features. An example may be the embracement of the principle of educational quality and the belief that it may be achieved through the propagation of non-streaming. In general it may be said that the charismatic head teacher wishes to promote social change. He may wish to change his pupils in a particular way, or he may wish to preserve in them qualities that he believes are essential but vulnerable. By changing or preserving certain qualities in his pupils he may hope to

[37] Etzioni makes the distinction between *achieved* and *ascribed* charisma, op. cit., 33.

initiate social change in the world outside the school. He may sometimes be the visionary of a new society.

A desire for social change often implies a special view of certain human qualities. A charismatic head teacher may believe that cognitive ability is not fixed and is susceptible to change, that each pupil has unique individual qualities that are valuable and should be preserved or even fostered. Such a head will arrange the social structure of his school to be highly differentiated, that is, it will be marked by non-streaming or a system of subject setting with free inter-set mobility. In a differentiated school the emphasis is on the individual pupil, not on groups of pupils with imputed similarities. Rituals are used to mark off groups and to deny certain individual differences, and so are not appropriate in such a school. The newly appointed charismatic head teacher is likely to progressively deritualize his school, reducing formality, addressing his pupils by their first names, modifying the prefectorial system. He is likely to be permissive about school uniforms, and may abolish corporal punishment. He may also abolish the house system, replacing it with a tutorial system of pastoral care. In the differentiated school the head teacher cannot be a ritualistic figure. He will tend to leave off his gown, eat with his teachers, and address them, too, by their first names. He may take on a substantial teaching load, often taking the least able pupils.

A charismatic head teacher may often promote the democratic government of his school, which entails the participation of teachers and pupils in the running of the school, and, more importantly, in decision making.[38] He may run a staff council on a regular basis, and, renouncing the use of the veto, allow real decisions to be made by majority approval. Many schools have pupils' representatives meetings, but the charismatic head is likely to give such bodies of pupils a little real power. Often this is the power to regulate pupil behaviour and the power to use sanctions for the breaking of school rules. It is the rare head teacher who allows his pupils to make decisions about academic or pedogogical matters. Any head teacher must take care that in the process of democrati-

[38] A discussion of democratization of organizations is to be found in *The Social Psychology of Organisations*, by Daniel Katz and Robert L. Kahn, Wiley, 1966.

zation, with the sharing of power with his erstwhile subordinates, he does not diminish his own authority to the point of ineffectiveness. Even when he has allowed others into the decision making processes, he is still responsible for the outcomes of those decisions.

The legitimation of charismatic authority is derived from the allegiance and response of the 'followers' of the charismatic 'leader'. The charismatic head teacher seeks the emotional approval of all his role-relations; his staff, his pupils and their parents. Because his power depends on personal influence he will try to interact with them as frequently as possible. Social control within his school will depend on the use of appeal, reason, the manipulation of approval and degree of positive response; all face-to-face techniques. It may be necessary, in a large school, for the head teacher to use a system of bureaucratic control in order to maintain a highly differentiated system of learning units, even where such bureaucratization and its attendant impersonality, is contrary to his essential ideology.

The head teacher who wishes to change the traditional social structure of his school must pay careful regard to the legitimation of the parents' approval. Many private 'experimental' schools, recruit their pupils on the basis of their parents' agreement with the ideology of the school and its head teacher. Much of a pupil's acceptance of the authority of the head teacher can be related to his understanding of his parents' acknowledgment of that authority. It is possible that the alleged distinctive qualities of some experimental schools derive as much from the unusual home backgrounds of their pupils, as the schools themselves.

In the maintained sector of education, charismatic head teachers are likely to be found in non-selective schools, especially comprehensive schools, since at this stage the comprehensive principle is still ideologically espoused, and comprehensive schools still regarded by many as potential agencies of social change. Often such schools have a high proportion of pupils from working class homes. Since there is a tendency for many working class parents to delegate responsibility for their child to the school, the charismatic head teacher may not have to depend on their legitimation. However, it is likely that he will recognize the important influence of a pupil's home on his school experience, and will try to engage parents in their children's education.[39] He will arrange his school to be easily permeable to parents. He may actively encourage them to see him, even without an appointment. He may try to engage their interest in their own homes by calling on them, or by persuading his teachers to do so. Whereas the ritualistic head teacher's Open Day will tend to be an idealized and often fictionalized representation of the school's work, the charismatic head teacher will invite parents into classrooms during authentic teaching sessions.

Charisma was originally used to refer to the personal power of individuals outside organizations. Charisma referred to power used to promote social change and would therefore not be susceptible to organizational routinization.[40] However, it is possible to defend the use of the term with reference to head teachers, in that they have a high degree of autonomy in defining their own role, and have the power to extensively modify the social structure of their schools. But there may come a time when the new ideology is generally accepted, when the desired-for social change has been accomplished. At this time the prophet becomes a priest, and charisma becomes routinized, even to the point of ritualization. It is not surprising that a few head teachers become apostles of change, and embrace the ideology of change as valuable for its own sake, as well as a preservation against the extinction of their own charisma.

Leadership and Authority

The concept of *leadership* within an organization is a difficult one to define.[41] Leadership, in head teachers, is often used to refer to charismatic qualities. It is sometimes used to refer to a head teacher who is efficient in the role of an executive or ritualistic figure. Leadership may refer to what has been called an 'influential increment'; something extra that is not part of the formally prescribed role of the head teacher.[42] Here, perhaps, the reference is to the *style* of the head teacher, the way he is able to prevent conflict by the use of evasion

[39] For class differences in parents' attitude to the school, see Jean Jones, op. cit., 19, and Basil Bernstein and Douglas Young, 'Social Class Differences in Conception and Uses of Toys', *Sociology*, 1, 1967.

[40] Weber, op. cit., 9.

[41] See Katz and Kahn, op. cit., 37.

[42] Katz and Kahn, op. cit., 37, p. 302.

tactics, such as avoidance and polite rituals of etiquette. Some head teachers are adept at the use of discretion and secrecy, the calculated leakage of information, and feigned ignorance. Others use humour, banter and irony. There exists a whole cabinet of these tricks for use in interpersonal behaviour.[43] Most head teachers use some of them. Where they are used successfully by a head teacher to support his authority, they may form part of the so-called leadership quality. This is especially true if he successfully initiates a difficult change, or solves an unexpected problem.

Variation in Authority

It is a truism to say that no two head teachers are alike in their authority. The three components or aspects of authority described here will vary in importance among head teachers. It has already been indicated that few head teachers can avoid the use of bureaucratic authority. However, schools may be bureaucratized to different extents, and in different ways. It would be tempting to postulate that the ritualistic and charismatic authorities represented the extremes of a continuum. Most head teachers use both kinds of authority, so they are certainly not dichotomous. There are many forms of ritualistic and charismatic authority. All established schools have a heritage of unique ritual, and a distinct cultural element that is bound up in that ritual. This might be an emphasis on music or a particular sport. The underlying ideologies of charismatic authority do vary. Rejection of examinations, and social service in the local community, are examples of ideas that may condition the precise nature of a head teacher's charismatic authority.

Quite apart from the relative importance of their different modes and styles of authority, head teachers vary in their effectiveness. There are many very efficient head teachers, but there are those who cannot construct a workable time-table, others who are figures of fun to their pupils and staff. There are head teachers who aspire to charisma but have no followers.

[43] Ronald G. Corwin, *A Sociology of Education*, Appleton-Century-Crofts, 1965, Chapter 10, 'Interpersonal Relations in Education'.

Authority and Social Change

In modern industrialized societies cultural change is the norm. The economic well-being of our society depends on rapid and continuous technical advances. The rapid, continuous changes in our material culture affect education in two important ways. Firstly, it is recognized that technical advance depends on a supply of appropriately educated people. Secondly, changes in our material culture lead to changes in our non-material culture.[44] It is necessary to have under almost continuous review those values which guide our actions, because the environment in which these actions take place is continuously changing. A changing world demands a changing way of life.

The continuous review of our social values, and the behaviour related to those values, means that the traditional elements of our culture are now more often questioned and sometimes rejected. The ritualistic authority of the head teacher is legitimated by tradition, and is now, more than ever before, questioned, and there are signs that it is in the process of modification.

The technical advances in medicine and birth control techniques have both contributed to the continuing fall in family size. The smaller family has undoubtedly been associated with an increase in parents' concern, for what may often be, their only son or daughter. Parents, as a source of legitimation for the head teacher's authority, have become more important, and increasingly approve the kind of authority structure which appears to allow their children to have as happy and successful a school experience as possible. To some extent the wish of parents that the individual needs and qualities of their children should be recognized in their education, is in conflict with the demands made on the educational system by our pluralistic work structure, which increasingly presses a selective function on to the school. The head teacher is often caught in the centre of this conflict. It requires a great deal of skill, in the use of his authority, to continue to receive full and wide legitimation of his power.

[44] William F. Ogburn and Meyer F. Nimkoff, *A Handbook of Sociology*, 5th edition, Routledge, 1964.

22

A. W. BATES[1]

The Planning of the Curriculum[*]

My previous work with the National Foundation for Educational Research took me round 50 comprehensive schools in England and Wales, to study the way they were internally administered. As an ex-teacher myself, I was not altogether surprised at the variety of the schools themselves, nor at the variety of ways in which they were administered. These differences reflected differences in policy and personality, and that is no bad thing. What did surprise and even alarm me, however, were the enormous differences found in the approach to what I took to be mainly a technical matter, namely the way policy regarding the curriculum was decided upon, and turned into practice through the school time-table. (Note that I am talking here about the method of reaching decisions and converting them into action—not about the decisions themselves.)

There are few areas where there is only one 'right' way of doing something, but there are usually some ways which are clearly seen to be much better than others, and I would have thought that over the years, by trial and error and the gradual accumulation of shared experience, an efficient technique of designing and implementing school academic policy would have emerged. Well, unless I went to a particularly unusual selection of schools, or unless my observations were very much distorted—and neither of these seemed likely from the information I gathered on my visits about other areas of school life—then each school had worked out its own indi-

[*] [From *Headmasters' Association Review*, Vol. LXX, No. 215, July 1972.]
[1] Thanks are due to the NFER for permission to use information first published in Monks (1970) and Bates (1971).

vidual approach to the problem with apparently little relationship to what was going on in other schools. This glorious individualism however rarely resulted in a procedure which took account of the requirements of all interested parties—parents, pupils, staff, and the school itself, as an entity. In short, few schools had come up with a good method of planning the curriculum.

There was evidence of all kinds to back up this statement —for instance, 26 schools gave information about when the time-table was *planned* to be finished (apart from minor adjustments). In eight schools this would be during the summer holidays, and in another nine schools it was hoped to finish the time-table by the last day of the summer term (an aspiration in fact rarely achieved). Of the nine schools with over 1,250 pupils for which information was available, two needed the whole of the summer term actually to compile the time-table once major policy decisions had been made, three managed it in about five to eight weeks, while four were able to compile it in less than five weeks. In 31 schools one person compiled the time-table, yet in the 19 schools where more than one person worked on the time-table, there was no evidence to show that this resulted in the time-table being compiled more quickly or thoroughly.

The most convincing evidence however came from those who actually compiled the time-table (usually the deputy head—32 out of 50 schools). I asked them to outline the procedures which led up to the construction of the time-table, or were necessary before it could be constructed. It soon became clear that when the timing or order of certain procedures changed, their significance or function altered considerably, and that procedures that were considered essential in some schools were completely omitted in others. It was as if there was only time for x procedures, but there was a need for at least $x+1$, and what was dropped depended on the relative importance attached to the various procedures by individual heads.

The fact that in these schools no depository of traditional wisdom was shared or acknowledged regarding curriculum planning worried me. Planning the total curriculum of a small school has not generally appeared to be a major problem in the past (although the actual decisions that have to be made are often difficult), because contact between all teachers

Fig. 22.1

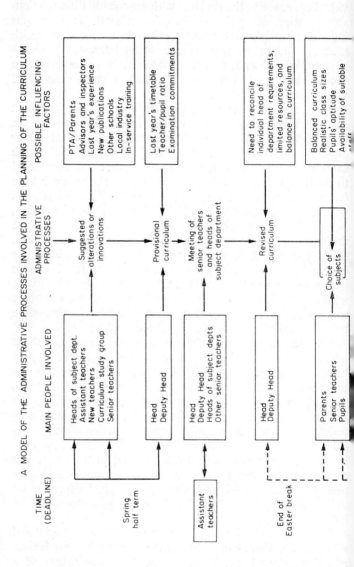

A MODEL OF THE ADMINISTRATIVE PROCESSES INVOLVED IN THE PLANNING OF THE CURRICULUM

TIME (DEADLINE)	MAIN PEOPLE INVOLVED	ADMINISTRATIVE PROCESSES	POSSIBLE INFLUENCING FACTORS
	Heads of subject dept. Assistant teachers New teachers Curriculum study group Senior teachers	Suggested alterations or innovations	PTA/Parents Advisors and inspectors Last year's experience New publications Other schools Local industry In-service training
Spring half term	Head Deputy Head	Provisional curriculum	Last year's timetable Teacher/pupil ratio Examination commitments
	Head Deputy Head Heads of subject depts Other senior teachers	Meeting of senior teachers and heads of subject department	
	Assistant teachers		
End of Easter break	Head Deputy Head	Revised curriculum	Need to reconcile individual head of department requirements, limited resources, and balance in curriculum
	Parents Senior teachers Pupils	Choice of subjects	Balanced curriculum Realistic class sizes Pupils' aptitude Availability of suitable staff

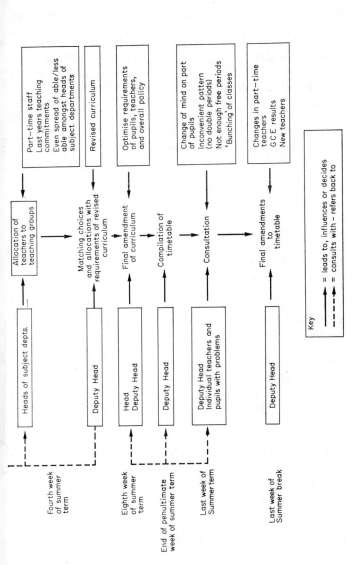

Part-time staff
Last years teaching commitments
Even spread of able/less able amongst heads of subject departments

Revised curriculum

Optimise requirements of pupils, teachers, and overall policy

Change of mind on part of pupils
Inconvenient pattern (no double periods)
Not enough free periods
'Bunching' of classes

Changes in part-time teachers
G.C.E. results
New teachers

Allocation of teachers to teaching groups

Matching choices and allocations with requirements of revised curriculum

Final amendment of curriculum

Compilation of timetable

Consultation

Final amendments to timetable

Heads of subject depts.

Deputy Head

Head
Deputy Head

Deputy Head

Deputy Head
Individual teachers and pupils with problems

Deputy Head

Fourth week of summer term

Eighth week of summer term

End of penultimate week of summer term

Last week of Summer term

Last week of Summer break

Key

⟶ = leads to, influences or decides

---- = consults with - refers back to

is relatively easy and frequent, and the range of subjects that can be offered is of necessity limited. Nor is it such a task in schools with a fairly homogeneous intake of pupils. In large comprehensive schools, however, it is obvious that planning the curriculum is—or should be—a major administrative task, because a wide range of differing, sometimes competing, objectives must be reconciled. The number of teachers may exceed 100, making communications difficult, yet the decisions reached must, as far as possible, suit the needs of pupils of all kinds. It seems important therefore that there should be some plan of campaign, logically worked out but tied closely to experience and what is practicable, which sets out to meet, or at least consider, the requirements of all interested parties. My strongly held opinion—and I would not like to rank it more highly than that—after having talked to those responsible for curriculum planning, in 50 schools, is that the whole process was never, in fact, explicitly worked out in advance, and consequently many crucial decisions affecting the lives and careers of individual children were wrongly made, either by accident or by default.

What I have tried to do therefore is to build up a model which incorporates most of the features found collectively in the 50 schools—but never all in one school—and structure these features in such a way that the necessary logical sequence of the processes and the constraints of time and demands on teachers derived from the interviews are all incorporated. In other words, I have set out in Fig. 22.1 a theoretical model derived from the data supplied during interviews, which, while reflecting no one school, nevertheless demonstrates clearly the kind of processes involved in the planning of the total curriculum of a comprehensive school. The various stages are discussed below.

(a) Suggested Alterations or Innovations

These might come from many sources, but primarily from individual heads of subject departments. Some schools in the sample had set up a curriculum study group, which met at intervals throughout the school year. In one school, this consisted of ten staff, appointed by the head, and included the deputy head, the three heads of school sections, and six heads of major subject departments. This appeared to me to be an excellent opportunity for pupil participation in policy-making. One or two sixth formers—particularly those contemplating teaching as a career—might be appointed or elected to be members of a curriculum study group. Thus not only would the views of pupils be heard at an early planning stage, but the hard realities of putting ideas into practice would be brought home to their representatives. A curriculum study group might take a topic such as whether to stream or not, examine relevant literature in detail, take advice from interested staff, send one or more representatives to another school where non-streaming, for instance, was practised and work out in detail the possible time-table consequences of changes. The study group would then report to the head, who in any case would probably have been kept in touch all along, and the group might suggest possible changes. Changes might also be suggested by new staff which may require allocation of more periods to their subject (and consequently more staff). Staff who had been away on courses or interested by new publications might also want to introduce changes affecting the curriculum.

Pressure for change may also come from outside the school. For instance, a large local firm may set up its own training scheme for school leavers, which might affect the provision of commercial sources in the fourth and fifth years; a nearby girls' school may lack suitably advanced science laboratories, and may wish to share resources; a college of further education may wish to avoid duplication of courses with the school; county council advisors or Her Majesty's Inspectors may be keen to implement new courses affecting the balance of the curriculum; or parents, through the parent-teacher association, may express their wish for the provision of more or earlier sex education for the pupils.

The head ultimately has the responsibility for sifting and assessing all these proposals, and presumably would spend much time discussing them individually with staff concerned. It will be seen, however, from Fig. 22.1 that if major changes are to be implemented in the following academic year, and are to be discussed fully with the people concerned, there is a deadline by which all these proposals must be submitted, to enable the head to assess them, and to see how the various proposals would interact, and their effect on the existing curriculum. In a large school, this date would probably not be later than the Spring half-term, if all the various processes identified in Fig. 22.1 are to be carried out.

(b) Production of Provisional Curriculum

On the basis of the various proposals put to the head, and the demands of the existing curriculum, the head and the deputy head would draft a provisional curriculum (perhaps incorporating a summary of the curriculum study group's work for the year). This would be drafted in a form to encourage discussion, with various alternatives set out. For instance, the effect of introducing a change in one area on other areas of the curriculum should be stated. This would be a tentative document, based on what is realistic, and therefore governed by the limiting factors of likely staff/pupil ratios, and the subjects to which the schools are already committed (e.g. examination courses). The help of the deputy head would be required, because of the role he would play later, and because of his knowledge of the practical difficulties in time-tabling. This document would then be circulated to the heads of subject departments and the heads of school sub-sections in time for them to study it fully before a meeting.

(c) Meeting of Heads of Subject Departments and Other Senior Staff

This meeting, to discuss the following year's curriculum, was held in nearly all schools in the sample. Its timing, however, and therefore its impact on determining the nature of the curriculum, varied considerably from school to school. At one extreme, the meeting occurred very late in the process, and acted merely as an endorsement of firm decisions already taken by the head or senior 'cabinet'. At the other extreme, the meeting was the first stage of the process, where ideas were asked for, or offered by the head for discussion. The head then went away, and, perhaps after discussion with individual heads of department, produced a curriculum which may or may not have reflected the views of heads of department.

In the model, however, proposals involving changes in the curriculum are put forward individually quite early in the school year, and documented in the form of a provisional curriculum, before this general meeting of senior staff and heads of subject departments. This would allow time for heads of subject departments to consider fully the implications of the proposals and consult, where necessary, with their departmental staff. Thus, the meeting itself would provide the head and deputy head with some idea of the strength of informed opposition or support for the various proposals.

(d) Production of Revised Curriculum

The head and the deputy head would then draw up a revised curriculum, incorporating new proposals where necessary. Inevitably, not all heads of subject department requests could —or should—be met, if a balanced curriculum is to be produced, and in any case, as already mentioned, the head is open to pressures from other than just heads of subject departments. The revised curriculum would be much more precise than the provisional curriculum, and where choice of subjects is to be made by pupils, the revised curriculum would indicate the range of subjects available to pupils. (In a large school, this range may nevertheless be very wide.) Pupils would then be informed what subjects they can choose from, and heads of subject departments would be informed what teaching commitments they are likely to have to meet within their departments.

(e) Choice of Course or Subjects

It could be argued that in a comprehensive education system, the most important decision made either by the school or by the pupils and their parents is which subjects or course to choose, and what level of examination (GCE, CSE, RSA, etc.) to work for. Reversing a decision once a course has begun can be very difficult, so a 'wrong' decision can have very serious and far-reaching consequences for the individual pupil. It is not surprising therefore that in 20 of the 48 schools for which adequate information was available, every pupil was interviewed individually about choice of subjects or courses by some senior member of staff. For most subjects and in most schools, major decisions were made when the pupils were about fourteen years old and again when they were about sixteen years old (i.e. towards the end of the third and fifth years). However, in a few cases some decisions, such as whether or not to take a second foreign language, were made even earlier than the third year.

It is interesting to note therefore that careers advice was usually given during the fourth and fifth years, *after* choice of courses had been made. While it was not possible to determine in my enquiry how much consideration was given to a career when pupils were advised about choice of subjects, it was clear that, except in most of the 11 schools in the sample with strong house systems, advice on careers was usually given by different staff from those who gave advice on choice of subjects.

As in the case of careers advice and care of the new intake, individual interviewing by senior teachers of every pupil concerning choice of subjects was more likely to occur in schools with strong subdivisions (14 out of 25)—and hence in larger schools—than in schools weakly sub-divided or not subdivided at all (6 out of 23). In 15 of the 28 schools where senior teachers did not individually interview all pupils, subject or form teachers were reported to have been responsible for this by the senior teachers interviewed. In these schools, only problems came through to senior teachers. Table 22.1 shows the involvement of senior teachers in advising pupils about choice of courses.

It became apparent during the interviews that in general it was not clear whose responsibility it was to advise pupils on choice of subjects in some of the schools where all pupils were not interviewed individually by senior teachers. Indeed, in these schools it was difficult to ascertain whether in fact individual advice was considered necessary or even a responsibility of the school. Certainly, individual advice on subjects and courses was in some schools left entirely to an ad hoc approach, and consequently, a comprehensive system of advice is a deliberate feature of the model.

Individual advice to pupils would be preceded by a parents' meeting or meetings, where choices would be explained. Each pupil would then be individually interviewed by a senior member of staff (house master, year master, senior mistress, etc.). Parents would also be able to attend the pupils' interviews, if an appointment system was used. This is feasible even in large schools. The model allows for a four-week period during which interviews could take place. In a school

Table 22.1

Number of Schools where Senior Teachers were Involved in Advice on Choice of Subjects

Administrative process	Head	Deputy Head	Senior master/ mistress	Head of school section	Head of House	Head of Year
All or most pupils individually	4	5	3	2	7	2
All pupils in classes or groups	—	3	1	1	—	—
Problems only	23	10	6	2	2	1
Aspiring sixth formers only	4	5	1	—	—	—
Very little involved in any process	18	23	29	1	1	3
TOTAL NUMBER OF SCHOOLS (for which information was available or relevant)	49	46	40	6	10	6

with 12 house staff, and 300 third-formers and 300 fifth-formers requiring advice (and it is unlikely that all fifth-formers would want advice at this point), each house teacher would have to advise about 12 to 15 pupils a week for four weeks—a maximum of three per day.

After interview, pupils would then make their choice, which would be passed directly to the deputy head, who would collate them. Some schools, particularly small schools, preferred choice of subject to be the first process in curriculum planning, asking fifth-formers what they wanted to do in the sixth form, given a free choice, and working back from there to the rest of the curriculum. However, many heads felt that experience from previous years provided a fairly accurate guide to the numbers likely to opt for each subject. (In one school the senior master analysed the choices made in the last four or five years and made a projection for the coming academic year.) These heads felt that further revisions could always be made to the time-table at a later stage in the process to accommodate any unexpected choices.

If four weeks are to be allowed for ensuring that all relevant pupils are properly advised, the revised curriculum would have to be ready by the beginning of the summer term, at the latest, to allow enough time after pupils have made their choice for the compilation of the time-table, and the other necessary activities that follow. On the other hand, many schools felt that the later pupils made their choice in the school year, the better, to prevent loss of interest in subjects being 'dropped' in the following year from affecting the pupils' work and behaviour. In any case, the revised curriculum would be difficult to complete in many schools before the end of March, since it is not until then that schools are informed by their local education authority of their quota of staff for the following academic year. Thus, it would seem likely that the parents' meetings would be in the first week of the summer term, and advice to pupils would take place over the first four weeks of that term.

(f) Provisional Allocation of Staff to Teaching Groups

Information was available from 34 schools on the deployment of staff. Within certain general constraints, this was usually decided upon within subject departments by the head of subject department (29 schools). Thus, in the model, heads of subject departments would be asked to suggest during the same four-week period how the staff who teach in their department might be allocated to the various teaching groups proposed in the revised curriculum. At the same time, requests for allocations of specialist rooms for staff and teaching groups, and for other special requirements, such as double periods, would also be made by heads of subject department. All these requests would be forwarded to the deputy head. The earliest time that this could be done for practical reasons would probably be the first week in April, since schools are likely to know by then their quota of staff for the coming year. The latest time for heads of departments to submit their requests would be the fourth week of the summer term.

(g) Matching Choices and Allocations to the Revised Curriculum

Having received over a four-week period choice of subjects

from pupils, and staff and room allocation requests from heads of subject departments, the deputy head would then be in a position to match the various pupils' choices and staff allocations with the revised curriculum. This would herald for the deputy head a period of intense consultation with pupils with 'awkward' choices, with heads of subject departments and individual subject teachers whose requirements cannot be met, and with the head, where departure from the revised curriculum seems necessary. This period would extend into the eighth week of the summer term, culminating in the head and deputy head making final amendments to the revised curriculum.

(h) Compilation of the Time-table

With regard to the technique of compiling a time-table, each school in the sample appeared to have its own method, although most relied heavily on pencil, rubber, and large sheets of paper. Manufactured time-table boards were used less than one would have expected, mainly because of their high cost, but also because teachers were not generally trained in using them. Although the compilation of the time-table is a major problem in many schools, very little has been published on this subject. Lewis (1961) discusses the decisions involved in determining the curriculum and some techniques of time-tabling. Davies (1968) has developed an interesting 'language' or shorthand for handling time-tabling decisions, and the Local Government Operational Research Unit (1967) surveyed the possibility of computers constructing time-tables. The latter study certainly indicated the possibilities in the future of a computer carrying out the routine time-tabling work for a number of schools, but at the moment computer-time-tabling would be extremely expensive in the case of large schools, and there are severe practical difficulties in computer-time-tabling schools where the time-table is 'student-based' rather than 'course-based', that is, where numbers of pupils each have a unique time-table, as sometimes occurs in schools with a large range of subjects to choose from. It is clear from the literature, however, that it is important to set up priorities for the order in which requirements are inserted, the most difficult requirements being entered first.

Whatever the possibilities of computer-time-tabling in the future, at the moment in each secondary school in the country, teachers set out every year to tackle the same kind of problem, guided only by their previous experience or by trial and error. There is obviously a great need for proper training in time-tabling techniques, based on research and wider dissemination of current practices.

In the model the length of time given for the construction of the time-table is between three and five weeks. This was all that was needed in 5 of the 13 schools with more than 1,200 pupils. However, certain pre-requisites are necessary before compilation of the time-table begins, if it is to be completed in this time:

(i) all the major decisions on the curriculum must have been made;
(ii) staff must have been fully consulted about these decisions;
(iii) the compiler must be freed of all other duties, including teaching, during this period.

The time-table is also more likely to be completed in time if it is begun in outline about half-way through the preceding process of matching choices and allocations to the revised curriculum, and if the deputy head is assisted with the room time-table, checking, and the production of individual time-tables for teachers and classes.

Heads and deputy heads gave some interesting reasons for condensing the compilation of the time-table into a comparatively short time towards the end of the summer term. Some heads felt strongly that teachers—and particularly newly appointed teachers—should know their commitments for the following year before the long summer holiday, so that they could use, if they wished, part of their holiday for preparation for the coming academic year. The view was also expressed that it was important for staff to know their commitments for the following year before the end of the summer term so that there was time for alterations to the time-table to be made if these commitments were completely unsuitable. Some schools even ran their 'new' time-table in the last week of term to discover snags and errors, so that the new academic year would begin smoothly. On the other hand, it was felt important to leave the choice of subjects as late as possible in the school year. Beginning the construction of the time-table any earlier would force all the other processes to begin earlier too.

Finally, it will be noted from the model that the deputy head is not only responsible for the compilation of the time-table, but is also involved in almost all the other stages in the planning of the curriculum. This, in fact, is based on empirical evidence from the interviews, but in addition, several interesting reasons were given as to why the deputy head should play such a key role in planning the curriculum, and particularly in the construction of the time-table. First, he is more free of teaching duties than anyone except the head, and consequently has the opportunity for frequent contact with other staff, and time to concentrate on the problems of curriculum. Second, he can be protected more easily than anyone (including the head) from interruption when compiling the time-table—a task which requires long spells of concentration. Third, as Burnham (1964) has pointed out, the deputy head is in a good position as an 'intermediary' between the head and the staff. Because of his closer contact with the staff, he well knows their individual requirements and viewpoints regarding the curriculum. Fourth, if the deputy head is involved with all the processes in the planning of the curriculum, he can resolve 'on the spot' many points of conflict between staff requirements and the planned or revised curriculum, whereas his close relationship with the head will enable him to judge which points involving funda-mental changes in the agreed curriculum need to be referred to the head for final decisions. Finally, several heads (and deputy heads) saw the deputy head's involvement with deci-sions on the curriculum and with the compilation of the time-table as an excellent training for headship, since difficulties with time-tabling bring home effectively the restrictions on policy decisions.

(i) Final Consultation

The remaining few days in the summer term would enable staff to inspect their individual time-tables for the coming year and to raise queries with their heads of department or directly with the deputy head. It would also enable a trial run to be made if required. In some schools, the deputy head finished the time-table early enough to discuss with each individual teacher his new time-table. However, in most schools where full consultation took place before compilation of the time-table, it was felt sufficient for the deputy head to be concerned at this stage only with those staff who had queries. These amendments were usually carried out in the last week of the summer holiday, by the deputy head.

The intention of setting out this model is not prescriptive —this is not the 'only' way in which the curriculum should be planned. It is more an example or a suggestion as to how the problem might be tackled to ensure that all parties involved are genuinely consulted. Each individual school would probably need to modify the model to suit its own particular circumstances. Furthermore, the model embodies many assumptions which may not be shared by individual heads. Nevertheless, I feel that before such a model should be rejected, the advantages of such an approach should be carefully examined.

The model emphasizes the need for increased formalization of school administration—the use of appointments, deadlines, study groups, the delegation of duties, etc. This tendency may be regarded as a further instance of large schools becoming bureaucratic. However, a formalized procedure such as that embodied in the model has certain advantages, and not only in large schools. There is no guarantee that ad hoc arrangements for planning the curriculum lead to effective consultation or more logical and flexible policy decisions, even in small schools where personal contact is easier. Formal arrangements, such as curriculum study groups and interviews for advising pupils, ensure that consultation, advice, and planning are systematically carried out, and that major decisions are laid upon to comment and criticism before they are finalized. In a large school, an *ad hoc* approach to curriculum planning, dealing with problems as and when they arise, can easily lead to unmanageable pressures on senior staff, and more importantly, to decisions—or non-decisions— which are unwittingly damaging to the future of individual pupils.

Another implication of the model is that it brings out clearly the need for deciding priorities in the way teachers' time should be utilized. For instance, the model requires the deputy head to be free of all teaching duties during the last four or five weeks of the summer term, but since all the deputy heads in this study taught at least four periods a week, and averaged 12 a week, even in schools with more than 750 pupils, this requirement may seem unrealistic. However, in several schools the deputy head was scheduled to teach mainly examination classes, particularly the sixth form. Pupils in these classes had, in fact, usually completed their examinations by the time the time-table had to be compiled, and could; therefore, be supervised by other staff during this period. Inevitably, however, there are likely to be conflicts between teaching duties and responsibility for the time-table, when the deputy head is heavily involved with both.

What was certainly clear from my enquiries was that a failure to delegate duties clearly, and dealing with problems on an *ad hoc* basis, resulted in senior teachers, particularly the head, in many schools being under considerable pressure from day-to-day and comparatively minor problems, which seemed to occur in a constant stream. Rather than the senior teachers running the school, some schools seemed to run the senior teachers! (. . . .)

I hope the model set out in this article, by stressing the need for careful timing of operations, and for the spacing of work-loads to avoid over-work of key personnel—including the head—at critical times of the year, might be of some practical use in easing one of the major burdens of school administration.

REFERENCES

Bates, A. W., 1971. *The Administration of Comprehensive Schools.* Unpublished. Ph.D. Thesis, Institute of Education, London University, London.

Burnham, P., 1964. *The Role of the Deputy Head in Secondary Schools.* Unpublished M.Ed. Thesis, Leicester University.

Davies, T. I., 1968. *School Organisation* (Pergamon, Oxford).

Lewis, C. F., 1961. *The School Timetable* (Cambridge University Press, Cambridge).

Local Government Operational Research Unit, 1967. *The Use of Computers for School Timetabling* (LGORU, Reading).

Monks, T. G. (ed.), 1970. *Comprehensive Education in Action* (NFER, Slough).

23

S. BENNETT and R. WILKIE

Structural Conflict in School Organization

There are a number of potential conflict situations in the school. Conflicts may occur within and between the three groups of participants in the school, pupils, teaching staff and ancillary staff, and also between groups inside the school and outside groups such as parents, local residents, the local education authority and the inspectorate. Certain types of conflict may derive from characteristics independent of the organization of the school, such as age, sex and colour. These, however, are less easily amenable to administrative modification, and are outside the scope of this paper.

There are many reasons for studying conflict in schools. First of all, there has been an increasing interest in educational administration over the last few years; secondly, corresponding with this interest, has been the realization that some conflicts can be constructive and likely to promote useful adaptations of the structure; thirdly, the understanding of conflict is generally recognized to be important in the understanding of human behaviour in general. In this paper, we intend to look at three types of structural conflict, conflict between subject departments, conflict generated by the introduction of a new system of pupil guidance* and conflict generated by the introduction of new administrative posts.

Conflicts may occur between departments for many reasons, ranging from personal dislikes to disagreements over the allocation of resources. At one Scottish school, conflict occurred because art and science were time-tabled together. The principal teachers of art brought up the question of curriculum choice at a meeting of principal teachers (heads

* [See the introductory footnote to S. Bennett and R. Wilkie 'The School and Organization Theory' at the beginning of this section.]

of teaching departments). He said that for years it had always been done the same way with subjects being 'confined' so that, for example, art and science could not go together because of the system of option blocks. He thought that perhaps the possibility of choice was too restricted, and that the system ought to be re-examined. There was immediate resistance to the idea from the headmaster who wanted to know what this suggestion was based on, and how many people it would affect. He thought that the principal teacher of art was thinking of the case of one pupil in particular who wanted to study architecture and who was very good at art. The boy who was about fourteen and in his second year, wanted to do art in his third year and presumably continue with it to Scottish Certificate of Education (SCE) level. The headmaster had pointed out to the boy that the University of Strathclyde, for example, would not accept art as an entrance qualification for architecture, and that they would require passes in physics and maths. The boy could not do art and physics at the same time because of the blocking system at the school. The headmaster also pointed out that the boy was not absolutely certain of what he wanted to do, he was still young, he might change his mind and therefore he should continue with the kind of course which would leave him with the most options at the end of the day—in other words, an orthodox academic course. He went on to say to the meeting that from bitter experience he had learned the wider the choice the greater the fragmentation until there could be people at the top of the school teaching two or three pupils only. He therefore did not believe in a wider choice of subjects, though he said that, of course, one way of increasing choice would be to decrease the number of periods devoted to a subject. This drew an immediate response from another principal teacher that the average pupil had too many subjects and not enough time to study them properly.

The head suggested that the principal teacher of art should 'put it all in writing'. Then the deputy headmaster suggested that he and the art principal should get together to talk it over. The headmaster asked the other principal teacher to join them. The deputy headmaster said that though it might be desirable to increase choice he did not think that the numbers would justify it at present. Another principal teacher said that it was a question of principle—did they want to increase the choice for pupils? Would they be able to manage with fewer periods? Finally, the headmaster said that it would be better if two or three of them discussed this instead of trying to talk about it in a large group.

It is obvious that the number of pupils in a school will affect the breadth of choice it can offer to its pupils. Similarly, if there is a shortage of staff this also will affect the school's capability of offering a wide choice of subjects. Nevertheless, the allocation of the school's resources inherent in the decisions bearing upon the time-table will reflect political decisions. Academic criteria will clearly play their part in the allocation of resources. Yet the fact that schools differ in their allocation of time and resources to the various subject areas indicates that there are other than academic criteria at work. Here we have an example of a subject department, art, being effectively denied access to many of the best pupils in the school. The latter would be encouraged by the headmaster to follow an orthodox academic course and since this included science it excluded art.

Another aspect of such a situation is that it may be perceived by the participants as having political aspects. In the present case some of the participants present at the meeting were of the opinion that, although the principal was professing concern at the lack of choice for pupils, in fact he was concerned at the low number of pupils taking Art. This meant that from an academic point of view they were not obliged to pay serious attention to the suggestions made. Similarly, the response was essentially a political one; that the suggestion should be discussed by a small group, most of the members of which appeared to be unsympathetic to the suggestions, instead of by the whole meeting, most of whom could legitimately be seen to have an academic interest in the proposal.

II

During the 1960s some Scottish schools introduced arrangements whereby teachers were appointed to posts of housemasters or housemistresses and charged with various aspects of pupil guidance. This guidance might consist of personal, vocational, curricular and social elements. In 1971 the Scottish Education Department (SED) published a Green Paper, 'The Structure of Promoted Posts in Secondary Schools in Scotland'. This paper proposed the establishment of such guidance systems on a formal and universal basis. The staff concerned were to be officially termed principal teachers (guidance).

In Scottish schools, principal teachers have traditionally enjoyed high prestige. This prestige has in the main been based on the fundamental requirement of an Honours degree, on many years of experience in teaching and, of course, on the fact that they were the heads of teaching departments. Over recent years, however, this situation has been changing. Not only has there occurred the phenomenon of teachers being appointed to the headships of departments after just a few years of teaching in those subject areas where there is a shortage of teachers, there has also been the dramatic introduction into schools of the new set of senior promoted posts in the form of posts of housemasters and house-mistresses. In general, the people appointed to these posts have been either university graduates with Ordinary degrees or other teachers without Honours degrees (for example, art teachers*).

The introduction of these new posts seems to have been accompanied in some cases by difficulties in the relationships between house staff and the rest of the teaching staff. A housemistress in one school said that there had been con-siderable amount of resentment at first. People asked what guidance staff did and when they tried to explain, which was difficult because of the nature of the job, people would say, yes, but what do you really do? As a result of this guidance staff felt isolated and tended to stick together, and relations between the house staff in this school had remained close. One major complaint made by the principals was that they did not know either what the house staff did or what the new system was supposed to do. One principal said that this applied to the other teachers who did not know what the guidance staff were up to and what they did not know they would fear, he supposed. You might notice a drop in certain conversations, he said, when the housemasters came into the staff room. There was a feeling that teaching roles were being expanded to include something akin to social work. One principal said that he knew that guidance was necessary but

* [The College Diploma in Art is recognized as a teaching qualification in Scottish secondary schools if it is followed by a period of teacher training at a College of Education—Ed.]

he was not sure that the house system was the best way of doing it. He was concerned about the possible consequences of the introduction of the system—in his opinion it was a question of whether the schools were to become social centres with 'education' as a secondary consideration, or whether 'education' should be the primary concern of the school. He was in favour of schools having an educational function with guidance only as an accessory. Another principal said that the schools had functioned well enough without the house staff. The way things were going, he thought, 'education' was suffering. They ought to get back to the three R's.

Another principal said that the system was supposed to allow a better knowledge of the pupils, so that teaching could be better oriented but in practice the information being gathered was confidential and therefore of no use to anyone. Even if he did know something which affected his attitude he could not treat one kid differently from the others in the teaching situation. This was so obvious to him that he could not understand why others had not realized it. He said that he was not antagonistic to the house staff and he would mention things to them, either for or against pupils, but he didn't know why—probably for something to talk about. The system was a waste of time but the staff were duty-bound to make it work, he said. Previously, before the house system, a teacher would, and still did, know quite a lot, and anyone seeking information would go to him. The housemaster had very little direct knowledge, except from those pupils he taught; thus his information was second hand. In any case, he said, most of the pupils were normal and neither required nor welcomed intrusion into their affairs. There were admittedly a few who benefited, but only a few, and he found it incredible to set up a tremendous structure for them alone. He also thought that guidance was an infringement of personal liberty. Another said of the system that he imagined that from a social point of view it was useful but it raised the question of what they were supposed to be—teachers of a subject or what?

It was not only the *raison d'être* of the scheme that was coming under suspicion, the actual workings were also criticized. Principals tended to see the house staff as excessively secretive. One said that there was an undercurrent of antipathy because of the secrecy and confidentiality. He attributed the unco-operativeness (as he saw it) of the principals to the mystery and apartness of the house staff. Another complained that they did not receive enough information from the house staff at times. He said that they took the confidential aspect of their work too seriously. Another principal, having said that contact with the house staff could be helpful, added that he was not happy about the feedback between house staff and principals.

The house staff, for their part, thought it necessary to know everything about a child; but did not see that it was necessary for other teachers to know all although they would tell them as much as they thought appropriate in certain cases. A housemaster made the point that they were prepared to release information to form teachers and subject teachers where the knowledge would be of use in the classroom situation, but not simply to make conversation. Some teachers would ask about the background of a child in the staffroom and would have to be fobbed off. He had on occasion said that if they wanted some information and would tell him why, he might be prepared to talk in private. A housemistress said that there was resentment over confidentiality. Many teachers felt that they were deliberately being told nothing. You must give some information otherwise you get no co-operation, she said.

A third difficulty concerned communications. There was no joint meeting of guidance and teaching staff and this was viewed unfavourably from both sides. One principal, talking about the 'cleavage' between the house staff and the rest said that there was no means of formal contact. There was a curtain between the two sides, he said. He meant no criticism of the house staff, they were very discreet, but he noted that there was a separate meeting with the headmaster for the house staff and for the principals. Equally, the house staff in this school were not satisfied with the system. The meeting they had with the head was not, in their opinion, very useful. They were not allowed to take part in policy decisions and the meeting had a limited usefulness for information purposes. It was bad policy not to sit in with the principals and the head, they thought. A housemaster said that there was an official instruction or recommendation that principals and house staff should meet together. The head, however, had said that the business of the two meetings was quite different, and also there was the problem of getting everyone in one room.

The house staff treated the separate meetings as a reflection on their status. A housemaster said that such meetings separated them from the rest of the promoted staff. Also, the fact that it was held in the lunch break put the status of the housemasters and their meeting on a different level. He thought they should have a definite say in the decision-making processes of the school. Principal teachers often had a subject-centred axe to grind and a narrow restricted view, he said, whereas the housemasters were more concerned with the school as a whole.

Most contact between principals and house staff was confined to informal meetings at lunch or while passing in the corridor, yet the nature of the job demanded that house staff be in contact with a large number of staff for one reason or another. The special circumstances of the school, however, meant that meetings were difficult to arrange. A teacher had to see people during his free time, but the people he wanted to see might be teaching. Many teachers therefore commented that a lot of meetings tended to be carried on in the corridors, in passing, because that may be the only time they can meet. If this is true of teachers in general it is equally true of house staff who have more people to see. They may often be late for classes as a result. Furthermore, the fact that they may be called away from classes to attend to parents, or children who are causing problems, means that their teaching is frequently interrupted. Some principals tend to interpret this as a conflict of loyalties on the part of the house staff. The house staff, it has been said, are not sufficiently interested in teaching, they are only interested in house business.

Headmasters reacted to the situation in differing ways and with varying degrees of success. One headmaster instituted a joint meeting of representatives of principals and house staff in an attempt to achieve the reconciliation of conflicting requirements. Another headmaster said that one of the reasons why meetings of house staff, which he chaired, took place outside school hours, was to make it plain to the other staff that the house staff had no soft job. Sometimes, however, the reinforcement backfired. Another headmaster sent a memo to all staff saying that his earlier instruction was being ignored, and that teachers should pass to the house staff information regarding achievements, poor attendance, illness of pupils or parents, bad behaviour, accidents, loss of parents, poor health, and the like; the passing of this information would not necessarily be taken as a reference for action, and they should please see that this most useful passing of information was carried out on the appropriate slip. A principal in this school later said that he could have had a great deal of contact with the house staff if he wanted. They were recommended to contact the house staff officially and to use forms at their discretion. The forms were not very much used, he thought. He could spend half his day doing this, telling them about various peculiarities of pupil behaviour, but he did not. He did not make official contact. Any contact was casual. Almost because of the headmaster's underlining of official contact he had stopped doing this, he said. He thought the house staff might be finding their jobs difficult, he did not know if they were getting information from the principals. He had had a boy recently who had refused the belt and he had had some difficulty in belting him although eventually, after taking him into a staff room, he had succeeded. He could have mentioned this to the boy's housemaster but he had not. This was partly because he could not be bothered filling in forms, it was easier to mention things casually.

The new house system has also had a profound effect on the career structure. As one principal teacher put it, there was quite a lot of resentment for irrelevant reasons. The house staff were seen as challengers for headships, they were a new set of candidates for the top jobs. A principal teacher at one school said that there was a residual unwillingness to accept the house staff because they cut across the traditional hierarchical organization of the school. Staff valued the opportunity to approach the head direct, he said, and also heads liked to keep in touch. He would probably send pupils to the head rather than to the house staff. There was, he said, a residual them-and-us feeling. On the other hand, a housemistress said that assistant teachers were mostly helpful, it was the principal teachers who were the main objectors. They feared for their status, she said. The strain mainly concerned principal teachers, said one housemaster—for example, it meant more people were eligible for promotion to assistant head. Another housemistress said that one problem was that you had to remember that you were an assistant in a depart-

ment. You may be 'agin' your principal teacher as to how
to deal with a pupil in your house. She made sure that there
was no friction with the principal teacher but she felt she had
to watch her step. 'It's a job where you have to watch carefully how you go.' The headmaster of one school mentioned
the fact that the guidance staff had got a room to themselves,
whereas the other promoted staff had no such room. In
another school, one principal teacher was reported to be
resentful of the fact that three of the members of his department who were house staff had accommodation of their own.

In spite of the difficulties in the situation some house staff
may be well regarded because of their personal abilities. One
principal teacher said that, in his school, he thought the
system was very useful because of the pupils at the school
and the house staff who were among the best he had known
of. He used them quite a lot and trusted them. At this school
he thought there were no status problems as far as he was
concerned. Although they might not have as high academic
qualifications as he had, he did not see why they should not
be paid as much; he admired their competence. In other
schools, he might be aggrieved. There were some unfortunate
appointments, he said, because for some it was their only line
of promotion and this was their only motive in applying for
the job. He thought his attitude would depend on his impression of the house staff. Other principals shared similar
opinions of the house staff themselves. One thought that
the success of the system depended on the personalities involved and that they were pretty lucky with their house staff.

III

The third example of conflict we want to consider is that of
the introduction of the new post of assistant headmaster in
Scottish schools. The Green Paper published by the Scottish
Education Department, to which we have already referred,
was the result of a study which had been made in session
1969–70 of 'the allocation of duties and responsibilities in
44 secondary schools, chosen to represent the different types
and sizes of schools likely to predominate in future, and also
to represent different parts of the country' (p. 7). In addition,
the Green Paper looked at 'some of the main areas of change'
in secondary education in Scotland and 'their implications for

the organization of secondary schools'. The authors concluded that their analysis has 'suggested that the present structure of promoted posts is inadequate' in a number of respects. First of all, there were too few posts just below that of the head teacher. The structure was also inadequate in the non-curricular field at the middle level, that is, at the principal teacher grade. Thirdly, the system of principal and special assistantships was 'no longer the most suitable arrangement for providing assistance to the principal teachers of large subject departments' (p. 18).

The Paper specified two requirements that should be met by any new structure of promoted posts. It must 'more effectively meet the existing and foreseeable demands of the schools' and it must also present teachers with an 'unambiguous career structure' (p. 18). The Paper proposed the setting out of minimum complements of promoted posts according to school rolls, recognizing that 'authorities would, quite rightly, not wish to be bound to a uniform pattern of internal school organization' and accepting that the authorities 'should have freedom to use a school's complement of promoted posts in whatever way would best meet its particular needs' (p. 19). The Paper envisaged a complement of up to five assistant headmasters in large schools of more than 1,500 pupils. These posts will clearly develop in a variety of ways depending on, among other influences, the objectives of the local education authority, the objectives of the headmaster of each school, the opportunities he allows for the development of the posts, and the personalities and capabilities of the holders of the posts themselves. In this paper, we want to look at certain general aspects of the job.

In the first place, the job involves two different major activities—teaching and administration. It is likely that his teaching will be interrupted by the demands of administration. If the interruptions are frequent then they will frustrate the sustained attention that good teaching usually demands. On the other hand, there will be occurrences in the school which have to be attended to immediately or which he would like to be able to deal with immediately but cannot because there may be a class waiting to be taught. Secondly, his administrative commitments may bring him into conflict with the principal teacher of the department. The fact that the assistant headmaster may find himself away from his classes frequently or late for his classes may annoy his principal teacher whose main concern, of course, will be the actual teaching done in the department. It is worth pointing out that some people would find the reconciliation of the two aspects of the job more difficult personally, but it is also possible that the head of middle school, for example, might be expected to have more discipline problems referred to him than, say, the head of the upper school, whose pupils may on the whole be more work orientated.

Thirdly, the fact that most members of the staff spend most of their time teaching makes it difficult for the assistant head to contact them. They may also not be directly accessible by phone. Consequently, a large amount of physical movement about the school is characteristic of the job. Fourthly, assistant headmasters are also assistant teachers in a department. The assistant head may have been a principal teacher prior to promotion and may therefore be more experienced than his head of department. In a few cases, principal teachers who have been promoted to assistant headmasters have found themselves acting as teachers in the same departments under new principal teachers who were previously their assistants. The assistant head will therefore be superordinate to the principal in terms of the school hierarchy and subordinate in terms of departmental hierarchy. In one case a new principal had as assistants in a department the deputy headmaster and an assistant headmaster, both of whom had been heads of that department prior to their promotions. In cases such as this, the assistant head may resist innovations made by the new principal and the latter may feel unsure about issuing directives to one who is only nominally his subordinate.

Fifthly, there is the professional dimension, the ideology of teaching. Assistant headmasters say that they like teaching and would not want a job which did not allow them to teach. It is interesting to conjecture whether they would refuse promotion to the headship of a large comprehensive school which would entail almost total devotion to the non-teaching aspects of the job. It is likely that this attitude is stimulated not only by their own past experience and by their no doubt genuine professional commitment, but also by the suspicion on the part of their colleagues, and in particular the principals, about the proliferation of posts not exclusively concerned with teaching.

Whereas the role of principal teacher is a teaching role with minor administrative tasks appended, together with some responsibility for teaching policy within the department (although the latter will also be influenced by the headmaster and outside bodies such as the examination board, the inspectorate, subject advisors and curriculum development committees), the role of the assistant head is more ambiguous. He retains substantial teaching commitments, spending more than half of the time teaching, yet he is clearly an important figure in the administration of the school and his teaching commitments may often take second place to pressing organizational or administrative demands. On the one hand, then, there is the difficulty faced by the person who is professionally trained to one job, being appointed to an essentially bureaucratic job and, on the other hand, there is the antagonism of the other senior professional people in the organization who stress the professional requirements of the job and ignore or undervalue the other requirements.

It is important to keep in mind that the situation is a new one. No consensus has been established about the role of the assistant heads; nor is there yet an established pattern of activities. The self-perceived ambiguity on the part of the assistant heads is obvious in these circumstances. Similarly, the principals are also unclear about the ways in which the new appointments will affect them. In one respect in particular they are fearful: they suspect that the creation of these new posts will lessen the availability of the headmaster, that the insertion of a new rank between them and the head will mean a loss of status. Some principals react to this by saying that they will go 'straight to the boss' if they have a problem which they cannot resolve themselves. Certainly they would go to the boss for some things which the assistant heads 'have no right to know about'. Or else they may acknowledge the increasing frequency of their contact with the assistant heads by saying that the latter consult them when they want information but that they never consult the assistant heads themselves. Moreover, this new situation has structural implications, regarding the position of assistant heads in the hierarchy of the school. They are subordinate to the headmaster and the deputy headmaster and superordinate to principals (and house staff), but they are not in a direct superior-subordinate relationship with the principals. They are perhaps assistants to the headmaster rather than assistant headmasters. They would appear to be in a co-ordinating rather than a directive or imperative role.

IV

These then are three examples of conflict within Scottish comprehensive schools. They differ in complexity but all three have lessons for those concerned with the problems of administration in schools. First of all, they illustrate the many-sidedness of organizational conflicts. The first example, an apparent case of competition for resources between Science and Art, was composed of elements of ideology (how much value is placed on Art or Science?), decision-making (who has the right to resolve the issue?), and power (who can in fact resolve the issue and how is the resolution brought about?). In the second case, the introduction of a new system of pupil guidance raised issues about the methods of introducing such a system into a fairly stable type of organization as well as the ideological implications of such an introduction. There were other issues, too, about the procedures for changing the goals of the schools and about the organizational consequences of introducing a new career structure inside the school. The third example again illustrated the problem of introducing new important posts and new career structures within the school, and also raised the issue of ideology (how much administration, how much teaching, how are these activities related?), and the importance of clarifying job responsibilities.

The second lesson which can be taken from these examples concerns the importance of the headmaster as the chief executive of the school. This has already been noted in the first example, but also in the second the role of the headmaster is crucial in mediating this conflict. In one school where the head appeared to make little effort to support the house staff, the conflict between them and the principal teachers was overt and influential. In other cases the conflicts have been kept in the background by the supportive attitudes of the headmasters concerned. In the third example, which is directly concerned with the increasing amount of administration in the comprehensive school, this is clearly the headmaster's special province, and his attitude will be of critical importance in determining not only the kinds of activities which the assistant headmasters become involved in but also the kind of reception which they will receive from the other, promoted staff in more established posts.

Thirdly, the three studies emphasize the importance to the management of the school of the understanding of conflict. Why, for example, does the introduction of a new system of pupil guidance create conflict? It is crucial that this question should be asked, particularly if the success of the pupil guidance system (or other innovation) requires the co-operation of the teachers (or other affected members of the organization). How is co-operation to be achieved? Should education authorities and headmasters spend a great deal of time attempting to convince their teachers of the value of the new systems prior to the introduction of these systems, or should they advance a programme of testing them by trial and error? Can they take the risks of the systems being resisted, halted or modified by opening up opportunities for discussion or inviting their subordinates into the decision-making process? Whatever the answers, such questions are important for the administration of schools.

Index